UNITING GERMANY: ACTIONS AND REACTIONS

For Leija, Tim, and Kai, in remembrance of our travels in Germany

Uniting Germany

Actions and Reactions

PEKKA KALEVI HÄMÄLÄINEN

Westview Press
Boulder • San Francisco

Published in 1994 in the United States by
Westview Press
5500 Central Avenue
Boulder, CO 80301-2877

Library of Congress Cataloging in Publication Data available upon request.

ISBN 0-8133-2536-6

Contents

Abbreviations

FAZ: *Frankfurter Allgemeine Zeitung*
FR: *Frankfurter Rundschau*
IHTr: *International Herald Tribune*
NYT: *New York Times*
SZ: *Süddeutsche Zeitung*

Acknowledgements

The completion of this book owes much to the contributions, impact, and help of many people who cannot all be mentioned here. They range from teenage friendships with young Germans forged on the highways, hikes, and in the youth hostels of a European youth, to later intellectual debts and discussions with Germans as well as with other Europeans and Americans from many walks of life. My contacts and encounters with Europeans have multiplied during the last few years as I seem to have returned in part to my roots, having spent almost equal amounts of time on both sides of the Atlantic during the last decade. Without resorting to a listing of names, I should nevertheless especially like to express my appreciation to my friend and colleague Theodore S. Hamerow of the History Department of the University of Wisconsin, Madison, for his encouraging and helpful comments on the manuscript. I also wish to thank Kathy McKeegan, Jane Williams and Ron Hawkins for their help, and last, but certainly not least, I thank my wife Patricia for patiently listening and contributing to the form of the narrative and the analysis at formative stages of the work.

P. K. H.
Madison, Wisconsin

Introduction

The story of German reunification is contemporary history at its most exciting. It displayed the tactics and strategy of a complex game. It embodied surprises, action and reaction, joy and fear, deception and pretence, and confidence. In it defiance, thrusts, counters, and tactical withdrawals followed one another in quick succession. Pursuit of freedom and democracy, of a better life and national identity, and the powerful, long-suppressed emotions they released were its driving force.

The stakes were high, a new order in Europe. This made the process of reunification the top game in recent history from the autumn of 1989 to the autumn of 1990. The following chapters attempt to make sense of this game and unravel the story of how it was played. Much of it was high drama full of raw emotion, but it also involved grandstanding and unconvincing theatre. Both emotions and pretensions reached headier heights than during more ordinary, humdrum times. Since so much was at stake, all the major players strived and strained to perform as effectively as they could. This they did within the limits set by their vision, by the means of their abilities, and by the resources at their command.

As always, some did better and some did worse and therefore their participation and the outcome were not equally satisfactory or pleasing to all. Some felt that they had won, and were happy and pleased. Others thought they had at least gained something in return for their concessions or at least avoided potential disasters. Yet others, however, had little reason to be pleased and emitted anguished cries during the game, but eventually they had to put a brave face on their disappointment. The reader can draw his own conclusions as to how these results applied to the main players and characters.

More than anything else, German reunification signalled and signalized a fundamental transformation in the distribution of power and correlation of forces in Europe. The curtain was closing on the post-war era of American and Soviet domination of their respective regions of the continent. The opening of the Berlin wall and Chancellor Helmut Kohl's speech and plan for a German confederation first symbolized this watershed. In this context it was both ironic and telling that the Malta summit of Presidents George Bush and Mikhail Gorbachev in December 1989 did not deal decisively with a development which was eroding the power both of the United States and of the Soviet Union in the very heart of Europe.

After over half a century of shared supremacy, both an American and Soviet pullback was in sight. Without fully realizing it, both were heading towards a door through which they had once entered with overwhelming power. Having struck a deal with one another at Yalta, they had proceeded to reorganize Germany and Europe to their liking. By the time of Malta, the Germans were starting to undo that reorganization. Malta was no Yalta.

German unity grew out of a peaceful popular revolt and the reactions to it. It resulted from interaction and synergy between East German crowds on the streets and high politics, buying and selling, and bargaining. A strongly felt and forcefully demonstrated public mood drove leaders, initiatives, and policies forward and helped to maintain a dynamic momentum behind the events. A close interplay at first between the domestic situation in East Germany and the international arena and later between the inter-German and the international scene characterized it.

This complex process gave birth to many questions and problems as it unfolded in a series of jolting and startling surprises. They included its origins and causation, the motivation of the participants, the relationship of their aims and available means, the distribution of resources, and the functioning of alliances. Making sense of German reunification also involves grappling with the role of the collective versus the individual, determination versus hesitation, and commitment versus vacillation. It necessitates tracing people's environment, expectations, visions, fears and hopes.

The following pages will explore how these various elements and factors interacted and analyse the main agents and players and their agendas. How strong of purpose and successful were they, and how clear and achievable were their aims? These were some of the key questions.

I arrived early at the hypothesis that German reunification resulted from a sometimes elusive combination of collective and individual elements. Of decisive importance were the economic, political and social conditions and the mood in East Germany. These influenced the leaders' perceptions and actions as well as the attitudes of their home constituents, as did the international correlations of economic resources and power. The key leaders' personal qualities also mattered a great deal at decisive moments.

Although the Germans played the principal role in their reunification, the process closely involved the broader European environment and both the United States and the Soviet Union. It did so primarily by signifying far-reaching changes in the international order, including changes in the relative weight and status among the major countries, and by creating a new kingpin at the centre of Europe.

In order to understand the process of reunification, I had constantly to keep in mind the dynamics of mutual dependency between its domestic German and international aspects. The same applies to the intimate connection between its socio-economic and political dimensions and the social psychology of the changing situations. Coming to grips with these different facets of the whole clarified how they depended on and reinforced each other. Reconstructing and interpreting the principal causative elements and factors thus lies at the very heart of the story.

A similar challenge confronted its leading players and participants. Coming to terms with it was a key to successful participation which resulted in the achievement of the desired results. The principal participants and players, however, not only had to tackle the various closely integrated and interacting elements of the process; they also had to act timely and decisively in order to achieve their aims.

What, then, was their role and what was the nature of their agendas, and how and why did the reunification take place?

The very first steps in the drama which evolved into the popular revolt in the DDR and the eventual reunification of Germany combined the internal conditions and mood of the DDR and international relations. Nevertheless, when young East Germans crossed the Austro–Hungarian border in August 1989, first in their hundreds and then in their thousands, without the Hungarians stopping them, no one yet knew where it would lead.

A few weeks later brave men and women of Leipzig gathered in and around their venerable old Nikolaikirche and defied and faced down thousands of police and militiamen armed with live ammunition. Then the old order in the DDR seemed doomed. The opening of the Berlin Wall on 9 November 1989, with the accompanying mass jubilation, confirmed its downfall. Empowered by such massively displayed popular sentiments, Chancellor Helmut Kohl's November plan of tentative steps towards a German confederation boldly put the question of German reunification at the centre of the international agenda.

There it remained, despite alarmed reactions, through the summits and the wheeling and dealing of the Ottawa meeting in February 1990, the Kohl–Gorbachev deal in July, and until the formalities of the Moscow benediction in September 1990.

Kohl did not let go until he reached his aim. Both in his dealings in the international forums and on his domestic stage, he was backed especially by the mood of the East Germans and the economic disintegration of the DDR. These provided him with a case for reunification to which no one had a viable alternative, and he advanced it with success.

The lead players in this complex game were thus the East German people and Chancellor Helmut Kohl. More than any other individual, Kohl, ably assisted by Foreign Minister Hans-Dietrich Genscher, also had a hand in directing it. Other key international leaders, including Presidents George Bush, Mikhail Gorbachev and François Mitterrand and Prime Minister Margaret Thatcher, played important roles, at times supporting and at other times obstructing the main game. They used their respective foreign ministers to test the waters and for much of the required international travel. Thus James Baker and Eduard Shevardnadze also became significant participants, as did, to a lesser extent, Douglas Hurd of Britain and Roland Dumas of France. All tried to protect and advance their countries' interests as they saw them, some more successfully than others.

Kohl held centre stage both because he had the most committed team and supporters and because of his personal qualities and position. He turned out to be both forceful and resourceful when those qualities were most needed, displaying a keen sense of timing, foresight, ability to take calculated risks, and tenacity in reaching his aims. Beside him he had a keen planner and fellow player in Genscher. Rivalry existed between the two men but they shared the same broad, basic aim. Yet with all their talents and assets, these two could not have won through without the co-operation and encouragement of the East German people and their West German supporters. Thus the German people in the end determined the outcome.

At the heart of the unfolding story thus lie not only the relations between the main individuals but their interaction with their people. In their dealings with other international leaders, Kohl and Genscher held an advantage in their team's commitment to their cause while the other leaders did not enjoy similar backing. Neither the Americans nor the Russians, neither the British nor the French, felt as strongly about the outcome as did the Germans. Furthermore, many of them were quite willing to let the Germans have their way.

The speed of German reunification took most observers and pundits by surprise. In its execution it resembled a political and economic *Blitzkrieg*, with Kohl as its commanding general and Genscher as the chief of staff of the victorious forces. However, they were not conquering foreign territory but rather carrying out their duties under the Basic Law of the Bundesrepublik which aimed at the reunification of Germany.

Among the German people the immediate result of the beginning of reunification was a short-lived emotional wave of exultation and celebration. This high gradually gave way to a more sober mood and to worries over the economic cost of unity. The West Germans worried about increased taxes and the East Germans about employment and rents. At the same time outsiders were still stunned and trying to come to terms with the speed of the unification process.

While a clear majority of ordinary people among the Western allies of the Bundesrepublik favoured German reunification, members of their élites were more hesitant or even opposed, though it was difficult to openly oppose for both practical and moral reasons. With the overwhelming majority of the Germans favouring it, outsiders' opposition would seem undemocratic and in many eyes immoral.

Acting as the brakeman, without the will or the strength to prevent the train of German reunification from reaching its destination, was thus largely a useless and thankless undertaking, yet it was a role tested by several before they gave up the task. They did it for various reasons: some out of fear, some to maintain their influence over Germany, some for relative parity, and at times these and other motivations were entangled together. While the Poles acted mostly from fear, Washington and Moscow were concerned with maintaining influence, and London and Paris with parity. Yet in the end they all came around to accept reunification. Overcoming the obstacles on the path to it was the job of the Germans shaping their contemporary history.

Contemporary history presents a great challenge to a historian. With contemporary topics he has access to only a small section of sources which will eventually become available, but he can also witness at first hand some of the events and developments about which he is writing and become in part a first-hand source himself. He may also have access to other people's recollections when they are still fresh and not distorted by the passage of time. He also knows that, even if historians do not write about contemporary history, journalists, other witnesses, participants and political scientists will.

One of the great challenges in writing contemporary history is to discern the essential from the less essential and to avoid trivia. Without the benefit and help of intervening time which helps the sifting process by consigning such forgettables to oblivion, the writer of contemporary history faces a tough test of judgement. His ability to see the essential, the relative importance of matters, and the process of causation in a long-term perspective and wider context is, after all, a fundamental criterion and quality of a competent historian. Historians therefore have all the less reason to leave contemporary history to others with perhaps less training and emphasis on such considerations.

Professional historians also need to deal more with contemporary topics of central and critical importance in order to retain their traditional relevance to the larger society and its decision-makers. If the profession shies away from confronting and grappling with the central contemporary international and national agenda and its concerns, while the representatives of other fields come to terms with them, so much the worse for the historians.

Within the scope of this study, I can only hope to achieve a preliminary analysis of the process of German reunification, though I can further indicate some directions which additional research could take. Directly and indirectly, through what it covers and does not cover, my own work suggests questions which need to be asked and problems to which answers need to be found for further clarification. Some of these matters will be long debated, but they will have to wait many years for conclusive answers, when all the relevant material likely to turn up will be available to scholars. Other matters can already be tackled by specialists in different fields.

The full story of the international ramifications of reunification will have to await the opening of archival documentation for research. The process of economic, social, cultural, and psychological reunification will continue long after the achievement of its political and monetary framework. This process of integration will last for many years, but its early phases and much of the political story can already be studied in considerable detail and quite systematically in specialized works and monographs. Much time will pass before the completion of many such studies, however, and before a broad historical synthesis based on them can be written.

Meanwhile, preliminary analyses and syntheses are much needed. It is for such a purpose and for my own urge to understand a fascinating and decisive historical watershed which I could follow partly at first hand that I have written this book. It has been an exciting enterprise, I have enjoyed working on it and I hope that my readers will share some of that excitement and enjoyment.

1 The Players and the Stage

The leading individual players in the game of German reunification had all been marked by the Second World War. They had lived through it and the war had implanted lessons in their minds and in their emotional make-ups. These experiences influenced some of their attitudes and actions when confronted with reunification.

The German Chancellor Helmut Kohl and the Soviet President Mikhail Gorbachev grew up during the war from childhood to early adolescence. Both also lost an older brother in the war. The American President George Bush became the youngest pilot in the US Navy. The French President François Mitterrand fought first as a soldier and then in the resistance, suffering the national humiliation of surrender and occupation. The British Prime Minister Margaret Thatcher reached young womanhood inspired by the fighting speeches of the wartime British Prime Minister Winston Churchill. The Polish President Wojciech Jaruzelski fought in the Polish forces organized by the Soviet Union.

Both as its victims and participants, they had an outlook on the world which was influenced by the war. Experiencing the war at first hand could give one a strong sense of the fragility of existence and the need to act when the opportunity arose, since it might not last long or be repeated.

Helmut Kohl was born and reached adolescence in an undivided Germany, where he lived on Hohenzollernstrasse, named after the old imperial family, in the small industrial city of Ludwigshafen on the River Rhine. To regard Germany as a natural entity, whose division was utterly artificial and unreal, was therefore more visceral to him than to Germans who were born and raised in a divided country. Born 3 April 1930, Kohl had barely turned fifteen by the time of the collapse of the Third Reich and the end of the Second World War. He had at a tender age seen his home town bombed and has painful memories of digging the dead and wounded from its ruins.[1] From such beginnings it had been a long journey for him to the heady moment of standing at the Reichstag building in Berlin cheered by a jubilant, massive crowd, waving a sea of German flags, on the night of reunification. Implanting the image of that moment in the mind and memory of millions, the German mass circulation weekly *Der Spiegel* headed its cover picture with the caption 'The Happy Giant'.[2]

Like other men and women of great power, Kohl has awoken strong and contradictory feelings. Before his striking performance and success in the game of German reunification, he was not infrequently sneered at as a mere provincial politician, with all the implications of limited ability and vision. After Kohl's forceful display of initiative and decisiveness, a rapid change took place in many assessments of him. Both words of admiration and fears and suspicions poured forth. Kohl was praised for almost singlehandedly having achieved German reunification, but he and the new Germany were also pictured as a threat to the stability and the well-being of the European continent.

Kohl has been both mocked and praised, often for the same qualities, including his physical appearance. To his detractors, he is a heavy, ponderous, self-satisfied, small-town bumbler with a narrow vision who is utterly lacking in sensitivity and sophistication; a man both obtuse and utterly unintellectual, inarticulate and devoid of a sense of history and appreciation of the importance of symbols. In short, a man totally undeserving and incapable of performing the historic role he actually fulfilled with skill and success (to some of his detractors' embarrassment).

Others have seen in him a powerfully built and powerful yet unpretentious and even unassuming man, self-confident enough not to be embarrassed by his modest background, a German patriot who is also a convinced European; the European leader perhaps most firmly and sincerely committed to a European union who possesses a good knowledge and grasp of history and a sophisticated sense of political intuition and timing. They have credited him with foresight and shrewdness, thoroughness and wisdom, as well as generosity and sensitivity in giving credit to whom it belongs.

Kohl's lack of fluency in foreign languages has frequently been held against him by both his German and foreign detractors; they have publicized it as a proof of his provincialism and limited abilities. Such criticism sounds less than fair when voiced by foreign journalists and commentators whose own leaders as a rule only speak their native tongues, without this being deemed worthy of comment.

Those with a low opinion of Kohl found it difficult even to credit him for his accomplishments in the drama of German reunification. Some preferred to give most of the credit to either Foreign Minister Hans-Dietrich Genscher or to Mikhail Gorbachev, or claimed that almost any politician could have presided over it. Such a lack of appreciation has wounded him but he has also benefited from being underestimated. Kohl himself likes to repeat some jokes and stories which throw light on this dilemma of his.

In one of the better ones, he prays to God to help him convince people that they underestimate him. God takes pity and agrees to help once with a miracle. Kohl ponders long and hard what kind of miracle would best help him to win the appreciation of the people. Finally he tells God that he wishes to be able to walk on water to cross the Rhine, and God goes along with the request. Huge crowds gather on the river banks to witness the miracle as, beaming and happy, Kohl walks across the river. But he hears no cheering or applause; instead there is only a stunned silence. Then he hears derisive laughter and someone shout, 'Look at that, there goes poor Helmut Kohl, he doesn't even know how to swim.'

In the game of German reunification Helmut Kohl achieved what he wanted, and his historic achievement sets him apart and distinguishes him from the other leading individual participants. Some of them gained or preserved much of what they set their sights on, but others misjudged the situation and the forces shaping its outcome for so long that they were largely left out or received only little for their losses.

George Bush caught on to the true correlation of forces, including the will to use them, early enough to preserve much of America's role. He quickly realized that its price was not only to pull back from efforts to throw obstacles in the path of Kohl but to help him along, and by such co-operation Washington hoped to secure a continuing role for itself in Europe. In the new Europe which would take shape with German reunification it would need German acceptance and agreement for its continued presence in ways which mattered.

Not only Bush but Gorbachev also realized early on his need of future German co-operation. Perhaps because his personal need of it was more pressing and imminent, Mikhail Gorbachev indirectly made even earlier decisions which turned out to be decisive milestones on the road to German unity; such a milestone was his decision not to back up the Honecker regime by force when it was confronted by massive demonstrations, as was later his acceptance of free elections and the non-Communist government of East Germany or the DDR and eventually reunified Germany's membership in NATO. In return, Gorbachev secured a massive infusion of German cash to the Soviet Union to shore up his own tottering position.

François Mitterrand and Margaret Thatcher struggled for some time against or alternatively to at least slow down the process of reunification. They saw no gain in it. Instead, they saw it leading to a relative loss of status and weight for their countries and themselves. Furthermore, the memory of the Second World War lived within them as they belonged to the war generation. Nevertheless, neither Mitterrand nor Thatcher, either publicly or openly, took a decisive stand against the reunification, nor did they have much success in throwing obstacles in its path. Eventually, having little other choice, both endorsed it.

*　　　　*　　　　*

In a way, German reunification repeated an enduring pattern of German history. Among major European nations Germany was late in reaching political unity, and it largely lacks a tradition of highly centralized government. Unlike many other European nations which emerged earlier as unified states, Germany has not had, over the centuries, a steady historical core area or region in the sense of a continuing centre of power. In contrast to England, France or even Russia, Germany has had no one single long, enduring and outstanding political, economic and cultural focus. It lacked an exact counterpart or anything even close to the dominance of London, Paris, Moscow or St Petersburg before the creation of the German Empire in 1871 which raised the Prussian capital, Berlin, to the status of a German capital.

This lack of a definite core and centre both explains and reflects the virtual historical absence of a centralized and unified German state. The only exception to this was Nazi Germany for some twelve years, and in this sense at least it was an aberration in German history. The Germanic Holy Roman Empire which incorporated most Germans from the tenth to the beginning of the nineteenth century was in essence a loose federation. Its emperors' powers over the semi- and at times virtually independent member states and their ruling princes were uncertain and shaky despite their occasional attempts to consolidate their hold.[3] Voltaire, the French eighteenth-century philosopher and writer, aptly needled the pretensions of this state formation as, despite its name, being neither holy, nor Roman, nor an empire.

The German Confederation which replaced it after the Napoleonic Wars by the Congress of Vienna in 1815 was an even looser organization of, in practice, sovereign states. Even the German Empire forged on the Franco–German battlefields in the war of 1870–71 was a federal state, as was its successor the Weimar Republic of the inter-war years.[4] Yet the German Empire amounted to a higher degree of German unification than had existed previously, and this unification was achieved under Prussian leadership. The Prussian kings became the German emperors and Prussia dominated the new German state to an extent that no *Land* or member state of reunified Germany does or can do.

Not only are centralizing and unifying political and administrative framework and institutions missing in the longer German tradition and history. For centuries Germans also lacked a unifying ideology. Religion and the

Church had provided such a unifying ideology for the English, French, Poles, Russians, Spaniards, Swedes and others in the past. The Germans had no equivalent of the Anglican or the Russian Orthodox Church. Neither Roman Catholicism nor any branch of Protestantism served as a unifying ideology for them as did Catholicism for the Poles and Spaniards and, after initial conflicts, for the French, or Lutheranism for the Swedes.

Instead of unifying the Germans, religion divided them. Helped by outsiders, German Protestants and Catholics brought utter devastation, ruin, and deeper divisions to their country through the ferocious and savage excesses of the Thirty Years War of the seventeenth century. It could be argued that this war between the Catholics and the Protestants caused more suffering to Germany than any other war in its history, except perhaps for the Second World War. Like the Second World War, it created a power vacuum of sorts in the heart of Europe and made German internal affairs and foreign relations subject to interference by outside powers.

Then, as well as later, the German situation was intimately tied to the balance of power in Europe. The Congress of Vienna sought to restore such a balance.[5] Then, as sometimes later, outside powers with a stake in Germany strove to block any evolution there which was contrary to their own interests; so they did again after the Second World War and, more feebly, in 1989–90 when facing German reunification. In this sense their basic aims were constant and the same. Yet they differed, of course, in where they perceived their interests to lie and in how best to secure them. This accounted in part also for the variations in methods and tactics used to best achieve such aims.

Changes in the German borders had been frequently used as a means of influence in Germany both by the Germans themselves and by outsiders.[6] Changing borders reflected changes in correlations of power. In 1989 outsiders again became highly concerned with the increase in German power. This concern brought to the forefront a discussion of how to cope with it, including how to block it or how to at least put limits and boundaries to it. In this context it was hardly strange that the question of the German borders was revived once again. Fears of questioning the post-Second World War German borders caused requests and demands for reassurances.

German reunification would *ipso facto* shift the eastern border of the Bundesrepublik eastward. It also raised the prospect of the transfer of the German political centre once again in the same direction if and when Berlin replaced Bonn as the capital. Some feared that such changes might cause additional efforts to further readjust the borders in the east.

Germany's eastern border had never been firm. It had fluctuated for centuries and particularly during and after the two world wars. Before 1945 its fundamental movement had been eastwards following the migration of the German people which started in the tenth century. This eastward movement, *Drang nach Osten*, had taken many forms. Military conquest, crusades, economic expansion and settlement gave a German character to the former West Slavic and Baltic lands along the southern and south-eastern shores of the Baltic Sea. In this way Germany expanded from the shores of the Elbe river in the west to Prussia and the borders of Lithuania in the east. It is one of the ironies of history that a conquered Baltic tribe which disappeared from history, the Prussians, left their very name to their conquerors as a symbol which, to outside eyes in particular, became identified with the very core of Germanness and German militarism and nationalism.

As a natural result of the fluctuations, the German eastern boundaries did not faithfully follow lines of ethnic and language division. The ethnically mixed character of the border populations made this impossible in many areas, and the result was ethnic tensions and minority problems and eventual forced movements of people.

These mainly affected the German and Polish borderlands, where the border changes had historically created the most bitterness. The fluctuation in the German–Polish borders went back to the medieval period of German eastward expansion. The most recent massive changes in the borders, accompanied by expulsion and the forced movement of millions of people from their homes, took place during the Second World War and its immediate aftermath. During the war the Third Reich, Nazi Germany, seized large formerly Polish territories and set about Germanizing them by expelling much of the Polish population and settling Germans in their former homes. At the end of the war the Poles and Soviet forces in turn forced out those Germans who had not already fled, both from these formerly Polish as well as from their newly acquired vast pre-war German territories east of the new Oder–Neisse border.

The wounds left by these traumatic changes continued to fester in the post-war period and surfaced again when the prospect of German reunification became a reality.

Compared with the east, the German western, southern and northern borders have been less mobile over the centuries, and similar population movements have not occurred in those directions. Thus, while news and speculation abounded about her eastern boundaries during the process of reunification, no corresponding phenomena occurred over her western and northern frontiers.

Yet even these were not immutable. In the west and south the greatest changes had been the separation of the Netherlands and Switzerland from the Germanic Holy Roman Empire after the Thirty Years War at the Peace of Westphalia in 1648. In comparison to this constriction of German frontiers, the fluctuations in the Franco–German or Dano–German boundaries had been a cause of further international conflict and swells of emotion.

The fate of Alsace–Lorraine (Elsas–Lothringen) and Schleswig–Holstein had generated at times passions similar to those felt over the German eastern borders. German, French, and Danish soldiers had bloodied their fields and meadows in wars fought over them, but at the time of German reunification few if any worried about an encore. However, some muttering about Austria and the danger of an *Anschluss* could be heard.

This could be expected in view of the tragic European history of the first half of the twentieth century. German and Austrian bitterness and frustrations connected with the settlement after the First World War combined with the deep economic depression of the 1930s, and resulted first in the Nazi state and later the *Anschluss*. *Anschluss* also means union, though it is often loosely translated as 'annexation' in English. Favoured by much of the Austrian population at the time, in hindsight it loomed as a decisive step towards the Second World War.[7] The very term *Anschluss* acquired a negative ring in many ears. It could again be heard in the debate about German reunification in 1989 and 1990, this time connoting the DDR's absorption or annexation by the Bundesrepublik when used by opponents and critics of reunification.[8]

Wartime Allied plans for post-war Germany involved its dismemberment. Originally advanced by Henry Morgenthau, Jr, the American Secretary of the Treasury, this scheme also aimed at reducing Germany to an agricultural and pastoral economy and gained short-lived acceptance by the American President Franklin Delano Roosevelt and the British Prime Minister Winston Churchill. The French and the Soviets also for some time favoured German dismemberment.

At the end of the war the German state collapsed and ceased to function, as the Allies did not accept or recognize any all-German national government. Instead, they divided Germany into four zones of military occupation where their military commanders were in charge. The Germans were put in a subordinate role to simply follow the orders of the occupation authorities. The Soviet zone encompassed what had become post-war eastern Germany after its loss of the lands east of the Oder–Neisse line and their incorporation into Poland and northern East Prussia into the Soviet Union. The British received north-western and the Americans central and southern Germany. The French were given a smaller occupation zone in the Rhineland which was carved out of the original British and American zones when the Soviet Union objected to French participation. In addition, each gained a sector of Berlin.[9]

The new German eastern border became a source of aggravation and acrimony. It gave the Poles more German land in exchange for the loss of their former eastern territories to the Soviet Union than the West envisioned in the Allied wartime discussions in Yalta. The difference involved a sizeable territory, much of Silesia, between the two Neisse rivers. Disputes arose over which one should be the border. The Soviet leader Joseph Stalin got his way despite American and British protests, both to their and the Germans' frustration. Altogether the German losses of land in the east amounted to almost a quarter of her pre-war territory. Some ten million refugees and expellees forced from their homes there crowded into the devastated occupation zones in what was left of Germany. Arriving almost destitute except for what they could carry or drag along on their long and painful trek, where many perished, they put further pressure on scarce food supplies and housing.[10]

From the very beginning, squabbles and quarrels erupted between the Allies over the spoils of war. It soon dawned on the Americans and the British that dismemberment and further divisions of Germany had negative consequences for them. Their occupation zones became a drain on their resources as their populations could not feed themselves, and they also recognized that a permanent dismemberment of Germany and her productive capacity would mainly benefit the Soviet Union by creating a power vacuum in central Europe.[11]

Abandoning dismemberment schemes beyond the deepening east–west division of Germany, they agreed to the founding of the Bundesrepublik, or the Federal Republic of Germany, under the challenge of the Cold War.[12] Encompassing all the Western occupation zones and with Bonn as its temporary capital, it was to integrate most Germans in the Western camp under the leadership of Konrad Adenauer. Elected as the first chancellor of the new Federal Republic on 15 September 1949, the Christian Democratic leader held office for the next 14 years. Dominating West German politics for so long, he provided a sense of continuity and stability. Many of his countrymen longed for and welcomed it after the previous decade of war and turmoil. Adenauer became something of a father (or rather, a grandfatherly) figure for them, reflecting both this and his advanced age.[13]

The Soviet answer to the Bundesrepublik was quick. Moscow sponsored the Communist-dominated German Democratic Republic, or the GDR (often referred to as the DDR after its German initials), in their occupation zone on 7 October 1949. Its most powerful and enduring leader was Walter Ulbricht, who had spent the war years in the Soviet Union. Utterly dependent on Soviet backing and support, he did their bidding.[14]

The Germans regretted the formalizing of their country's political division but they were powerless to prevent it, though improved relations between the West Germans and the Western Allies were taking place, in part through an indirect Soviet contribution via the Berlin blockade.

Soviet efforts to gain control over all of Berlin through a blockade of West Berlin, and the Western Allies' answer to it in the form of a massive airlift of supplies to their besieged sectors, accentuated the East–West confrontation in 1948 and 1949.[15] It also persuaded the Western Allies and the West Germans increasingly to see each other as partners rather than as enemies and adversaries. This psychological transformation was important in easing or facilitating future co-operation between them.

Not only the political structure, the capital, and borders of Germany had changed several times. Its economic fortunes had also risen and fallen with dizzy and dramatic speed several times during living memory.[16] The relative prosperity of the Empire, the Kaiserreich, had been followed by wild inflation during the Weimer Republic in the 1920s, when money lost all value. Savings were wiped out and for a while people had to do their shopping with bags of worthless notes. After a brief recovery, the Great Depression with massive unemployment had followed in the early 1930s. Ambitious projects such as the construction of the autobahn or motorway network and the rearmament programme of the Third Reich produced another short period of economic recovery before the hardships of the Second World War. For much of the war, however, the exploitation of occupied countries and territories cushioned the Germans against shortages. So too did the relatively slow and gradual conversion of their economy to the requirements of war.

At the end of the war and during its immediate aftermath Germany experienced the deepest descent of its economic fortunes in memory. The Germans called this time 'zero hour' or *Stunde Null*. It was a time of undernourishment, near starvation, and humiliation to the Germans. Among them the amply fed Allied occupation troops were the new super race who, with a few cigarettes and chocolate bars, could quickly get services of all kinds, ignoring the original bans on mingling with the Germans.

Most German cities of any size were dominated by bombed-out ruins and shells of former buildings, and the occupying powers proceeded to further dismantle the remaining industrial and even transportation capacity. The motivation for this activity was in part the same as for the schemes of German dismemberment. A thirst for retribution and the spoils of war dictated both a need to weaken Germany to preclude future aggression and a need for her to make good for past aggression through war reparations.

Except for the Soviet zone, the industrial dismantling fell far short of the original plans and did not, in fact, go very far. The Americans and the British at first reduced the programme and then abandoned it when they realized that, on balance, it did not pay for them. The more they took, the more they ended up giving. Dismantling made the Germans in their occupation zones increasingly dependent on the occupiers for survival. Their heavily industrial populations could not grow enough food to feed themselves, and dismantling their industrial capacity removed their ability to earn their keep through exports to pay for necessary food imports. The Western Allies soon realized that the dismantling of German industries also hampered reconstruction elsewhere in Europe, and it put additional pressures on American resources.[17] Neither did the dismantling fit the requirements of the emerging Cold War.

Economic considerations, a sort of crude cost–benefits analysis, and the East–West conflict thus played an important role in the Allies' changing policies towards the political form and industrial status of post-war Germany. They were also going to do so during the process of German reunification.

After the establishment of the Federal Republic, recovery and reconstruction was rapid in West Germany. Of key importance to the economic recovery was the currency reform of June 1948 of Ludwig Erhard, successor to Konrad Adenauer as chancellor of the Bundesrepublik. The currency reform was drastic and painful to many people. It allowed the exchange of only a pitiful 60 old Reichsmarks to the new Deutschmarks at a one-to-one rate; for the rest, rates of one to ten or later even one to fifteen prevailed.

It was for the second time within a generation that German currency lost almost all its value. That habits of frugality and saving survived such jolts testifies to the strength of these cultural characteristics among the Germans and perhaps to their necessity for survival through their harsh experiences. Painful as it was, the currency reform was a necessary precondition for economic and financial stabilization and future recovery and growth.[18] Together with the more distant memory of the superinflation and currency reform of the 1920s, it imbued the Germans with a determination to follow economic policies of moderation in order to avoid any future repetition of such traumatic experiences. People who had not shared these German traumas, however, found such preoccupations exasperating after economic success had made them a force and power to reckon with in the international economic community.

The rapidity and success of West German economic reconstruction struck many people as something almost magical and was christened an economic miracle, the *Wirtschaftswunder*. It seemed all the more startling to those who had believed in the effectiveness of the Allied carpet bombing during the war in destroying German industrial might. Despite the seemingly enormous destruction, witnessed by the ruins of once thriving cities and industries, the bombing was fairly ineffective in destroying industrial capacity and potential. Estimations have varied concerning the overall damage but the bulk of the productive capacity of even primary targets survived the onslaught. In the heartland of German heavy industry, the Ruhr valley, most of the industrial capacity remained by the time of the Allied occupation.

The wheels of West German economic recovery and reconstruction started to turn at full speed in the 1950s. Its annual economic growth rate averaged an astounding 8.6 per cent from 1950 to 1960. Unemployment disappeared in practice in the early 1960s, leading to an import of labour. The booming economy was reflected in the explosive growth of West German exports. From having a trade deficit in 1950, the Federal Republic grew to become the leading exporting country first in Europe and then in the world. It narrowly led the United States, both far ahead of Japan, in total exports in 1988 with a population roughly a quarter of the former and half of the latter.[19] This success and resulting wealth created the economic underpinning for reunification.

The economic prowess of the Bundesrepublik has, of course, provoked discussion as to its causes,[20] Marshall aid and the rapid modernization of its industrial plant following the wartime destruction being most frequently cited as basic explanations. While important, however, they do not account for the fact that the Bundesrepublik continually clearly surpassed its neighbours in growth rates. It received much less, $1.5 billion in Marshall aid, than Britain or France which received 3.1 and 2.7 billion respectively, and the wartime damage to its industry was not as enormous as first thought.

Clearly, other factors were at work. The rapid and considerable expansion of the West German labour force resulting from the waves of refugees and expellees from the east was the type of boost that Germany's neighbours did not share. While initially creating enormous difficulties and challenges, it gave a powerful shot in the arm to the economy in the long term. Combined with the wartime destruction, it necessitated immense efforts for the reconstruction of housing and a new infrastructure for the increased population. The refugees also brought with them skills and know-how and a determination to rebuild their lives. By 1950 some 9.3 million refugees added almost a quarter to the native-born population of West Germany and, although in smaller numbers, additional refugees arrived during the 1950s. In a sense they made a contribution to West German economic development which can be compared to the immigrant contribution to the United States, although they held less of an advantage in age structure. Young adults did not dominate among the refugees to the same degree.

A memory of the dynamics of this period of growth, and the contribution that the infusion of the new labour force from the east and the need of reconstruction had made to it, coloured many Germans' expectations of fruits from reunification. Many people expected it in time to result in a similar economic boost.

Of fundamental importance in explaining the West German economic success are the difficult to measure but nevertheless real characteristics of German culture and mentality. Oft-cited traits such as a capacity for methodical, systematic and disciplined work combined with an attention to quality go far in accounting for their economic achievements. When aggressive, efficient and dependable marketing and servicing are added, the key ingredients contributing to the striking export volumes are in place.

The West German economic and industrial machine operated within a political, social and legal framework which further contributed to and facilitated its success.[21] A higher degree of constancy and continuity characterized German economic policy on the governmental level than in Britain or France, while the federal structure of West Germany also worked against excessive concentration and encouraged competitive economic dynamics. Furthermore, a legal structure was constructed allowing for some employee participation in management which helped in labour relations. This contributed to a steady rise in production and to dependable and punctual deliveries which gave an edge in the international competition for customers.

Such conditions enabled the West German economy to gain maximum benefits from the new opportunities opening up with the birth of the European Economic Community, the EEC, in 1958. It brought vast markets within easier reach of West German products by reducing and abolishing artificial barriers of trade between its members. The most efficient firms were going to gain the most from this levelling of the odds, and they included many West German industries.

The success of the West German economy and the prosperity which resulted fascinated the East Germans. They were going to be both a powerful force of attraction and a tool that could be put to use when the opportunity for German reunification arrived.

In sharp contrast to the West German economic record, the East German performance appeared modest. Heavy reparations to the Soviet Union, at first in the form of massive dismantlement of her industrial and transportation capacity, hampered her recovery and reconstruction. This dismantling reduced by anything from 40 to 65 per cent her productive capacity during the first two post-war years, according to some estimates. Along with stripping the factories of their machinery, tearing up of railway tracks, and the transfer of rolling stock and shipping into Soviet hands, came exploitation. Taking the form of the forced relocation of engineers, technicians and highly skilled workers with their instruments and machinery to the Soviet Union, keeping prisoners of war as a captive source of slave labour for up to a decade or more after the war, forced unpaid deliveries of goods, and manipulation of pricing, it added up to a massive drain and transfer of economic assets and wealth from East Germany to the Soviet Union.[22]

The East German protests and demonstrations which led to the uprising of 17–18 June 1953, put down by Soviet tanks, was a desperate popular protest against the harsh conditions forced upon its people.[23] It destroyed the credibility of all pretensions of wide popular support for the regime and nakedly revealed its dependency on raw Soviet armed power and the will to use it against the people. This moved the leftist German writer Bertolt Brecht to comment ironically that since the people had forfeited the government's trust it should elect a new people.

Although East Germany also received an influx of massive waves of displaced German refugees and expellees from the east, she also suffered from a weakening drain of people escaping to West Germany. By 1950 some 4.5 million refugees had entered East Germany. They formed an even larger proportion of the population than in West Germany, creating enormous pressures on housing and other problems of absorption. Those who fled to West Germany were younger and better educated than the average, which added to polarization and inequality in the economic performance of the two Germanies.

The closing of the East German borders with the building of the Berlin Wall on 13 August 1961 was in a way a measure of desperation on the part of the East German regime to stop this debilitating drain.[24] Before then, some 2.5 million people had left the DDR since 1949 for the Bundesrepublik.

The Federal Republic continued to prosper through most of the 1960s. By the 1970s, under the impact of the oil shock, its economic growth slowed and, even after the recovery in the 1980s, it bore the burden of relatively high levels of unemployment. Yet in comparison with other major Western economies the Bundesrepublik was doing well.

The West Germans felt both pride and uneasiness over their new economic success and prosperity. They knew it evoked awe and respect but also envy, resentment and fear in many other nations. They were less persuaded that others not infrequently perceived them to be arrogant and tactless and suspected that the Germans considered most other people less effective and dependable than themselves. Such suspicions or convictions were more widespread among those Europeans who remembered the Second World War. Like many people, they tended to be on the lookout for anything that reinforced their earlier experiences and the beliefs based on them. German tourists sometimes fulfilled their expectations.

Yet most exasperating to the Germans was the realization that not only negative characteristics but also their positive qualities could arouse resentment and anger. Thriftiness and frugality could be mocked as stinginess, orderliness and sense of discipline could be seen as signs of intolerance and lack of imagination, exuberance as boisterousness and rowdiness. To some it seemed that, no matter what they did, they could not win acceptance and liking. Others behaved very carefully or increased their efforts to make friends.

The German post-war leaders shared the dilemma that their compatriots experienced both as individuals and as a people. Bonn generally trod carefully in dealing with other governments and international bodies. It knew it had constantly to consider not just the present but the impact of the past. Past memories could easily inflame minor routine disagreements with an emotional charge which had little to do with the issue at stake. Bonn became known for generally trying to maintain a low profile in international affairs except for its efforts to keep alive the idea of German unity. It refrained from criticism of other powers and from interfering in the internal affairs of other countries. In return, it had to suffer the humiliation of sometimes being called a political impotent or midget.

Such references reflected only in part Bonn's caution or passivity. They were also born out of the perceived discrepancy between German political and economic assertiveness in the international arena and, to no small effect, they mirrored others' exasperation with the economic success and wealth of the Federal Republic. Thus it was doubtful whether greater political assertiveness by Bonn would either have pleased or satisfied the critics.

The European Economic Community and, after 1967, the European Community had been primary vehicles for the economic success of the Federal Republic and its integration to and acceptance by much of Europe. This was helped by the fact that in many ways it was like the well-behaved student of the class, whose conscientious homework the others copied. It was in many respects a model citizen of the European Community. Its standards and regulations were widely emulated and often became the yardstick to which other members of the Community aspired. It willingly footed a major share of the Community budget and it frequently and eagerly promoted new initiatives and measures for further increased Community cohesion. As the most successful exporter of its goods to the other Community nations, however, it also reaped major rewards from further consolidation of the Community.

None of this would have been possible without the co-operation of France. Without France the European Community would not have come about, and without the Germans it could not have become viable. The two countries needed each other to achieve what neither could achieve alone. Their co-operation became the axis of the European Community without which its wheels could not turn. Where the Germans could provide energy to spare, the French could get away with open political thrusts that the Germans would have hesitated to undertake on their own to consolidate and to move the Community forward. Acting together, the two could dominate it.

The question of the future is whether, after German reunification, they still can work together closely for European unity.

Notes

1 Filmer and Schwan, *Helmut Kohl*, 1985, pp. 16, 18–19; Maser, *Helmut Kohl: Der deutsche Kanzler*, 1990, p. 28.
2 *Der Spiegel,*, 19 Nov. 1989.
3 Buschmann (ed.), *Kaiser und Reich*, 1984.
4 Koch, *A Constitutional History of Germany in the Nineteenth and Twentieth Centuries*, 1984.
5 Kissinger, *A World Restored*, 1957.
6 Demandt (ed.), *Deutschlands Grenzen in der Geschichte*, 1990.
7 Cf. Diwald, *Deutschland einig Vaterland*, 1990.
8 DDR stands for Deutsche Demokratische Republik or East Germany. Bundesrepublik stands for the Federal Republic of Germany or West Germany before the reunification.
9 See, e.g., Morgenthau, *Germany is Our Problem*, 1945; Kimball, *Swords or Ploughshares?*, 1976; Gaddis, *The United States and the Origins of the Cold War, 1941–1947*, 1972; Kuklick, *American Policy and the Division of Germany*, 1972; Sharp, *The Wartime Alliance and the Zonal Division of Germany*, 1975; Willis, *The French in Germany, 1945–1949*, 1962; I.D. Turner (ed.), *Reconstruction in Post-War Germany: British Occupation Policy and the Western Zones, 1945–1955*, 1989; Peterson, *The American Occupation of Germany*, 1978; Gimbel, *The American Occupation of Germany: Politics and the Military, 1945–49*, 1968; Sandford, *From Hitler to Ulbricht*, 1983; Nettl, *The Eastern Zone and Soviet Policy in Germany, 1945–50*, 1951.
10 De Zayas, *Nemesis at Potsdam*, 1989; Benz (ed.), *Die Vertreibung der Deutschen aus dem Osten*, 1985; Grünwald (ed.), *Sudetendeutsche: Opfer und Täter*, 1983.
11 See, e.g., Graml, *Die Allierten, und die Teilung Deutschlands*, 1985; Treue, *Die Demontagepolitik der Westmächte nach dem Zweiten Weltkrieg*, 1967; H. Thomas, *Armed Truce*, 1986, pp. 337–40; Maier and Bischof (eds), *The Marshall Plan and Germany*, 1991, pp. 1–39, 71–114.
12 See, e.g., Clay, *Decision in Germany*, 1950; Schwartz, *America's Germany*, 1991; H. Thomas, *Armed Truce*, 1986.
13 See, e.g., Augstein, *Adenauer*, 1964; Koch, *Adenauer: Eine politische Biographie*, 1985; Baring, *Im Anfang war Adenauer*, 1988; Birke, *Nation ohne Haus*, 1989; Hans-Peter Schwarz, *Die Ära Adenauer, 1949–1957*, 1981.
14 See, e.g., Birke, *Nation ohne Haus*, 1989; Childs, *The GDR: Moscow's German Ally*, 2nd edn, 1988; McCauley, *The GDR since 1945*, 1983; Staritz, *Geschichte der DDR, 1949–1985*, 1985; Weber, *Geschichte der DDR*, 1986; Stern, *Ulbricht*, 1964.
15 Davison, *The Berlin Blockade*, 1958.
16 Cf. Hardach, *The Political Economy of Germany in the Twentieth Century*, 1980.
17 Treue, *Die Demontagepolitik der Westmächte nach dem Zweiten Weltkrieg*, 1967; cf. Gimbel, *Science, Technology and Reparations: Exploitation and Plunder in Postwar Germany*, 1990.
18 Cf. Hardach, 1980, pp. 107–8, 143–6.
19 The respective export volumes amounted to some 323, 322, and 265 billion dollars.
20 See, e.g., Maier and Bischof (eds), 1991; Backer, *Priming the German Economy: American Occupation Policies 1945–1948*, 1971; Abelshauser, *Wirtschaft in Westdeutschland, 1945–1948*, 1975; Berghahn, *The Americanization of West German Industry, 1945–1973*, 1986.
21 Cf. Hardach, *The Political Economy of Germany in the Twentieth Century*, 1980, pp. 163–78.

22 Cf. ibid., pp. 110–38; Leptin and Melzer, *Economic Reform in East German Industry*, 1978; Staritz, *Die Gründung der DDR*, 1984, pp. 37–151; Lenz, *Die Wirtschaftsbeziehungen DDR – Sowietunion*, 1979, p. 31.

23 Baring, *Uprising in East Germany*, 1972; Spittmann and Fricke, (eds.), *Der 17 Juni 1953. Arbeiteraufstand in der DDR*, 1988; Diedrich, *Der 17 Juni 1953 in der DDR*, 1991.

24 Schwarz, *Berlinkrise und Mauerbau*, 1985.

2 Neighbours and Partners

The Germans faced their most formidable obstacle to reunification in the fact that no one else saw it as being in their interests or really wanted it. Through its Basic Law the Federal Republic was formally committed to seeking German unity, but its leaders repeatedly had to come to terms with the stark reality that at most they received only the support of words in this aim – and even on this level, support was waning. In the 1950s it was still there but already in the 1960s it was weakening.

Originally the Bundesrepublik envisioned a reunification which would also include some territories lost to Poland. This seemed quite impossible or unacceptable to others, but even a more modest reunification limited to the Bundesrepublik and the DDR seemed for long to have few realistic prospects. Washington's determination under the impact of the Korean War to rearm the West Germans and to incorporate them in the Western defence system and its acceptance by Adenauer precluded reunification short of Soviet surrender.

The prospect of the Bundesrepublik acquiring arms alarmed the Soviet Union. It instead proposed German reunification to the Western Powers on 10 March 1952, the reunified Germany to be a neutral, essentially unarmed state. The Western Powers did not enter serious negotiations over the matter, being anxious to incorporate the growing West German strength into the Western Alliance. Rather, they demanded free all-German elections and insisted on freedom for the ensuing all-German government to choose its own allies.[1] In short, they rejected the Soviet conditions for a reunified Germany. Subsequently these East–West positions on German unity remained essentially the same, despite renewed later exchanges.

In the Federal Republic the Soviet proposal intrigued in particular the Social Democrats, opposed to West German rearmament and inclusion in the Western military alliance.[2] It was rejected by Chancellor Adenauer, who was committed to the integration of the Bundesrepublik with the West. He was above all worried about German isolation and sought to guard against it, yet it was not within German power at the time to decide the fate of reunification one way or another. Although the West Germans could express their sentiments on it, they would have to abide by the decision of others.[3]

As neither Bonn's Western allies nor Moscow favoured German unity, its division increasingly became a widely accepted central aspect of the balance of power. The longer this situation lasted, the more it became regarded as part of a stable political order in Europe. Attempts to change or even seriously question the division of Germany were increasingly viewed through this prism as destabilizing and even a danger to peace. The failure of the West to intervene first in the Hungarian uprising of 1956 or later in the suppression of Czechoslovakia in 1968 concretely confirmed the dominance of such attitudes. Stability in Europe had become identified with the maintenance of the existing East–West division.

This was a highly frustrating situation to those wishing for German reunification. The realities of power and prevailing attitudes in both East and West forced Bonn to pursue more modest, shorter-term aims than actual reunification but related to it. These involved various efforts to question and undermine the validity of the existing division and a search for and build-up of potential support for its eventual weakening and abolition.

Such efforts included the so-called Hallstein Doctrine which, with the exception of the Soviet Union, sought to prevent other countries from recognizing the DDR by raising the prospect of Bonn's retaliation.[4] Building and maintaining friendly relations with concerned parties and the use of the increasing economic power and resources of the Bundesrepublik also potentially served the aim of a possible eventual reunification.

A basic precondition of reunification was its at least tacit acceptance, or refrain from forceful resistance to it, by the wartime Allies and the neighbours of Germany. Their post-war relations with the Bundesrepublik illuminate their attitudes towards reunification. The closest partner of the Federal Republic in the European Community was France, and France felt perhaps more affected by German reunification than any other of the former wartime Allies.

The Franco–German relationship has been long and complex. Modern German nationalism emerged and grew in part in reaction to the strong role of French culture and political power in Germany. Resentment sprang up against the presence and prestige of the French language and culture among the German upper classes in the eighteenth century. An increasing emphasis on the value of German culture also turned into a powerful political force under the impact of the Napoleonic wars and French occupation in the early nineteenth century. The Franco–German war leading to German unification in 1870, the First World War and the French occupation of the Ruhr valley, the Second World War and the German occupation of France and post-war French occupation policies in Germany, all in turn stirred powerful emotions. This heritage influenced attitudes and behaviour long afterwards.

It shaped the post-war developments both for and against increasing co-operation and unity in Western Europe. Fear and resentment of Germany worked against acceptance of German unity and of West Germany as an integral and equal member of the European family. Yet it also counselled binding West Germany closely to Western Europe for preventive purposes. The West Germans themselves were anxious to participate in joint ventures and eager to reassure and find acceptance.

The powerful emotions derived form the past and current calculations could be seen at play both in the post-war saga of the European army and the early steps towards the future European Community. Fear of what path Germany would take if left outside countered the fear of West German power and domination if it were allowed inside. This dilemma, combined with the unwanted division of their country, also added to German difficulties in determining their policies.

Thus various and contradictory pressures divided opinion among the Germans and urged caution on them not to aggravate old fears. Bonn felt it had little room to manoeuvre. Concerned that it was likely to be suspected and possibly resented if it asserted itself vigorously, it followed a very cautious line most of the time.

Where the Germans hesitated or refrained from disagreeing with their neighbours or challenging the Americans or the Russians, the French took more risks without much fear of retaliation. They neither carried burdens from the past like those of the Germans, nor perhaps were they watched as avidly and taken as seriously. For the Germans, the shadows of the past long seemed to cover the present.

The French at first favoured German dismemberment after the Second World War, but eventually accepted the setting up of the Federal Republic. They preferred a West Germany to a unified Germany, as the power relationship would then be more in balance, and soon accepted West German participation in the European Coal and Steel Community, which was established 18 April 1951, in part to keep a close eye on German heavy industry, mindful of its military potential.[5] This co-operation opened the way for subsequent and more substantial Franco–German collaboration. The European Coal and Steel Community eventually evolved into the European Economic Community in 1958, from which in turn emerged the European Community and the European Union in Maastricht in December 1991.

As a fitting symbol for the budding Franco–German co-operation in overcoming shadows of the past, an active force behind it had been Robert Schuman, the French Foreign Minister. A German citizen in Alsace before its return to France in 1918, he had powerful personal reasons to strive for reconciliation between the two countries.

Limits nevertheless remained. French Premier René Pleven proposed the creation of European armed forces including West German troops under international control on 26 October 1950, its purpose being both to strengthen West European defece against the Soviet Union in reaction to the Korean War and to keep the Germans on a leash by preventing the emergence of a separate West German army. Adenauer accepted the proposal, but in the end the French parliament rejected it on 30 August 1954. French fears of German military might and unwillingness to give up national military sovereignty still remained strong.[6]

A special complication in Franco–German relations involved the fate of the economically important Saarland with its vast coal resources, which the French originally entertained hopes of incorporating into France after the Second World War. The Saarland remained under French supervision until a plebiscite held in the area in 1955 which overwhelmingly favoured its full return to the Bundesrepublik. It was almost a rerun of a similar situation in the inter-war period and its resolution through a vote twenty years earlier, in 1935. Bonn had refrained from forcefully claiming the return of the area, being unwilling to risk serious tension with Paris, yet in the end the French accepted their loss without rancour, although the return of the Saarland could also be seen as a step towards eventual German reunification.[7]

Franco–German co-operation made a considerable advance after the imperious French leader, Charles de Gaulle, agreed with the long-serving West German Chancellor Konrad Adenauer that it was to their countries' mutual advantage. De Gaulle recognized that France was too weak alone either to lead Western Europe or to measure up to the United States or the Soviet Union. With the help of German muscle, however, it could hope to play a role unattainable through its own resources. By co-operating closely with West Germany, it could also keep a close eye on it, and the developing ties could prevent the Germans from going their own separate way.[8]

As many French leaders envisioned the co-operation, West Germany would be the engine and France the driver, and without the driver the engine could go nowhere. Eager to smooth over and to prevent the reappearance of fears and resentment of Germany, while also supporting further West European integration, Adenauer and subsequent West German leaders cultivated the French connection.[9] It reduced their dependency on the United States, and the French withdrawal from NATO also strengthened Bonn versus Washington by increasing the importance of the Bundesrepublik as an ally of the Americans. The Franco–German alliance was anchored in close acquaintance and personal relationships between the respective leaders after they started meeting at frequent intervals. In the 1970s President Valéry Giscard d'Estaing and Chancellor Helmut Schmidt got along particularly well.

The durable contemporary national leaders, Chancellor Helmut Kohl and President François Mitterrand, have seen each other regularly and have cordial relations. Lending their support to Franco–German co-operation they have made joint appearances at occasions symbolic of past conflict; in one memorable and moving scene, on 22 September 1984, they stood clasping hands at Verdun, perhaps the most blood-soaked Franco–German battleground in the First World War, where among others Kohl's father had fought.

Nevertheless, all the meetings and such gestures did not prevent a rift from opening between them during the process of German reunification. This was not an accident or even surprising. A basic aim of Bonn's foreign policy, reunification, had never actually been welcome to the French leaders. It ran counter to the very basic rationale of Franco–German co-operation as the latter envisioned it. A French aim was, after all, to prevent the emergence of a much stronger, potentially unpredictable rival rather than to help German reunification.

On the matter of reunification the Germans also had their doubts about the French. In the 1960s the ebullient and optimistic Chancellor Ludwig Erhard and his successor, the courtly Kurt Georg Kiesinger, were wary of de Gaulle's activism in Eastern Europe and cultivation of the Soviet Union, concerned that it could lead to deals at Germany's expense. In turn, the French fretted about Bonn's Ostpolitik in the 1970s, suspecting that it could result in an agreement with Moscow which would bring German reunification and neutrality and weaken the position of France.[10]

France did not have the industrial base to compete with Germany. It had suffered from a chronic imbalance in its trade with the Germans and held little prospect of catching up.[11] Yet, despite its weaker economy, France had been successful in asserting itself in the European Community, and had, in fact, laid claim to a leadership role which it may find difficult to sustain in the future. West Germany had to a large extent acquiesced in such French assertiveness in the past, but a reunited Germany freed from former constraints would demand a greater say. At the very least, the French would have to share their claim to a role of leadership; it was more likely that they would have to relinquish most of it to Germany.

As geographical neighbours, the Germans and the French developed intimate ties and were also emotionally engaged with each other. Both physical geography and their degree of mutual involvement helped to maintain more distance between Germany on the one hand and Britain and the United States on the other.

Traditionally the British had been more self-confident and relaxed than the French concerning the Germans, a result of both geography and history. Although they were neighbours, the British and the Germans were also separated by a sea. Together with their naval and air power, this fact had helped the British to avoid the French experiences of destruction and occupation by the Germans. Instead, they had twice defeated the Germans with the help of coalitions. Thus the British did not historically have the same degree of anxiety and fear of the Germans as did the French.

The Germans in return had displayed a certain envy, respect and even grudging admiration of the British in the past. Certainly they did so during the height of British power in the nineteenth century, and even Adolf Hitler was not immune to such feelings. The world wars, and in particular the Second World War with its terror bombings, had created mutual hatreds and left a long-lasting impact on the war generations, yet the British soon abandoned vengeful policies toward the Germans after the both world wars.

In the post-war years suspicions and resentments lingered between the wartime adversaries, and with the rapid German recovery a keen sense of rivalry re-emerged between the British and the Germans.

More long-lasting than wartime hatreds, this economic and political rivalry had been keen since German unification and the creation of the German Empire in 1871. Originally far behind, the Germans had gradually caught up with and overtaken the British in many spheres of economic activity and modernization well before the First World War. Continuing in the inter-war period, the rivalry surfaced again after the creation of the Bundesrepublik.[12]

Behind British attitudes lay difficulties in coming to terms with the reversal of British and German fortunes in the post-war decades. Where Britain had suffered from relative economic decline, the Bundesrepublik had prospered. While the Germans had invested heavily in education, technical training and hard work, at the same time maintaining good labour relations, the British had coasted along somewhat cushioned by inherited capital accumulations and by North Sea oil, engaging in repetitious and wasteful labour conflicts. Germany emerged as the leading economic power in Europe, while Britain was falling out of the first tier of the West European nations in per capita income, sinking between them and the poorer Mediterranean group.[13]

Additional problems and tensions arose from British coolness towards West European integration and West German enthusiasm for it. Their different attitudes towards West European co-operation kept the ties between Britain and Germany from becoming as close as the Franco–German relationship. Originally, in contrast to Bonn's enthusiasm for the EEC, London showed little interest in it. Then, when the British wanted to join the Community, Adenauer acquiesced to de Gaulle's wish to keep them out. This angered the British but they got along better with Adenauer's successors, Ludwig Erhard and the north German Social Democrat Willy Brandt, who had supported the British bid for membership.[14] As in the Franco–German relationship, so personalities mattered in British–German relations.

Prime Minister Margaret Thatcher thought highly of Helmut Schmidt but did not develop a similar regard for Chancellor Helmut Kohl. Although they shared many views about the East–West conflict and the need for close ties with Washington, they did not develop a close personal rapport. Thatcher credited Kohl with 'a strong sense of history' but also put him down as a 'provincial politician'. Neither did she find in Kohl an ideological soul mate. This mattered as, in comparison with the rather pragmatic Kohl, she was an ideologist – common ideological views and fervour explain in part her closeness to President Ronald Reagan. She thought Kohl viewed the world far more like socialist Mitterrand than would any British conservative.[15]

As well as such matters and different views concerning European integration, their relations with Washington caused friction between London and Bonn. The British were attached to their special relationship with the Americans – it was a source of additional influence. The missile controversies of the 1980s and Thatcher's apprehension of neutralism in Germany brought further strains. Advocating a harder line than Kohl, who was under heavy domestic pressure to yield more to the Soviets, she had 'acrimonious' discussions with him;[16] since they both tended to be blunt, their exchanges could indeed become direct.

Neither the British nor the American attitudes towards the Germans were complicated by the experience of the humiliation and sense of vulnerability and weakness that wartime occupation and exploitation had given to Germany's continental neighbours. Its absence meant that they did not have to overcome the same trauma in establishing relations with the Germans. To them the risks seemed smaller and the past was a smaller hurdle to overcome if present needs called for it.

American–German relations had historically not been as important on the level of high politics as had been the relations between Germany and Britain or France before the two world wars and the Cold War. American attitudes towards the Germans had vacillated a great deal over time and also showed much segmental variation.

Originally, largely positive attitudes owed much to the impact of German immigrants and German universities. More negative attitudes, however, emerged before the First World War, in part due to their emerging rivalry. During the war intense anti-German propaganda strongly influenced popular attitudes, leading to suppressive actions against the German heritage in America. More balanced attitudes reappeared briefly during the Weimar Republic, but the emergence of the Third Reich with its unsavoury characteristics again increased negative American perceptions of Germany. The Second World War and the Holocaust strongly intensified them.

The needs of the Cold War and a shared dread of Communism pulled the Americans and the West Germans together, and the passage of time inevitably reduced negative American sentiments about the Germans despite constant reminders of the Holocaust. Gradually, more positive attitudes towards the Germans reappeared and were reciprocated. Eventually these feelings were affected by a sense of economic rivalry sharpened by a gradual change in their relative economic fortunes. Anti-American sentiments also arose among the Germans, in particular among the left.[17]

In addition to these variations in attitudes which were connected with crises, and the passage of time, remarkable differences existed between many segments of Americans in their perceptions of the Germans. Official polls conducted in 1966 indicated that far more men than women, educated people than the less educated, Protestants than Catholics or Jews, midwesterners and westerners than north-easterners or southerners, liked Germans. Differences in attitudes among some of these groups varied quite sharply between the extremes, the more educated and the Protestants liking the Germans best, the southerners and the Jews liking them least.[18]

Despite fighting the Germans in the two world wars, the Americans had little reason to fear them on the basis of the past. They were the quickest to wish to incorporate the West Germans into the Western Alliance as an answer to the needs of the Cold War.[19] The Korean War had given a sense of urgency to West German rearmament for fear of Soviet military moves in Europe when America was heavily engaged in the Far East. This American pressure had persuaded the French to propose their own plans for integrating the Germans in the Western defence structure without the revival of a German military threat.

After the French had opted out of the planned European Defence Community, which they had devised as a way of thoroughly integrating German forces under international authority, a new method had to be found for West German rearmament. The French refusal to follow this through had been in part due to the British refusal to join the planned defence community, an early example of persistent and enduring British aloofness to continental co-operation. It fell, then, on Washington, London and Bonn to find another way for West German participation.

The result was West German entrance into the North Atlantic Treaty Organization (NATO) in 1955. Increased sovereignty for the Bundesrepublik with an end of the Allies' occupation rights on its territory and their pledge to support German reunification accompanied this new acceptance of the Germans. Yet the promise to back German unity went little beyond words and, in accordance with Bonn's wishes, refraining from recognizing the DDR.

Konrad Adenauer, the West German chancellor, had been eager to anchor his state in the Western alliance system and especially sought close ties with

France and the United States. A man of strong will and strong feelings, he kept a close personal rapport with General de Gaulle and the American Secretary of State, John Foster Dulles, but less so with such contemporary Western leaders as the British Prime Minister Harold Macmillan or Presidents Dwight D. Eisenhower or John F. Kennedy. Adenauer was wary of British attitudes towards the European Economic Community and of Kennedy and any possible understanding between Washington and Moscow at German expense,[20] as ultimately West German defence depended on the Americans.

The Adenauer era came to end in 1963. After the chancellorship of the post-war monetary reformer Ludwig Erhard, a grand coalition government of the Christian Democrats under Kurt Kiesinger and the Social Democrats led by Willy Brandt took over in 1966. In the 1960s Washington and Bonn were growing apart. Bonn felt that Washington was increasingly preoccupied elsewhere in the world than in Europe. American President Lyndon B. Johnson bluntly discouraged Bonn from expecting active American support for reunification, and let Kiesinger know that the United States would not fight a war over it.[21]

With Willy Brandt as its foreign minister and since 1969 the new chancellor, in coalition with the Free Democrats and their leader Walter Scheel as foreign minister, the Federal Republic was pursuing an increasingly independent eastern policy. Brandt, a sensitive and charismatic leader with a great deal of natural charm, had directly experienced the German division most starkly and at its most unnatural location as the mayor of West Berlin. He had witnessed that the West, short of verbal protests, accepted the construction of the Berlin Wall and the sealing off with it of the one remaining opening between the two Germanies. Here Kennedy's show of solidarity by the Berlin Wall with his much-quoted words, 'Ich bin ein Berliner', made no difference. They remained a gesture unbacked by deeds. If the Federal Republic wanted to maintain contacts between the West and East Germans, a new policy was clearly called for. Here lay the reasons and the rationale for Bonn's Ostpolitik or its new eastern policy.[22]

The construction of the Berlin Wall was essentially a defensive move by the leaders of the DDR who wanted to hold on to their subjects. During the 1950s some three million East Germans moved west, for it was simple to slip through the some forty-kilometre gap in the iron curtain which existed in Berlin. In the long run the DDR could not survive the continuation of such a haemorrhage. On the night of 12–13 June 1961, the East German police and militia sealed the border between East and West Berlin, and the construction of barbed wire obstacles and the wall started. In charge of the operation was Erich Honecker, the future leader of the DDR. Eventually a double wall was erected with a booby trapped and mined death strip in between. The Berlin Wall was 105 miles (169km) long and 13 feet 6 inches (4.10m) high. It had 295 observation towers, 243 guard dog tracks, and 43 bunkers. The DDR regime called the wall a protection against imperialist and Fascist aggression.

The building of the Berlin Wall convinced the East Germans that they had no alternative but to try to make a life for themselves within the confines of the DDR. Efforts to adapt to its totalitarian order distanced many mentally from the West, and this became easier with the economic improvement following the end of the continual drain of skilled people to the West. The DDR's reputation as the most prosperous and technically competent and developed country in the Soviet bloc also contributed to the seemingly increasing acceptance of it by its people.[23]

The wall also affected the West Germans. Its building starkly revealed to them the limitations of their Western allies' commitments to German interests. Kennedy might walk up to the wall and empathize with the besieged Berliners, but he was not ready to take the risk of knocking it down. If the wall could not be knocked down, some way would have to be found around it to maintain connections between the two Germanies. The very logic of the situation was to work for increasing support to Ostpolitik in the future. Since its allies could not prevent increasing isolation between the two German states, clearly Bonn had to seek another approach if it was not simply to accept passively and barrenly the new *status quo*. The key to the other way lay in the east.

In spite of his efforts, Brandt made little headway with Ostpolitik *vis-à-vis* the DDR as long as the dour old goatee-bearded Walter Ulbricht remained at its helm. A survivor of the massive bloodletting and purges that the German Communists had suffered in Stalin's Soviet Union, he early foresaw dangers to his position and rule. One of the earliest and most eager advocates of the suppression of the liberalizing Prague Spring in 1968 in which East German troops participated, he clearly made no easy partner for Brandt. Ulbricht had reason to be concerned about his subjects. Surveys indicated that three out of four East German youths felt themselves primarily German, while only one in four primarily held to the identity of a citizen of the DDR.

Ulbricht, however, was no independent master of his land. He in turn had his masters in Moscow.[24]

Working through Moscow channels, Brandt also made some headway in the DDR. By March 1970 he found himself standing together with Willy Stoph, the prime minister of the DDR, on a square in Erfurt in East Germany hearing a crowd cheering 'Willy', and they were not cheering Stoph.[25] It was a stirring moment, all the more so because Erfurt had given its name to the classical nineteenth-century programme of the German Social Democratic Party which became a model for many other party programmes in other countries.

Ostpolitik also signified Bonn's growing independence from its Western allies. Facing their doubts, reservations, and suspicions it nevertheless sought their approval, pointing out the advantages to be gained.[26] Washington did not like Bonn's independent ambitions. It wanted both Bonn's eastern policy to fit its own Soviet policy and also to retain a check on it. Henry Kissinger, the American Secretary of State, was very wary of Brandt's Ostpolitik although he recognized its advantages to the Germans.[27]

The formal foundation stones and achievements of Brandt's Ostpolitik were the signing of treaties between Bonn and Moscow in August 1970 and the subsequent four-power agreements on Berlin in 1971, treaties between the two Germanies in 1972, Bonn and Warsaw in December 1970, and Bonn and Prague in 1973. These treaties normalized and regularized relations between the signatories and opened the way for further advances.[28]

In essence, Ostpolitik signified Bonn's acceptance of the post-war boundaries of Germany and *de facto* acceptance of the East German state. In return, Bonn gained increasing access to the markets of Eastern Europe and the Soviet Union, practical arrangements with the DDR which eased access between the two German states, and clarification of the status of West Berlin including its ties to the Federal Republic.

At the time of its emergence, Brandt's Ostpolitik came under harsh attack from the Christian Democrats, the CDU, as a sell-out and abandonment of German reunification,[29] though eventually they embraced its essentials under the leadership of Helmut Kohl. From the point of view of German interests, Ostpolitik simply had no sensible alternative.

Brandt's chancellorship lasted until May 1974. Ironically, in view of his Ostpolitik, he was brought down by the revelation of a close collaborator, Günter Guillaume, as an East German spy. Brandt resigned office and was replaced by party comrade Helmut Schmidt, formerly minister of defence, a caustic and intellectual realist who had gained much regard for the way he conducted his work. Schmidt's high reputation for competence was quickly put to a severe test. Economic difficulties gripped the Bundesrepublik and the rest of the world as a result of the oil crisis with its sudden dramatic increase in the price of this basic source of energy and the accompanying inflation. Although the Federal Republic had to import virtually all its oil, in contrast, for example, to Britain or the United States, it weathered the crisis well under Schmidt's determined and purposeful management.[30]

As a result of the Ostpolitik, Bonn was becoming more assertive of specific German interests at a time when Washington's prestige and influence in the world weakened because of the war in Vietnam and the parallel internal American divisions and turmoil. Bonn's Western allies were originally wary of its Ostpolitik, but America's declining relative economic power and affluence and its repeated calls for more burden-sharing by Bonn and its other European NATO allies also pointed towards greater equality between Bonn and Washington. So did the growing expectation that Washington placed on Bonn's economic and fiscal policies for relief and stimulation of the American and world economy.[31] Yet Bonn was also careful enough not to trample on Washington's sensitivities by seeking its backing for its openings to the east.

The relative economic status of the Federal Republic continued to strengthen in relation to the United States, of which one indication was a substantial increase in the value of the German Deutschmark versus the dollar. German–American relations tended to fluctuate and were not helped by cool relations between Chancellor Helmut Schmidt and President Jimmy Carter. Schmidt was critical of Carter for weak leadership and lack of consistency – he was disturbed, for example, by Carter's vacillations on the neutron bomb. In contrast, the highly self-confident and assertive Schmidt continued to get along well with the French President Valéry Giscard d'Estaing, which facilitated Franco–German co-operation.

Further development of Bonn's Ostpolitik ran into problems with the Soviet placement of new middle-range missiles, which was countered by a Western decision to follow suit. Schmidt was a strong advocate of a firm Western response, despite massive popular protests and opposition to it in his own party. Additional difficulties arose from General Wojciech Jaruzelski's military coup in Poland on 13 December 1981. Carried out under the threat of an otherwise looming direct Soviet intervention against the liberalizing challenge of Lech Wałęsa's Solidarity movement, the coup was welcomed by Erick Honecker, who had replaced Ulbricht as the East German leader and was concerned about the spread of liberalizing ideas from Poland to his bailiwick.[32]

Broad consensus had nevertheless evolved in the Federal Republic in support of the Ostpolitik. The Christian Democrats who had initially opposed it became, under the leadership of Chancellor Helmut Kohl in a coalition with Foreign Minister Hans-Dietrich Genscher and his Free Democrats, its new executors and agents in the 1980s, while under Honecker the East German leaders of the DDR became in part unwitting participants in the Ostpolitik. Persuaded by their own decaying economy and needs, they were seduced by West German economic concessions and aid to lower the barriers of movement and travel between the two Germanies. The resulting increase in movement of people undermined the DDR. First-hand exposure to the glaring differences in the living standards between east and west increased the dissatisfaction of the East Germans.

Honecker had originally tried to buy popularity by petty material bribes and concessions. Hard currency shops, where much-wanted Western goods were available, spread around the DDR. Thousands of Volkswagen Golfs were imported to please well-off East Germans. In the DDR this West German everyman's car passed as a luxury automobile. His mass-level bribes were more modest – otherwise unavailable exotic fruits like bananas and oranges were imported at special holiday seasons – but such concessions could not buy legitimacy for the regime.

A child born from Soviet soldiers, bayonets, and tanks on German soil and led by people who had arrived in their wake from Moscow, the DDR faced a fundamental problem in how to legitimize itself to its population and to outsiders. This it strove eventually to do by finding roots in German history.[33] From originally identifying itself only with traditions of radical social protest, in time it threw its net in wider and deeper waters, catching bigger and heavier fish.

From early claiming as its own Thomas Müntzer, the radical social and religious reformer of the German peasant wars in the 1520s, it advanced to embracing Martin Luther at the fifth centennial of his birth on 10 November 1983.[34] Six years later, the East German Lutheran Church and its clergy were to play a significant role in the revolutionary challenge to the DDR.

Despite previous often-repeated damnations of historical Prussia and what it stood for, the DDR also eventually reassessed this long-standing whipping boy. An earlier view of Prussia as a nest of reaction and militarism became more nuanced. Positive progressive aspects were found in the Prussian state and its policies. Traditional Prussian characteristics, such as a sense of duty and service, austerity and discipline, hard work and frugality, were brought forth and emphasized as a precious heritage.

Honecker himself participated directly in this re-evaluation of Prussian and German history. In his autobiography he speaks with appreciation of Martin Luther, Carl von Clausewitz and Frederick the Great, and this latter embodiment of the greatness of Prussia returned soon afterwards to grace the Unter den Linden, the parade street of East Berlin from which he had been banned since the war.[35] Yet some lingering reservations remained, and with them went new efforts to falsify history. Sitting on his horse, Frederick was now charging westwards where originally he had charged eastwards. However, few remembered that; what mattered most was that the equestrian statue of the Prussian hero was back in a position of honour.

In the DDR the acceptance of German and Prussian history remained selective, but clearly less selective than before. Some physical symbols of this broader approach could be restored, but others remained beyond retrieval. The medieval Wartburg castle associated with Luther was restored, but of the Berlin castle of the Prussian Hohenzollern kings and German emperors only a balcony remained. The East German Communists had blown up the restorable ruins of the castle after the Second World War but they had saved one of its balconies and stuck it incongruously into the glass façade of their modernist Palace of the Republic on Marx-Engels-Platz – not, of course, to honour the Prussian kings but in memory of the revolutionary Marxist message that had once, allegedly, been spoken from this balcony.

Otto von Bismarck, the Iron Chancellor of Prussia and Germany, and the architect of German unification in the nineteenth century, had been an enemy of the Marxists, yet their later East German heirs eventually also included him in their rehabilitation of Prussian and German history. They belatedly praised the statesmanship of this Prussian *Junker*, the pivotal statesman of the Europe of his time. Kurt Hager, the chief ideologue of DDR, and Ernst Engelberg, a leading East German historian, commended both his foreign policy and its long-term domestic results as opening the way for the rise of the working class.[36]

These attempts to come to terms with such giants of German history as Luther, Frederick the Great and Bismarck bespoke the East German regime's sense of insecurity and vulnerability. It felt that the continuity of German history and its most prominent figures were too formidable and strong potential opponents to fight or to ignore. Discrediting them had not worked and was risky; ignoring them was not practicable. To try to join and co-opt to its own cause what it could not beat was the logical conclusion. The illegitimate East German leadership and state was seeking rescue and legitimacy from pillars of the German past.

Yet the East German regime's very efforts to legitimize itself by embracing heroes of German history also reminded its subjects of the joint German past and the historical ties that bound them to the Germans in the west. They knew that Luther had made a fundamental contribution to German unity through his powerful impact via the creation of a standard unifying German literary language, and they shared widely other Germans' respect for Bismarck because of his role in German unification. Thus the regime's resort to history also undermined the cultivation of a separate East German identity and the very existence of the East German state.

Gordon A. Craig pointed out in his classic *The Germans* how the East German Communists vacillated in their stated views about German unity. They favoured a socialist version of it in word until the end of the 1960s. In 1954 Walter Ulbricht, the leader of the DDR, enthused in sentimental terms, 'We are for the unity of Germany, because the Germans in the west of our homeland are our brothers, because we love our fatherland.'[37] Such verbal ardour soon cooled, however. In the early 1970s the overtures of Bonn's Ostpolitik created nervousness in the DDR's leadership. It started increasingly to speak of the two nations of Germany, and a rewriting of the DDR constitution in 1974 dropped all previous references to German unity.[38]

Henry Ashby Turner, Jr, observed that Bonn under Kohl's leadership put renewed stress on German unification after the low profile of the preceding Schmidt and Brandt administrations on the matter. He also noted the quid pro quo between West German economic help to the DDR in 1983 and the subsequent East German dismantling of its most murderous border installations and easing of travel restrictions across it.[39]

Both the renewed emphasis on unification and the successful use of economic might to gain concessions foreshadowed important developments during the critical years for German reunification in 1989 and 1990. The former pointed at a future policy difference between the Kohl–Genscher government and the West German Social Democrats, and the latter at a way of dealing with the Soviet Union.

Helmut Kohl had replaced Helmut Schmidt as the chancellor on 1 October 1982 when the Free Democrats of Hans-Dietrich Genscher switched sides. Abandoning his coalition with the Social Democrats and linking himself with the Christian Democrats, Genscher retained his post as foreign minister. Genscher had his roots in East Germany, and Kohl's wife also came from there. Both these leaders were keen on cultivating ties between the two Germanies.[40] Some observers have stressed a distinction between the aims of reunification and such an emphasis on human contacts, but in the long run they were merely two sides of the same coin. After many years of broken or weakened human contacts following the building of the wall, their renewal and maintenance was simply essential for keeping alive and fresh the hope and wish for eventual territorial reunification.

In the 1980s Bonn's ability to pursue Ostpolitik was complicated by the general East–West tensions associated with the placement of a new generation of nuclear missiles in Europe. NATO's countering of the new Soviet SS-20 intermediate-range missiles with Pershing II missiles went ahead with the combined support of the principal West European leaders Kohl, Mitterrand and Thatcher, despite massive demonstrations against it in the Bundesrepublik and Britain.

Although Bonn had backed the placement of the new missiles, it favoured greater flexibility and was more willing and even eager to negotiate with Moscow than was Washington, where President Ronald Reagan had come to power on 20 January 1981. Reagan's tough talk about the Soviet Union alarmed many Europeans, including the Germans. The Germans of both East and West were keenly aware that they would probably be the first and the worst victims in a military conflict or war in Europe. With the deteriorating general East–West climate and the accompanying war scares, this shared awareness built foundations for their co-operation, despite harsh and tense East–West relations.

Kohl had met the East German leader Honecker at the funeral of the Soviet leader Yuri Andropov in Moscow in February 1984. They met again at the funeral of Andropov's successor Konstantin Chernenko on 18 March 1985.[41] The funerals of both the former KGB chief and the 'heroic border guard' became occasions of a large gathering of international leaders which gave Kohl and Honecker a chance to exchange views without all attention focused on them. Speaking in the regional dialect they both shared – Honecker grew up in the Saarland in West Germany – they became acquainted and established some degree of rapport. These and other contacts between the Germans bore fruit in the form of West German credits to East Germany and the easing of travel restrictions from east to west, and an agreement on a visit by Honecker to the Federal Republic. The Germans had, however, moved too fast and too far for Moscow. After an aggressive Soviet media campaign against the Bundesrepublik, accusing it of efforts to destabilize Europe, Honecker cancelled his visit in September 1984.[42]

Yet important results followed from the agreed easing of travel. A truly dramatic increase in the number of East German visitors to the West ensued, bringing their numbers to the millions. Before the mid-1980s, few East Germans other than pensioners had been allowed to visit the West. The East Germans' increased opportunities to make first-hand comparisons between the conditions in the East and the West hardly made them more fond of the DDR.

Honecker's planned visit did not materialize until after Mikhail Gorbachev came to power. Gorbachev's reforms influenced both the general East–West relationship and the situation in the whole Soviet bloc, and the resulting relaxation and liberalization also enabled the two Germanies to further their mutual co-operation. When Honecker finally arrived on his long-delayed visit to Bonn on 7 September 1987, Kohl received him, at the same time speaking of the unity of the Germans and the need of more human rights in East Germany.[43]

He was here touching a sensitive nerve. Growing signs of exasperation with the oppressive conditions in the DDR followed the following year. These took the form of both open demonstrations and smaller informal meetings in which demands for more freedom were raised. Police countered demonstrators in East Berlin on 17 January 1988, the demonstrators using the occasion of an officially sponsored demonstration to present their own demands for freedom, and again in Dresden on 13 February 1988.[44]

While Honecker had accepted a certain limited amount of *rapprochement* with the Federal Republic when he saw some gains for his regime, he was not willing to follow Gorbachev's example of limited and cautious internal liberalization. Nevertheless, he and his regime were eventually caught up in the maelstrom of reform and liberalization which was sweeping the Soviet bloc in powerful currents and which in the end would demolish both the bloc and the Soviet Union itself.

Parallel with the emerging challenges to Honecker's system in the DDR, reform demands and concessions dominated neighbouring Poland and nearby Hungary during 1988. After increasing demonstrations and strikes, the Polish Communist regime entered negotiations with Solidarity which resulted in an agreement in April 1989 whereby the Communists gave up their monopoly on political power and other fundamental reforms were initiated. The consequent parliamentary elections turned into a convincing victory for Solidarity on 4 June 1989, and Solidarity leader Lech Wałesa's close collaborator Tadeusz Mazowiecki became the Polish Prime Minister on 24 August 1989. The era of Communist domination was over in Poland.[45] These dramatic Polish changes both encouraged opposition to the regime in the DDR and weakened the Soviet position there.

In Hungary, reform-minded Communists themselves carried out a far-reaching liberalization of the country. After veteran Communist leader Janos Kádár was ousted on 22 May 1988, the pace of reform and liberalization rapidly accelerated.[46] Eventually it also had decisive importance for the evolution in East Germany. Kádár, who had been in power since the Hungarian uprising of 1956, had himself carried out considerable liberalization without relinquishing the Communist monopoly on political power, but his successors opened the gates for a stream of reforms which eventually swept them from power.

The following year, 1989, was to be a fatal year for the Honecker regime. It opened with demonstrations in Leipzig on 15 January, and Leipzig was where the wave of demonstrations was going to be most persistent and massive the following revolutionary autumn.[47] Meanwhile, the Honecker regime pursued its previous path of easing travel to the Bundesrepublik while simultaneously maintaining tight internal control. Despite obviously growing dissatisfaction, it claimed to have gained the support of 98.85 per cent of the voters for its list of candidates in the local elections of 7 May 1989, to the frustration of many voters who were convinced that the results were falsified.[48]

However, it was ultimately not just the situation in the DDR which was to determine the future of Germany but also German relations with the superpowers, the United States and the Soviet Union. These in turn were increasingly influenced by the growing economic weight of the Federal Republic and the relative economic decline of both the United States and the Soviet Union. The upsurge of German prosperity and America's relative economic decline simply changed the traditional power relationship between them and called for new attitudes on both sides. Bonn would no longer accept Washington's tutelage and leadership as in earlier years.

A widening gap between American ambitions and resources became increasingly visible and apparent to the Germans and other Europeans, undermining American hegemony. Watching the political polarization in the United States, and its transformation from a creditor to a debtor nation owing to its massive international trade deficits, the West Germans contrasted it with their own increasing resources, economic and monetary stability, and growing influence in Europe.

These opposite trends in the fortunes of the two countries would alone have caused strains in their relations, but so did different attitudes and different perspectives on the international scene and what was most important to each. Bonn, rather earlier than Washington, tended to see a reduction in the Soviet threat and an opportunity to strike mutually beneficial deals with Moscow.[49] Bonn was also far more Europe-centred in its outlook than Washington. Where the decision of the European Common Market in 1988 to seek a higher degree of West European unity by the end of 1992 was warmly greeted in the Federal Republic, it caused shivers of alarm in Washington, fearful of a fortress Europe which would shut out American goods and cut down American influence. Yet at the same time Washington increasingly needed and called for co-operation from Bonn in managing its own and influencing the world economy.

If Washington needed Bonn's co-operation in economic policy, Moscow stood in need of direct German investment of technological know-how and funds in its stagnating economy and industrial plant. Its needs were so dire that Moscow stood ready to grant major concessions in return for such an infusion of West German resources and capital.

In this the Ostpolitik came in handy, providing a linkage with the past history and traditions of German involvement in Russia. Historically, the Germans had in many ways stood for the impact of Europe on Russia in trade, technology, and currents of thought and philosophy. The German Hanseatic merchants had carried on extensive trade with the Russians in the Middle Ages and maintained a permanent presence in the leading Russian trading city of Novgorod. Peter the Great had first learned about European ways and technology in his boyhood in the German suburb of Moscow. After Peter the Great, German blood ran in the veins of Russia's rulers. German universities heavily influenced the Russian universities in the nineteenth century. German settlers and fortune-seekers brought new knowledge and skills to Russia, and officers and civil servants of German origin played a major role in the armed forces and administration of Tsarist Russia.

This background goes far to explain why and how certain German achievements and characteristics have traditionally deeply impressed the Russians. They have long been in awe of German science and technology, and have long compared German effectiveness and organized and orderly behaviour with their own more relaxed and lackadaisical ways and characteristics. All this helped Bonn when it was ready with its Ostpolitik to begin to make a major effort to rebuild relations and ties with Moscow, just as Helmut Kohl and Hans-Dietrich Genscher were to do when they readied themselves to strike a bargain with Moscow for German reunification. The Germans knew that the Russians wanted to trade with them and would appreciate their products and technical advice.

Notes

1 See, e.g., Alfred Grosser, *Geschichte Deutschlands seit 1945*, 1974, pp. 457–8; Hillgruber, *Deutsche Geschichte, 1945–1982, Die 'deutsche Frage' in der Weltpolitik*, 1983, pp. 51–3; Steininger, *Ein vertane Chance: Die Stalin Note vom 10 März 1952*, 1985; Steininger (ed.), *Chance zur Wiedervereinigung? Die Stalin Note vom 10 März 1952*, 1985.
2 See, e.g., Albrecht (ed.), *Kurt Schumacher*, 1985, pp. 905–7.
3 See, e.g., Adenauer, *Erinnerungen*, vol. 2, pp. 63 ff; Hanrieder, *Germany, America, Europe*, 1989, pp. 153–7, 436–9.
4 Hanrieder, 1989, p. 160
5 Friend, *The Linchpin: French–German Relations, 1950–1990*, 1991, p. 17.
6 For the defence and security policy considerations, see, e.g., Fursdon, *The European Defence Community: A History*, 1980; Wettig, *Entmilitarisierung und Wiederbewaffnung in Deutschland*, 1967; Dockdrill, *Britain's Policy for West German Rearmament, 1950–1955*; Friend, 1991, pp. 20–24.
7 Friend, 1991, pp. 15, 24–5.
8 See, e.g., Hanrieder, pp. 13–14; Kaiser-Lellouche, *Deutsche-Französischen Sicherheitspolitik*, 1986; A. Grosser, *Frankreich und seine Aussenpolitik, 1944 bis heute*, 1989, pp. 225–57; Schwarz (ed.), *Adenauer und Frankreich*, 1985.
9 See, e.g., Friend, 1991, pp. 29–40.
10 Hanrieder, 1989, pp. 14–19; Friend, 1991, pp. 44–5, 54–5.
11 Kennedy, *The Rise and Fall of the Great Powers*, 1989, pp. 428–9.
12 Cf. Kennedy, *The Rise of Anglo-German Antagonism, 1860–1914*, 1980; Mommsen, *Two Centuries of Anglo–German Relations*, 1984; Birke, *Britain and Germany*, 1987.
13 Kaiser and Morgan (eds), *Britain and West Germany: Changing Societies and the Future of Foreign Policy*, 1971; Kennedy, *The Rise and Fall of the Great Powers*, 1989, pp. 425–6.
14 Friend, 1991, pp. 38–40; Brandt, *People and Politics*, 1978, p. 117; Laitenberger, *Ludwig Erhard*, 1986, p. 161.
15 Thatcher, *The Downing Street Years*, 1993, pp. 257, 263, 477, 552.
16 Ibid, pp. 786–7.
17 See Konrad Jarausch, 'Huns, Krauts, or Good Germans? The German Image in America, 1800–1980', in Harris (ed.), *German–American Interrelations. Heritage and Challenge*, 1985, pp. 145–59.
18 Ibid. pp. 156–7.
19 For American–German relations see also, e.g., Cooney, Craig, Schwartz and Stern (eds), *The Federal Republic and the United States*, 1984; Gatzke, *Germany and the United States*, 1980; Hanrieder, *Germany, America, Europe*, 1989; Jonas, *The United*

States and Germany– A Diplomatic History, 1984; Morgan, *The United States and West Germany, 1945–1973*, 1974; Trommler and McVeigh (eds), *America and the Germans*, vol. 2, 1985.
20 Hanrieder, 1989, pp. 174–5, 444–5.
21 Hersh, *The Price of Power*, 1983, p. 416.
22 Brandt, *Begegnungen und Einsichten*, 1976, p. 17.
23 Impressions from conversations with East Germans over several years.
24 See, e.g., Lange (ed.), *Aspekte der deutsche Frage*, 1986; Stern, *Ulbricht*, 1965.
25 *Frankfurter Rundschau*, 20 March 1970.
26 Helmut Schmidt, 'Germany in the Era of Negotiations', *Foreign Affairs*, Fall, 1970, pp. 45–6.
27 Kissinger, *White House Years*, 1979, pp. 211, 409–10.
28 See, e.g., Griffith, *The Ostpolitik of the Federal Republic of Germany*, 1978; Keithly, *Breakthrough in the Ostpolitik*, 1986; Plock, *The Basic Treaty and the Evolution of East–West German Relations, 1986.*
29 Werner Link, 'Aussen- und Deutschlandpolitik in der Ära Brandt, 1969–1974', in Bracher et al. (eds), *Geschichte der Bundesrepublik Deutschland*, vol. 5, 1986, pp. 206–13.
30 One gets a good sense of him through Helmut Schmidt, *Menschen und Mächte*, 1987 and *Die Deutschen und ihre Nachbarn: Menschen und Mächte*, II, 1990.
31 Hanrieder, 1989, pp. 370–72.
32 *Neues Deutschland*, 16 Dec. 1981.
33 Johannes Kuppe, 'Das Geschichtsbewusstsein in der DDR', in Weidenfeld (ed.), *Geschichtsbewusstsein der Deutschen*, 1987; Venohr, *Die rote Preussen*, 1989; cf. Brinks, *Die DDR-Geschichtswissenschaft auf dem Weg zur deutschen Einheit*, 1992.
34 *Neues Deutschland*, 10 Nov. 1983; R.F. Goeckel, 'The Luther Anniversary in East Germany', *World Politics*, vol. 37, Oct. 1984.
35 Honecker, *Aus meinem Leben*, 1982, pp. 613–14.
36 Engelberg, *Bismarck*, 1985.
37 Craig, *The Germans*, 1991, p. 307.
38 Ibid., p. 308.
39 Turner, Jr, *Two Germanies since 1945*, 1987, pp. 203–4.
40 Heinz-Joachim Melder, 'Endstation: Bundeskanzleramt', in Filmer and Schwan, *Helmut Kohl*, pp. 182–3; Maser, *Helmut Kohl*, pp. 73–4; Wolf Siedler, 'Vorbemerkung', in Genscher, *Unterwegs zur Einheit*, 1991, pp. 9–11.
41 Hanrieder, 1989, 214–15.
42 *FAZ, SZ, NYT*, 5 Sept. 1984.
43 *FAZ, SZ, NYT*, 8 Sept. 1987; Kohl, in *Bulletin*, 10 Sept. 1987.
44 *FAZ, SZ*, Jan. 1988; *Welt am Sonntag*, 14 Feb. 1988.
45 *NYT*, 5 June 1989, and *IHTr*, 25 Aug. 1989; cf. Ash, *The Magic Lantern*, 1990, pp. 25–46.
46 *IHTr*, 23 May 1988; cf. Ash, 1990, pp. 48–60.
47 *FAZ* and *SZ*, 16 Jan. 1989.
48 *Neues Deutschland*, 9 May 1989.
49 See, e.g., Genscher, *Unterwegs zur Einheit*, 1991, pp. 137–50.

3 Needs and Anxieties

They kept on coming, worn-looking men and women with their children, speaking old-fashioned-sounding German. The poorly dressed emigrants with their archaic dialects were one of the earliest telling signs of the dramatic changes soon in store for Europe. Rolling across the frontiers of Eastern Europe, they were fleeing from bleak conditions in the Soviet Union, Poland and Romania for a better life in the Bundesrepublik. Single adults and family groups with grandmothers, parents, boys, girls and babies, carrying shabby bags and parcels, they were entering the welcoming camps both bewildered and relieved. At least the trials and tribulations of the departure and the journey were at last behind them. Both serious and smiling adult faces and wide-eyed, curious children, all wondered what the future would bring.

The year 1988 saw a rapid increase in the number of ethnic Germans allowed to leave the Soviet Union and Eastern Europe and move to their ancestral homeland. For the most part they were descended from settlers who had arrived from Germany centuries ago, and for generations they had maintained their identity as a testimony to their cultural cohesiveness, persistence and ethnic pride. They believed themselves, by tradition, to be more advanced and accomplished than their eastern neighbours as they had originally been settlers largely invited for their desirable skills or knowledge. They had been invited to Transylvania in the twelfth century and to Russia by Catherine the Great in the eighteenth, though many Germans had settled in Russia much earlier. The maintenance of their ethnic identity had not been easy. The inevitable pressures of assimilation are the common lot of minorities, and at times there had been forceful pressure and oppression, as in particular in the Soviet Union during and after the Second World War and in Eastern Europe in the post-war period.

After the massive flight and forced initial expulsion of Germans from the eastern territories in the closing stages and the aftermath of the Second World War, the borders were shut with the clamping down of Communist control. Millions of Germans had fled or had been forced out of the territories of post-war Poland and Czechoslovakia, along with smaller numbers from elsewhere in Eastern Europe. They had left their homes in Prussia, Pomerania and Silesia, formerly German territories which went to Poland, and East Prussia, much of which went to the Soviet Union, with the Oder–Neisse line as the new German–Polish boundary.[1]

Some, nevertheless, managed to stay behind. These territories also had sizeable populations of mixed and uncertain ethnic backgrounds and less than firm or undivided loyalties. Their price for staying in their homes and for acceptance in post-war Poland had been at least the outward suppression of German identity, but recently many had rediscovered it. It offered them the ticket to the Federal Republic and its citizenship. Fleeing the economic misery and lack of ethnic minority rights in Poland, they were the single largest contingent among the ethnic German immigrants, the *Aussiedlers*. Estimates of the number of people who claimed German heritage in Poland vary because of the lack of reliable statistics, but they could amount to as many as 500,000.

Hardships had marked many of them, and some had strange and tragic tales to tell about their lives. A fiftyish, stocky, greying Polish German, for example, had spent his childhood suppressing two heavy burdens and liabilities. As a small boy he had seen his mother and sister raped by Soviet soldiers, and the cries and violence of the scene continued to haunt him in nightmares for years, though he long felt too shamed to talk about it. He had to hide the memory, just as he felt that he had to suppress his German identity and background, to avoid more hurt.[2] Over three million Germans had been forced out of Czechoslovakia after the war. There also some of mixed ancestry had remained, but they were not numerically or statistically a significant element among the recent newcomers to the Bundesrepublik.[3]

The largest potential pool of new arrivals were the estimated two million ethnic Germans in the Soviet Union. Often referred to as the Volga Germans, the largest concentration had lived in farming villages in the Volga region until the German invasion of the Soviet Union, when they had become widely dispersed. Although many of them belonged by tradition to religious sects with a reputation for non-violence and pacifism, Stalin distrusted them. The men were shipped to vast slave labour camps, which became death camps for many. The women and children were scattered in harsh and hostile surroundings through the wilds and arctic cold of Siberia and the dust and heat of Soviet Central Asia. That they managed to survive and pass on their German heritage, including their language, in these conditions was a considerable feat, though this achievement was not always appreciated. The old-fashioned German spoken by many Soviet German immigrants to the Federal Republic is sometimes an object of wonder and source of amusement in their new surroundings, where it is not always understood what its preservation had demanded and cost in endurance.

The middle-aged or older Soviet Germans' lives had been harsh. An aging couple recalled a bleak childhood spent with their mothers and other German women and children in an Arctic community in the north of Siberia under terrible conditions which took a heavy death toll. Together with others they had been expelled from their home village along the Volga river. Members of the NKVD, the security police, had banged on their doors one night and taken their fathers away for forced labour. That was the last time they saw their fathers, who were starved and worked to death like so many others in slave labour camps. They remembered wondering as children why people were so mean to them and their families just because they were Germans. Both had learned to read German with the help of family bibles rescued by their mothers, an invaluable skill in their new surroundings.[4] Similar stories were common among the Soviet Germans.

When Helmut Kohl had come to power as chancellor in 1983, he had pledged to work for the freedom of more Germans to leave the Soviet Union. It took the better part of the decade before larger numbers were allowed out, but by 1989 close to a hundred thousand entered the Bundesrepublik, while those remaining behind were gaining increased cultural rights and opportunities to use their mother tongue.

Besides Poland and the Soviet Union, Romania was also a significant source of *Aussiedlers*. These descendants of the builders of the picturesque and impressive medieval towns of southern Transylvania had been better able to maintain their German identity than the others. Bearers of an urban culture among their originally rural Romanian and Hungarian neighbours, they had benefited from their status over many centuries. They had been able to leave the nightmare of Ceauşescu's land in a steady stream due to the monetary generosity of the Bundesrepublik. Ceauşescu had been selling his Germans to the tune of some 100 million Deutschmarks a year.

A gracious older German woman remembered an early childhood in a comfortable family villa in an old historic Transylvanian town before the Communist takeover in Romania. Afterwards her family had to give up their villa at short notice to a local Romanian Communist official and move to small, cramped quarters shared with others. She had grown up taunted for being a Saxon and a bourgeois brat. Looking back on the past, she felt that she had suffered from constant heavy stress during much of her childhood and youth without quite realizing what it meant.[5]

These newcomers to the Federal Republic from Poland, from the far-flung corners of the vast Soviet Union, and ancient towns and villages of Romania were both a challenge and an asset to it. Money and effort had to be spent to get them settled. Housing and jobs had to be found. Instruction in German also had to be offered, in particular to the people from Poland whose grasp of it was often almost rudimentary or next to non-existent. Even if fluent in their dialects, others had to learn many new concepts of modern life in the Bundesrepublik. Alongside generous attitudes and helpfulness, however, there was also resentment and jealousy of the aid extended to the newcomers.

Yet they were not just a burden. The very fact that they had survived and overcome the many frustrations and obstacles on the path of emigration to the Federal Republic vouched for their persistence and sense of purpose. Clearing the immense and formidable hurdles of bureaucracy, ill will and hostility in their former homelands would have sapped and exhausted the energy and will of those less determined and tenacious. The leap to the virtually unknown new land demanded daring and a spirit of enterprise. Thus, whatever the shortcomings in their practical preparednes, the newcomers possessed positive qualities to begin a new life in the Bundesrepublik. They also brought a helpful infusion of younger blood and willingness and skills for manual labour. Young adults among them were far more dominant than among the greying population of the Federal Republic, and they were ready and eager to take up the kind of hard labour that many others shunned.

The newcomers could draw courage from knowing that the highest leadership of the Bundesrepublik recognized both its obligations to them under the constitution and their value. Chancellor Helmut Kohl had urged generous acceptance of the newcomers whom he wanted welcomed 'with opened arms'. In his view, both national solidarity and recognition of their value dictated a warm welcome. Such words put to shame those who wanted to put curbs on the inflow of the new German citizens.

Why were they, then, allowed to leave after all the decades of denials? The decision reflected the economic and political difficulties of the Communist authorities. In desperate need of an infusion of cash and know-how from the West, they increasingly saw the Bundesrepublik as the closest and likeliest provider of such needs. Loosening the bonds of the ethnic Germans was a way of courting Bonn. The Germans had a reputation of being hardheaded people, and the Federal Republic was doing quite well in competing for the title of the leading exporting nation in the world. It had little need of the meagre and bankrupt markets and economies of the Communists. Only about 5 per cent of its exports went to the Communist countries, hence the need to cultivate and please the Germans.

Through his conciliatory policies and disarmament proposals Gorbachev had achieved enormous popularity in the Federal Republic, gaining astonishing results in popularity polls by far surpassing any foreign rivals. The enthusiastic persistence of Hans-Dietrich Genscher, the Bonn Foreign Minister, in supporting Gorbachev's policies and overtures had helped to warm relations with Moscow, and Genscher expected high returns in the future.[6] Yet Moscow might have remained cool and unreceptive to his eagerness for co-operation if it were not for the pressing Soviet need of what the Bundesrepublik could offer it. Gratifying Moscow had never alone been enough to guarantee Soviet favours. If combined with a Soviet need, however, it could help.

Gorbachev was nevertheless going to try to drive as hard a bargain as he could in his steadily declining situation. Before a much-awaited meeting with Kohl in Moscow, the Soviet leader uttered dire warnings to those who aspired after German unification. They were playing with fire, he said on 24 October 1988, with a face-to-face encounter with Kohl imminent.[7] He was playing hard to get. No warm, traditional gift of Russian bread and salt for Kohl here, but instead a jab where it hurt. The German chancellor is a difficult man to intimidate, however, and can be as persistent and stubborn as anyone. Kohl talked of the German wish to end their artificial division.[8] The man with the iron teeth, as Gromyko, the former Soviet foreign minister and president once characterized Gorbachev, had met his match in political toughness and cunning.

In addition to the sparring, a certain amount of business was accomplished, but nothing truly earthshaking. The Germans granted credits to further their exports and promised know-how and technical expertise for the modernization of the Soviet nuclear, medical equipment and consumer-good industries.[9] It certainly did not amount to something which would rescue Gorbachev and the Soviet Union from their economic difficulties. If Gorbachev wanted to get more from Kohl, he would have to give more in return. That was the lesson of the meeting.

Before the meeting, anxiety gnawed at the allies of the Bundesrepublik over a possible deal between Kohl and Gorbachev. For some time they had been concerned about an exchange of German unification for German neutrality. These anxieties weakened and subsided after Kohl's return, but lingered to some extent and had some basis in public opinion polls taken in the Federal Republic and in sentiments among the German Social Democrats.[10]

The French in particular were subject to such worries in spite of their close contacts with their German neighbours. French President François Mitterrand and Kohl met frequently and got along well, as did their respective foreign ministers. Yet the worry persisted. Although the division of Germany was acceptable to them as it was to other non-Germans, the French leaders realized how strongly the Germans felt about it. The French were thus anxious to bind the Bundesrepublik to themselves and to the European Community with unbreakable ties. In the French attitudes towards Germany, however, the element of rivalry was also present, for the Federal

Republic was becoming increasingly superior in its growing economic might and a united Germany would leave France further behind. Like his towering predecessor General De Gaulle, whose ego rivalled his physical height, Mitterrand did not like to play second fiddle to anyone. He also was a proud man.

In view of the enthusiasm and support of the Federal Republic for the European Community and for achieving its tantalizing goals of 1992 for a higher level of European unity, French concerns regarding German neutrality seemed far-fetched. Kohl had made his commitment to the Community quite clear both by deed and word. Furthermore, the prosperity of the Bundesrepublik rested heavily on free access to the markets of the Community. They absorbed over half its exports. Kohl also had said that he thought that Community membership could advance rather than block additional ties with East Germany. It gave the Federal Republic additional leverage in dealing with both the DDR and the Soviet Union, as both were eager for more access to trade with the Community.

With his sound instincts for politics and keen sense of German and European history, Kohl appreciated the anxiety about Germany. He strove to reassure France in particular by throwing his weight behind increasing and intensifying Franco–German co-operation. Before his meeting with Gorbachev in Moscow, he sought to reassure all Germany's neighbours. Only by their agreement could German unity come about.[11]

Yet doubts and apprehension persisted among the Western allies of the Bundesrepublik. Foreign Minister Genscher rather than Kohl was a cause of it through his enthusiasm for Gorbachev and advocacy of concessions and favours to the Soviet Union. Genscher was hugely popular among his countrymen and he was defying those who persisted in regarding the Soviet Union as a threat. In Genscher's view, Gorbachev's policies offered unique opportunities for co–operation which should be grasped and used while they lasted. Gorbachev should be encouraged rather than hindered,[12] as this would weaken Soviet hard-liners and produce gains to the Germans and the West.

In spite of his longevity as the foreign minister of the Bundesrepublik, however, Genscher certainly could not singlehandedly determine its foreign policy. He represented after all a minor party, the liberal Free Democrats, the junior partner of Kohl's Christian Democrats in the ruling coalition. Furthermore, with the resignation of his hand-picked successor as the party chairman, Genscher's hold on his party had weakened. Its chairmanship had passed from Martin Bangemann to Count Otto Lambsdorff. The count, a strong-willed and assertive man, was more wary of the Soviets than Genscher and got along well with Kohl.

The occasionally different agendas of Kohl and Genscher were not the only cause of Western apprehensions concerning Germany. As the winter and spring of 1989 rolled along, Kohl's position weakened when support waned for both parties of his coalition, and received a severe blow in local elections in West Berlin on 29 January. Its loss of local power there to a new coalition of the Social Democrats and the Greens raised the spectre of similar results elsewhere. In Berlin the vote for Kohl's party sank from 46 per cent to 38 per cent, and the same trend persisted elsewhere.[13] Support of Kohl's Christian Democrats dropped to an all-time low in the public opinion polls. The combined support for the Social Democrats and the Greens overtook Kohl's coalition, the Social Democrats alone having the backing of 41 per cent of the population.[14]

Such figures, together with the rapidly waning fear in the Federal Republic of any potential threat from the Soviet Union, made the future direction of German politics uncertain. A real threat was emerging to Kohl's ruling coalition in Bonn, and its repercussions were unpredictable. Yet one thing was certain. If somebody was going to replace Kohl, the very change would cause severe palpitations in many a political chest in Germany and elsewhere.

The prospect of Kohl's downfall delighted his many critics and opponents. They had frequently heaped scorn and derision upon him, but time after time he had disappointed those waiting for and predicting his political demise. Now, however, he seemed to be in real trouble. The normally confident and self-assured chancellor had reason to worry. His party was under pressure from left and right simultaneously as both extremes were gaining popularity, which made it difficult to move clearly in any direction. On the other hand, Kohl was known as a tough fighter when cornered. Furthermore, he had a long record of coming out from difficult scrapes on top. He certainly could not be counted out.

Sagging popularity polls and a series of defeats in state elections encouraged a search for a scapegoat among the Christian Democrats. Pressures against Kohl thus spread from outside into his own party. Muttering concerning a need for change at the top would grow if the defeats continued. Nervousness and tension would increase before the party had to face the next general election in 1990. Although not yet a full-scale rebellion, the potential for growing disaffection was there.

In Washington and London, consternation was intensifying with Kohl's problems. The American President George Bush and the British Prime Minister Margaret Thatcher were frustrated and unhappy with Kohl's willingness to go faster and further than they were in the disarmament negotiations with Gorbachev, yet they were reluctant to press him too hard. The disagreements focused on short-range nuclear weapons. Bush and Thatcher knew that these weapons were unpopular in Germany, as the Germans of both east and west recognized that they would be the main victims if the weapons were ever put to use. A head-to-head encounter between Kohl and Thatcher failed to bring a solution. Aware of Kohl's political problems, Bush and Thatcher realized that by adding to his burdens they might in future face a German administration much harder to deal with over such issues. Thus they preferred Kohl's Christian Democrats to its Social Democratic alternative.

The uneasiness of the leaders of the Bundesrepublik's Western allies was not relieved by the wave of massive enthusiasm that greeted Gorbachev on his visit to Bonn in June 1989. A joint declaration by Kohl and Gorbachev spoke of all nations' right to self-determination. This pleased the Germans, although Gorbachev stopped short of promising anything specific concerning possible future German unification.[15]

The prospect of German unification was bound to cause both a quickening pulse and consternation in many quarters. It was a matter of fundamental and historical importance not only to Germans but to all their neighbours and all Europeans as well as to the general East–West relationship. The Western allies of the Federal Republic were on record as being in favour of peaceful German unification, but they had done little to advance it over the decades.

In fact, everybody outside the two Germanies seemed in practice to accept and even embrace the German division as a more or less permanent feature of the political balance in Europe. The period of German dominance during the Second World War had left many persistent fears, and the economic prowess of the Bundesrepublik had inspired new ones in the post-war decades. Old resentments and new jealousies combined with anxiety about the potential impact of German unification on the East–West balance.

Such concerns were born out of the recurring fear that the Federal Republic would drift out of the Western camp towards neutralism in exchange for Soviet acceptance of closer ties between West and East Germany. In the Western alliance such fears continued to feed mainly upon the neutralist traditions and sentiments of the West German Social Democrats. When the Social Democrats were in power, Chancellor Willy Brandt's so-called Ostpolitik had built upon the Social Democratic tradition of striving for a relaxation of relations with the East. He had won goodwill there by recognizing the existing frontiers of West and East Germany. In return, with the additional help of financial and economic carrots, East Germany had become increasingly tied to the Bundesrepublik.

Its Western allies had intermittently worried about the future path of the Federal Republic ever since Brandt had begun to promote his eastern policy.[16] The Ostpolitik built bridges to the east and via increasing economic, political, cultural and human contacts it reduced the wall of separation. The Bundesrepublik had evolved into the most important trading partner for the

Soviet Union and Eastern Europe. Forming only a marginal share of its total foreign trade, trade with the Communists was small in Bonn's trade statistics yet it had greater significance than was indicated by the current figures.

It held a promise of something much larger in the future. Trade with the East had been important to Germany by a historical tradition which preceded its division. Furthermore, it was of great interest to the Soviet Union and Eastern Europe, thirsting for German know-how and specialized products. Their growing economic difficulties also made them hunger for German credits, loans, and investments to help them out of their mess. A prewar saying in Eastern Europe, in a nutshell, threw light on the region's faith in German know-how and skill: when your car broke down on its bad roads, you asked for the local German to fix it.

The Christian Democrats had originally criticized the Ostpolitik, but when they returned to power with the bearlike Chancellor Kohl at the helm in 1982 they continued to pursue the opening to the East. These efforts were spearheaded by Foreign Minister Genscher,[17] a highly intelligent and far-sighted politician. The fact that Genscher survived as the perennial foreign minister of the Bundesrepublik for almost 20 years from 1974 is indicative of his political acumen and skills. A leader of a very minor party, he navigated successfully through shifting coalitions with the Social Democrats and the Christian Democrats, all the time managing to hold on to the most prestigious cabinet post next to the chancellorship.

The *rapprochement* with the East held a lure for the Federal Republic beyond the prospects of increasing ties with East Germany. In fact, it was turning into a veritable economic *Drang nach Osten*, a drive to the East, to the power vacuum evolving between Germany and Russia in the wake of crumbling Communist and Soviet power. With the Communist hold of Poland and Hungary collapsing, German business was rushing into those two countries in particular.[18] The Bundesrepublik had emerged as by far the single most important economic prop for the Hungarian and Polish reforms. Investments in Hungary and aid to Budapest also turned into a 'thank you' to the Hungarians for early opening its frontiers to East German refugees. The help to Poland further served the purpose of putting pressure on the East German regime to proceed with reform as the returns were now clearly visible.

The Federal Republic was also becoming the leading exponent of Western economic co-operation with the Soviet Union. It wanted to help to assure the survival of Gorbachev and his policies of *glasnost* and *perestroika*. Considering their survival the best available guarantee of the relaxation of East–West relations and German interests, Bonn was willing to support its words with deeds.

It could well afford it. The Bundesrepublik had the most powerful economy in Europe, and on the world stage its recent economic prowess rivalled that of Japan. With the leading economy and technology in Europe, it could also afford the strongest army on the continent short of the Soviet Union and nuclear weapons. Both the Americans and Russians had been wooing and complimenting it. Hearing both Bush and Gorbachev saying nice things about them on their own soil had boosted German pride, confidence and assertiveness.[19] One increasingly heard and saw the word 'fatherland', virtually banned from public use for many years because of its association with a nationalistic past. The Germans were also becoming increasingly interested in their history, parts of which many had long avoided. New generations of Germans, born long after the Second World War, were coming to terms with their heritage unburdened by any sense of personal guilt over what had happened during their grandparents' time half a century before.[20]

Notes

1 See, e.g., de Zayas, *Nemesis at Potsdam*, 1989.
2 Personal account, Berlin, July 1990.
3 Grünwald (ed.), *Sudetendeutsche: Opfer und Täter*, 1983.
4 Personal accounts, Munich and Berlin, July 1990.
5 Personal accounts, Munich, Aug. 1989.
6 Genscher, 1991, pp. 137–50.
7 *Pravda*, 25 Oct. 1988.
8 Doder and Branson, *Gorbachev: Heretic in the Kremlin*, 1991, p. 64; Maser, *Helmut Kohl*, 1990, p. 268; *FAZ* and *Die Welt*, 25–26 Oct. 1988.
9 *Der Spiegel*, 31 Oct. 1988.
10 Ibid.
11 *FAZ, SZ*, 19 Oct. 1988.
12 Genscher, 1991, pp. 137–50.
13 *FAZ*, 30 Jan. 1989.
14 *Der Spiegel*, 27 Feb. 1989.
15 German television, 12–15 June 1989; *FAZ* and *Die Welt*, 13–16 June 1989; *Der Spiegel*, 19 June 1989; Karl Kaiser, *Deutschlands Vereinigung*, 1991, pp. 32–5, 143–8.
16 See, e.g., Kissinger, *The White House Years*, 1979, pp. 405–12, 529–34; Renata Fritsch-Bournazel, 'The French View', in Moreton (ed.), *Germany between East and West*, 1987, pp. 64–82.
17 See, e.g., Genscher, *Unterwegs zur Einheit*, 1991.
18 See, e.g., *The Economist*, 29 April 1989.
19 See, e.g., *Rheinischer Merkur/Crist und Welt*, 2 June 1989; *Der Spiegel*, 5 June 1989.
20 Impressions from Germany in 1989 and 1990.

4 Turmoil in the East

Some of the grandparents' generation still held the reins of power and they were confronted with the massive accumulated problems of the DDR. There the sickly, aging Communist leader Erich Honecker at 77 and the other septuagenarians around him seemed increasingly out of touch and at a loss. While their subjects voted with their feet against the failures of Honecker's bailiwick, the object of this tangible vote of non-confidence prepared to celebrate its fortieth anniversary as a triumph in the autumn of 1989. Honecker was letting his people go as never before, hoping this would reduce the potential for disruption. Yet at the same time he kept a tight leash on those who remained behind. The growing contrast with the reforms in Poland, Hungary, and even the Soviet Union, was meanwhile causing the intense frustration of his subjects to grow into a quiet despair and even fury.[1]

Some were finding a way out during the summer and into September of 1989. In increasing numbers they were drawn to a gap in the fence that had hemmed them in. The gap was the Austrian–Hungarian frontier. Hungarian soldiers had been busy clearing the barbed wire and mines in May, conveniently just before the start of the summer holiday season. Thousands of East Germans holidaying on the shores of Lake Balaton and elsewhere in Hungary learned of the new opportunity to head west. Decamping and piling up their children and belongings in their little Trabant cars, they took off westwards towards their promised land of the Bundesrepublik. Reaching the border and crowded crossing points, many simply abandoned their cars and what they could not carry and walked across the frontier. Scenes of East Germans literally pushing and rushing across the border testified to the strength of the urge for freedom and opportunity. As a young woman said, 'You grabbed the chance because it might not last long.'[2]

While many East Germans defied the need of papers and permits to cross the border, others were besieging the Budapest Embassy of the Federal Republic for visas and Hungarian authorities for exit papers. On 10 September the Hungarian Foreign Minister Gyula Horn announced that Hungary would no longer block East German emigration via its territory, and thereby won Bonn's gratitude. The clearance of the last obstacles brought thousands in a surge to Austria. From enthusiastic receptions there they continued their journey to an even more enthusiastic welcome in their new homeland. Many were well-educated, energetic young adults determined to make their fortunes. They were clearly a gain for the Bundesrepublik and a very real human and psychological loss to East Germany. Such a mass escape witnessed by the world through dramatic pictures in the mass media was a humiliation for Honecker and his colleagues and a powerful testimony to the bankruptcy of Communism.[3]

That Hungary was the first Soviet bloc country to allow East German refugees to flee to the West across its borders was no accident. It reflected the extent of its internal liberalization and search for ties with the West. Having moved furthest from the Soviet fold in many ways, the Hungarians much liked Bonn's hints of their future inclusion in the European Community. They also benefited from Chancellor Helmut Kohl's gratitude for opening their western border to the East Germans. Kohl's gratitude went beyond words and took a substantial, concrete form: the West Germans underwrote a billion Deutschmark loan for Hungary and became the Hungarians' influential friends in the IMF, the International Monetary Fund.[4]

The East German refugees' mass escape through Hungary triggered a debate about the German question in the Bundesrepublik. Anxious warnings against attempts to destabilize the DDR alternated with predictions of its impending collapse and speculation about the prospect of reunification.[5] This debate anticipated future changes in Bonn's policy towards the DDR. It had rested on a *de facto* acceptance of the existence of two German states and strove to improve their relations since the launching of Willy Brandt's Ostpolitik. By September 1989 Brandt had also become ready to move beyond that policy, stating prophetically: 'It will surely not be possible to separate for ever what belongs together.'[6] Some other leading Social Democrats shared Brandt's views. The party chairman Hans-Jochen Vogel thought the same way and encouraged contacts with the East German opposition, reversing previous Social Democratic policy of working with the ruling East German Communists.[7]

Yet such changes by no means signified a sudden West German confidence in reunification in the early autumn of 1989. Widespread doubts remained. Some continued to believe in the East Germans' genuine acceptance of the DDR.[8] Others worried about a re-emergence of the wartime anti-German alliance in reaction to possible German assertiveness about reunification.[9] Continuing their mass flight, however, the East Germans made concrete to everyone their alienation from their rulers and their system; its extent surprised many.

In the face of growing demands for reforms in the DDR, caution long prevailed in the west. It did not challenge the Honecker regime and offered little support to the East German opposition. In Bonn this approach reflected Foreign Minister Hans-Dietrich Genscher's thinking and influence. He believed that only international stability could bring reforms in the east and was therefore wary of exploiting what were possibly passing troubles in the DDR.[10]

Yet the continuing refugee flow and turmoil in the DDR fanned talk of the German right of self-determination. It served as a code for reunification, as the former was assumed to result in the latter. To many commentators, adjustment to the new reality clearly caused problems as they found it difficult to fit their old views to it.

From Hungary the East German refugee drama shifted to Czechoslovakia. The palatial Prague Embassy of the Bundesrepublik was overrun and crowded by waves of young East Germans looking for a way to get to the west.[11] When the embassy was packed full, thousands had to camp outside on the squares and pavements. Some found refuge under the stately bridges and in the parks of the ancient city. They shivered during the chilly nights but the Prague Communist authorities turned a cold shoulder, withholding help.

Eventually the Honecker regime agreed to let sealed trains take the trapped refugees through East German territory. This enabled the DDR to try to save face by clinging to the fiction that it was actually expelling disloyal citizens. The pathetic transparency of this attempt became all the more glaring when many other East Germans besieged the train on its stops along the route and tried to climb on board yelling, 'Wir wollen raus', we want to get out.[12]

Flashing night after night across the television screens and front pages of all Europe, the plight of the East German refugees became an unbearable embarrassment to the Honecker regime. Occurring just before the birthday celebrations, they pointed sharply to the hollowness of its accompanying boasts and claims of accomplishments. Honecker lived in a never-never land.

The East German regime had been unable to create a natural sense of national identity and loyalty to itself in the part of Germany that had fallen under Soviet occupation. Not that it had not tried. Attaching itself at first to every expression of left radicalism in the German past and sponsoring the most high-powered athletics and sports programme in the world had not been enough. Only belatedly had the regime cast its net wider, seeking acceptance and legitimacy by restoring statues of the heroes and luminaries of German history from Martin Luther to Frederick the Great.[13] It was almost with desperation attempting to suggest some continuity and connection between itself and such heavyweight symbols of the German and Prussian tradition.

Luther, however, was a reformer and Honecker was not. Frederick the Great perhaps was the foremost of the Enlightened Despots and Honecker may have been a despot but enlightened he was not. He simply did not even come close to either the rebel against Catholic orthodoxy or the sage and sophisticate of the palace of Sans Souci or the later version, *alte Fritz*, of the parade grounds of Potsdam. He had neither the imagination of a reformer nor the sophistication and strength of a successful authoritarian. He even failed to try on the jacket of the great reformer of his time, Gorbachev. Not only neglecting to test the workability of the reform ideas, he went further: banning reform-minded Soviet media or subjecting it to strict censorship, he actively strove to exclude or at least to minimize its impact on East Germany. In a country whose population had easy and ready access to West German media with its reporting of the Soviet reforms, this was both sheer stupidity and grossly ineffective. Although East Germany was a police state second only perhaps to Ceauçescu's Romania and Albania in Europe in the tightness of its police surveillance, this was not enough.

Honecker had stayed in power beyond his time. Like many aging men, he preferred the past to the present. Confronted with the disturbing signs of today, he fled to the glory days of his youth – but the time of building Communism was long gone.

Witnessing the drama of the mass flight of their countrymen on their television screens in programmes broadcast from the Bundesrepublik fired up the East Germans. They took to the streets in their thousands in Leipzig in mass demonstrations for democratization, and exposed and drove home the emptiness of the fortieth anniversary celebration of the DDR. They were spoiling the self-congratulatory pleasure of Honecker and his companions whose tentative grins were reduced to sour scowls.

Emerging as the centre of what amounted to a revolutionary change, the people of Leipzig marched forth as the principal catalyst for the undoing of the old order. By bravely taking their destiny in their own hands, they were changing not only their own lives but East Germany as a whole. Giving the decisive push to the eventual collapse of the rotten edifice of the East German state, they emerged as a primary force for German reunification with all that it meant for Europe and the world. It was a role worthy of an ancient historic centre of the Protestant tradition in Germany. Some 470 years earlier it was in Leipzig that Martin Luther challenged the doctrinal monopoly of his time in a historic debate in 1519. From there the challenge had spread all over Germany and beyond, and thus it was fitting that this time also there was an association between church and protest. The Nikolaikirche of Leipzig was the earliest notable meeting place for opposition and protest groups. Later it became the gathering and starting-point of demonstrations when participants far exceeded the space available in the church.

Leipzig had also been a centre of a mid-nineteenth-century nationwide protest movement, that of the German liberal nationalists who had risen against the repressive rule of the many German princes and the division of the nation into several small or medium-sized principalities and kingdoms. Their dream and aim had been a liberal, united Germany. In their time they had been defeated, but some 140 years later dreams of freedom and national unity were again in the air. Once more crowds of demonstrators were surging through the narrow streets between the ancient buildings with their high pitched roofs and gables in the old German centre of publishing and music. In the past eminent German writers and intellectuals such as Johann Wolfgang von Goethe and the philosopher and mathematician Gottfried Leibniz and composers such as Johann Sebastian Bach, Robert Schumann, Richard Wagner and Felix Mendelssohn had walked the same streets and seen the same (or almost the same) sights. Under Communist rule this venerable old centre of German culture had become run down and blackened and fouled by pollution from the burning of brown coal. While its centre remained reasonably presentable, many of its ancient buildings and quarters were literally falling apart for lack of upkeep. The state of its buildings reflected the state of the order and society that was failing. The people of Leipzig had reason to protest.

The first large demonstration in Leipzig took place on Monday, 25 September 1989. Subsequently demonstrations became a regular Monday focus of activity for the people of Leipzig as the ranks of participants snowballed in size. At first the police tried to break up the demonstrations and the spirit of the opposition by the use of force. Arresting people *en masse*, beating them with sticks and setting dogs on them, the police and the Communist militia sought to intimidate and contain rising waves of dissent. It was as useless as trying to calm a stormy sea. The people were afraid but overcame their fear. From twenty thousand strong on 2 October, the demonstrations grew to number fifty to seventy thousand on 9 October and a hundred thousand a week later. From Leipzig they spread to other cities and towns across East Germany. Crowds poured onto the streets of Dresden, East Berlin, Halle, and that symbol of the ruling ideology, Karl-Marx-Stadt.[14]

The police and militia had used force against the relatively small earliest demonstrations, but they seemed to lack the will to try to overpower or even contain the demonstrations as they grew massive in size. At least in Leipzig preparations were in place for the use of firepower to subdue the crowds on 9 October, but in the end there was no feared repetition of the massacre of Peking's Square of Heavenly Peace, still fresh in the mind of everyone.[15] This perhaps more than anything else testified to the steadfast courage and strength of purpose and will of the people of Leipzig and other East German demonstrators, as they well remembered how their Communist bosses had congratulated and praised their Chinese colleagues for their butchery.

With the East Germans becoming increasingly restive during the autumn of 1989 and many leaving one way or another, demands for democratic reform were becoming bolder and more insistent. Encouraged by the permissiveness of *glasnost* in the Soviet Union, by the examples of their next-door neighbour Poland and the familiar nearby holiday destination of Hungary, the challenge to the repressive East German regime was spreading rapidly. It undermined the aging and ailing Honecker, who had looked forward to the anniversary celebrations of his state. Judging by the eagerness of so many to leave, his subjects did not see what there was to celebrate.

Joining a growing stream of ethnic Germans from Eastern Europe and the Soviet Union, they were heading for the booming Bundesrepublik, which was emerging more and more as the economic powerhouse of Europe. For years, neighbours and trading partners had called on the West Germans for faster economic growth so that they could absorb more imports, but the Federal Republic had cautiously held back, ever mindful and fearful of the return of the monstrous inflations of the distant past. By 1989, however, the West German economy was really becoming alive. Its industry was working at close to 90 per cent capacity and the growth rate of its GNP was far exceeding predictions. The West Germans were getting ready for the increase in demand for their goods expected from European integration by the end of 1992. Furthermore, they were not just preparing themselves: as major exporters of capital goods, they were also helping others to prepare themselves by meeting their needs for retooling. The result was a massive West German trade surplus and a massive accumulation of wealth.

While the economic boom rolled in the Bundesrepublik, the East German birthday party on 6 and 7 October had turned into a nightmare. A showy military parade and torchlight procession on the Unter den Linden in East Berlin, reviewed by Gorbachev and Honecker, was designed as the high point of the celebrations, but while the torch-carrying masses greeted Gorbachev they ignored Honecker. This was a forewarning of what was to come.

The hypocrisy of the self-satisfied and self-congratulatory leaders infuriated the gathered masses. Encouraged by their own sheer numbers and knowledge of previous, smaller protests generated by the fraudulent local elections of the previous May, the angry crowds surged through the streets. Demanding democracy and freedom, they gathered outside the state news agency shouting 'Liars!' They braved massive formations of police, militia and troops, calling them 'traitors'. Attacked and beaten bloody by the police swinging sticks, people were hauled away by the truckload. Later they were submitted to humiliating and intimidating procedures: stripped of their clothes, they had to stand or squat for hours in the cold under police guard.[16]

This violent end to the anniversary celebrations nakedly revealed their emptiness. What had already taken place and ensuing protest demonstrations exposed both the artificial nature of the regime's claims and the bitter reality. They signalled the end of the DDR.

The guest of honour, Mikhail Gorbachev, lectured his host Honecker on the need for changes. His very presence encouraged demands for reform and thousands and then tens of thousands of demonstrators to take to the streets beyond East Berlin, in Leipzig, Dresden, Halle and Magdeburg. Battling against them, swinging sticks and with the help of snarling dogs and water cannon, the Communist police sought in vain to quell them. If it had temporary success in dispersing the demonstrators in one place, new demonstrations broke out elsewhere. These massive public shows of discontent and protest were the largest in East Germany since the Soviet tanks crushed the popular East German uprising on 17 June 1953. On this occasion, however, such aid was not forthcoming to the discouraged and demoralized East German Communist leaders.

They had to face their subjects by themselves and the day of reckoning was approaching fast. This prospect was cracking the solidity of the leadership, where increasingly voices were heard demanding concessions. The cracks were also becoming visible in the formerly tightly controlled press of East Germany.[17] Disagreements over tactics in dealing with the demonstrators and the growing opposition were dividing the regime, although it clung to its monopoly of power.[18] Despite the turmoil on the streets, the regime still seemed to be in charge and few yet expected its collapse.[19]

It was not only in the streets and among the Communists themselves that the signs of change were visible. Citizen groups and other formerly submissive or non-existent political parties were asserting themselves. Originally the opposition had only a loose and vague organizational base, and many of its spokesmen and women seemed out of touch with the East German masses. In the early autumn of 1989 New Forum emerged as the most publicized opposition organization. It voiced largely democratic left socialist opinions sprinkled with some Green influence. Inspired by the Czech reformers' ideas of the Prague Spring of 1968, the Hungarian Communist reformers, and Gorbachev's reforms, it dreamed of creating a so-called third way in the DDR combining democracy and socialism. Clearly to the left of the West German Social Democrats, New Forum was and remained cool to reunification, opposing it vocally.[20]

Organized political opposition to the DDR regime was not limited to New Forum. Signs of it also emerged among the formerly docile auxiliary parties of the dominant SED, the Socialist Unity Party. Both the previously submissive and the re-emerging parties were asserting themselves. East German Christian Democrats, Liberals, and Social Democrats had seen the writing on the wall and were awakening from a long-enforced stupor. Proposals for reform had been voiced among the Christian Democrats and the Liberal Democrats in September 1989.[21] These early signs pointed towards their future as alternatives to Communist domination of the DDR. An independent East German Social Democratic Party had also emerged and during the fortieth anniversary weekend it called for democratization.[22]

Although they were talking of reforms, none of these organizations yet voiced demands for German reunification.[23] This reflected the burden of its prolonged past denial, for reunification had over the years become taboo. Even the original lines of the DDR's national anthem referring to a unified German nation had been dropped.

While the organized East German opposition did not first publicly raise the issue of reunification, some perceptive West German political leaders early foresaw the wider implications of the turbulence in the DDR. One of the first to grasp and record its potential significance for the post-war political order was Professor Kurt Biedenkopf, a prominent Christian Democrat. He thought the closing of the post-war era also ended the justification for the division of Germany. Yet its reunification and stability also demanded massive economic efforts to bridge the gap in living standards between east and west. In Biedenkopf's widely shared view, the West Germans had a moral duty to help the East Germans economically since the latter had carried a much heavier burden after the war through falling under Soviet control and being saddled with heavy reparations.[24]

The sharp disparity between the living standards of the two Germanies undoubtedly helped to undermine the stability of the DDR. Yet it did not as such trigger the demonstrations and turbulence in the autumn of 1989 which brought the eventual collapse of the Communist regime. The DDR had weathered and survived severe economic strains before. They had preceded the uprising of 1953, the construction of the Berlin Wall in 1961, and the ousting of the DDR's veteran leader Walter Ulbricht and his replacement by Erich Honecker in 1971. None of these economic difficulties had resulted in a change of the system.

Shortly after the anniversary celebrations and the accompanying demonstrations and clashes, it was Honecker's turn to go, but this time a change of leaders could not save the system. Something had fundamentally changed in the equation in comparison to the DDR's previous crises. The system had changed or was rapidly changing in the neighbouring or nearby Poland and Hungary, and eventually even Czechoslovakia. This reduced the strategic value of the DDR to the Soviet Union, which also was weakened by internal turmoil. Its ability, reasons, and will to maintain its grip on the DDR were undermined. As the credibility of the ultimate guarantor of the Communist regime in the DDR was being shaken, the regime's prospects of survival grew dim.

The beleaguered East German Communists dumped their ailing veteran leader Honecker on 18 October 1989 in a vain effort to cling to power. Having lost the support of Mikhail Gorbachev, he had become disposable. Replaced by his long-time protégé Egon Krenz, Honecker faced an uncertain future.[25] In a few weeks the once all-powerful boss of East Germany would be reduced to a homeless old man with a threat of prosecution hanging over his head. The sacrificing of Honecker was not going to pacify the snowballing opposition, however. It wanted a change of substance, not one of mere faces and names. It sensed that it had the Communist bosses on the run. In Bonn, Chancellor Helmut Kohl reminded his people two days after the fall of Honecker that 'we hold fast to the unity of the nation' and that 'freedom and the right of self-determination for all Germans remains our aim'.[26]

Formally, Krenz had as much power as his predecessor but the substance of power eluded him. The fear was gone on which Communist power had rested. Originally it held many in its grip, and they had to struggle within themselves to overcome it enough to dare to join the demonstrations. Anger and curiosity helped many to make up their minds. The more that joined, the weaker the restraining hold of fear became until it largely disappeared. Parallel with its weakening went the Communists' and the Soviets' leverage on the people.

As increasing numbers of East Germans overcame their fear and hesitation, the street demonstrations grew ever more massive. Some 300,000 demanded free elections and other democratic reforms in Leipzig on 23 and 30 October. From the streets and the masses the open opposition was spreading to the formerly docile rubber-stamp East German parliament.[27]

Mikhail Gorbachev had apparently favoured Honecker's deposition, feeling that he had become a liability,[28] yet he was unwilling to underwrite either democratization of the DDR or German reunification. Krenz's replacement of Honecker held the promise of neither and was approved by Gorbachev. Honecker had at least grown up in a united Germany and had a sense of the Germans as one nation. He had revealed some inclination to put German interests ahead of Soviet interests during the missile crises of the 1980s, while Krenz had no such record. To the Germans, he was no improvement on Honecker.[29]

Little was known about Krenz in the West but enough had seeped through to secure him a cold reception. The West German press called him an 'election rigger' and 'China friend', referring to Krenz's role in fixing the local election results the previous May and his pronouncements about the massacre of the Chinese dissidents in the Square of Heavenly Peace.[30] Born in 1937 as the son of a Pomeranian tailor, Krenz had proper proletarian origins and, although trained as a teacher, he had devoted himself to a party career. His long service as head of the DDR's Communist youth organization earned him the nickname of a professional juvenile. He smiled and grinned easily, and some said he even smiled when recommending death sentences in connection with his work with the state security organs.[31] Krenz tried desperately to contain the mushrooming criticism and opposition with promises of concessions – but promises of curbing police brutality against the demonstrators and of a new electoral law meant little from a man who had little credibility and commanded less respect.

Having been in charge of internal security, Krenz was directly and even personally connected with the harassment and suppression of people who dared to speak up against the East German regime. He had manipulated elections and had extolled the brutal massacre of Chinese reformers. When a man with that kind of record inherited power from Honecker, the East Germans saw little reason to listen to him or to hope for any significant improvement under him in their lifetime. With the fear factor gone, even the chilling aspects of Krenz could no longer help him to assert control. When demonstrators numbering hundreds of thousands were on the streets in Leipzig, such a mass of humanity defied the nerve of the cornered Communist hardliners to try to block it with bullets. The resulting bloodshed in the heart of Europe would have caused the recent bloodiness of Beijing to pale in comparison.

The promises of Gorbachev's *perestroika* encouraged many East Germans to expect and demand more at home, yet even prospects of such improvement were not enough for many others – they continued to pour into West Germany. The Gorbachev reforms not only affected the Germans in the East. They also had a profound impact on the Bundesrepublik, reassuring it that there was little to fear from the Soviet Union. The relieved West Germans had offered a startlingly enthusiastic welcome to the Soviet leader during his June 1989 visit to Bonn, and in West German public opinion polls his popularity was flying high. They had also some concrete, visible evidence of beneficial results specifically for Germans of Gorbachev's policies – the enabling of ethnic Germans of Eastern Europe and the Soviet Union by the hundreds of thousands to emigrate to the Bundesrepublik. Joining the newcomers from East Germany, they were a potential additional shot in the arm to the already roaring West German economy.

By its example in aiding and abetting reform in Eastern Europe and by espousing relaxation in East–West relations, Soviet policy was actually undermining the justification for and the existence of a separate East German state. Shorn of its distinct ideology, that artificial creation had little reason to exist. Thus the Soviet Union was, in fact, unintentionally putting the issue of German reunification to the forefront of the international stage. This caused the leaders of Bonn's Western allies a dilemma. They were slow in addressing in public the implications for German reunification of the East German turmoil and the flow of refugees. They had paid lip-service to it for decades but had not supported their words with actions. Their words in favour of German reunification had cost them little as long as it seemed an impossible prospect. In the autumn of 1989, the formerly impossible began to look possible.

Washington's attitudes towards German reunification were affected by its concerns about the Soviet Union. Fearing the unknown and the unpredictability resulting from the liberalization of the Soviet bloc and Soviet reactions to it, Washington's stand was cautious and even baffled. President Bush was wary of weakening Soviet President Mikhail Gorbachev's position, and old apprehensions about Germany and the Germans also revived among the American establishment.

Uncertain over their Western allies' and Moscow's reactions, the Germans hesitated to bring up reunification during the early autumn of 1989. Many worried that it would put at risk the prospects rising out of the turmoil in the DDR.[32] The Germans had not forgotten the unspoken mission of NATO which its former secretary general, Lord Ismay, had once conceded included control of them.[33]

Bonn's uncertainty over its Western allies' reactions also led Chancellor Kohl and other West German leaders to repeatedly pledge loyalty to the Western Alliance. Knowing their concerns, Bush distanced himself publicly from commentary fearful of German reunification, though neither did he want to commit himself to a timetable for it.[34] The Germans would also have to obtain British and French agreement on reunification.[35] This was easier said than done. While both the British and French establishments included those who favoured it, they were not in charge at the time. Among others, the former French Foreign Minister Jean François Poncet and a prominent French specialist on Germany, Alfred Grosser, expressed support for German aspirations. Grosser found it 'hard to understand the French attitude, which consists of saying the whole world must practise self-determination – everyone, that is, but the East Germans'.[36] To many other British and French leaders the winged words of the Nobel Prize-winning French writer François Mauriac applied even better. He had declared himself so fond of Germany that the more German states that existed the better.[37]

Before the fall of the Berlin Wall hardly anyone had foreseen or expected German reunification in the near future. Even after its fall, many authoritative commentators and prophets of German affairs predicted that reunification would take years. This lack of foresight rested in part upon a lack of understanding of the situation in the DDR. Outsiders, including West Germans, believed it to be a far more viable and even successful entity than was the reality.

Intellectuals in particular but also politicians made gross misjudgements. Many held as an article of faith that the DDR was a successful socialist experiment which rivalled the living standards of the United Kingdom, and statistics seemed to bear this out as well as establish the DDR as the tenth industrial power in the world. It was as if holders of such views had never travelled in the United Kingdom and the DDR with at least one eye open. From such beliefs it was easy to arrive at the conclusion that the people of the DDR were satisfied with their lot.

The belief was also widespread that the DDR was not only an international necessity but in time had become a natural entity. In this view its existence was necessary for the stability of Europe and the precarious balance between the East and West and it had succeeded in creating its own identity embraced by its people.

The East German economy had the reputation of being the most prosperous and best performing among the economies of the Soviet bloc, but what did that mean in practice? Did it mean at least a modicum of success or simply that East Germany suffered less from economic stagnation than the rest of the bloc? Whatever it meant, the East Germans were not satisfied with their material condition. To them it was no consolation that they were better off than the poverty-stricken Poles or the Soviets – they were comparing their lot with their fellow Germans in the Bundesrepublik.

Furthermore, the stagnation, even decline, was there for everyone to see with their own eyes. East Germany seemed unable even to keep up the economic infrastructure that it had inherited from Nazi Germany. Visible symbols of this inability were long stretches of closed lanes on the autobahns, roads overgrown with bushes and trees, collapsed bridges, decaying buildings and streets in towns and villages. Those who knew more about the economic situation from the inside knew that it was far worse than was told by the statistics or even the testimony of one's own eyes. For lack of necessary investment in plant and machinery, the economy was living on capital assets and borrowed time.[38] As elsewhere in the Soviet bloc, the system was also running out of assets and drive. The resulting lowering of living standards and quality of life created a potentially explosive situation.

Clearly, many people wore blinkers, or at least rose-colored spectacles, when looking at the DDR. In some ways perhaps most amazing was the blind or wilful overlooking of the enormous environmental destruction and pollution there by intellectuals otherwise extremely sensitive to such matters. Leftist intellectuals in particular seemed willingly to overlook or tolerate various evils and failings in the DDR for which they had a very sharp eye and low tolerance in their own societies.[39]

In the case of leftist West German intellectuals, a certain degree of idealization of and selective blindness to the reality in the DDR resulted from their discomfort with and criticism of their own part of Germany. With their subjective views, intellectuals both in the east and the west certainly underestimated the Federal Republic's power of attraction to the ordinary East Germans. Here West German Social Democrats and East German New Forum intellectuals shared the same astigmatism. They seemed to have little appreciation of the East Germans' desperate desire, soon to become quite apparent, to escape their sense of being second-class Germans, grounded in the oppressiveness and poverty of the DDR.

Many East German intellectuals were either out of touch or lacked empathy with their people's aspirations and the extent of the alienation between the people and the system and the privileged in the DDR. This was not often fully realized by Western reporters and observers who overestimated both the East German intellectuals' following and their acumen to assess the mood of their fellow East Germans. Accordingly, the actions and reactions of the East German masses repeatedly surprised them both.[40]

Both tended to entertain exaggerated notions of most East Germans' attachment to the DDR and the strength of their sense of separate identity. This was a common mistake among the intellectual New Forum critics of the Honecker regime and a primary cause of their failure to retain a mass following.[41] Such misconceptions were persistently reflected in reports and dispatches which spoke about the East German nation, sometimes empathizing with those mourning its impending death. Although the DDR was a state, its people neither were nor regarded themselves as a separate and distinct nation. Rather they were and felt themselves to be part of the German nation.

These misconceptions also led to conclusions that it was merely the lure of the material abundance of the Bundesrepublik that led the East Germans to support reunification. Certainly a strong desire to improve their material conditions of life was an important factor, but not the only factor in this drive. A strong urge to improve the quality of their lives involved many other and often intangible matters for many East Germans. Freedom from official pressure, harassment and restrictions, as well as a sense of German identity, were also of fundamental importance.[42]

Outsiders' inaccurate assessments of the East German attitudes towards the system in which they had to live and, before 1989, even towards their rulers, were sometimes due to ignorance or a general ideological empathy with socialism. Ignorance or blindness concerning the degree and magnitude of police surveillance, intimidation and blackmail within the DDR was common among outsiders. Even more lacking was appreciation and understanding of their powerful impact and the corrupting role of the associated reward system on East German lives.[43] Lack of knowledge or a disregard of these made the essence of the East German society and state elusive and left the real feelings and mood of its people a riddle.

Yet it was obvious that the DDR was a police state *par excellence*. It was at the core of the system that the Soviet Union had sponsored in its zone of occupation in Germany. It was the fundamental nature of the society which its inhabitants had come to so abhor that most wanted to either leave it or destroy it. In the DDR the agents or informers of the state security police, the Staatsicherheit or the Stasi, were everywhere.[44] After its demise it was discovered that the Stasi had roughly twice the personnel of its Nazi counterpart to control a captive population which amounted to less than a quarter of the Third Reich. Security police know-how was perhaps the most successful export item of the DDR to the oppressive regimes of Marxist Third World countries.

After the fall of the East German Communist regime, increasing numbers of people felt that those it put in power were criminals not fundamentally different from the bosses of Nazi Germany. They had constructed a police state of omnipresent informers, corruption, lies and decaying economy. The Stasi served as the enforcer of the ruling Politburo from which power flowed downward. It had informers in every workplace and on every residential block or highrise apartment building. Persuaded by ideological zeal and material rewards or a sense of power and importance or pressured by blackmail, they kept a sharp eye on their colleagues and neighbours. Their minutely detailed reports kept an army of some hundred thousand full-time Stasi employees busy in reading, interpreting, classifying and processing them. Acting as informers, joining the party and praising the leadership, these were the ways to get ahead in a career, to gain privileges and material rewards not available to others.[45]

Official and private lies were everywhere. The official mass media was so distrusted that for reliable information virtually the whole population turned to the media of the Bundesrepublik. Teachers were forced to lie to their pupils in schools and were pressured by the Stasi to extend punishments of parents to their children in classrooms and playgrounds. One way was the freezing out or isolation of these children from their classmates. The Nazis had practised the same chilling methods.[46]

This was the background that produced the mass flight of East Germans to the Bundesrepublik in the summer and autumn of 1989 and the huge demonstrations on the streets of East German cities. The bloodletting of the mass flight crippled the already run-down East German economy, as many of those who left were young adults with skills vital for its functioning. Repeatedly the massive street demonstrations defied efforts at intimidation and police intervention and brutality. Increasingly confident, the demonstrators became bolder. Their slogan, 'Wir sind das Volk', we are the people, served notice to the ruling clique that they were fast becoming irrelevant in the minds of their people. It was not long before a new rallying cry thundered and echoed in the streets from hundreds of thousands throats. 'Wir sind ein Volk', we are one people, meant that the time of German reunification had arrived.

It was clear that things could not continue as before. If Moscow had had the will, Soviet tanks could have bloodily crushed this popular East German uprising, as they had in June 1953, but they could not have repaired the broken-down economy. However, Moscow seemed to have lost its will and stomach for using tanks to solve political and economic problems. It had not worked in Afghanistan and nothing seemed to work in the Soviet Union. In desperate need of a shift of resources from military to civilian use, Western credits, know-how and help, Moscow simply could not afford to use tanks to try to maintain its grip on East Germany or the rest of Eastern Europe. The men in the Kremlin knew that much of what they most needed they would have to try to get from Bonn. This was the reality behind the surrender of Communist power in East Germany.

The heir of Honecker's power, the ever-grinning Egon Krenz, made concession after concession in a panting, nervous effort to cling to his newly won position. They were too little and too late. He was trying to hang on to the old order as much as possible, to the point of letting all those opposed to it leave in the hope of weakening the opposition. The East Germans did not trust his promises, which seemed grudgingly given only for tactical reasons.[47] Real power was already beyond him. It had passed to the crowds on the streets. Some one million demonstrated in East Berlin against the Communists' monopoly of power. They openly mocked Krenz and other Communist leaders who attempted to speak to them on 4 November 1989. Millions of East Germans followed this mass action on television.[48] Witnessing the massive show of popular strength and the humiliation of the Communists, other political forces took increasing courage. New forces started to emerge and assert their independence from the Communists. Left out on a limb, the East German cabinet headed by Prime Minister Willy Stoph resigned on 7 November 1989.[49] In a telling testimony to the political stagnation of East Germany, the 75-year-old Stoph had served as Prime Minister since 1964, except for a short interlude in the mid-1970s.

The very same day that the East German cabinet resigned, anti-government demonstrators in Moscow revived a historic Bolshevik slogan against the Tsar. But this time the signs stating 'Fish begin to rot at the head' were aimed against the Communist rulers in the Kremlin.[50] In the streets of East German cities and towns, demonstrations of hundreds of thousands continued as practically daily occurrences, and continually built up the strength of the challenge to the old Communist order. Defying the widely held notion of Germans as submissive people they nevertheless remained basically orderly, thus reinforcing another cherished German characteristic. Truly it was a German revolution of the people. In contrast, the East German cabinet was a mere creature of the ruling Politburo. Its resignation followed on 9 November.[51] Krenz attempted to salvage what he could by retaining some members in the new Politburo, yet it was becoming clear that no mere tinkering with the old order could maintain Communist power. Krenz was grinning in vain.

Notes

1 Impressions from conversations with East Germans in 1989.
2 Ibid.
3 West German television and *SZ*, 10–13 Sept. 1989; *Der Spiegel*, 18 Sept. 1989; Horn, *Freiheit die ich meine*, 1991, pp. 308–33.
4 *FR*, 16 Sept. 1989; *Stuttgarter Zeitung*, 21 Oct. 1989; Horn, 1991, pp. 308–33; Jim Hoagland, 'Europe's Destiny', *Foreign Affairs*, 1989/1990, p. 40.
5 See, e.g. *SZ*, 12 Aug.; *Kölner Stadt-Anzeiger*, 2 Sept.; *Stuttgarter Zeitung*, 12 Sept.; *FAZ*, 21 Sept. 1989.
6 *SZ*, 23 Sept. 1989.
7 Ibid.
8 Ibid.
9 *FAZ*, 21 Sept. 1989.
10 *FR*, 2 Oct. 1989.
11 See, e.g., Darnton, *Berlin Journal, 1989–1990*, 1991, pp. 67–73.
12 *Der Spiegel*, 2, 9 Oct. 1989; *SZ*, 5 Oct. 1989.
13 See, e.g., J. Kuppe, in Weidenfeld (ed.), *Geschichtsbewusstsein der Deutschen*, 1987, pp. 175–7; Honecker, 1982, pp. 613–14.
14 *FAZ*, *SZ* and *Die Welt*, 26, 27 Sept.; 3, 4 Oct.; 10, 11 Oct.; 17, 18 Oct. 1989; *Der Spiegel*, 2, 9, 16 Oct. 1989.
15 Kuhn, *Der Tag der Entscheidung*, 1992.
16 *Welt am Sonntag*, 8 Oct.; *Bild Zeitung*, *Der Tagesspiegel*, *Die Tageszeitung*, *FAZ*, *FR*, *SZ* and *Die Welt*, 9, 10 Oct. 1989.
17 See, e.g., *Berliner Zeitung* and *Die Junge Welt*, 10, 11, 12, 13 Oct. 1989.
18 *FAZ*, 12 Oct. 1989.
19 *SZ*, 7 Oct. 1989.
20 *FAZ* and *Die Welt*, 4 Oct. 1989; Knabe (ed.), *Aufbruch in eine andere DDR*, 1989; Rein (ed.), *Die Opposition in der DDR*, 1989; *Deutschland Archiv*, Dec. 1990, pp. 1935–41.
21 *Rheinische Post*, 30 Sept. 1989.
22 *General-Anzeiger*, 9 Oct. 1989.
23 *Die Welt*, 7 Oct. 1989.
24 Kurt Biedenkopf, in *Rheinischer Merkur/Christ und Welt*, 6 Oct. 1989.
25 *Neues Deutschland*, 19 Oct. 1989; Doder and Branson, *Gorbachev: Heretic in the Kremlin*, 1991, pp. 387–8; Beschloss and Talbott, *At the Highest Levels*, 1993, p. 133.
26 Kohl, in Seewald (ed.), *Helmut Kohl: Deutschlands Zukunft in Europa*, 1990, pp. 45, 66.
27 *FAZ*, *SZ* and *Die Welt*, 29, 31 Oct. 1989.
28 *Westdeutsche Allgemeine*, 19 Oct. 1989.
29 *General-Anzeigner*, 19 Oct. 1989.

30 *SZ*, 20 Oct. 1989.
31 *General-Anzeiger* and *Stuttgarter Zeitung*, 19 Oct. 1989.
32 *Der Tagesspiegel*, 12 Oct. 1989.
33 Jan Reifenberg, in *FAZ*, 18 Oct. 1989.
34 *Rheinischer Merkur/Christ und Welt*, 3 Nov. 1989.
35 Josef Joffe, in *SZ*, 28 Oct. 1989.
36 *Die Welt*, 30 Oct. 1989.
37 Ibid.
38 Impressions from the DDR and occasional conversations with East Germans in 1989 and 1990.
39 Cf. Andrei S. Markovits, 'The West German 68-ers Encounter the Events of 1989', *German Politics*, vol. 1, no. 1, 1992, pp. 13–29; Melanie Drane, 'A Divided Left Faces German Unity: A Response to Andrei Markovits', *German Politics*, vol. 1, no. 2, 1992, pp. 274–81.
40 Personal impressions; sociological research has backed up these early observations. See, e.g., John Torpey, 'Two Movements, Not a Revolution: Exodus and Opposition to the East German Transformations, 1989–1990', *German Politics and Society*, Summer, 1992, pp. 21–42, especially 31–7.
41 Ibid.
42 Ibid; cf. Schneider, *Leipziger Demontagebuch*, 1990; Schüddekopf (ed.), *Wir sind das Volk*, 1990; Laurence McFalls, 'The Modest Germans; Towards an Understanding of the East Germans' Revolution', *German Politics and Society*, Summer, 1992, pp. 1–20.
43 Based on conversations with East Germans, Berlin, July 1990.
44 Cf. Fricke, *Die DDR-Staatssicherheit*, 1989, and Fricke, 'The Power of the Stasi', *German Comments*, October, 1990, pp. 16–23; Gill and Schröter, *Das Ministerium für Staatssicherheit*, 1991; Schell and Kalinka, *Stasi und kein Ende*, 1991; Christiane Lemke, 'Trials and Tribulations: The Stasi Legacy in Contemporary German Politics', *German Politics and Society*, Summer, 1992, pp. 46–7.
45 Cf. Gauck, *Die Stasi-Akten*, 1991, and Schäuble, *Der Vertrag*, 1991, pp. 265–83; conversations with East Germans, 1989–90
46 Based on conversation with East Germans in 1990.
47 *FAZ* and *Rheinischer Merkur/Christ und Welt*, 3 Nov.; *FR*, 6 Nov. 1989.
48 German television, 4, 5 Nov. 1989; *Welt am Sonntag*, 5 Nov. 1989; Mitter and Walle (eds), *Ich liebe euch doch alle*, p. 249.
49 *Neues Deutschland*, 8 Nov. 1989.
50 *IHTr*, 8 Nov. 1989.
51 *Neues Deutschland*, 10 Nov. 1989.

5 A Breakthrough and Reactions

While these momentous and historic events were taking place in East Germany, Chancellor Kohl wasted little time in coming to terms with them. Seeking to guide and shape the continuing process in Germany, he addressed the Bundestag on 8 November 1989, extending a helping hand to the East Germans, saying:

> Free self-determination for all Germans – that was, is and will be also the wish, yes, the longing of our compatriots in the DDR. Who of us is not touched and moved seeing pictures of several hundreds of thousands of people peacefully gathered in Berlin, in Leipzig or in Dresden, in Schwerin, in Plauen and in other towns of the DDR? They call out: 'We are the people!' and I am sure their call will not fade away.

He tied together free elections in East Germany, German self-determination and German reunification as parts of the same issue. Calling for reunification in freedom, he said confidently of the East Germans, 'I am certain that if they get the chance, they will choose freedom and unity.'[1]

In an effort to realize these aims, he promised massive aid to bankrupt East Germany after free elections and economic reforms, and sought to reassure his Western allies. Thus, while making it clear that German unification was an urgent matter on his agenda, Kohl also pledged continued allegiance to the West. The core of Kohl's message was nevertheless German unity: 'We have less reason than ever to be resigned to the long-term division of Germany into two states.'[2]

Kohl was confident, yet some Western commentators feared that in desperation the Communists might resort to violence. Without fully realizing the mood of the East German army, they thought the use of it was still an option for Krenz. Others dreaded the possibility of a Soviet military coup in the face of the failures of *perestroika* and the impending disintegration of the Soviet hold on Eastern Europe.[3]

Then there were those who did not know what to fear most, a crackdown in East Germany or German reunification. The latter prospect was most unsettling to the British and French political power élites as, in some ways, they stood to lose most by it. Already concerned by and resentful of the growing might of the Bundesrepublik, many were displeased with the idea of a united Germany.

The economic weight of the Bundesrepublik had left both Britain and France clearly behind, but a united Germany would be in a different league. The size of its economy would be close to the size of the British and French economies put together. It would have a population about 40 per cent larger than either Britain or France. At a time when economic might seemed to be replacing military power as a measure of influence in the world, British and French nuclear weapons could hardly make up such a gap and maintain a balance. For both Britain and France it would be next to impossible to preserve the kind of near equality with a united Germany that they had had with the Bundesrepublik. Nobody enjoys a reduction in their relative status, a prospect that the British and French leaders were facing with German reunification.

The idea of German reunification was not only upsetting because of what it meant for the balance of power between what had formerly been near equals. It was also disturbing because of uncertainty as to where a unified Germany would stand in the future. What would its relations be with its partners in the European Community? Would it stay in the Community or would unification come in exchange for neutrality? And even if it stayed in the European Community, how would its enhanced stature affect the very nature of the Community? In short, what was the future role of a united Germany in Europe?[4] With so many anxious questions hanging nervously in the air, no wonder potential German reunification caused very mixed feelings.

While Britain attempted to maintain its traditional aloofness towards the continent, France had entered into very close co-operation with the Bundesrepublik over the years. The Bonn–Paris axis had been a key to the political and economic structure of Western Europe, the burying of the ancient Franco–German hostilities having enabled Western Europe to enjoy an era of political stability and economic prosperity. Some feared that German reunification might undermine this political stability.

The anxiety over this prospect which emerged among the ruling circles in Paris and London in particular did not pass unnoticed elsewhere. The French President François Mitterrand sought to reassure the Germans during a visit to Bonn, claiming that he was 'not afraid of reunification', and conceding that reunification should be left entirely to the Germans.[5] Yet such words did not overcome all the anxieties and reassure everybody. To some, they revealed what they sought to deny.

France had hoped to maintain a certain political and cultural leadership in a Western Europe increasingly dominated economically by the Bundesrepublik. Now that hope was slipping, and with it an uncomfortably increasing sense of inferiority to Germany was spreading among the French. With the possibility of German reunification, Germany stood not only to grow greatly in strength and resources *vis-à-vis* France, but with the retreat of Soviet power from Eastern Europe, Germany would emerge as the pivotal central power in Europe. While its partner and rival would become the kingpin of the continent, France faced the prospect of its central role in Western Europe being reduced to a more marginal role in Europe in the shadow of Germany. Not only differences in human and material resources but differences in geographical and geo-political location would predicate a shift in favour of a united Germany. Geography put Germany at the heart of Europe. To counter such developments, the French tried to advance rapidly a more intense integration of Western Europe. While conceding the German right of self-determination in theory, some French spokesmen were very verbose in connecting it to and emphasizing Germany's neighbours' rights and the abstract interests of peace in Europe.[6]

Mixed with a certain nostalgia about the 'stability' of the past decades went wishful thinking that the East Germans might want to maintain their own state if only they received more freedom, but that was not to be. There were, of course, socialist idealists in Eastern Germany who dreamed of their own democratic state, and adherents of such sentiments were disproportionately represented among vocal intellectuals active in their opposition towards the East German Communist regime. Highly audible and visible, their views were taken to be fairly representative of the popular mood among the East Germans. People tend to believe what they want to believe. Numerous elements of the power élites in London, Paris and Rome preferred the idea of two German states to the vision of a reunified Germany, and hence they were quick to echo the idea of an East German state shorn of its repressive apparatus. 'We like Germany so well that we want two of them,' was a cynical refrain often repeated among political operators.

The people of East Germany were not a nation who wanted a separate state of their own, however. They felt German. They wanted not only freedom from oppression but the reunification of Germany and prosperity. They were leaving at the rate of 10,000 to 11,000 souls a day in early November 1989, before this flood of humanity broke the dam. Large numbers were fleeing through a narrow neck of Czechoslovak territory that jutted between East Germany and the Bundesrepublik, taking advantage of the reopening of the Czechoslovak borders on 1 November 1989. Sad and tearful scenes were typical of these departures. Mothers and fathers, sons and daughters, were taking leave of one another without knowing when they would meet again.

Many were leaving everything behind, convinced that their window of opportunity could soon be closed again.[7]

In a desperate, last-minute manoeuvre, Krenz finally authorized the opening of the border to the Bundesrepublik in November 1989. It was a way to try to win acceptance but was also an effort to open a safety valve to let off steam. Krenz and other East German Communists hoped that, once their countrymen saw that they could go as they wished, the fever to leave would ebb in most people and that those most irreconcilable would leave for good. On 9 November the East Germans started to clear the barbed wire and knock down the Berlin Wall, which drew massive and enthusiastic crowds and led to an incredible and wonderful scene. Young Germans from east and west were climbing and pulling each other up onto the hated wall, joyfully hugging and dancing. Happy throngs were milling around the Brandenburg Gate in the heart of old unified Berlin, toasting and waving German flags. Millions were crowding the streets of Berlin and other German cities in an outpouring of emotion rarely seen. West Berlin welcomed with open arms, tears of joy, sekt, and flowers the East Berliners pouring through the wall.[8]

The stunning news reached Helmut Kohl in Warsaw while he was on a state visit to Poland. Aware of world attention focusing upon Germany, he felt both confident and the need to be careful. Knowing that both East and West were closely watching the Germans, he was anxious to get in touch with Bush, Gorbachev, Mitterrand and Thatcher as soon as possible. He sensed the possibility of German unification drawing closer as 'the wheel of history is turning faster'.[9] Interrupting his Polish visit, he dashed to Berlin in order to share the great moment with his compatriots.

Together with Willy Brandt, who had been the mayor of Berlin when the wall was built, Kohl addressed the German people outside the Schöneberg Rathaus, the West Berlin city hall. Both men were deeply moved and expressed similar sentiments, with Kohl declaring, 'We are and remain one nation. We belong together.' Brandt thanked the Lord for having lived long enough to experience the happy day, and exclaimed that the 'unnatural division of Germany' could not last, and added the famous words, 'we are now in a situation where what belongs together will grow together', to the delight of the cheering crowd.[10]

Afterwards, Kohl mixed with the crowds of East Berliners near Checkpoint Charlie where he met overwhelming enthusiasm. Tears flowed, hands were extended in greeting and repeated calls, 'Helmut, Helmut, unite the country and the people', filled the air. This spontaneous warmth and trust deeply impressed and moved Kohl, who observed, 'Here one sees what the people really think.'[11]

While still in Berlin, Kohl received a confidential message from Gorbachev asking him to help avoid 'chaos' at any price. The message made the

Germans at first wonder whether it was more a sign of genuine concern or a veiled warning. Upon learning that Gorbachev had also advised the SED leaders to contribute to a 'friendly transformation' in the DDR, Kohl felt reassured. At least the Soviet Union was not contemplating the use of force[12] to save the DDR regime which was tottering and desperately hoped for West German economic aid. Calling Gorbachev, Kohl assured him of economic support for his reforms and in return was gratified to receive 'no threat, no warning, only a request to let prudence rule'. Until then Kohl, despite all earlier contacts, seemed to have had some doubts; his foreign policy adviser Horst Teltschick reported that after the call tension fell from Kohl who laughed and said, 'The hay is in the barn.'[13]

When the news of the opening of the border reached them in Bonn, the members of the Bundestag, carried away by emotion, stood spontaneously in their plenary session and began to sing triumphantly the German national anthem. Choked with emotion, some had tears in their eyes.[14] Clearly, German feelings had been deeply stirred. Comparing the joy he felt at the opening of the Berlin Wall to his joy when he was reunited with his wife after the war, Helmut Schmidt gave a human and poignant dimension and expression to many Germans' emotions at that time.

Intense human emotions can make history and so they did on 9 and 10 November 1989 in Berlin. The excitement of that night, transmitted by TV broadcasts all over Germany, uncorked desires and urges which could not be bottled up. Those with eyes to see and a willingness to understand knew that after this Berlin night things in Germany could not remain the same. Something irrevocable had happened which precluded the survival of the old regime and system in the DDR.

Insisting on the Communists' continuing hold on power, Krenz did not seem to realize that the curtain was coming down for him and them. Piecemeal reforms would not be enough for the East Germans who had tasted freedom; they would demand a full voice in their own destiny, and the future changes in East Germany would affect not only the DDR but all of Germany and, beyond it, Europe and the world.

All along the inter-German border, mile-long lines of East German cars, Trabants and Wartburgs, were crossing the formerly insurmountable forbidden frontier as millions headed west for the first time in their lives. The people of the Bundesrepublik welcomed their fellow Germans generously. There was welcome money, free shopping, concerts, and theatres for the more than three million East Germans who rushed to make use of the opportunity, the first in a lifetime for many, to come to the west. After the jubilation they went back to their homes and work and the number of daily emigrants to the Bundesrepublik decreased sharply. The East Germans now felt that they had options and were no longer constrained like the inmates of a closed camp from which it was difficult or impossible to receive permission for a leave.

While much of the mass media of the world reported on and reflected the enthusiasm and exuberance of the Germans over the opening of the wall, the reactions of political leaders and establishments were more cautious and muted. Some reactions were not pleasing to the Germans. While assuring Kohl of his friendship, Mitterrand planned to go ahead with a state visit to the DDR, while the British Foreign Minister Douglas Hurd distanced himself from German reunification. The Germans were particularly vexed by Israeli Prime Minister Yitzhak Shamir's statements which received wide circulation in the American mass media. He had doubts about German reunification and, recalling the Holocaust, expressed fears of its repetition if Germany again became the strongest power in Europe. Bush informed Kohl on the telephone of differences in views on the part of Bonn's allies, but was ready to meet him only after the forthcoming summit with Gorbachev in Malta in early December 1989.[15]

Kohl took note of the mood among his allies and, although he spoke of the Germans' right to self-determination, he did not bring up German unification at the EC summit arranged by Mitterrand as he did not want additional difficulties for his freedom of action on the matter.[16] Meanwhile, he found encouragement in the opinion polls and the continually growing demonstrations in the DDR. The polls indicated that 70 per cent of West Germans supported reunification and believed it could occur within ten years. A call for reunification was also heard for the first time loud and clear in the DDR where the earlier slogan 'We are the people' was evolving into 'We are one people'. It echoed in huge mass demonstrations involving some 250,000 people in Leipzig and additional tens of thousands in other East German cities on Monday, 20 November 1989.[17]

Perhaps impressed by the same phenomena, both Soviet and American representatives passed conciliatory messages to Bonn. A Soviet representative mentioned the possibility of a German confederation and Washington confirmed in principle its support of German self-determination and unity. The first Bonn ally to do so, Washington yet remained apprehensive and wary of its timing and manner and concerned with Gorbachev's reactions to it. Bush impressed on Kohl that Gorbachev was anxious about German unity. Kohl in turn attempted to link German unification to further European integration in a speech to the EC parliament in Strasbourg.[18] This was a clever move to overcome the hesitations and apprehension of Germany's neighbours, and it became an oft-repeated Kohl refrain to smooth the way and to reassure the doubtful and fearful.

Among the Germans, Kohl faced a growing need to provide leadership on the question of unification. This became imperative when the belief spread that it was a real possibility, as otherwise political rivals might act first and steal the show. On the eve of Kohl's public presentation of his ten-point plan, his road map for German unity, *Der Spiegel* reported that many politicians no longer doubted unification but rather wondered when and how it would take place. Estimations in this regard varied widely. Kohl himself thought unification would come in five to ten years.[19]

While most Germans were exhilarated by the opening of the border and celebrated it with joy, it caused some to worry and depressed others. Among these were the East German Communists. In an effort to boost its sagging morale the party gathered its supporters to a massive rally in Berlin even as its members were resigning in droves. Those remaining met with increasingly open anger and hostility. The stress and pressure were getting too much for some party members, who found their only refuge in death.

The Communists tried to rescue what they could by promoting the Dresden party leader, Hans Modrow, the new Prime Minister on 13 November. He was elected by the Volkskammer, the DDR legislature, in a secret ballot in use for the first time. Modrow had received favourable publicity in the Western media because of his relatively modest lifestyle. He was believed to have more credibility with the people than the other Communist leaders as he was unpopular with the Honecker's old guard and had a reputation for being receptive to reforms.[20]

It did not help. Massive demonstrations against the Communist regime and for free elections continued. Soon cries for 'Ein Deutsche Vaterland', one German fatherland, and 'Wir sind ein Volk', we are one people, echoed on the streets. It was rapidly becoming clear that not only the end of the Communist regime but also that of the East German state was near. The people on the streets rather than the budding alternate self-proclaimed leaders represented the mood of the majority of East Germans. Furthermore, on the desire for reunification there was little difference between the Germans of the east and west. By an overwhelming majority, both wanted it. Public opinion polls taken in November 1989 showed 67 per cent of the former and close to 70 per cent of the latter in favour of it.[21]

Combined with the events and mood in the DDR and the opening of its borders to the west, such polls caused some consternation outside Germany. Although Kohl and the Polish Prime Minister Tadeusz Mazowiecki had hugged one another and attended a church service together during Kohl's Polish visit, the Poles in particular were wary of German reunification. Kohl and Mazowiecki had met in a highly charged symbolic reconciliation at the former estate of Count James Helmuth von Moltke in Silesia. The count was a key figure in German anti-Nazi resistance and a victim of Hitler, which gave him all the right credentials, but he was also related to Field Marshall Helmuth von Moltke, the military brain behind nineteenth-century German unification.

Wary as the Poles were of German reunification, they also needed German help. In exchange they were willing to grant some hitherto forbidden cultural rights to the German minority in Silesia.[22]

The opening of the inter–German border emboldened the Germans while it alarmed many others. During the high that immediately followed the opening of the frontier, the Germans also took notice of and commented (often caustically) on their allies' reactions. As they coolly calculated that the seeming Soviet acceptance of self-determination in its former satellites was rooted in a new cost–benefit analysis, they noted their allies' bafflement, fears and alarm.

Recalling that American presidents from John F. Kennedy to Ronald Reagan had called for demolition of the Berlin Wall, the Germans commented that George Bush's Washington seemed alarmed over its unpredictable consequences just at the time that reunification no longer seemed totally unrealistic. To the Germans, the Americans appeared confused over what policy to pursue. Aware of a gap in the attitudes of ordinary Frenchmen and their leaders toward German reunification, the Germans thought the latter were trying to persuade the public to share their own alarm. They noted the efforts of French politicians, newspapers and television to alert the public to the threat posed by a 'Greater Germany', and also noted the meagre results. Neither did the British Prime Minister Margaret Thatcher's warnings to the DDR not to pull out of the Warsaw Pact, and about the East German events' impact on Mikhail Gorbachev's situation (her preference being the survival of the DDR rather than reunification) escape German attention.[23]

Mrs Thatcher hoped to delay German reunification through Anglo–French co-operation, though such co-operation faced a formidable obstacle in their very different views on European integration. Where Thatcher preferred a loose European Community, Mitterrand wanted it to be more centralized and united as a means of checking Germany. Since the French and the Germans worked closely together in the EC, Mrs Thatcher wanted to separate them from each other. She believed that a more integrated EC would rather enhance German influence and power than hold it in check.

In her desire to slow down the Germans, Mrs Thatcher felt forced to turn to Mitterrand since Bush did not share her approach to the German question. Bush saw the Bundesrepublik as the Americans' main partner in Europe, 'a partner in leadership', as he had said to Bonn's delight and Mrs Thatcher's chagrin in May 1989. She took it very hard and felt she could no longer depend on Washington as she had done before. Bush tried to mollify her later, telling her that 'we too were partners in leadership', but she felt that 'the damage had been done'. [24]

After the opening of the Berlin Wall, Mrs Thatcher suggested to Bush that priority should be given to the democratization of East Germany rather than to reunification. Bush agreed at first,[25] but later it became clear that they did not think the same way about the German question.

Displaying his sound instincts for political timing, Kohl was quick to sense the historic opportunity that the mood of the Germans offered. Once again seizing the initiative and grasping hold of the issue of reunification, he boldly outlined a broad plan towards achieving it in a speech to the Bundestag on 28 November 1989.[26]

Kohl's ten-point plan called for sweeping changes both in Germany and Europe as a whole, the two being tied together. It cleverly anchored his proposals in earlier pronouncements by both Bonn's Western allies and Mikhail Gorbachev. Kohl cited Nato documents stating that 'A final and stable settlement in Europe is impossible without a solution to the German Question … which must remove the unnatural barriers between Eastern and Western Europe, which are revealed most clearly and most cruelly in the division of Germany.' He associated Gorbachev with his plan by referring to their joint declaration of the previous June pledging respect for peoples' right of self-determination.

Kohl's proposal also outlined a plan of action which the Germans could set in motion without needing the immediate consent of outsiders, and offered enticements to Germany's neighbours in the east. This was a way of minimizing or neutralizing from the very beginning outsiders' objections and interference and efforts to block the plan at the outset. In view of prevailing German sentiments in favour of reunification, it could also serve Kohl well in the next general elections, to be held in about a year.

Stressing the need for immediate action because of the East German situation, Kohl gave a sense of urgency to his proposals. He based his plan on free elections in East Germany. Next, confederal structures were to be developed between the two German states with the aim of creating a federation. Joint governmental and parliamentary committees would be set up to develop further institutional co-operation by stages. Making use of historical confederal precedents would lead to a reunified Germany. As an incentive for quick and decisive action on his plan in East Germany, Kohl promised generous economic help once the East Germans had set up the framework for free elections.

Kohl's plan was carefully worded in a way which sought to place it firmly in the traditions of nation-building in German history. It was fitting that, as a former student of history, he sought to legitimize and validate his vision in this fashion, but although national historical experiences provided a base and guidance for unification, it was the will of the Germans that would have to make it a reality. Kohl sought to fill his fellow Germans with confidence to that effect by stating, 'I am sure, however, that unity will come, if it is wanted by the German nation.'

He was not only speaking to the Germans. Trying to address the concerns of others, he strove to reassure both his Western allies and the nations of Eastern Europe. Thus he drew parallels between the further integration of the European Community and German reunification and pledged German loyalty to NATO. To the East Europeans he held out the promise of supporting their access to the European Community.

Thus, from the very beginning, Kohl associated his efforts to achieve German unity with a search for European unity. His ten-point plan for action spoke of overcoming the divisions of both. Specifically, he advocated the integration of the DDR into the European Community and the creation of associations tying the reforming East-Central European nations to it as well. He stated, 'The EC must not end on the Elbe, but must remain open to the East.'

Besides connecting German reunification to European integration, Kohl also connected it via freedom and self-determination with stability. As Kohl put it, 'Freedom does not cause instability, but rather the oppression thereof.' It was an attractive and powerful message, difficult to resist or oppose, at least openly. This was all the more so as his call for action was also carefully couched in terminology previously used by the other powers in order to minimize any potential irritation and opposition. With this plan, Kohl took the centre of both the German and the European stage just before the scheduled Malta summit meeting between Presidents George Bush and Mikhail Gorbachev at the beginning of December 1989.

While Kohl's unilateral action with his ten-point plan provoked criticism and even anger among the other powers,[27] their options for countering its aims were unattractive. They could have dealt much more easily with a challenge by the Bonn chancellor if it had been an isolated phenomenon, but this was not the case. Kohl had instead positioned himself simultaneously as the spearhead and the lightning conductor of the East German masses who had smelled and tasted the heady lure of freedom after decades of incarceration. Having allied himself with them, and backed by the majority of the West Germans, Kohl was virtually immune to ordinary outside pressures. As long as he was clad in this shining armour, the chancellor was a tough opponent for anyone on the German question.

Kohl had read well the mood of his countrymen, as befitted a master politician. He was roundly applauded and praised, and his foreign minister and sometime rival Hans-Dietrich Genscher congratulated him, saying, 'Helmut, that was a great speech.'[28] Even the Social Democratic opposition endorsed the essence of his vision. In East Germany, Krenz sounded a sour note and some opposition spokesmen there were also less than enthusiastic;[29] neither reflected the wishes of the clear majority of East Germans on the issue of reunification.

Kohl's confidence rested in part on a widespread German belief that other powers and their leaders lacked the practical means to block the road towards German unity. They could not stop the popular drive towards it short of a massive use of force and the resulting bloodshed. This in turn was inconceivable in view of their prevailing domestic attitudes with regard to German reunification and the general international climate. The outside powers' lack of options in dealing with the German question also left them with very little bargaining leverage in negotiating with Kohl and Genscher.

Developments in the DDR soon overcame the gradualism and moderation of Kohl's November ten-point plan. The massive and rapidly increasing haemorrhage of the East German population to the west after the border opening brought the DDR to the point of collapse. There was insufficient time for a slow build-up of the kind of elaborate mechanism envisioned in the Kohl plan for reaching eventual German unity. The DDR was bankrupt. The East Germans would not simply wait patiently for a slow and gradual lowering of the barriers between the two German states in anticipation of binding them closer together in the future. They wanted and demanded immediate action, and their pressure was hurrying statesmen and politicians along in both the East and West.

Outside Germany the reactions to Kohl's bold move were mixed. There was much hand-wringing and gnashing of teeth. Mixed with genuine or pretended concerns was indignation and anger that Kohl had acted on his own without consulting the other powers first.[30] Yet Kohl's foreign policy adviser Horst Teltschick, who had played an important role in drafting his plan, found the international reception on the whole satisfactory, having expected no enthusiasm and remembering recent history.[31] Perhaps shrewdly anticipating endless objections and warnings, Kohl had, by a single stroke, put German unification openly on top of the international agenda.

Instead of risking being hamstrung behind the scenes by prior consultation with the other powers on the issue, he was forcing them openly to take a position on it. For years the Western allies of the Bundesrepublik had been on record as being in favour of German reunification, but over the years it had remained only a theoretical possibility. Now suddenly they were asked to be as good as their word. Whether the issue involved only a request to put their cards on the table or a collection of long-standing debts, it felt unsettling.

Yet for the Western allies of the Bundesrepublik it was highly risky to oppose reunification when it was becoming a realistic possibility. It would embitter and alienate the Germans, and the results of that would be unpredictable. The Germans would be looking for alternatives. They might try to strike a deal with the Soviet Union, and there could be an upsurge of frustrated nationalism. The result of all these mixed feelings and calculations was often a remarkable gap between public statements and private views about the reunification in élite circles. The degree of hypocrisy was therefore far more than normal.

In the United States and Britain, élite opinions ranged from more or less calm and sober acceptance of German reunification to open hostility harking back to the Second World War, and memories of the Nazis and the Holocaust. The Americans in particular worried over its impact on NATO.[32] The future viability of the organization would depend heavily upon whether Germany remained a member. Broader public approved of the reunification much more clearly. In the United States 67 per cent and in Britain 61 per cent favoured it.[33]

French élite reactions were on the whole cautious and circumscribed. Knowing how closely connected French and German fortunes were in many ways, the French mandarins were wary of openly offending their neighbours and partners. Yet competitive anxieties and resentment were also coming to the surface. Expressions of shock over Kohl's action were voiced. Warnings not to rush too fast or push too hard could be heard, but they were combined with resigned recognition of Germany's power and ability to decide its own future.

A harsh public reaction came from the French Defence Minister, Jean-Pierre Chevénèment, who sought to discourage the Germans by claiming that neither the United States nor the Soviet Union wished for German reunification.[34] Yet President Mitterrand's close adviser Jacques Attali passed the word to Teltschick that the French could live with the ten-point plan. Such assurances did not altogether convince the Germans. Aware of impending visits by Mitterrand to the Soviet Union and the DDR, they wondered and worried about possible Franco-Soviet co-operation aimed at blocking German aspirations.[35] Eager to push quickly for further integration of the European Community, the French were also anxious that German reunification did not get in its way.

In France as in the United States and Britain, public opinion was far more generous and acceptive of reunification than was the élite. For years, more Frenchmen had thought their eastern neighbours to be their best friends than had cherished similar notions of their historical allies, the Americans and the British. Thus it was no surprise that an even larger majority of the French, 80 per cent, than of Americans or the British approved of German unification.[36] The long years of close Franco–German co-operation on many levels, including widespread exchanges of students and delegations of all kinds, was clearly bearing fruit.

Many had thought that Soviet reactions would be decisive to the prospects of the Kohl plan of action. The Soviet Foreign Minister, Eduard Shevardnadze, wasted no time in rejecting it the day after Kohl's speech, on

29 November 1989; warning of German 'revanchism', he opposed any European border changes. In support of his position, Shevardnadze said that 'facts must be accepted' and 'we have two Germanies'[37] – this at a time when a rapidly snowballing international opinion had come to doubt that very fact, and the people of East Germany were doing away with it. In reality, two Germanies were going to be a fact only if the Soviet Union was able and willing to maintain it, and that ability and will no longer seemed to exist.

It was not immediately clear how solid the Soviet opposition to German reunification was or whether it was a mere bargaining ploy. The Soviets were talking about the need to maintain the decades-old post-war balance in Europe when this structure was clearly changing rapidly and radically. These changes were so fundamental that out of them a new order was rising on the continent.

The strongest fears and resentments concerning German reunification were to be found among the Poles and the Jews,[38] which was understandable as the two had suffered more at German hands during the Second World War than any other people. The Poles had the additional fear of possible future German claims on eastern territories they lost to Poland after the war. However, neither the Poles nor the Jews had the power to block reunification, though the resulting feelings of frustration further increased the intensity of their reactions.

The Poles were also painfully aware that they needed German capital, yet fretted about their country turning into a German economic dependency. Recipients of massive credits from the Bundesrepublik, they knew that they needed further German investment. The Germans were simply the likeliest source for much of the funds necessary for retooling and reconstruction if Poland was to pull itself out of economic misery, but many Poles feared that Germans would end up as the owners of the choicest assets in Poland. Others, in contrast, worried that the needed German investments would instead go to East Germany. The Poles had reason for such fears as there had been rumbles of discontent in the Bundesrepublik about the size of the West German aid package to Poland. They had not kept up the payments on their previous massive loans and some West Germans were therefore unwilling to lend them more. Efforts to tie the aid to better Polish treatment of the German minority, and German expellees' resentments over the loss of their homes, further complicated matters.[39]

The very emergence of a German minority where none officially existed in formerly German territories of Poland stoked further fires under the growing Polish anxiety about German reunification. The Red Army and the Poles had expelled the bulk of the local Germans at the end of the Second World War. Those able to remain, often of mixed ancestry, could stay only by at least outwardly turning into Poles. Vengeful and embittered by their wartime suffering under the Nazis, the Poles took revenge. Trying to wipe out as much as possible of the German character and heritage of their newly acquired western territories, the Poles ruthlessly pursued policies of Polonization. That not only meant refusal to grant any basic services in German but extended to extremes such as a ban on the public use of German.[40]

As a result of the spectacular and stirring events in Germany, a long-submerged German minority in Polish Silesia was reasserting itself. It called for elementary minority rights, such as the establishment of a German cultural society. Even such a modest request met with deeply anxious and hostile Polish reactions, and many Poles took it as a sign of eventual efforts to return Silesia to Germany. They remembered that during Kohl's Polish visit in early November 1989, which included Silesia, some local Germans had greeted him as 'our chancellor'.[41] There lay an irony in all of this, as the intention of Kohl's visit had been German–Polish reconciliation.

Jewish reactions to the prospect of German reunification received prominent expression in Israel and in such flagships of the American media as the *New York Times*[42] with its notable influence on opinions in the United States, in particular in liberal and academic circles. The experience and memory of the Holocaust, actively kept alive by Jewish communities around the world, caused a special anguish and anxiety among them about Germany. Some Jews wanted to prevent German reunification, among them being prominent figures such as Elie Wiesel, a winner of the Nobel Peace Prize, and leading Israelis. Wiesel's early tragic experiences as a youth gave his voice a special resonance. At the age of fifteen he had been shipped to a concentration camp and his parents and younger sister perished in the camps. Such memories inevitably influenced Jewish reactions to German unity.[43]

Notes

1 Kohl, in *Bulletin, Presse-und Informationsamt der Bundesregierung*, 9 Nov. 1989.
2 Ibid.
3 Cf. Szabo, *The Diplomacy of German Unification*, 1992, p. 114.
4 For French concerns over these issues, see, e.g., *Le Figaro*, 1 Oct. 1989, and Renata Fritsch-Bournazel, 'German Unification: A Durability test for the Franco–German Tandem', *German Studies Review*, 3, 1991, pp. 579–81.
5 Mitterrand, in *Le Monde*, 5 Nov. 1989.
6 See, e.g., David Yost, 'France in the New Europe', in *Foreign Affairs*, 69, Winter, 1990/1991, p. 111; Walter Schutze, in *Europa-Archiv*, 25 Feb. 1990, pp. 133–8.
7 *SZ*, 2–5 Nov. 1989; *Der Spiegel*, 6 Nov. 1989.
8 German television, 9, 10 Nov. 1989; *Bild Zeitung*, 10 Nov. 1989; *Der Spiegel*, 13 Nov. 1989.

9 Teltschick, *329 Tage*, 1991, p. 15.
10 *Bild Zeitung*, *FAZ*, *FR*, *SZ*, *Der Tagesspiegel*, and *Die Tageszeitung*, 11 Nov. 1989; *Der Spiegel*, 13 Nov. 1989.
11 Kohl, in Teltschick, 1991, p. 21.
12 Ibid., pp. 19, 23.
13 Ibid., pp. 28–9.
14 *FAZ*, 11 Nov. 1989.
15 *NYT*, 16 Nov. 1989; Teltschick, 1991, pp. 26, 32–4, 36.
16 Teltschick, 1991, p. 38; Thatcher, 1993, p. 793.
17 German television, 20 Nov. 1989; *FAZ*, *SZ*, and *Die Welt*, 21 Nov. 1989.
18 Teltschick, 1991, pp. 44, 47–8; *Der Spiegel*, 27 Nov. 1989.
19 Teltschick, 1991, p. 52; *Der Spiegel*, 27 Nov. 1989.
20 *Neues Deutschland*, *FAZ*, and *Die Welt*, 14 Nov. 1989.
21 *Der Spiegel*, 20 Nov. 1989.
22 *General-Anzeiger*, 13 Nov. 1989.
23 *Rheinischer Merkur/Christ und Welt*, 10 Nov. 1989; *FAZ* and *Handelsblatt*, 13 Nov. 1989.
24 Thatcher, 1993, pp. 759–61, 768, 784, 789, 796.
25. Ibid., p. 793.
26 Published, e.g., in H. Seewald (ed.), *Helmut Kohl*, 1990, pp. 115–23; Kohl's 'Zehn-Punkte-Program zur Überwindung der Teilung Deutschlands und Europas', *Europa-Archiv*, 24, 1989; *Bulletin*, 134, 29 Nov. 1989, p. 1141–8.
27 See, e.g., *Der Spiegel*, 11 Dec. 1989; Wickert (ed.), *Angst vor Deutschland?*, 1990, p. 11.
28 Teltschick, 1991, p. 58.
29 *FR*, 29, 30 Nov. 1989; *Neues Deutschland*, 30 Nov. 1989.
30 Cf. Wickert (ed.), 1990; *Der Spiegel*, 11 Dec. 1989.
31 Teltschick, 1991, p. 60.
32 Ibid.
33 *The Economist*, 27 Jan. 1990.
34 Chevènement, in *Le Figaro*, 30 Nov. 1989.
35 Teltschick, 1991, pp. 60–61.
36 *Eurobarometer*, 32, Dec. 1989, p. 33.
37 TASS, 29 Nov. 1989.
38 Cf. *IHTr*, 30 Nov., 1 Dec. 1989; *The Economist*, 27 Jan. 1990; Ammon Neustadt, 'Israelische Reaktionen auf die Entwicklung in Deutschland', *Europa-Archiv*, 11, 1990, p. 352; Michael Wolffsohn, 'Fear of Germany and Security for Europe', in Dieter Grosser (ed.), *German Unification: The Unexpected Challenge*, 1992, pp. 163–76, 178–9.
39 See, e.g., Jozef Misala, 'Deutsche-polnische Wirtschaftsbeziehungen vor und nach Erreichen der Deutschen Einheit', *Osteuropa Wirtschaft*, 37, 1992, pp. 225–36.
40 Cf. Grzegorz Ekiert, 'The Return of the German Minority to Poland', *German Politics and Society*, Summer, 1992, pp. 90–108.
41 Ibid. and *The Economist*, 18 Nov. 1989.
42 See, e.g., *NYT*, 18 Nov. 1989.
43 Neustadt, *Europa-Archiv*, p. 352, and Wolffsohn, in *German Unification: The Unexpected Challenge*, 1992, pp. 165, 167–76, 178–9; Wiesel, in *Der Spiegel*, 1 Jan. 1990 and *Spiegel Spezial. 162 Tage Deutsche Geschichte*, 1990, pp. 34–7.

6 Summits and Germans

The rapid pace of events and changes in Germany left the Western allies of the Bundesrepublik groping for a workable policy with regard to reunification. Mere words did not suffice for a policy when events stripped them of their power to guide and shape the unfolding historical process. The train of German reunification had set off, and it was not going to stop until it reached its destination. The vague and cautious comments of both Bush and Gorbachev on the German issue at their Malta summit meeting on 3 December 1989 reflected their uncertainty over their ability to influence it decisively. Not only had Kohl taken them by surprise with his plan just a few days before their meeting, but at the same time the DDR as a state was rapidly falling apart.

As Bush and Gorbachev sat on board the Soviet ship *Maxim Gorky* at the dockside in Malta, a statement came from East Berlin announcing the resignation of Secretary General Egon Krenz and the whole Politburo and the impending arrest of former leading East German Communists.[1] Challenged by the press to give his views on Germany, Bush reasserted his adherence to the Helsinki Agreements of 1975 on the permanence of European borders and his wish to reassure Gorbachev: 'I made clear to President Gorbachev that we, for our part, do not want to do anything that is unrealistic, and cause any country to end up going backwards, or end up having its own people in military conflict, one with the other.'[2] The question by then, of course, was what was or was not unrealistic concerning the German issue. Besides being mindful of Gorbachev, Bush also did not want to offend Kohl and the Germans. He disclaimed any intention of trying to interfere in the German question: 'I don't think it is the role of the United States to dictate the rapidity of change in any country. It's a matter for the people to determine themselves.'[3]

Gorbachev also tied the German issue to the Helsinki process and emphasized the existence of two sovereign German states as a legacy of history. Yet in a departure from the language of his own foreign minister Shevardnadze a few days earlier, he stopped short of using harsh words of warning. Beyond philosophizing on history, he merely stated that 'We don't want to do anything to accelerate these changes artificially for the people of these two great German states'.[4] This was less than coming out totally and openly against German reunification. Rather it was a delaying action. The Soviet leader wanted a chance to reassess the situation and to give new instructions in an effort to turn an adverse tide. Clearly, both leaders were groping for the right tactics and strategy on the German question.

In German ears and eyes Bush's comments did not exactly reflect enthusiastic support for Bonn's dreams of unity. Gorbachev's words in turn sounded to them like a clear warning against unilateral acts. Yet they also found both Bush's and Gorbachev's reactions to the German question and Kohl's ten-point plan generally surprisingly restrained.[5] With dramatic events and changes unfolding not only by the day but by the hour in the DDR, it was hardly surprising that Bush and Gorbachev felt ill at ease to state a position on Germany. Sitting on the windswept little island in the middle of the Mediterranean, they were probably uncertain of what might be happening in Germany at the very moment they were asked to state their view on the subject.

Increasingly, many Europeans were coming to the view that the American and the Soviet leaders had little business anyway to pontificate about Europe, and still less to try to impose their will on the continent. With the loosening of the Soviet grip on Eastern Europe and the winding down of the Cold War, many Europeans were rapidly losing both their fear of Moscow and their need of Washington. The liberation of Eastern Europe and the growing prosperity and confidence of Western Europe with its plans for further integration led to a new European assertiveness. From it followed a lower tolerance of interference by what more and more Europeans had come to regard as not only outsiders but declining and unneeded outsiders.

By skirting key issues such as German reunification, Bush and Gorbachev were reducing their Malta summit to a non-event. They seemed impotent to shape the momentous changes in Europe. Tellingly, a tone of mockery entered European discussion of the summit. It was called historic only because it coincided with a historic turning point, and when high winds kept the two leaders from getting together, this caused no small amount of amusement. Having journeyed so far to meet, only to be kept apart by a few hundred yards of surging waves in Valletta harbour, each a captive in his own ship, the two travellers inspired chuckles rather than awe. Even the intended symbols of their power, the anchored warships, seemed out of date as an appropriate setting. Popular will and economic muscle seemed to matter more than armaments in shaping Europe. A wicked wit called the summit newsworthy, but only because the President of the United States had almost drowned.[6]

Malta was no Yalta. Many Europeans had derided the results of both these summits, but while Yalta deeply affected their continent and their lives, Malta could make no such claim. This time it was not the leaders of the superpowers who decided the liberty of tens of millions of Europeans. Rather, ordinary Europeans were setting limits on the liberty of the leaders to make decisions about their continent. The millions of demonstrators in Central and Eastern Europe had succeeded in establishing a new framework for what was considered possible or realistic.

The very same day that Bush and Gorbachev were making their comments on Germany, the peaceful climax of a popular revolution was taking place in the DDR. Millions of men and women and boys and girls of all ages were holding each others' hands, forming an enormous human chain across the land in a moving and orderly demonstration for liberty and democracy. It was a powerful show of mass action and solidarity, allowing millions of ordinary East Germans simultaneously a sense of personal participation in making history. It was also an act of power; the same day, 3 December, the supposedly reformed East German Politburo, with Krenz at its head, resigned.[7]

Under the fresh impact of these events and his summit with Gorbachev, Bush had supper with Kohl in Brussels the very same evening, preparing for a NATO summit conference. Telling Kohl that Gorbachev had thought that the Germans were moving too fast, he also assured him that he had vouched for him. Everything would be well taken care of and no unrealistic rush would lead to things getting out of hand. To what extent this soothed Gorbachev remains doubtful, the more so since Bush also mentioned that he had added that the speed of change in the DDR was the business of its people.[8]

Kohl in turn estimated that creating a German federation would take perhaps five years and reassured Bush everything would occur in agreement with Germany's neighbours and allies. He was keen on finding common ground with Bush, who stressed the importance of keeping the West together and not causing problems for Gorbachev. To the assembled heads of the NATO states, Bush expressed support for German unification with a number of qualifications, stressing the need for caution and everyone's agreement, and said that he knew his friend Kohl shared his convictions.

Some summit participants gave vent to alarm about the speed of events, the power of the popular action, and governmental loss of control of the German situation. Giulio Andreotti of Italy and Margaret Thatcher shared these views, though Premier Ruud Lubbers of the Netherlands seemed friendlier to the Germans.[9]

On the eve of the Malta summit, on 1 December 1989, the East German legislature had abolished the Communist, SED, monopoly of power. It had also opened the way for the criminal prosecution of the leading Communists for corruption and graft. The action came in response to continually growing revelations and exposure in the media of bribe-taking and corruption which enraged not only the ordinary people but also the rank and file Communists.[10]

Krenz had tried to save himself by denying any knowledge of the corruption, but he was booed and shouted down by a disgusted and furious crowd the evening before his resignation. He suffered this humiliation on the Marx-Engels-Platz in a scene which surely would have made those two prophets of Communism avert their eyes from the sight. On 5 December Honecker was placed under house arrest suspected of corruption, and the following day Krenz resigned as president and chairman of the National Defence Council.[11]

The huge crowds demonstrating on the streets and public squares of the cities, towns, and villages of East Germany week after week and month after month were persistent. They provided the primary pressure for German reunification, and it was intensifying. Among their signs and shouts for free elections, calls for reunification were multiplying. An increasing display of West German flags and slogans for a united German fatherland symbolized the mood of the people.

Yet the fervour for reunification was even higher among the West than the East Germans. According to Wickert-Institut polls in early December 1989, 88 per cent of West Germans and 64 per cent of East Germans supported reunification. In the east support varied notably among different age groups, being highest among those over 50 or under 30. Among the easterners support for the introduction of a market economy was much higher, reaching 91.7 per cent according to Infas-Institut polls conducted at about the same time.[12]

The earlier demonstrations for free elections and democracy had already implied reunification. Nobody expected the East German Communists to win free elections, and the abolition of the Communist system in East Germany would leave no excuse or foundation for the existence of a separate East German state. Yet the growing directness and explicitness of the push for reunification was speeding up the process of disintegration of the DDR. So was the growing public furor over ever-increasing revelations of the sordid corruption of the Communist leadership.

These daily exposés gave rise to demands for punishment of the offenders. Such demands and the mass resignation of the Communist leaders focused attention on the previously omnipresent oppressive enforcer of the old order, the Stasi, the state security police. Instead of upholding the law, it had engaged in spying and bullying as an obedient servant of the corrupt leaders. By December 1989 the glory days of both the masters and the servants were over. Only the previous October, Honecker had been smiling with pride and joy and a sense of his own importance, highly conscious of his central role in the East German fortieth anniversary as its head of state. By December he and his gang were sitting gloomy and forlorn under house arrest and in disgrace.

The Stasi was at the same time beginning to lose control even of its own secret files. Enraged citizens forced their way into its offices to investigate and secure the police dossiers. Again the citizens of Leipzig led the way, as they had in initiating the massive street demonstrations. Their example emboldened others to follow suit. The citizens had good reason for their actions, for Stasi members and agents had been busy destroying and removing revealing and compromising documents for fear of the consequences if these fell into the victims' hands.[13]

One file had long remained beyond the reach of everyone except one man. It was in a mysterious red leather briefcase which lay in the personal safe of Erich Mielke, in Stasi headquarters. Mielke, the boss of the Stasi, used this material in the same way as the Stasi used much of its information, for blackmail. He was blackmailing Honecker. The material included compromising Nazi documentation concerning Honecker during his imprisonment from 1935 to 1945. It indicated that he had given away his comrades under interrogation.[14]

With the ordinary East Germans not only defying the Communist regime and the Stasi on the streets but invading the Stasi nests as well, the end of the regime was near. A clear power vacuum was emerging in East Germany. The people on the streets were calling for the abolition of the Communist party, while the leaders of East German opposition groups such as New Forum were unable to establish leadership and new authority among their countrymen. They had spoken in favour of a continued separate East German existence as a reformed democratic socialist state, but most ordinary East Germans saw their salvation and fulfilment rather in the reunification of Germany.

The Communists had grasped at their last straw with the appointment of a new reputedly reformist Communist prime minister, Hans Modrow, on 17 November 1989.[15] He tried to hang on to whatever shreds of authority remained, and Gorbachev clung to him as the sole remaining East German agent through whom lingering Soviet influence could be exercised. Neither amounted to much. Under the pressure of the continuing haemorrhage of the DDR, Modrow seemed to discern the writing on the wall. He was cautiously moving to the idea of some kind of German confederation in the future, as could be seen in a widely discussed interview he gave to *Der Spiegel*.[16]

Yet the Soviet leadership once more condemned in harsh words all efforts at German reunification on 5 December 1989, attacking the Kohl plan for interfering in the internal affairs of the DDR which remained a 'friend and ally' of the Soviet Union. By harking back to memories of the Second

World War and talking of the vital Soviet interests at stake, it underlined the seriousness of its warnings. Accusing Kohl of trying to impose his will despite potentially 'dangerous consequences', the Soviet leaders attempted to reassert their waning influence in Germany while also preparing for the visit by Genscher the same day.[17]

Genscher tried to reassure Gorbachev and Shevardnadze, arguing that Bonn was not proceeding on its own or according to any timetable. Kohl's plan was merely an offer to the DDR. Such soothing words could not reassure the Soviets. They were keenly aware of and unhappy over the decisive impact of the continuing massive outflow of people from the DDR in undermining it, and complained to Bonn that the mass media caused people to leave illegally. Efforts to slow down or to stop this outflow may have lain behind Gorbachev's green light to Modrow to pursue additional agreements with Bonn while at the same time rejecting German reunification. Anxious to secure economic co-operation with Bonn, Modrow reacted reasonably positively to Kohl's ten-point plan, thus somewhat parting ways with the Soviets.[18]

Over the following few days East German Communist officials complained of crowds attacking police and army installations and the re-emergence of the Nazis and of anti-Semitism. These complaints and warnings caused fears that such accusations amounted to deliberate provocation, a standard, traditional Communist tactic. The complaints about mob actions could be turned into an excuse for a last-minute use of force to stop the disintegration of Communist power.

Yet that would have amounted to a desperate gamble, for the prospects of success were minimal or even non-existent. The Communists could no longer count on the army and were themselves in the process of dissolution as a party. Even the soldiers and officers of the most trusted élite units were thoroughly demoralized. Soldiers were simply leaving their units and many officers were utterly dejected by the collapse of their ideals and their own personal futures.

The Communist rank and file were in many cases as furious about the exposed corruption and greed of their fallen leaders as other East Germans. Disillusioned and embarrassed, they were turning in their party cards in their thousands. Some 1,000,000 out of 2,300,000 had resigned their membership by early December 1989. Clearly, party membership would not be the kind of valuable asset in the future that it had been in the past. At the same time the East German Communists were rushing to reorganize and rename themselves, tacking on to SED the Party of Democratic Socialism, the PDS. They were making a desperate effort to disassociate themselves from their former discredited leaders and the graft with which they were associated, but they still aimed at preserving the East German state.[19] For that, however, a mere change of name and leadership was not enough.

Gregor Gysi, the new leader, claimed that the changes were to be more than cosmetic, yet his predecessors' hypocrisy and corruption had aroused such anger that all Communists were stigmatized by their past associations. An intensifying bitterness was gripping the East Germans. New revelations of official wrongdoings were coming to light as the winter cold was settling in, with increasing use of brown coal for heating polluting the air and making it harder to breathe.

Gysi was cultivating a new image for the party and calling for a break with its Stalinist past, though that was hardly anything new. Communist leaders had long been in the habit of unburdening themselves and their parties of the worst sins of their past by dumping them in the lap of the dead Soviet dictator, a safe thing to do as the old monster had for long been thoroughly discredited. For the Soviet leader Nikita Khrushchev it had taken some courage when he started the practice back in the 1950s, sowing the first seeds of the future *glasnost* of Gorbachev. Since then it had been repeated too many times by too many people to provide many dividends for Gysi.

Lionized as a brilliant lawyer by many sympathizers, Gysi came from a well-established intellectual Communist background – his father had served as the East German Minister of Culture – but it would take more than such accolades and lawyers' tricks to save Communism in East Germany. Gysi's declarations of change, his sporting of a sailor's cap and not wearing a tie could not win over the East Germans. Besides anger and fury, strong feelings of disgust and a sense of betrayal were gripping them the more they learned of their past Communist leaders. Most were in no mood to listen to and to accept the assurances of any kind of Communist.[20]

It was not just the past that made them unreceptive to Gysi's message but the present as well. Gysi talked about wanting to save his country, and was against German reunification before general European unification in some vague and distant future. He predicted that German reunification would destabilize Europe by leading to a series of demands for boundary revisions. By continuing to insist on a separate East German state and opposing national reunification, the Communists were in fact lining up with the outsiders who were opposed to it. To side with foreign powers on the highly emotion-charged issue of the nation's unity was alone enough to maintain a wide gap between the Communists and most East Germans. Like most Germans, they not only wished for reunification but had increasingly come to regard it as inevitable.

In view of the realities of the situation and the mood in Germany, it was futile for outsiders to persist in throwing obstacles in the path of German unity if they were not ready to block it by force, which they were not. Yet this is exactly what they did. Already, at the opening of the Berlin Wall on 9

November, anxious allies of the Bundesrepublik had hurried to state that reunification was not imminent. The second jolt was the Kohl plan of 28 November. Kohl's plan had startled them just as it had startled the Soviet leaders and the East Europeans. None had recovered when they witnessed the rapid unravelling of the East German state before their very eyes. It made many feel uncomfortable, as they had mixed feelings about it.

The spontaneous rising of the East German people for liberty evoked warm feelings of empathy and sympathy. Yet by raising the spectre of German reunification and visions of a future Europe dominated by a powerful Germany, it brought forth caution and even fear of where it would all end. Yet short of shedding blood and gunning down peaceful Germans on the streets, what could stop their drive to national unity?

The belief that Germany's gain was others' loss had many adherents among political leaders outside Germany. For a while it seemed to revive the ghost of the wartime alliance against the Germans, and made for some strange bedfellows. Kohl's old associate and partner in the Paris–Bonn axis of the European Community, President François Mitterrand, was climbing into bed with Gorbachev. On a visit of the two leaders to Kiev, the Ukrainian capital, Mitterrand cautioned the Germans in quite strong terms on 6 December 1989 about reunification. He warned that it might 'poison' the situation in Europe by upsetting the balance and the process of integration of the European Community. Gorbachev joined Mitterrand in warning about the dangers of tampering with the existing international order.[21]

The sight of their supposed ally and friend Mitterrand in a Russian fur hat beside Gorbachev, both echoing each other's negative views and words of warning about German unification, did not make Kohl and the Germans happy. Mitterrand had been wavering on the issue in public but was apparently ready 'to tell the truth', as he put it, to the Germans.[22] Against the background of the Kiev meeting of Mitterrand and Gorbachev, some fireworks and hard bargaining could be expected at the summit of the leaders of the EC countries in Strasbourg on 8 and 9 December 1989.

During the summit Mitterrand and Thatcher had private discussions about Germany at Mitterrand's suggestion. According to Thatcher, Mitterrand was even more concerned than she and very critical of Kohl's ten-point plan. He had a sympathetic listener. Over a historical map of Germany which Mrs Thatcher had pulled from her handbag, the two worried leaders of the Second World War generation wondered what they could do. Mitterrand recalled how, at times of past dangers, their two countries had pulled together and needed to do so again. Thatcher concluded that, although they did now know how, they both wanted to stop the Germans.[23]

Germany was on everybody's mind at the summit. The more the events in Germany seemed to point towards eventual German reunification, the more the talk of the need for stability and the strengthening of existing international structures intensified. Mitterrand stressed the wartime Allies' prerogatives in Germany and held that European integration should take priority over German reunification. Mrs Thatcher also reminded the gathering of the wartime Allies' remaining powers in Berlin. Many reservations were made and frustrations aired but in the end the summit backed German unity, though with many qualifications.[24] It was made dependent on the approval of the former Allied powers, which could potentially conflict with a German right of self-determination, and the integration of the DDR into the European Community. Yet considering the mood of other leaders on the issue, Kohl basically achieved his aims. In spite of the Kiev meeting he had reason to smile.

The outcome was not only good for Germany, it was also good for Europe. The European Community would hardly have faced a bright future if its leaders had tried to block German reunification. In fact, if the Germans had come to see it as an obstacle rather than an asset for their deepest national wishes, the Community could hardly have survived. Mitterrand had backtracked, and in return Kohl had compromised on the tricky and contentious issues of a joint European currency and a European central bank. For the Germans this was no small concession. They valued highly the stability and prestige of the Deutschmark and the discipline and independence of their central bank. The results of the Strasbourg summit rested on mutual needs: the other members of the European Community simply could not afford to deeply wound and anger the Germans, for their fortunes were so intertwined.

The relationship between the Bundesrepublik and the United States was not as many-sided and close, and the Americans had more power. Hence Washington was freer than Bonn's European Community partners to push its views on the German issue within certain limits. Yet mutual dependency also worked here.

The sheer economic weight of the Federal Republic had made it the major preoccupation of Washington in Europe, apart from the Soviet Union. James Baker, the American Secretary of State, had learned much about German economic power during his days of overseeing the US Department of the Treasury. The weak and declining American economic situation further increased Washington's sensitivity to Bonn. By December 1989 the dollar had dived sharply against the Deutschmark,[25] which emphasized Bonn's economic strength at the expense of the American currency. It impressed international investors who bestowed a resounding vote of confidence upon the Bundesrepublik through their currency transactions. They seemed to have more faith in the German than the American economy.

Furthermore, the future American role and presence in Europe were closely connected with German attitudes toward it. Bonn in turn could use any

American backing it could get in dealing both with its European Community partners and with Moscow on the matter of German reunification. Even American neutrality on the issue could be put to good use, but American procrastination or opposition meant further hurdles and burdens for the Germans. While not necessarily fatal to reunification, they could cause a slowdown and complications in the process.

Bush had been equivocal on German reunification in Malta. Afterwards he hurried to the NATO summit meeting in Brussels where, over a dinner with Kohl, he had a chance to amplify his views. Meanwhile, the American ambassador to Bonn and a close associate of Bush, Vernon Walters, had predicted German unification within five years. Asked to comment, Bush said, 'I think it's better to let things move on their own and without the United States certainly setting some kind of time deadline.'[26] He seemed to concede indirectly the Germans' right to proceed, yet refrained from definitely endorsing or even accepting any timetable for reunification. Instead, he had set various preconditions for it, such as continued membership of a reunited Germany in NATO and the European Community, and free elections. Reunification had to also take place gradually and peacefully, and respecting the Helsinki Agreement of 1975 which guaranteed the borders of Europe.[27]

The topic of Germany had preoccupied both the NATO summit in Brussels and the EC summit in Strasbourg. Talk of Gorbachev's concerns about Germany were entwined with preconditions for eventual German unity. Some German observers commented, perhaps only half ironically, that they almost got the impression that most participants felt that NATO and the Warsaw Pact were needed because of the Germans rather than because of the East–West division.[28]

Washington seemed to them to advocate both its own and Soviet interests with its emphasis on stability. Its other aim was to broker its allies' interests in face of the turmoil in Germany, a task which was by no means easy when some favoured stemming popular desires for fundamental change and national unity. A potential conflict was emerging between the foreign policy ambitions of the various powers and the right to democracy and self-determination of the Germans.

It remained to be seen whether the lid of stability could be kept on the changes deriving their dynamics from popular desires. At the moment the driving forces of history seemed to reside on the streets rather than in the traditional corridors of power.

Nobody admitted openly that they were opposed to German unity, but warnings to the Germans not to rush matters abounded and a growing list of preconditions was waved in front of them. Ultimately they had more to do with preoccupations with status and balance of power than with anything else.

The British felt that their pivotal position, due to their claimed special relationship with America, was threatened and undermined by the emerging new constellations of power of Europe in the wake of a unified Germany. Paris had based its post-war Franco–German co-operation on West Germany, which was more in balance with France with regard to its resources than a united Germany, and tied to the Western alliance systems. Reflecting the dismay of the French élite at the prospect of German unity, President François Mitterrand and his Foreign Minister Roland Dumas kept on insisting upon the subjection of German self-determination to the approval of the rest of Europe and America.

While displaying understanding of the concepts of balance of power, the Germans could hardly accept a lesser right of self-determination for themselves than that which others enjoyed. To them, the post-war decades of perceived inferiority were more than enough. Here lay the crux of the dilemma facing both the allies and the Germans.

Meanwhile, the East German Communists once more rejected reunification on 9 December 1989 at an extraordinary party conference of the SED. Modrow called reunification an anachronism yet held out for a confederate structure. In Moscow Gorbachev insisted that the Soviet Union would not abandon its strategic ally, the DDR. He urged the acceptance of the post-war reality of two German states. Departure from it threatened destabilization.[29]

By early December 1989, however, the Germans were moving fast in changing East Germany and building new links between it and the Bundesrepublik. Speaking to a meeting of the Christian Democrats, the CDU, in West Berlin on 11 December 1989, Kohl sought both to encourage the East Germans and to meet the doubts, fears and protests of others. To the East Germans he said, 'You are not alone. We are one people. We belong together.' To the rest of the world his message was that neither Bonn nor the other powers but the East German people shaped the development of the DDR. They should be free to choose, but Kohl had no doubt that they would choose unity. As if to soften the challenge his words involved, Kohl once again affirmed his wish to solve the German question by taking into consideration everyone's security and within a wider European context.[30]

The rapid process in Germany left both Western allies and the Soviet Union behind. They were grasping for a lever to reassert themselves. Looking for a way of giving themselves a place in the process under way in Germany, they agreed to a Soviet initiative for a meeting of their ambassadors in Berlin. The meeting had little substance and had to share the limelight with Kohl's speeches the same day.[31] Harking back to the prerogatives of the wartime Allies over the Germans, the meeting seemed strangely out of date. It looked like an effort to resurrect a ghost from the long-moribund and distant past.

The very nature of the meeting was indicative of the frustration and irresolution of the participants. They could see the Germans making rapid preparations for reunification on their own and bypassing their former victors in the war. The reunification of Germany amounted to the destruction of the kingpin of the post-war settlement. The Germans were thus, in fact, not only proceeding to reunify their country but, from another viewpoint, were shaping a new order for Europe. The fruits of their victory in the Second World War were slipping from the control of the wartime Allies. This shared fate had brought the long-time adversaries of East and West together in Berlin, for their remaining power in Germany was flowing out of their hands. The Russians' ability to bully and the need and credibility of the Western Allies as protectors were rapidly disappearing.

The ambassadors' meeting did not please the Germans. They saw in it interference with both their rights and a natural process.[32] It reminded the Germans both of a painful past and also of the irksome Allied privileges and practices that were still in force. Among other matters, stubborn Allied insistence upon exclusive control of the air routes to West Berlin angered the Germans a great deal. They found it humiliating not to have the choice of flying a German airline, Lufthansa, to their traditional capital, and with the heady feeling of national reunification in the air, such symbolic reminders of second-class status in their own country were rapidly becoming less tolerable. The Germans wanted to get off their knees, and thus a potential clash was emerging between the wartime Allies and the Germans over the process of reunification.

While the ambassadors were conferring in Berlin, Baker met Kohl. He expressed his satisfaction with the situation in the DDR evolving in a controlled manner and having Kohl, a friend of the USA, in charge of German policy. He also assured him that the USA had from the beginning supported German reunification but that the Soviet Union, Britain and France were highly nervous about it. Tying united Germany to the West would reduce this nervousness. Baker also wanted to couple the security of the United States and Europe in the future, and change NATO more into a political organization, as well as to overcome the division of Europe and Germany peacefully but gradually, with everybody's agreement and respecting the existing borders. Under these conditions, the United States would co-operate actively to achieve German unity and a new order in Europe. Kohl in turn stressed the East Germans' growing popular wish and impatience for German unity. He was not doing anything to complicate the situation, he said, but that did not change the ever-increasing East German demands for unification.[33]

Baker also paid a visit to the ambassadors' meeting as if to lend further prestige to the assembly. Baker's visit and words were an American effort to climb back onto the locomotive of the train of German reunification. Washington wanted to at least have significant input in the process even if it could not control it. By emphasizing in public that reunification involved not only the Germans but also Germany's allies, neighbours, and the Soviet Union, Baker also underlined the differences between Kohl's and Bush's blueprints for German reunification. Although he demanded consultations and the right of influence on the process of reunification by the interested parties, Baker stopped short of explicitly claiming Allied veto rights.[34]

In the short term, Baker's assertiveness seemed to have some effect, but its long-term impact was riskier and less clear. Facing alarm and anxiety among the leaders of both his Western allies and the Soviet Union over German reunification, Kohl made some soothing gestures and promised to consult with them. Yet he also defiantly pointed out the decisive role of the popular clamour for reunification; the decision for it was made in the streets, not in the chancelleries.[35] Quite clearly, Kohl felt strongly about German unity. Furthermore, he was staking his political success heavily on that issue in preparation for the elections of 1990.

As had happened many times before, Kohl's political instincts were again proved to be sound. The issue of national reunification obviously captivated the Germans and, predictably, an intense rivalry emerged between politicians and political parties about initiatives and gestures which seemed to advance the cause. A sense of me-tooism was spreading across the land, but it was Kohl with his November plan who had made the deepest impression and left the clearest imprint. He became in the public mind most closely identified with the national aspiration and potentially also a major beneficiary of it.

Huge demonstrations were demanding reunification in Eastern Germany at the very same time that the ambassadors of the wartime Allies were meeting in Berlin and Baker was delivering his words of caution. Slogans such as 'Wir sind ein Volk', we are one people, or 'Wir wollen ein neues Deutschland', we want one new Germany, were carried on banners or against the background of German maps in the national colours of black, red and yellow. Opinion polls taken in Leipzig indicated that 75 per cent of the population favoured unification.[36]

Such enormous demonstrations of support strengthened both Kohl's hand and German resolve. In contrast, they undermined the efforts of others to interject themselves into the reunification process as the decisive factors. While all the EC and NATO partners of Bonn had, at least in principle, expressed support for German unity recently, Moscow was holding out. Kohl sought to reassure Gorbachev and impress upon him the importance of the growing East German pressure and impatience due to lack of reforms in the DDR. Proposing a meeting, he strove to keep the initiative and to make further progress in overcoming resistance to German unity. Gorbachev's unhappiness with the existing level of German–Soviet co-operation provided both an opening and an invitation.[37]

The events in Germany and in Eastern Europe were causing gloom behind the massive red brick walls of the Kremlin. It was from Moscow that the most persistent and insistent repeated warnings had come against tampering with the existence of its client, the East German state. Moscow feared that German unification would erode the Warsaw Pact. Gorbachev warned Kohl not to interfere in the internal affairs of the DDR by telling him that Soviet Union would do everything in its power to neutralize such interference. He stressed again that the DDR remained a strategic ally of the Soviet Union and a member of the Warsaw Pact. Gorbachev's warning did not cow the Germans, however. They felt that the train of German unification had already left the station and could not be stopped.[38]

As Moscow's grip on Eastern Europe was slipping, less and less heed was paid to its rumblings and grumbling, yet the Western allies of Bonn continued to make use of them in trying to influence Kohl. In part these efforts were inspired by concern regarding the political fortunes and staying power of Gorbachev at the helm in the Soviet Union and the continuation of the relaxation in East–West relations. In some cases they were just a matter of finding an excuse to slow down the Germans, and sometimes they reflected, some Germans thought, pure and simple hostility.

Gorbachev had reason to feel beleaguered. Concurrently with the critical developments in Germany, a surging challenge to the Communist monopoly on power was gathering strength in the Soviet legislature. He was also under pressure because of the crumbling of Soviet power in Eastern Europe. People close to the two new East German Communist leaders, Modrow and Gysi, passed the word that Gorbachev had told them that the problems of East Germany were a threat to his reform programme and his leadership in the Soviet Union. If that was true, Gorbachev must have been pleased with Baker's promises to prop up the Modrow regime. Meeting the East German Communist prime minister in the splendid resort and garrison town of the Prussian kings, Potsdam, on 12 December, Baker promised economic aid in exchange for reforms.[39] It was the first such high-level contact ever between the American and East German governments, and revealed the intensity of American concern about the rapidly changing situation in Germany and Europe.

Bush and Gorbachev and the men around them shared some uneasy feelings. They sensed a reduction of their traditional influence in Europe and were hurriedly looking for ways in which to restore as much as they could. Aware of a powerful current for unity in both Germany and Western Europe, and also of the attraction of the European Community to Eastern

Europe, Washington wanted to make sure that some of the benefits also accrued to the USA. Such notions, besides the immediate events in Germany, were a central aspect of the Baker mission. This concern of Washington emerged from Baker's efforts to link transatlantic ties to increasing European integration and co-operation. Tellingly, Baker also spoke 'of a need for an active United States role in Europe, a need even acknowledged by President Gorbachev'.[40] The two superpowers felt they needed each other to help prop up their influence in Europe.

Although both Bush and Baker reaffirmed American support for German reunification, such affirmations sometimes tended to get lost in the litany of qualifications, cautions and warnings which accompanied them. The same was true of Bonn's other Western allies' less than enthusiastic endorsements of it. All this left many Germans unhappy and resentful. Among them the feeling spread that they were being let down by their supposed friends. When their Western allies stressed the need to proceed slowly, paying heed to Moscow, this seemed like deliberate delay masquerading as something else. True, the Western cautions were often motivated by the need not to cause difficulties for Gorbachev, whose position was regarded as being vulnerable to an internal challenge in the Soviet Union, but such pleas not to rock the boat seemed to many Germans to subordinate their wishes and aims to those of others.[41]

The German estimation as to their Western allies' preferences was close to the mark. After the Malta summit both Bush and Gorbachev felt they were close in their views on Germany, and Bush put *perestroika* ahead of German unification;[42] yet among the Western leaders Bush was the most receptive to unification. Bonn's Western allies were nevertheless unwilling to make any commitment to the Soviet Union jointly to block German unity although Moscow persisted in serving notice that it was not ready to accept reunification and warning that it would destabilize the European situation. Kremlin spokesmen also continually claimed that reunification would cause difficulties for Gorbachev and would result in renewed East–West tensions. It was as if the Bonn's Western allies and Moscow were echoing each other's warnings.

One result of all these warnings was a growing sentiment among the Germans that they had to act on their own to make the most of their historical opportunity to re-create a unified Germany. History did not wait for ever, and the opportunity might not last long enough to suit others' timetables. Kohl became the embodiment of the idea of national unity when he visited East Germany to meet Modrow and to give a speech in Dresden on 19 December 1989. He knew he was walking a tightrope. On the one hand he needed to meet the aspirations and emotions of his East German audience, on the other he had to weigh the reactions of the other powers who would be listening and watching closely. Moscow was concerned enough to have its Bonn ambassador request Kohl to prevent disturbances from breaking out in Dresden[43] – an indirect but candid admission of its lack of confidence in the Modrow regime and its own impotence in the situation in the DDR.

Kohl was greeted by applauding and cheering crowds waving West German and green and white Saxon flags. Shouts of 'Helmut, Helmut', 'Deutschland, Deutschland', and 'We are one people' were mixed with demands for unity. This enthusiastic reception began on his arrival at the airport and continued along the streets and outside his hotel, and reached a climax at his speech. Visibly moved by the responsiveness of the crowd, Kohl responded to the mood. He spoke with emotion about his commitment to his compatriots in the DDR and how they would together find the way to the German future. His aim remained 'the unity of our nation'. It had to be reached in co-operation with their neighbours and the road would be difficult, but Germans also had a right to self-determination. Speaking by the ruins of the Frauenkirche, Kohl evoked the tragedy of the war and of the German commitment to peace, yet 'true peace' was 'not possible without freedom'. Praising the East German struggle for freedom, he also gave credit to Gorbachev's reforms, Polish Solidarity, and the Hungarian reformers for contributions to is progress.[44]

Kohl's speech was well received, and not only by the people in the DDR. It was widely praised and approved in the Bundesrepublik and beyond the borders of Germany for its statesmanlike qualities. Kohl also engaged himself in wide-ranging talks with Modrow about the future course of action in Germany. The two men agreed upon opening up the Brandenburg Gate, a highly emotion-charged symbol of Berlin located in the heart of the city on the border of east and west. Modrow was very concerned about the situation in the DDR and anxious to obtain economic help. Kohl wanted further reforms in the DDR. New agreements on economic co-operation and promises of further reforms and free elections in May 1990 resulted from the meeting, which appeared to many as a major new step towards Germany unity.[45]

On the heels of Kohl, President Mitterrand arrived to meet Modrow in East Berlin on 20 and 21 December with words of caution about German unity. While he maintained that the Germans should be free to decide their fate, he also once again spoke of the inviolability of borders. He was not sure that the majority of East Germans wanted reunification, and stressed the rights of Germany's neighbours and the victorious wartime allies. Mitterrand was the first Western head of state to visit the DDR. His visit did not please Bonn, however, for he seemed more of a hindrance than a help to the cause of German unity.[46]

It was not the first time during this decisive period for reunification that the Germans were annoyed with French behaviour. They felt that the French leaders were not only holding back support for reunification but siding with others against the Germans on specific disputed issues. In particular, pronouncements by the French Foreign Minister Roland Dumas and the repeated French stand on the borders had disturbed Bonn,[47] but the Germans were also unhappy with Mitterrand's actions and words. Mitterrand had cancelled an agreed breakfast meeting with Kohl, and had also talked about the inviolability of European borders at the Brussels NATO summit in early December. The Germans took that to include the inter-German border. When meeting Gorbachev in Kiev, Mitterrand had made it clear that he thought that the Germans should not interfere in the East.[48]

Modrow, who to many eyes merely headed a caretaker government, was perhaps slightly startled by the amount of personal attention he suddenly received from international leaders. Where Western leaders, with the exception of Bonn, had ignored his predecessors, now they were suddenly paying him visits and promising aid.

In German eyes Kohl and Mitterrand had opposite missions in mind when seeing Modrow. Where Kohl was seeking German unity, Mitterrand was looking for a way in which to block it or at least to slow it down, fearing its impact on the relative status of France. As one German paper put it, 'Is that the reason why septuagenarian M. Mitterrand is at present one of the world's most active statesmen? Within ten days he met Mikhail Gorbachev, George Bush and Hans Modrow ... he would undoubtedly like to slow down Herr Kohl a little, by extensive diplomatic travels if need be.'[49]

The sudden interest of Washington and Paris in the DDR, which they had previously largely ignored, looked to some suspiciously like a last minute, desperate effort to resuscitate a terminally sick patient, the East German state.

Not that it made much difference. The day after Mitterrand's arrival, Kohl returned to attend with Modrow the festivities accompanying the formal opening of the Brandenburg Gate on 22 December which symbolized another step towards German unity. The occasion echoed the joy and celebrations accompanying the fall of the wall. The enthusiasm of the mass reception for Kohl was unprecedented in its degree and size in East Germany, and amounted to a great personal triumph.[50] Clearly he was riding a wave of massive popular approval with his vision and pressure for national unification. Other leading Germans were captivated by the same wave and also helped it to grow to an ever more massive swell. The venerable and well-liked senior Social Democratic leader, former Chancellor Willy Brandt, was doing his share and was also enthusiastically received in East Germany, and outshone the official leaders of the Social Democrats, including Oskar Lafontaine, the hapless challenger to Kohl.

Brandt was largely responsible for persuading the Social Democratic Party to eventually back German unity. Perhaps the most stirring character in German public life, he was prodding his party to embrace unification as its goal, while Lafontaine had remained cool to national unity. Brandt had grown up in a united and Lafontaine in a divided Germany, but it was not only this that separated the two men on the issue of national unity. Where Brandt came across as an intensely alive and sensitive human being, Lafontaine projected the image of an analytical, thin-blooded theoretician who preferred to talk about a world community and internationalism rather than German unity. The difference between the two men came into sharp focus at the Social Democratic party congress in Berlin held in the shadow of Kohl's and Modrow's Dresden meeting in December.[51]

The Bundesrepublik was experiencing an economic boom, yet Lafontaine had been complaining about the cost of helping German refugees and emigrants from the east as well as of the costs of reunification. By doing so he had committed a cardinal sin for a politician – he had misread the dominant mood of his countrymen. His concerns and his parsimonious attitude did not fit the extraordinary times in which the Germans were living. When many felt generous and the touch of something greater than their ordinary existence, Lafontaine's chosen tactics revealed a small man in their eyes.

German reunification was emerging as the dominant issue and preoccupation in both the Bundesrepublik and East Germany. With it overshadowing all other topics and issues, Kohl had reason to smile and Lafontaine to look worried. It gave a boost to Kohl and his Christian Democrats and Free Democratic allies and hurt the Social Democrats. Following Kohl's example, lesser lights among the West German politicians were also venturing on forays to East Germany. West German parties were mobilizing to give aid and encouragement to their soul mates in the east. All this was rapidly leading to a merging of German politics between east and west. It amounted to a growing display of German assertiveness against the dictates by outsiders on the fundamental issue of national unity. German patriotism was far from dead, although it was often under the surface.

Taking their destiny in their own hands, the Germans were changing from objects to subjects of history. Their striving for unity frequently met with suspicion, pretending to be suggestions of caution and prudence. Yet neither persuasion nor threats stopped the drive to German self-determination and reunification. The popular mood defied outside interference.

As the Germans saw it, the Western powers had accepted the goal of German reunification through treaty commitments, and furthermore could not deny the Germans the right of self-determination without violating or ignoring their democratic convictions. Some warned about the consequences of resisting reunification, harking back to the memories of the impact of the Versailles Peace Treaty upon Germany. Attempts to block reunification would create ' a wave of nationalism'.[52]

Far from being intimidated by open Soviet resistance and what they felt to be procrastination by their Western allies, the Germans were challenging them on the matter of reunification. Adding to German confidence was the resounding boost from the international financial community through heavy demand for the Deutschmark and investment in the Bundesrepublik. It translated into a remarkable upsurge in the value of the mark against the dollar and a number of other national currencies. These economic moves not only reflected investors' optimism about Germany as such but their expectations of Germany emerging as a major economic as well as political beneficiary of the liberation of Eastern Europe.

Notes

1 *FAZ* and *Neues Deutschland*, 4 Dec. 1989.
2 Bush, as quoted in *NYT*, 4 Dec. 1989.
3 Ibid.
4 Gorbachev, as quoted in *NYT*, 4 Dec. 1989.
5 See, e.g., Thomas Meyer, in *Kölner Stadt-Anzeiger*, 4 Dec. 1989, *FAZ*, *SZ*, and *Die Welt*, 4 Dec. 1989.
6 Personal impressions from Europe and the European media in December 1989.
7 German television, 3 Dec. and *Bild Zeitung*, *FAZ*, *SZ*, and *Die Welt*, 4 Dec. 1989.
8 Teltschick, 1991, p. 62.
9 Ibid., p. 63, and *FAZ*, *IHTr*, *SZ* and *Die Welt*, 5 Dec. 1989.
10 See, e.g., *Berliner Tagesblatt*, *Neues Deutschland* and *Bild Zeitung*, 23, 24 Nov., 2 Dec. 1989.
11 See, e.g., *Welt am Sonntag*, 3 Dec. and the above papers for 4, 5, 6, 7 and 8 Dec. 1989.
12 Maser, *Helmut Kohl: Der deutsche Kanzler*, 1990, pp. 301–2.
13 See, e.g., *Berliner Tagesblatt*, *Bild Zeitung*, *FAZ*, *SZ*, and *Die Welt*, 16 Jan. 1990.
14 *FAZ*, 19 Nov. 1990.
15 *Neues Deutschland*, 18 Nov. 1989.
16 Modrow, in *Der Spiegel*, 4 Dec. 1989.
17 TASS, 5 Dec. and *Pravda*, 6 Dec. 1989.
18 Teltschick, 1991, pp. 67–9.
19 See *Neues Deutschland*, 9, 10, 11, 17 and 18 Dec. 1989.
20 Impressions from East Germany.
21 *Le Monde* and *Pravda*, 7 Dec. 1989.
22 Ibid.
23 Thatcher, 1993, pp. 986–7.
24 *FAZ*, *Le Monde*, *The Times*, 9 Dec., and *Le Monde*, *Sunday Times*, *Welt am Sonntag*, 10 Dec. 1989.
25 The Bundesbank helped this along. See, e.g., *The Economist*, 13 Jan. 1990.
26 Bush, as quoted in *IHTr*, 5 Dec. 1989.

27 Ibid.
28 See, e.g., *FR*, 6 Dec. 1989.
29 See, e.g., *Neues Deutschland* and *Pravda*, 10 Dec. and TASS, 9 Dec. 1989.
30 *FAZ* and *Die Welt*, 12 Dec. 1989.
31 Cf. Szabo, *The Diplomacy of German Unification*, 1992, p. 43; *FAZ*, *IHTr*, *Le Monde*, *Pravda* and *The Times*, 12 Dec. 1989.
32 Cf. Karl Kaiser, 'Germany's Unification', *Foreign Affairs*, 1991, p. 189; *Der Spiegel*, 4 Dec., *Stern*, 21 Dec and *Die Zeit*, 15 Dec. 1989.
33 Teltschick, 1991, p. 77.
34 See James Baker, in *Current Policy*, 1233, 12 Dec. 1989.
35 *IHTr* 12 Dec. 1989.
36 See, e.g., *Bild Zeitung*, *Der Tagesspiegel* and *Die Tageszeitung*, 12, 13 Dec. 1989.
37 Teltschick, 1991, pp. 80–81.
38 Ibid. pp. 83–5.
39 *FAZ*, *IHTr*, *Neues Deutschland* and *Die Welt*, 13 Dec. 1989; *Der Spiegel*, 18 Dec. 1989.
40 *NYT*, 13 Dec. 1989.
41 Such widespread German attitudes were expressed, e.g., in *Der Spiegel*, 4 and 11 Dec. 1989, respectively pp. 24–9 and 16–19.
42 Beschloss and Talbott, *At the Highest Level*, 1993, pp. 168–9.
43 Teltschick, 1991, p. 86.
44 Kohl's speech appears in Seewald (ed.), *Helmut Kohl, Deutschlands Zukunft in Europa*, 1990, pp. 127–31.
45 Teltschick, 1991, pp. 87–92; Robert Leicht, in *Die Zeit*, 31 Dec. 1989; *FAZ* and *Neues Deutschland*, 20 Dec. 1989.
46 *Neues Deutschland*, *FAZ*, *SZ*, *Die Welt*, and *Le Monde*, 21 Dec. 1989; *Der Spiegel*, 1 Jan. 1990.
47 Teltschick, 1991, pp. 75–6; *FAZ*, *SZ* and *Die Welt*, 13 Dec. 1989.
48 *FAZ*, *FR*, *SZ* and *Die Welt*, 6, 7 Dec. 1989.
49 *Kölner Stadt-Anzeiger*, 22 Dec. 1989.
50 *Bild-Zeitung*, *FAZ* and *Die Welt*, 23 Dec. 1989.
51 *Der Tagesspiegel*, *FAZ* and *FR*, 19, 20 and 21 Dec. 1989.
52 Johannes Gross, in *FAZ*, 3 Jan. 1989.

7 The Quickening Pace

In November and December 1989 Helmut Kohl had placed himself in the driver's seat of the train of German reunification. With his November plan he had seized the initiative in the emerging political game around the issue. After that he moved fast, seemingly always a step or two ahead of the other players. It was a remarkable performance and a political feat difficult to both swallow and admit by the many pundits used to denigrating Kohl.

Belying his supposed reputation of a bumbler, Kohl proceeded adroitly. His detractors, cultivating an image of Kohl as a provincial blunderer with narrow vision and concerns, unintentionally helped the object of their scorn. Widely underestimated, Kohl had a better than average chance to take his opponents by surprise and, as any player knows, the element of surprise can be a valuable tactical advantage. Surprise can lead to success, as Kohl was going to demonstrate once again. Kohl is more concerned with substance than image, and those more preoccupied with his image than the substance of the man were simply wide of the mark. Deluding themselves and misleading others, they unwittingly made Kohl's task somewhat easier than it might otherwise have been. Kohl recognized the advantage. As he put it, 'I make my living by being underestimated.'[1]

Kohl had not generally fared well in popularity polls, but at the end of 1989 a telephone survey put him ahead of both Brandt and Genscher, previously often rated as the most popular German politicians.[2] The approbation he received earlier in Dresden and Berlin had already given a foretaste of how Kohl had risen in his compatriots' esteem as the result of his leadership in pursuit of German unity. Kohl's message of hope and optimism was striking responsive cords in their hearts and minds.

Early in January 1990 Kohl visited Mitterrand at his country retreat in Gascony, south-western France. Reports about French attitudes towards German reunification from Bonn's Paris embassy preceded the visit. While Mitterrand believed that reunification would take place, French officials applied the brakes; whether France would be constructive or oppose it remained open. The leaking of this information to the press caused frustration in both Bonn and Paris, and provided an incentive for Kohl and Mitterrand to try to patch things up.[3]

Both leaders recognized that they needed each other and were anxious to reassure one another of their friendship and co-operation. Kohl had been frustrated by French pronouncements and actions but wanted to avoid a rift. He had a long history of successful co-operation with Mitterrand over many issues and he did not want to risk an estrangement. His attitude was conciliatory and he sought common ground. Germany would not pursue unification alone. France would be her partner, Kohl assured Mitterrand; furthermore, a reunited Germany would remain committed to act with France in pursuit of further European integration.

Mitterrand was concerned over German press reactions to some of his statements and actions, although he claimed to accept that the two German states would unite. The Germans thought he was purposely vague on several matters in order to preserve and increase his options. Thus when Mitterrand spoke of the inviolability of borders, they were not sure whether he also meant the inner German border. Tying German unification to the internal Soviet situation and Gorbachev's fate, he said the Russian nationalists were unwilling to yield on reunification and it must not benefit the Soviet hard-liners; Gorbachev had been concerned over the speed of it all. Mitterrand thought that the biggest obstacle to reunification was the membership of the two German states in the separate alliances, and connected this with the danger of German neutrality. Time was needed to think matters over, he advised, and hinted that not all Germans supported speedy reunification, though he also said that it would proceed in one form or another.[4] Thus the French president seemed both ambiguous and perhaps fatalistic.

Soon after his talks with Kohl, Mitterrand met Mrs Thatcher in Paris, where they continued their Strasbourg discussions. Both were preoccupied with the topic of Germany and unhappy about the way matters had been evolving. According to Thatcher, Mitterrand was utterly frustrated. He did not want to give top priority to German reunification, but complained that the Germans treated any words of caution as criticism or hostility and thus saw no way of blocking reunification. Thatcher proposed slowing down the process by all possible means.

The two leaders agreed to explore further the question of German reunification and Anglo–French co-operation, but nothing much came of these joint consultations. In the end, Mitterrand shied away from putting the British before the Germans, or choosing co-operation with Thatcher rather than Kohl. Thatcher naturally thought he had made the wrong choice for France and was unhappy over the discrepancy between Mitterrand's words to her in private and his public utterances and policies on the German issue.

Yet she had to admit that Mitterrand's judgement concerning their inability to block the Germans turned out to be correct.[5]

Mitterrand's activities and statements concerning German reunification had repeatedly caused sour comments in the West German press. His warnings about premature and hasty action and his emphasis on the wartime Allies' prerogatives had embittered the Germans. Feeling that Mitterrand's pronouncements challenged their right of self-determination, some contrasted his behaviour with the behaviour of another neighbour, the Czechoslovak President Václav Havel, who had made conciliatory and supportive comments about German reunification. While embittered by Mitterrand's efforts, the German media could also view them with a certain irony when it was clear that they were ineffectual. Widespread public support for reunification among their Western allies helped to reduce and contain German anger and bitterness concerning the lack of early support by the allied political leaders.[6]

Soon after his visit to Mitterrand, Kohl had received an opening which could bind Gorbachev to his plans. The Soviet leader appealed for food aid. Kohl responded at once, recognizing both the chance to improve relations and Gorbachev's importance to German reunification. He was eager to meet Gorbachev to remove possible misunderstandings and causes of friction and to clarify what could be achieved and when.

Laying the groundwork beforehand, Kohl impressed upon the Soviet ambassador to Bonn the negative impact of the refugee outflow on the DDR and connected it to continued efforts to revive the Stasi. He promised support for Gorbachev and underlined their mutual interest in preventing things from getting out of hand.[7]

Kohl's determination to deal directly with Gorbachev probably increased when he heard via Genscher from Baker that the Soviet Union had proposed a high-level four-power meeting to prepare the way for agreements between the Bundesrepublik and the DDR. His comment on this piece of news was telling and cutting: 'We don't want any midwives.' To Kohl the matter involved the German right to self-determination. He instructed Genscher to urge the three Western allies to consult closely with Bonn before answering Moscow,[8] a request which showed Kohl's self-confidence.

In his drive for German reunification, Kohl also received important support from another German political leader of strong emotions and capable of rousing them – the former Chancellor Willy Brandt. A leading figure in the international Social Democratic movement, Brandt engaged himself wholeheartedly and with enthusiasm in the campaign for reunification. He exclaimed to an approving audience of fellow Social Democrats in Berlin that 'nowhere is it written that the Germans have to stay stuck in a siding until the all-European train has reached the station'.[9] He also warned that Allied efforts to erect obstacles on the path of reunification could result in an upsurge of German nationalism. Having left Nazi Germany in the 1930s to spend the war years in Norway and Sweden, Brandt was well known for his long-standing internationalism and his words carried weight in Europe far beyond Germany.[10]

In Germany resentment was growing with the Western allies. Their joint action with the Soviet Union in the ambassadors' Berlin meeting in December 1989, their lecturing and statements and their repeated cautions on the need to give consideration to Gorbachev's situation caused bitterness. The Germans reminded their Western allies that they had pledged to support peaceful German unification in exchange for the NATO membership of the Bundesrepublik. Such reminders reflected a spreading feeling among the Germans that their Western allies' warnings and words of caution resulted mainly from self-interested fears of losing ground and jealousy of a reunited Germany.[11]

Kohl's bold unilateral move in November 1989 with his plan towards eventual reunification and his subsequent actions won increasing support even among those Germans who had originally been hesitant or even averse. In face of their allies' attitudes, the opinion gained increasing ground among the Germans that they had to reach unity by their own determination and their own strength. Many of those originally critical of Kohl for not consulting the Western allies before publicizing his plan also embraced the view that such consultation would simply have led to verbose objections and warnings, but little effective support.[12]

What was further strengthening and accelerating the German drive for unity was the intensifying crisis in the east. While the flight of East Germans to West Germany had declined with the opening of the wall and the borders, the exodus continued to drain the east of its people. They were fleeing not merely from economic misery but also from the signs of Communist efforts to retain control. The supposedly reformist Communist leader Hans Modrow, as the new prime minister, was evading reform and moving to consolidate his own and Communist power.[13]

Tensions were growing as a feeling spread that the SED and the Modrow government continued to resist reform. The mood also affected West Germany. Modrow had produced little of what he had agreed with Kohl in Dresden. Instead, he was trying to secure the power of the Communists through manipulation of the election regulations and tried to revive Stasi under a new name, justifying it by the danger of neo-Nazism. When demonstrators increasingly called for a united fatherland, he proclaimed that reunification was not on the agenda, but kept asking for financial aid. With such declarations and with plans to re-establish a successor to the Stasi and to exclude West German help from his opponents in the emerging election campaign, Modrow was evoking fear and anger.[14]

Only massive pressure wrested concessions from the SED. It looked as though the comrades just would not let go but clung to power wherever they could. They hung on tooth and nail to the economic possessions they had amassed during their monopoly of power, including much of the mass media. Using their access to media, they suddenly secured wide international attention for claims of a serious neo-Nazi threat in East Germany, though previously they had claimed that such a threat existed only in West Germany. Under the circumstances, these claims did not sound convincing.

Modrow's stalling and efforts to keep the Stasi afloat under a new guise produced a powerful reaction. Demonstrators stormed the Stasi headquarters in East Berlin on 15 January 1990, and a wave of demonstrations against the Stasi took place in many East German towns at the instigation of New Forum. The disintegration of the DDR was accelerating. Combined with calls for a united fatherland were demands for the outlawing of the SED. The Modrow regime's collapse was at hand. Unable to govern and under intense pressure, it finally agreed to bring forward free elections from the original May to 18 March 1990.[15]

Modrow's manoeuvring had also contributed to the continuing flight from the east and provoked fears of worse to come. These signs of renewed desperation in the east after the wave of joy that had accompanied the opening of the inter-German frontier had put Kohl in a difficult position. His dilemma was how to help the people but not the SED; how to get enough help and hope to the east without unduly supporting the Communists who were still in charge there. A massive outflow of anti-Communist East Germans was also causing increasing concern in the Bundesrepublik because of its costs, and some politicians were exploiting the issue.

The most prominent among them was Oskar Lafontaine, who was making a bid to become the next chancellor. Lafontaine's formative years had been spent in a Jesuit-run school and at the University of Saarland at the height of the 1960s student disorders. Known as 'Cheeky Oskar', the sharp-tongued Lafontaine had to first ensure his re-election as Minister-President of the Saarland to achieve nomination as the candidate of the Social Democratic Party, which would them make him officially the challenger to Kohl. In these efforts the ambitious Social Democrat was playing on and using the resentments and fears of those West Germans who were less than generously disposed towards the newcomers from the east. Fear of competition for employment, housing and social benefits loomed in the background.

They seem to have loomed especially large in the Saarland, where Lafontaine and the Social Democrats soundly beat the Christian Democrats on 28 January 1990.[16] The victory boosted the Social Democrats' hopes of a victory in the federal elections in December and Lafontaine's dreams of replacing Kohl as chancellor. Lafontaine had not only turned a cold shoulder towards the refugees from the East; he was also clearly anything but enthusiastic about German reunification. His appeal to the more niggardly instincts and pocketbook concerns of the electorate, while Brandt appealed to their loftier aspirations and dreams of national unity, allowed the Social Democrats to work both sides of the street at the same time.

Kohl thought that sacrifices comparable to the post-war burden-sharing were needed, yet he feared that they would change the country's mood. Perhaps this fear, combined with the current favourable West German economic situation, in part led him to make what turned out to be too optimistic economic assumptions. He did not want to endanger public support for Germany unity,[17] and the Bundesrepublik continued manoeuvring under his leadership towards reunification. Kohl was striving to keep different options and timetables open in order to gain the maximum advantage of any opportunities as they arose in a fluid situation. Accordingly, he avoided getting pinned down on formal legal and political details.

At the same time, the German people and institutions were developing close ties and co-operation across the east–west border. East and West Germany were growing together. Closed-off old country roads were recommissioned. Teachers with school classes, local choirs and orchestras and all kinds of delegations passed back and forth.[18] The Germans were effectively starting in practice to construct the necessary physical and institutional base and infrastructure for eventual reunification. Road and railway crossings across the border were rebuilt and improved, inter-German flights were put in place, and neighbouring towns and villages were forging links with one another.

Border-crossing back and forth had become so commonplace and frequent by early 1990 that even the formerly tense and at times threatening East German border guards had relaxed. No longer toting sub-machine-guns, they had become civil and even frequently pleasant towards the people passing the checkpoints. Cross-border traffic had become so thick and frequent that it fostered ever closer ties. Friendships were born and romances conducted across the formerly closed frontier. Various organizations and institutions sought co-operation with their counterparts across it, and the more prosperous West Germans were donating equipment and know-how to their eastern cousins. Universities were sending professors, other institutions specialists in various skills and branches of information, libraries books, hospitals and laboratories ambulances and scientific equipment and materials, and colleagues were increasingly socializing across the border. In short, the two Germanies were growing into one through innumerable ties uniting ordinary and not so ordinary people quite spontaneously and apart from the negotiations and decisions of politicians and governments whose actions lagged far behind.

All this naturally did not pass unnoticed by the rest of the world. While for the most part ordinary people favoured German unification, the élites persisted in being more dubious and sceptical about it. Fears of a repetition of the past mingled with concerns of drastic changes in the international balance of power and resentment of a stronger Germany combined with a relative weakening of its partners and rivals.

A notable example of such sentiments surfaced in public in Margaret Thatcher's comments towards the end of January 1990. She saw German reunification mainly as a destabilizing force and a source of many problems. It was a threat to Gorbachev whose downfall would be a calamity to all, and it would destroy the economic balance of the European Community, already dominated by the Germans. She accused Kohl and Genscher of ignoring wider European interests in favour of narrow nationalist aims.[19] This was ironic, as her EC partners had repeatedly subjected her to similar criticism. Kohl took this public scolding hard, particularly as Thatcher had not addressed such views to him in person. He was determined not to let it pass but would take the matter up personally with her.[20]

Mrs Thatcher was not altogether out of tune with British public opinion on German reunification. While more in favour of it than opposed to it, its supporters were fewer and the opponents more numerous among the British than among other major Western allies of the Bundesrepublik. In them a clearer majority of the public favoured German reunification, according to public opinion polls conducted between 19 and 22 January 1990. Such majorities were the largest and the share of people opposed to German unification smallest in the United States and France – in both, 61 per cent favoured and in the United States only 13 and in France 15 per cent opposed reunification. In Britain and in Poland the number of those in favour was clearly smaller and those opposed clearly larger. Only 45 per cent of the British and 41 per cent of the Poles favoured German reunification, while 30 per cent of the British and 44 per cent of the Poles opposed it.[21]

Germany's European neighbours worried more about a unified Germany emerging as the dominant power in Europe than did the Americans. While the Poles were by far the most concerned, half of the British and the French shared such sentiments. The reasons behind these concerns varied a great deal. The major British fear was a revival of some form of Fascism, while the French feared German economic power more and the Poles almost equally German territorial expansion and a revival of Fascism. A clear majority of the British sought reassurance in the continuing future membership of Germany in NATO, while most Frenchmen put their trust in a deepening political unity within the European Community. Most Poles saw in the continuing presence of American troops in Europe a better counter to increased German power.[22]

Such mounting concerns with German reunification resulted from a growing perception that it would take place sooner rather than later. After strong popular opposition spearheaded by the New Forum movement had blocked the ill-considered efforts of Modrow and his Communist supporters to keep alive the hated Stasi in a renewed and reduced form, the East German Communists were on the run. They were scrambling in desperation for ways in which to retain something of their former hold.

The Communists hoped to survive by making scapegoats of the generation of leaders who had taken over after the removal of Honecker. Krenz's turn came on 21 January.[23] He had sought credit and survival from his role in the changes that followed Honecker's deposition, but Krenz had learned his theory of revolution poorly. He had not realized that revolutions rarely stop halfway and stay with transitory leaders but rather tend to run their course, and that leaders between the beginning and the end are merely transitory. The East German Communists had not come to power in the first place on the shoulders of a popular revolution but had been backed by foreign bayonets and tanks. Thus it was perhaps too much to expect them to understand and cope with a popular revolution when they were confronted with one in their own country. From formerly powerful and feared figures they were reduced to worrying and whining about the hardships of finding employment and making a living.

Disintegration in East Germany was forcing reforms and a revision of the plans for elections, as chaos was emerging as a serious alternative. The Communists' efforts to appease and curry favour with the angry East Germans with belated concessions did them little good. These gestures were too little and too late, as had been the Communists' earlier attempts at appeasement. The Modrow government, dominated by the so-called reform-minded Communists, could not gain the trust of the people and was unable to govern. Like their counterparts in Poland, Hungary and Czechoslovakia, the East German Communists could only hope to cling to power by co-operating with their challengers. Everybody was talking about impending collapse and chaos in the DDR.[24] Gorbachev also drove home the hopelessness of the DDR's future to Modrow during his Moscow visit at the end of January 1990.[25] By indicating that there was, in practice, no doubt of German unification, he was clearly departing from his previous stands, though by saying that it had to be settled responsibly and not on the streets he reserved his bargaining leverage. Although he seemed to regard reunification as inevitable, Gorbachev wanted to extract a price for it.

Modrow wasted no time in echoing Gorbachev's change of course on German reunification. He started immediately to talk in terms of Kohl's November plan and a united German fatherland, though in preparation for it he proposed the neutrality of both the German states. Kohl rejected German neutrality, believing that it would isolate the Germans and knowing Bonn's Western allies would bitterly resist it. Modrow later confessed to Kohl that neutrality was no absolute requirement.[26] Modrow's talk of German neutrality was a trial balloon for Gorbachev in preparing the ground for his forthcoming meeting with Kohl. They agreed on 2 February to meet a week later in Moscow. The very next day Modrow confided to Kohl that even local government was falling apart in the DDR and said that the growing together of the two German states was inevitable.[27]

This was music to Kohl's ears as he was getting ready for his Moscow journey. He had many things on his mind. The deteriorating situation in the DDR and Soviet requests for food improved his bargaining power with Gorbachev, though he also worried about things falling apart in the DDR and the resulting chaos which could have unforeseen results. He was also concerned about Gorbachev's mounting problems, lest a less co-operative leadership replace him in the Kremlin. Fresh in his mind was Gorbachev's prediction in Kiev, according to Mitterrand, that in the event of German reunification, a marshall would replace him.[28] Simultaneously, surging restlessness and large demonstrations in the Soviet Union testified to its instability.

Intimidated by the signs of economic and administrative collapse and massive demonstrations not only in the DDR but also surging through the Moscow streets on 4 February, Modrow was ready to surrender. Backing for his government was rapidly disappearing in both the DDR and the Soviet Union. It was forced effectively to share power with spokesmen of the opposition forces and to reschedule the intended elections to 18 March 1990. On 5 February 1990, the government and the opposition agreed on an interim coalition government. The new coalition government included opposition leaders from the right to the left but was clearly only a transitory caretaker body to fill the vacuum before a new legitimate authority emerged from the March elections.[29]

With the change of the election dates the accelerated election campaign in East Germany quickly also became a proxy vote about reunification. Most East German parties campaigned for reunification and, sharing the same aim, West German parties and politicians entered the arena, pouring out financial aid and electioneering know-how to their eastern counterparts. West German political big guns participated in person in the campaigning, which was shaping up as a practice run for the December elections of the Bundesrepublik.

The disintegration and electioneering in East Germany were rapidly making reunification seem all the more imminent and the most realistic solution.

The day after the formation of the new coalition government in the DDR, Kohl announced his decision to pursue monetary union with it. This was a new and major step towards reunification. Once again, as with his November plan, Kohl acted without apparently consulting with the other powers and displayed his self-confidence. Kohl had long been worried about the deteriorating situation in the DDR and the refugee flow's impact on opinions. He hoped monetary union would alleviate both by giving new hope of a better future. The prospect of another politician, Lothar Späth, raising the issue perhaps triggered the timing of his announcement. Kohl had also secured prior agreement from Count Otto Lambsdorff and Theo Waigel, the leaders of his coalition partners, the Liberals and the Bavarian Christian Social Union.[30]

On 6 February 1990 Hans Haussmann, the economics minister of the Bundesrepublik, formally announced the plan for extending the Deutschmark to the DDR. Monetary union would mean East Germany's surrender of its monetary and economic and a large part of its political sovereignty to the Bundesrepublik. As the financial cost of rescuing the East Germans loomed higher to the West German taxpayers, and with general elections ahead in December in the Bundesrepublik, Kohl was taking a considerable political risk in the eyes of many observers. Yet he pushed boldly ahead against the warnings and opposition of economic specialists.[31] He clearly had a vision of the order of importance of matters which went beyond the horizon of the bookkeepers.

After the opening of the inter-German border, Herr and Frau Deutsch from East Germany had visited the Bundesrepublik and had seen with their own eyes the enormous gap separating their living standards and their buying power from what their cousins enjoyed in the west. The East Germans were also shocked to discover that even West Germans who were dependent on social security were better off than many working East Germans. They decided that the only way to bridge that gap quickly and effectively was to join their cousins, as did over 2,000 East Germans daily even in early February 1990. They wanted a better life to start today and not in an uncertain tomorrow for themselves and their children.

Sensing that the momentum towards reunification was gathering strength and accelerating, Kohl set up a ministerial committee of 'German Unity' under his chairmanship on 7 February 1990. The same day the Central Committee of the Soviet Communist Party voted to relinquish the Communist monopoly on political power. Entering into discussions with the East Germans about German monetary unification, Kohl's committee started the serious practical construction of German unity. Kohl was overriding the advice of the Bundesbank and its president Karl Otto Pöhl, who was concerned about the stability of the German currency and warned that the move would weaken the Deutschmark. Once the political decision had been made, Pöhl went loyally along and made the best of it. He expressed confidence in the strength and stability of the German currency and the ability of the Bundesbank to manage the transition.[32]

Kohl had felt he had to move fast to reassure the East Germans who were facing an increasingly desperate economic situation and saw German reunification as the only solution. The East German leadership had come to the same conclusion. As late as January Modrow had insisted that German reunification was not on the agenda, but by February he was singing a different tune. By then he was echoing Kohl's November plan and talking about the united fatherland of the German nation.[33] Modrow was looking for a survival role for himself and the East German Communists. However, times had changed, and both the events and the mood had already outrun such an echo of the past. What had been bold and innovating then was now outdated and not enough.

The pressure for reunification was relentless both in the form of massive demonstrations and continued flight to the West as well as erosion of the East German Communist Party. Recognizing the dynamics of the situation in Germany, Gorbachev was also groping for a way to cope with it, though the neutral Germany that Moscow was proposing in exchange for reunification was not acceptable to the Bundesrepublik and its Western allies. The proposal harked back to what Stalin had once suggested back in 1952 and it was no more palatable to the West now than it was then. The Western allies wanted to keep the Germans tied to themselves. As some of their spokesmen put it in their more candid moments, 'The Germans have to be watched.'[34]

Notes

1 *IHTr*, 27 Nov. 1989.
2 *Kieler Nachrichten*, 30 Dec. 1989.
3 *FAZ*, *SZ* and *Die Welt*, 4 Jan. 1990; Teltschick, 1991, p. 98.
4 Teltschick, 1991, pp. 97–100.
5 Thatcher, 1993, pp. 797–8.
6 See, e.g., *FAZ*, 13 Nov. 1989; *Kölner Stadt-Anzeiger*, 22 Dec. 1989; *FAZ*, *SZ*, *Die Tageszeitung* and *Die Welt*, 3, 4 Jan. 1990.
7 Teltschick, 1991, pp. 101–2.
8 Kohl, in ibid., p. 105.
9 Brandt, in *The Economist*, 13 Jan. 1990.
10 For Brandt's career and personality, see, e.g., Brandt, *My Road to Berlin*, 1960; *People and Politics*, 1978; *Reden über das eigene Land: Deutschland*, 1984; *My Life in Politics*, 1992; and Binder, *The Other German: Willy Brandt's Life and Times*, 1990, *passim*.
11 Impressions from Germany, Dec. 1989 and Jan. 1990.
12 Ibid.

13 Cf. Arnold, *Die ersten hundert Tage des Hans Modrow*, 1990, *passim*, and Thaysen, *Der Runde Tisch*, 1990, *passim*.
14 Cf. *FAZ*, *SZ*, *Die Welt* and *Der Tagesspiegel*, 10–13, 16 Jan. 1990; *Welt am Sonntag*, 14 Jan; *FR* 18 Jan. 1990; Glaessner, *The Unification Process in Germany*, 1992, pp. 60–61; Thaysen, 1990, pp. 163–72; Arnold, 1990, *passim*.
15 German television, 15 Jan. 1990; *FAZ*, *SZ*, *Die Welt* and *Der Tagesspiegel*, 16, 24, 29 Jan. 1990.
16 *FR*, 29 Jan. 1990.
17 Teltschick, 1991, pp. 103–4.
18 See, e.g., *Rheinische Merkur/Crist und Welt*, 22 Dec. 1989.
19 Thatcher, in the *Wall Street Journal*, 26 Jan. 1990.
20 Teltschick, 1991, p. 116.
21 *The Economist*, 27 Jan. 1990, pp. 29–34.
22 Ibid.
23 *Neues Deutschland*, 22 Jan. 1989.
24 See, e.g., *FAZ*, *Neues Deutschland*, *SZ* and *Die Welt*, 30, 31 Jan. 1990; *Der Spiegel*, 29 Jan. 1990.
25 Teltschick, 1991, p. 120.
26 *FAZ*, *Neues Deutschland*, *SZ* and *Die Welt*, 31 Jan. 1990, 2 Feb. 1990; Teltschick, 1991, pp. 120, 123.
27 Teltschick, 191, pp. 124, 126.
28 Ibid., p. 109
29 *FAZ*, *IHTr*, *SZ*, *Neues Deutschland* and *Die Welt*, 5, 6 Feb. 1990; *Der Spiegel*, 5 Feb. 1990.
30 *FAZ*, *SZ* and *Die Welt*, 7, 8 Feb. 1990; Teltschick, 1991, pp. 129–30.
31 See, e.g., *FAZ* and *Handelsblatt*, 7 Feb. 1990.
32 *FAZ*, *SZ* and *Die Welt*, 8 Feb. 1990; *Der Spiegel*, 12 Feb. 1990.
33 *Neues Deutschland*, 12 Jan. 1990, 2 Feb. 1990.
34 Comment by an American official in Jan. 1990.

8 Selling, Buying, Soothing

Kohl had kept the Western leaders on their toes by continually reminding them of their long-standing verbal support of German reunification. Now they were called to show if they measured up to their words or whether they had spoken with a forked tongue. Both implicitly and explicitly, Kohl and other Germans were posing the threat that by not delivering on its words on reunification the West risked a rift with Germany and an intensification of the crisis in the DDR. Kohl also brandished a carrot to reassure the West, however, by pledging that a united Germany would stay in NATO.

To deliver on that promise he needed Gorbachev's co-operation. Although hard-pressed at home by the internal problems of the Soviet Union, Gorbachev could still exact a price for not throwing sand in the wheels of German reunification. Kohl in turn could try to buy Gorbachev's and Moscow's agreement by promising an economic return or by withholding it from thc impoverished Russians. He could also convincingly argue that, for all practical purposes, blocking reunification was not a realistic option.

Yet Gorbachev could still try to drive a hard bargain. Having repeatedly voiced its opposition to NATO membership of a united Germany, Moscow could hardly be expected to yield everything on the security issue without getting something in return. If it did not get German neutrality it could at least insist on other military concessions, such as the withdrawal of all foreign forces, as the price for the withdrawal of Soviet troops from Germany. This was all the more a real possibility as the German Social Democrats for the most part favoured cutting ties with military alliances. Thus the future of foreign troops in a united Germany did not look promising. A possible removal of Soviet forces from Poland would leave the Soviet troops in Germany extremely vulnerable. Without secure supply lines they would cease to be an asset, which made it easier for Gorbachev to bargain them away.

After Gorbachev had sent signals of his willingness to negotiate a deal about the German issue during Modrow's visit to Moscow, Kohl and Genscher took advantage of the opening. They prepared themselves for a trip to meet Gorbachev in early February 1990. The Germans received some significant aid from Bush who, in his State of the Union address, proposed disarmament measures which could help to solve the security problems connected with German unity. Envisioning reductions of conventional forces in Central Europe, they could pave the way for cutting the Soviet military presence in the DDR. As Kohl's Moscow journey drew closer, Bonn's Western allies became increasingly supportive. As if sensing that a potential breakthrough could be in store, they were climbing on a winning bandwagon. Mitterrand asserted anxiously that no problems existed between him and Kohl, although the press claimed the opposite, and that he wanted close consultation, while Foreign Minister Dumas predicted publicly that the reunification was near. Thatcher was more reserved, but admitted publicly that reunification was probable.[1]

Of all the allied leaders, Bush was clearly the most co-operative towards the Germans. On the eve of Kohl's departure he pledged support in specific terms. Assuring Kohl that he would not allow Moscow to pressure the Germans via four-power meetings, he also conceded that its people should decide about unified Germany's role in the alliances. At the same time, he was satisfied with Kohl's rejection of neutrality and keeping Germany in NATO. Agreeing to a specific status for East German territory in NATO, he also promised close information on the talks between Baker and the Soviet leaders which was to immediately precede Kohl's arrival in Moscow, and expressed his admiration of the way Kohl had met recent challenges as a leader.[2]

Bush accepted Genscher's proposal that, while a unified Germany would remain a member of NATO, no NATO troops would be stationed in former East German territory in order to make the reunification palatable to Moscow.[3] Washington needed to make a commitment to quick reunification. It was faced with elections in East Germany which, by all the signs, would bring to power a government that would without delay proceed towards national unification. Another urgent consideration also influenced Bonn's Western allies. They had to consider the impact of Soviet and East German talk of a unified neutral Germany upon the West Germans. If the Western allies withheld their support for reunification and frustrated the Germans, the consequences were unpredictable.

Gaining Moscow's agreement to German reunification on terms acceptable to the Bundesrepublik and its Western allies remained a major hurdle that Kohl had to overcome. In preparation for his mission to Moscow, Kohl's adviser Horst Teltschick was engaging in a little psychological political warfare, helped by the situation in East Germany and alarming reports of it in the German media. On the eve of Kohl's departure for a meeting with Gorbachev on 10 February, he was passing word that East Germany was facing imminent economic and political collapse. Kohl himself spoke of his need to bring home the 'dramatic' situation of East Germany to Gorbachev. Bonn also announced that it was sending massive food aid to the Soviet Union.[4] Kohl still had a selling job to do and, as a careful tactician, he was doing his utmost to lay the groundwork for the best possible outcome of the visit from his point of view. Adding to the uncertainty were charges by the German Social Democrats that Kohl and his advisers were fanning panic and hysteria.[5]

As Bush had promised earlier, Baker informed Kohl of his prior talks with Gorbachev and Shevardnadze upon the German delegation's arrival in Moscow. These talks had produced agreements on substantial progress in reducing weaponry and the numbers of American and Soviet troops confronting each other in Europe.[6] Such agreements obviously benefited the Germans and improved the prospects of a Soviet retreat from the DDR. This time an American–Soviet deal seemed to help the Germans, unlike some occasions in the past. It did not pass unnoticed by them. Baker's report was thus encouraging and helpful to Kohl. Not only had Baker made progress in arms control, but he said that Gorbachev and Shevardnadze regarded German reunification as inevitable, although they were concerned that it could lead to instability in Europe.[7]

When meeting Gorbachev in the Kremlin a little later, Kohl stressed the urgency of a quick reunification in view of the alarming situation in the DDR. He said that neutrality was not acceptable to him as a price for it, but he also indicated that NATO would not have to extend to East German territory. Gorbachev asked what kind of timetable Kohl had in mind, but Kohl could not give a definite answer. He noted that in December he had talked of reunification taking years but the people had disagreed with their feet. Gorbachev then said that there was no disagreement about German unity between the Soviet Union, the Bundesrepublik and the DDR, and the right of the people to pursue it. This was the decisive breakthrough, or concession.

In return, Gorbachev wanted assurance on the Oder–Neisse border, the honouring of the DDR's economic obligations towards the Soviet Union and further future economic co-operation, to all of which Kohl indicated agreement.[8]

The Kohl mission to Moscow was a resounding success for the chancellor. Gorbachev had, in fact, agreed that the Germans themselves could solve the form, timing and conditions of German unity.[9] He realized and acknowledged that the crumbling of the Soviet empire in Eastern Europe made the Soviet hold on the DDR untenable and pointless. Recognizing this and that he could not block German unification short of using force, which would wreck the very foundations of his foreign and internal policy, Gorbachev gracefully made the best he could of the situation. Giving the green light for reunification, he was still trying to exact a price for it. As he put it, reunification was not to offend 'the legitimate interest' of others. What these interests were and how high a hurdle they would constitute remained hazy.

This very vagueness could potentially be used to complicate matters in the future if needs and opportunities to do so emerged. On the very day of Kohl's arrival, Soviet Foreign Minister Shevardnadze had still been talking of a neutral Germany. Gorbachev had mentioned it as remaining a possible solution, but Kohl ruled it out. Elated and beaming, Kohl could claim that Gorbachev had agreed to German reunification, leaving it up to the Germans to decide about its progress. It was indeed 'a great day for Germany', as triumphant Kohl declared.[10]

What may have helped the Kohl mission was Soviet preoccupation with the internal restructuring of the political machinery and redistribution of power in the Soviet Union. Moscow certainly was not only unenthusiastic about German reunification but, more than anyone else, it had been voicing public reservations about it. Internal Soviet opposition to German reunification persisted. Spearheaded by Yegor Ligachev, the main opponent of Gorbachev, it had support among the Soviet hard-liners.[11] Furthermore, nobody could overlook the Soviet troops in East Germany, long thought of as among the élite of the Soviet armed forces. Thus the success of Kohl's Moscow mission brought a great sense of relief to the Germans.

The increasing likelihood of German reunification inevitably brought uneasiness and trepidation to many other Europeans. It did, after all, upset an international order that had lasted some 45 years and, despite the tensions of the Cold War, this had been the longest uninterrupted period of international peace that Europe had ever enjoyed. Because of the sheer weight and central location of the country, German reunification would fundamentally change the balance of power on the continent. Through its economic strength Germany would emerge as the leading European power, at least in time of peace. Many leaders and spokesmen of Germany's neighbours displayed apprehension at the prospect of a resurgent Germany because of lingering memories of the Nazis and the Second World War. However, the Bundesrepublik had been a successful and stable democracy since its origins over 40 years. No extremist party had gained a significant following there, and its stable economy and progressive welfare legislation had created a basically harmonious and peaceful society not essentially different from its neighbouring prosperous welfare states.

This did not, nevertheless, necessarily put everyone's concerns to rest. To many it was not the nature but the power of a reunited Germany that mattered. Talk of fears rooted in the past sometimes simply camouflaged and covered jealousies and rivalries of the present. Thus everybody was not agreeable. The very day that Kohl was meeting Gorbachev in Moscow, British Prime Minister Margaret Thatcher urged caution about German reunification. She wanted 'massive consultation' about the matter and the approval of no less than 35 nations.[12] Such proposals spelled complications to the Germans, and Thatcher's words did nothing to warm the coolness that already prevailed between her and Kohl. They echoed similar sentiments to those of an earlier proposal by Soviet Foreign Minister Eduard Shevardnadze that there should be a referendum on German reunification among Europeans and North Americans. Both proposals were stillborn. Kohl had wasted no time in countering Shevardnadze, saying that German unity was a German issue, but he did not convince Thatcher.

There remained further hurdles on the path of German reunification. The Soviet Union as well as the Western allies and partners of the Bundesrepublik were anxious to receive all the assurances and promises they could from the Germans. In a telephone call to Modrow, Gorbachev still insisted after his meeting with Kohl that he had 'clearly told' Kohl that a reunited Germany could not stay in NATO.[13] That kept him on a collision course with the West, but he had a weak bargaining position. Kohl was already starting to speak for all of Germany with the authority that the overwhelming support for reunification in East Germany gave him. Recognizing the sentiments of their countrymen and facing elections 18 March, all the significant political parties there were declaring themselves in favour of unification.

The Soviets were getting the message and hedging on their opposition to NATO membership of a united Germany. At an East–West conference in Ottawa a dejected and forlorn-looking Shevardnadze, shrugging his shoulders, refused to comment on it on 13 February.[14] The Soviet leadership knew that its empire was crumbling and that it was also making sudden major one-sided concessions to the West in disarmament negotiations. On both the German issue and the disarmament issue it was giving in on matters which it knew it would shortly lose but was now asked formally to concede.

The Ottawa conference between the NATO and Warsaw Pact foreign ministers turned into another milestone on the path to Germany unity. At the end of November, just a few months earlier, Kohl's ten-point plan had triggered anxious and even angry objections. Since then, much water had flowed under the bridge and efforts to stop it had proved to be futile. In Ottawa the wartime Allies together with the two German states formally accepted German unity.

By then, everyone agreed that the division of Germany was destabilizing Europe; before that, everyone (other than the Germans) had talked of how reunification threatened stability. This turnaround in views was no mean achievement for the East German people and the German leaders who drove it home time after time with their foreign counterparts. The Ottawa participants also agreed on the so-called two-plus-four process to deal with the external aspects of German unity while its internal dimensions were left to the two German states.[15] This procedure ensured the participation of the four principal wartime Allies – the Untied States, the Soviet Union, Britain and France – and the Germans in shaping the future of Germany and Europe.

The Ottawa meeting confirmed a growing general conviction about the inevitability of German reunification. Only the matter of its form, timing and reassurances to other countries remained to be decided. Bonn's Western allies saw their best available reassurance in continuing German membership of the EC and NATO, and sought to sell the same notion to the Soviet Union and the East Central European neighbours of Germany. Poland, Czechoslovakia and Hungary accepted it quickly, but Poland wanted additional assurances. It wanted to participate in future discussion about German reunification and demanded guarantees for their common border.[16]

The smaller western and northern neighbours of Germany found it relatively easy to accept German reunification, having already long grown accustomed to close co-operation and a degree of economic dependency on the Bundesrepublik. Thus the Netherlands, Belgium, Denmark and Luxembourg were not going to cause complications, although they grumbled about not being invited to take part in the unification negotiations.[17]

Even Israel was coming around to accepting what seemed inevitable. The Israeli Foreign Minister Moshe Arens arrived in Bonn and expressed to Kohl his hope that 'misunderstandings' over Israeli Prime Minister Shamir's statements concerning German unity on American television had not burdened German–Israeli relations. He said Shamir's pronouncements had to be understood against the background of his having lost all his family in the Holocaust.[18]

For Britain and France, German reunification was also a hard pill to swallow. Both stood to lose more in their relative status than the smaller countries. The élites of both Britain and France felt strong frustration in sensing their power and influence slipping to Germany, and yet at the same time recognizing that prudence dictated acceptance of it. Painful as it was, eventually both had to approve reunification.

Both Britain and France knew, by the time of the Ottawa meeting, that nothing was likely to block German reunification. They were adjusting to what seemed inevitable. Mitterrand had realized that Gorbachev was in no position to block it or even to drive a hard bargain. He was concerned about the future of allied troops in Germany after the Soviet withdrawal and anxious over whether the Germans would in future honour their pledge not to acquire nuclear, biological or chemical weapons. Kohl sought to reassure Mitterrand and pledged continuing Franco–German co-operation.[19]

Mitterrand's concerns were indicative of his preoccupation with the future balance of power between Germany and France. Its possession of nuclear weapons was about the only thing left where France could still in the future hold an edge on Germany. The same was true of Britain. Seeing Ottawa as a turning-point, Foreign Minister Douglas Hurd announced unconditional British support for German unification in an interview with a German newspaper – at which Kohl's foreign policy adviser Teltschick jotted down in his diary, 'It has taken long enough.'[20] The comment expressed intense German frustration with British actions and attitudes on German reunification. Despite Hurd's assurance, problems between the two countries lingered, as was soon to become obvious.

In advance of her allies, the United States had adopted a realistic view of German reunification. Bush and Baker could then move to actively help to shape the process around it. This enabled them to make a positive contribution to it and to American–German relations, which Kohl appreciated. This decision by the American President spoke well of his sense and acumen in adapting to the changing situation.

What really mattered, however, was the kind of deal that the Germans and the Russians would strike. The British and the French impact was negligible. The American influence was stronger once Washington had concluded that reunification was inevitable and decided to make the best of it and, indeed, positively helped it along.

This American policy was aided by calls for neutrality and unification from German Social Democrats. Arguing that the end of the East–West confrontation was changing the meaning of neutrality, they were raising fears in the West. For Washington, one way of countering such arguments for neutrality was to contribute positively to German reunification and at the same time to insist on continued German participation in NATO. Bush and Baker pleased Kohl and Genscher by helping to persuade the British, the French and the Soviets to agree to the 'two-plus-four' formula, whereas these three had originally favoured a so-called 'four-plus-zero' formula which left the Germans out of the negotiations.[21] Such high-handedness held the promise of all kinds of delays concerning reunification and was unacceptable to the Germans.

While reunification was the Germans' primary concern, its impact on international security arrangements was a preoccupation of their negotiating partners and neighbours. Although the West insisted upon NATO membership of a united Germany, it agreed to a temporarily continued Soviet military presence in eastern Germany. The Soviets in turn wanted to tie reunification to its acceptance by all Germany's neighbours and to guarantees of the post-war borders and a peace treaty. Facing German unification, Moscow could find some reassurance and consolation in the potential popularity of the Social Democrats in a united Germany because of their neutralist leanings. Public opinion polls showed strong support for them in East Germany close to the East German elections of 18 March. In a united Germany this presumed strength could conceivably translate into a Social Democratic victory in the elections.

While this was something that the Soviets could hope for, it was something that Bonn's Western allies dreaded. In addition, at least in London and Paris, a frustrating and uneasy feeling of impotence prevailed in face of the rapid progress towards German unification. There was a sense that Bonn was pressing ahead on its own and that the sheer momentum and dynamics of the situation were forcing all the others along. Such uneasiness caused a fair amount of worried talk but no effective intervention.

This left the politics of reunification largely in German hands. The Americans offered help to the Germans. The Soviets were a coy and not too convincing opponent that was constantly shifting its position, sometimes holding more than one position on the issue at the same time or speaking with more than one mouth and voice. Gorbachev and Shevardnadze, like Mitterrand and Thatcher, protested that German unification was advancing too fast and felt left out, as they were unable to control the process.[22] Both among the Germans and on the international scene the dominant mover was Kohl. Kohl was looking towards the future and knew clearly what he wanted to achieve. His fellow players both in the West and East only knew what they wanted to prevent. They were haunted by the past, or at least they acted or pretended as if they were.

Even after having embraced a quick German reunification, Washington strove to minimize any possible consequent reduction of American influence in Europe. As NATO remained the major vehicle for projecting and exercising that influence, the securing of future German participation in it and the prevention of its breakdown became a major American preoccupation. This was a tall order.

The liberation of East Central Europe from the Soviet grip and the relaxation of East–West rivalry and confrontation dramatically reduced the relevance and appeal of NATO in particular to the Germans. Among the Germans especially but also elsewhere in Europe there was increasing questioning of the role and need of NATO and a search for alternative security arrangements and structures. Oskar Lafontaine, the Social Democratic challenger to Kohl, had argued that, like France, Germany should walk out of the integrated chain of NATO military command. Ridiculing Kohl's and other Christian Democrats' pledges of loyalty to NATO as 'anachronistic', he sought to ride the anti-NATO sentiments.

Kohl was anxious to soothe American concerns about these matters in order to keep the process of German reunification on track. Bush in turn was as anxious to be reassured of continued German membership of NATO and commitment to the future presence of American troops in Germany and Europe. To take care of these mutual anxieties, Kohl journeyed to Washington on 24 February 1990, when he sought to ease Washington's wariness by assuring Bush that unified Germany would remain a full member of NATO and that American troops should remain in Germany and elsewhere in Europe. Bush wanted to prevent a Soviet troop withdrawal from forcing the American troops to leave as well. While he expressed support for German unity, he also stressed the importance of close consultation between the allies to overcome anxiety about the unification. He said Thatcher had come round to accepting it, which was not the case three months earlier.[23]

Kohl's reassurance was timely in soothing Washington's worries. Facing an impending Soviet retreat from East Central Europe, Washington worried acutely about the future of the American military presence in Europe. On 26 February the Czechoslovaks and Moscow agreed on the withdrawal of all Soviet forces from Czechoslovak territory, starting immediately.[24] Accompanying a similar Soviet–Hungarian understanding, such a Soviet retreat from the borders of Germany weakened the case for maintaining American troops there. Having directly confronted the Soviet army on the German–Czechoslovak border, the American troops in the Bundesrepublik would only face the Soviet forces remaining in the rapidly crumbling and disappearing DDR, where their increasing isolation made their positions untenable with the withdrawal of the Soviet forces behind them in neighbouring East Central Europe.

From time to time in the past significant political bickering and dissension had disturbed NATO. Repeated quarrels about burden-sharing had occurred, with the Americans often feeling that they were carrying more than their fair share and accusing other members of trying to get a free ride at their expense. In the internal American debate even the spectre of the unilateral withdrawal of American troops from Europe was raised more than once to force the Europeans to do more for their own defence and security. Unimpressed and unconvinced by such American pressures and threats, the Europeans had in turn often complained about American high-handedness in running NATO and not consulting sufficiently with their allies. Most of this quarrelling had not been serious in the sense of threatening to undermine the very existence of the organization. The one serious exception was the French withdrawal under Charles de Gaulle from the command structure of NATO in 1966, which had weakened the co-ordination and integration of the defence of Western Europe.

None of these past quarrels had led to serious questioning of the very existence of NATO, but the dramatic reduction of an imminent Soviet threat struck at the original reason for the birth and continued life of the organization by creating a new situation in Europe. While Chancellor Kohl continued to pledge and profess his and Germany's loyalty to NATO, other Germans spoke ever more boldly of alternative security structures for Europe. These structures were to bridge the East–West gap and replace the alliance systems inherited from the Cold War. Such ideas were increasingly heard not only from German Social Democrats but also from Genscher's German Foreign Ministry. Furthermore, they were ideas which held wide appeal for many Europeans. Public opinion polls in turn suggested that a clear majority of Germans preferred not to be part of any alliance system after reunification.

Prominent among those questioning the continuing need of NATO was Lafontaine. To him, both NATO and the Warsaw Pact were relics of the Cold War which belonged to the past.[25] The spread of such views further increased Kohl's bargaining power with Bush as they intensified American anxiety about the future of NATO. Seeing it as the best vehicle available for the continued exercise of American influence in Europe, Bush grew ever more determined to back Kohl and to do what he could to ensure Kohl's re-election.

Washington was visibly and audibly hard put to find reasons for the perpetuation of NATO which were persuasive to the sceptics. In the short term, important support existed for the continuation of the organization, yet even many of its backers for the immediate future were looking for alternative longer-term security arrangements.

In Europe the strongest support for NATO persisted in Britain. Mrs Thatcher and the British Foreign Secretary Douglas Hurd repeatedly emphasized its importance and the need of continued German membership for the security of Europe. The French also backed NATO, at least for the time being. Publicly, both the British and the French spoke of the necessity of maintaining NATO because of uncertainty regarding the future of the Soviet Union and Gorbachev and the continuation of his policies towards the West. One could not be sure that the thaw in East–West relations would last for ever – or, as French Prime Minister Michel Rocard stated bluntly, 'Mr Gorbachev will die one day. He will have a successor, and army marshals cannot be excluded.'[26]

Yet it was not only the Soviet Union but also unified Germany that loomed as a potential, although usually an unspoken, threat, and as another justification for the continued existence of NATO. Behind much of the talk about the need to keep up NATO and insistence on continued German membership were hidden concerns and fears of a unified Germany and a need to keep her tied and under surveillance. To some extent such concerns agitated her neighbours and partners. They all shared memories of the Second World War and they all were confronted with the prospect of increased German power in the near future. They may have reconciled themselves to accept German reunification but such acceptance did not preclude continued anxiety.

Because of its geographical proximity, the immediacy of its ties to the Bundesrepublik, the size of its resources, and its pivotal role in the European Community, the attitudes in France were of special importance among Germany's neighbours.[27] Paris vouched for its trust of Bonn and for its wish to co-operate with the Germans. The French recognized that this long-lasting co-operation had been a pillar of stability and prosperity in Western Europe after the Second World War. Furthermore, they regarded it as necessary to meet the economic challenge of the United States and Japan. So far it had been largely a co-operation of equals. France's status as a nuclear power and its prominent role in the EC bureaucracy had in part balanced German economic superiority.

How long would such a balance last? Facing the changes in Germany, alarm and apprehension were spreading in France, on both the right and the left, about increasing German power. Among the French élite and leadership a keen sense of rivalry and suspicions and fears of the Germans surfaced from time to time. President Mitterrand had thrown obstacles in the path of speedy German reunification. The former French Premier Michel Debré commented darkly about his neighbour: 'We French, who know our neighbour well, how can we not remind all Europeans and the world ... of the need to guard against abuses which Germany commits in all areas when it sees an opportunity?'[28] In an article in *Le Figaro*, he even expressed suspicions of Germany again dreaming of world domination.[29]

The shadow and memories of the past had left their traces in the psyche of the French, and these burdens of blood and humiliation affected their attitudes towards Germany. The bold and fast-paced moves towards German reunification and the prospect of facing an increasingly more powerful Germany in the near future created uncertainties and revived old fears, especially among those alive during the Second World War. As Dominique Moïsi, the prominent French scholar of international relations, put it: 'The French are deeply insecure. ... The Germans are asserting themselves, and we are growing fearful. Our fears may not be well founded, but we have them none the less, and a fearful people will not always distinguish carefully between myth and reality.'[30] Among younger Frenchmen born after the war, such fear and the burdens of the past based on them seemed to have largely lost their grip, judging from the overwhelming support among them for German reunification, but they were not yet the French leaders and the past loomed large in the minds of the war generation.

Other European leaders shared the desire of Washington, London and Paris to keep a united Germany in NATO. Thus all the 15 NATO members expressed their support for German unity. The Italian Foreign Minister Gianni de Michelis spoke in strong terms of the need for Germany to stay in NATO. A man who loved to talk and quip, he was reported to have repeated the refrain that he loved Germany so much that he preferred two of them.[31]

The Soviet Union remained the only major power to hold out against a united Germany's membership of NATO. After returning from Ottawa, Shevardnadze said that finding a solution to the problem would take years but that he was not opposed to German membership if fundamental changes took place in NATO policy. Gorbachev was quoted in *Pravda* on 21 February 1990 as saying that the Soviet Union did not oppose German unification, though he complained that it was advancing too fast. He was backtracking from his comments to Kohl in Moscow, saying that unification was not a matter purely for the Germans to decide but that they had to consider their neighbours' interests.[32] He clearly wanted to be part of the action. Only a week later, on 27 February, Shevardnadze said that German membership of NATO would destroy the European balance of power. Stating 'That is absolutely out of the question', Gorbachev imperiously ruled it out in an interview on German television on 6 March. Shevardnadze even excluded the compromise of not placing NATO troops in East German territory as an artificial device and called Western pronouncements on German NATO membership 'tactless'.[33] Harsh as these statements sounded, neither Gorbachev nor Shevardnadze any longer categorically and specifically ruled out German unification, as they had done earlier. Their bark was worse than their bite, perhaps for bargaining purposes and because of Soviet internal politics. They were concerned about unmet East German economic obligations and criticism by Soviet hard-liners for too easily giving up the fruits of victory in the Second World War.

The Soviet Union had remained opposed to German reunification for as long as possible. Both Gorbachev and Shevardnadze had vocally and pointedly originally ruled it out. Shevardnadze had even used exceptionally emotional and strong language for diplomatic discourse, painting dark images of threatening 'sinister shadows of the past … militarism … [and] revenge'.[34]

By contrast, the majority of Soviet public opinion, as expressed in polls, early accepted German reunification.[35] Such generosity of spirit was remarkable in a country which had lost by far more lives in the war against Germany than anyone else, or all the others combined for that matter, and whose people had constantly and continually been bombarded by reminders of that war.

The pressure of events and persuasion gradually and eventually also pushed the Soviet leadership to reconsider and amend its position. The persuaders included Bush and Baker, who were trying to sell Gorbachev and Shevardnadze the notion that membership of NATO by a united Germany was also in the Soviet interest since it prevented unilateral German action in the sensitive sphere of security policy. This was no easy task, as the Soviet leaders hardly thought that they needed advice as to what was in their interest. It was going to take more than words to persuade them. They wanted something concrete in return which only the Germans could deliver.

The notion that NATO should be preserved as an insurance against a resurgent and potentially threatening Germany was risky. In fact, it was self-defeating and downright dangerous to the health and longevity of the very organization whose survival it ostensibly sought. With only a minority of Germans supporting continued membership of NATO, any suggestion that the organization was somehow not in their interest could stir further opposition to it in Germany. With the foundation of popular support for NATO already precarious, it could make German membership untenable. Kohl's seemingly wholehearted embrace of NATO and assurances of German loyalty to it would not be enough if the popular mandate for it disappeared, and strong opposition to it developed in Germany. Such strong opposition could grow from the resentment felt by the Germans who saw themselves as no threat to anyone, having absorbed all the lessons of the past. Nobody likes to stay in a group where one's fellows are obstructive or antagonistic, and in the long run Germany was strong enough not be forced to keep company which it did not want. The unstated but often implied notion that part of NATO's mission was to check the Germans could become fatal to the organization.

If German enthusiasm for NATO was less than overwhelming, its commitment to the European Community was beyond reasonable doubt. The Bundesrepublik was, after all, a major beneficiary of the EC, traditionally running a trade surplus with its other members. Compared with this the sums it contributed to the EC were relatively modest. Nevertheless, the spectre of German unification caused anxiety among the partners of the Bundesrepublik in the Community. In particular, fears abounded about the impact of German reunification on the prospect of achieving a higher degree of EC unity as planned by the end of 1992. The Germans were commonly expected to become so preoccupied with the complications and tasks of national integration that they would have less interest and energy left for the European Community.

Some were concerned about an upsurge of German nationalism and its impact on the EC. Others fretted about the economic consequences of the incorporation of East Germany into the EC via the Bundesrepublik. The penny-wise were vexed about who would pay for what share of the cost of German unification and integrating East Germany with the EC. Together with such concerns went anxieties about competition for markets, funds and investments.

It was generally recognized that East Germany would have to be subsidized and granted exceptions from many EC standards and rules for some time. The big question was at whose expense, to what extent and for what length of time. The Spaniards and the Portuguese fretted about possible losses of potential German investment going to East Germany. The British worried about competition from subsidized East German companies; giving open expression to such fears, British Foreign Secretary Douglas Hurd proclaimed, 'The rest of us will need protection from the entry into our markets of subsidized East German goods.'[36]

It would take time before the answers to such questions would become clear, which did not lessen the levels of nervousness and anguish. The most enthusiastic proponents of further EC integration were especially concerned that, under the weight of all these new complications and burdens, the whole process would lose momentum, slow down, and possibly stop altogether. They included notably the French, most prominently the President of the European Commission Jacques Delors, President François Mitterrand, and Foreign Minister Roland Dumas. To them further EC integration continued to be the best promise of maintaining and asserting the French role and influence in the face of a resurgent Germany. Mitterrand saw no insuperable problem in extending the EC into East Germany,[37] and Bonn's decision not to seek additional EC representation based on the East Germans undoubtedly helped.

Those less enthusiastic about further integration within the EC were not altogether displeased with the additional complications. Those downright opposed to more integration were frankly cheered by them. Notable among these groups were many Britons and most prominently Mrs Thatcher. Mrs Thatcher was, of course, not enthusiastic about German unification either, the potential perceived source of further complications for the EC, but she was even less enthusiastic about the further loss of British sovereignty which loomed largest in her mind among the unfortunate results of further EC integration.

In addition to the specifics of the immediate and short-term impact of German reunification, the EC members also held longer-term worries. These varied from fears of German domination of the EC to Germany turning eastwards and concentrating its investment and trade heavily in Eastern Europe, to the detriment and neglect of its EC partners. Contradictory as such fears sometimes were, they were nevertheless real to those who were haunted by them. Fears of German domination harked back to Adolf Hitler's New Order in Europe. They had to do not only with perceptions of German arrogance and 'Besserwisser' (know-all) mentality, but also with the mere German reputation for superior efficiency and hard work. Linked with these went simple astonishment at the German economic performance and doubts of being able to compete with the Germans in world markets.

In a sense many of these fears and doubts rested on realities already in place. The economy of the Bundesrepublik was already the powerhouse of Europe, and the Deutschmark and the policies of the German Central bank powerfully affected other European currencies and economic policies – for example, higher Deutschmark interest rates forced interest rates higher elsewhere in Europe. This was an indirect way for the Bundesrepublik to make others share the costs of German reunification and reconstruction of eastern Germany. Germany also contributed by far a larger share of the EC budget than any other member, however, and Kohl had tried to meet in part the economic concerns of Germany's EC partners by stating that EC monies did not need to be used to pay for the costs of reunification but that the Germans would pay their own bill. Nevertheless, such assurances could not overcome all the deeply rooted apprehensions.

Notes

1 *IHTr* and *FAZ*, 1 Feb. 1990; Teltschick, 1991, pp. 123, 128; *Die Welt* and *The Times*, 9 Feb. 1990.
2 Teltschick, 1991, pp. 134–5.
3 See, e.g., Hans-Dietrich Genscher, 'German Unity within the European Framework', *Statements and Speeches*, 13, 2, 6 Feb. 1990, or Genscher, 31 Jan. 1990, Tutzing, *Unterwegs zur Einheit*, 1991 and Szabo, 1992, pp. 56–62.
4 See, e.g., *FAZ*, *Die Welt* and *Der Spiegel*, 5 Feb. 1989, and *FAZ*, *SZ* and *Die Welt*, 8, 9 Feb. 1989.
5 *FR*, 10 Feb. 1989.
6 Reuters and TASS, 10 Feb. 1990.
7 Teltschick, 1991, p. 137.
8 Ibid., pp. 139–41.
9 TASS, 11 Feb. 1990.
10 German television, 10 Feb. 1990; *Welt am Sonntag*, 11 Feb. and *Die Welt*, 12 Feb. 1990.
11 *IHTr* and *Pravda*, 8 Feb. 1990.
12 *The Times*, 11 Feb. 1990.
13 ADN, 12 Feb. 1990.
14 CNN, 13 Feb.; *FAZ*, *IHTr*, *SZ* and *Die Welt*, 14 and 15 Feb. 1990.
15 Ibid.
16 *The Economist*, 17 Feb. 1990; *Time* and *Newsweek*, 19 Feb. 1990.
17 Ibid.
18 Teltschick, 1991, p. 150.
19 Ibid. pp. 150–51 and *Die Welt*, 20 Feb. 1990.
20 Teltschick, 1991, p. 153.
21 Szabo, 1992, p. 61.
22 *Pravda*, 21 Feb. 1990.

23 Claus Genrich in *FAZ*, 24, 26 Feb. 1990; Teltschick, 1991, pp. 159–61.
24 *IHTr*, 27 Feb. 1990.
25 See, e.g., Karl Kaiser, 'German Unification', *Foreign Affairs*, 1, 1991, p. 195; Lafontaine, in *Time*, 2 April 1990.
26 Rocard, in *Time*, 2 April 1990.
27 On French views and policies, cf. Ronald Tiersky, 'France in the New Europe', *Foreign Affairs*, Spring, 1992, pp. 131–9.
28 Debré, in *Time*, 26 March 1990.
29 Debré, in *Le Figaro*, 15 March 1990.
30 Moïsi, in *Time*, 26 March 1990.
31 *FAZ, IHTr, SZ* and *Die Welt*, 9 March 1990.
32 Shevardnadze, *The Future belongs to Freedom*, 1991, p. 137, and Gorbachev, in *Pravda*, 21 Feb. 1990.
33 TASS, 27 Feb. 1990; German television 6 Mar. 1990; Shevardnadze in *Neuen Berliner Ilustrierten*, 8 March 1990.
34 Shervardnadze, in *Time*, 26 March 1990.
35 *Libération*, 19 Feb. 1990. Some 51 per cent were in favour.
36 Hurd, in *Business Week*, 2 April 1990.
37 Teltschick, 1991, p. 151.

9 Growing Alarm

To the Germans, the sinking East Germany economy and the resulting mood of its people were rapidly becoming the imperatives that could not wait. Fanned by alarming media accounts and rumours about economic breakdown and foreseeable utter collapse, the East Germans' notion of the state of their economy was sinking even faster than was warranted by its actual performance during the winter of 1990. Driven by desperation, the East Germans created a situation where anything short of reunification seemed unacceptable.[1] Their economic despair and anxiety to snatch at the lifeline of the Bundesrepublik was so strong that for most it overcame their fears of losing the modest security they had enjoyed through their savings, pensions, and jobs.

Some were, of course, unhappy with the prospect of the demise of the DDR. Those most unhappy were its major beneficiaries, the recipients of power, status and perquisites. Facing a potentially less comfortable future, they regretted the passing of their fountain of welfare. Among them were officials of the party and state, favoured cultural and sports figures, and possessors of knowledge and skills soon to become obsolete: officers of the Stasi and the political officers of the East German armed forces, teachers and professors of Marxism and Leninism as well as Russian, all knew that after reunification there would be little if any need of their services. Most of these people looked forward to an uncertain future. Some were bitter and fearful. A few were defiant, among them the phenomenal figure-skating star Katarina Witt of Karl-Marx-Stadt who had dazzled the world with her poise and skill. 'I'm no cheap turncoat,' she declared to critics of her continued adherence to the Communists.[2]

Instead of teachers of Marxism and Leninism, East Germany badly needed people capable of starting and running small and medium-size companies that could offer employment. Called the *Mittelstand*, such companies were the backbone of the West German economy and the trainers of much of its highly skilled labour force. Although parts of East Germany had had a similar tradition, the Communists had stamped it out long enough ago to make its revival difficult. The former entrepreneurs for the most part would be too old or had been away too long to begin again in the much changed circumstances, and had not had an opportunity to train and pass on their knowledge and skills to successors. Meanwhile, the Communists had created a system which not only discouraged but made virtually impossible any independent economic activity beyond the smallest scale. A remaining alternative was to try to attract *Mittelstand* from the west after reunification.

This alternative was increasingly becoming a reality during the weeks that preceded the East German March election of 1990. Co-operation between West and East German companies was growing, and West German companies were increasingly looking for investment opportunities and markets in the DDR. In turn, East German companies were hungry for advice and know-how in order to be able to function within the free market economy they expected in the near future.

However, there were also fears of West German claims for the return of business and private property once expropriated by the Communists. Such claims added to the insecurity felt by many about their future employment and housing. The East Germans who became most disturbed and upset were those who found West Germans knocking on their doors and introducing themselves as the owners of their homes.

East Germany had experienced massive confiscations and transfers of property since the war. The Soviet authorities had taken the first measures, confiscating and expropriating the larger landed properties, and by these actions they had broken the economic backbone of the Prussian *Junkers*, among others. The East German authorities later carried out additional takeovers of property, and over the years the status of such property had become complex. A long time had passed since these measures had taken place; former owners had often settled in the Bundesrepublik where they had received some compensation for their losses, and over the years these properties might have passed through several hands.

The East German occupants or owners of such properties at times agreed and even freely admitted that the original owners had suffered an injustice, yet they also felt entitled to their existing occupancy conditions and contracts. They argued that new injustices should not replace old ones. Uncertainty concerning the disposition and ownership of much East German property was eventually to become perhaps the single most important impediment to prompt economic reconstruction in eastern Germany after reunification. It was a major obstacle to the selling and merging of businesses as well as new investment.[3]

With the approach of the March elections and the seeming inevitableness of speedy German reunification, insecurity on a larger scale was also intensifying among some of Germany's neighbours, most strongly among the Poles. They worried and fretted increasingly about possible future German claims upon territories lost at the end of the Second World War. The Poles of Pomerania, Prussia and Silesia wondered whether Germans would some day return and claim their lost lands and farms and town houses in places like Szczecin (Stettin), Poznan (Posen), Worchlaw (Breslau), and even in Gdansk (Danzig), and in numerous smaller towns. Many were refugees from the former Polish territories in the east lost to the Soviet Union[4] as a result of Hitler and Stalin's division of Poland in August 1939 and the subsequent Soviet invasion on the heels of the German onslaught. After the Allies had swallowed this result of the Nazi–Soviet Pact of August 1939, these refugees had no place they could call home to return to and were haunted by the fear of once again becoming uprooted and homeless. The older ones did not want to start all over again in a new place, and the younger ones had grown up in the former German territories, the only home they knew.

To most Germans, who had accepted as permanent the loss of their former eastern lands, the Polish fears seemed exaggerated and irrational but they were nevertheless there. They became a reality of international relations when Poland demanded renewed firm guarantees of its western border in the face of German reunification. Poland was also the only country in Europe where a clear majority, about two-thirds according to some public opinion polls, opposed the reunification of its neighbour.[5]

Some of the uncertainty and anxiety among the Poles and others about the future attitude of Germany towards its Polish border was linked with Kohl's statements on the issue. While Kohl had not made any claims on border revision, neither had his pronouncements on the topic fully reassured everyone. Kohl linked the recognition of the Oder–Neisse line to Polish renunciation of reparations – they had demanded some 200 billion Deutschmarks – and a treaty concerning the rights of the German minority in Poland. Furthermore, he thought that only a reunified Germany could conclusively and finally recognize the border. This did not satisfy the Poles, who wanted recognition before reunification and strove to be included in the two-plus-four talks in order to achieve their aim.[6]

During Kohl's visit to America in late February 1990, Bush indicated to him that greater clarity on the Polish border issue would help unification. He was pressed hard on the border topic in a news interview but once again he failed to assuage the doubters. In frustration Kohl affirmed in vain, 'I have again and again declared, during the past months … nobody wants to link the question of national unity with changes in existing borders ... in the Federal German Parliament, we have already pronounced on ourselves and confirmed our line about the non-changing borders.'

Appearing together with Kohl, Bush interpolated by stating directly that 'the US respects … the inviolability of current borders in Europe, and the

US formally recognizes the German–Polish border'. As Kohl appeared to take the position that the final settlement of the issue would have to wait for German unification, Bush supported him when confronted with queries about differences between the two leaders: 'I think we are in alignment. I would not interpret what he said as equivocating at all. And I have just given you the US position ... I prefer to look at Germany's 45 years of contribution to democracy, and to the security of the West.'[7]

There they stood side by side, Bush, the tall, spare, and lean Connecticut Yankee turned Texan, and Kohl, the big burly Rhinelander, in fact staking out different positions on the border issue without, however, admitting it.

Kohl's caution and ambiguity on the matter reflected his reading of the internal German political situation. According to current polls, he was facing a closely contested election. He had reason at the time to think that he could not afford to offend and alienate the millions of Germans and their descendants who had fled or who had been expelled, often by brute force, from their former homes in the east. If he appeared too easily and readily to jettison their concerns, many might vote for the nationalist right-wing Republicans or simply stay at home at election time, even if they would normally have voted for Kohl's Christian Democrats.

The votes at stake here were not few but amounted potentially to more than was usually realized outside Germany. Originally close to eleven million Germans had been ejected from their homes in the east, and the survivors and their descendants traditionally made up a sizable proportion of the support for Kohl's party. Many of them belonged to organizations through which they could make their voices heard. It was not just a matter of border revision to them, as many realized that this was unlikely, but they hoped that a compromise could be struck which would bring them some compensation for their losses and minority rights for the Germans who had stayed behind, often by hiding the national identity which they now wished to claim back and to assert.

Outside Germany many saw the issue from a different angle and in a different light. Theirs was the perspective of the former victims of Nazi Germany. Some were angry at Kohl, and some even saw something sinister behind his attitude. To them, Kohl's hesitations and his and many other Germans' ambiguity on the border issue raised the prospect of future German revanchism and expansionism. While the greatest anxiety on the matter existed in Poland, some of it found an echo in the United States. Spokesmen for Polish–Americans called on Bush to urge Kohl to unequivocally recognize the Oder–Neisse line as the German–Polish border. In particular, Kohl was criticized by American politicians whose constituencies included many Polish–American and Jewish voters or contributors. Senator Paul Simon of Illinois, with many Polish–American voters in Chicago, voiced his concerns and Clairborne Pell, chairman of the Senate Foreign Relations Committee, took issue with Bush's and Kohl's statements. Confronting and directly challenging Bush's denial of any 'equivocating' on Kohl's part, he told the president that Kohl's 'equivocation on Poland is unacceptable'. Pell was also giving voice to other fears caused by German nationalism. To him, Kohl's and even Hans Modrow's talk of the German people and fatherland was disturbing as it also raised the vision of the incorporation of Austria into Germany.[8]

In fact, the border issue divided the Germans. Among them the Social Democrats and the Free Democrats, as well as many Christian Democrats, were prepared to immediately give the reassurances needed to pacify the Poles and others on the matter. Some openly criticized Kohl for not straightforwardly guaranteeing the border and putting Polish fears to rest. Others simply declared their acceptance of the existing border. Among the most prominent West German leaders they included Richard von Weizsäcker, the aristocratic President of the Bundesrepublik and a Christian Democrat, and Foreign Minister Genscher.

It was not among the Germans but rather among the Poles that the border issue awoke the most intense feelings and most emotional and extreme responses and talk across the political spectrum. It united Poles, from the supporters of Solidarity to the Communists, in a passionate espousal of national interests. *Rzeczpospolita*, the Polish government newspaper, described as 'wretched' the results of the Bush and Kohl meeting as far as the border issue was concerned.[9]

The Polish President Wojciech Jaruszelski met the Soviet Ambassador, Vladimir I. Brovikov, to insist on Polish participation in any negotiations about Germany affecting Poland. Janus Onyszkiewicz, the Solidarity-aligned chairman of the Foreign Affairs Committee of the Polish parliament, warned that 'the only way to change that [the boundary] is war'. Recalling painful historical experiences he said that 'We want to break certain patterns that have been established for many years, such as the Molotov–Ribbentrop pact and Yalta, of smaller nations having their fate decided by big ones. ... Nothing about us without us.' Other prominent Poles echoed the same or similar sentiments. Bronislaw Geremek, the leader of the Solidarity group in parliament noted, 'Despite Polish military participation in the Second World War, the shape of the Polish borders was decided at Yalta and at Potsdam without Polish participation,' and Adam Michnik, another leading Solidarity member, bluntly upheld the threat, 'Any attempt to change this border simply means war.'[10]

Such Polish concerns also translated into a renewed tolerance of Soviet troops' continued presence in Poland. They were seen as a form of reassurance against the Germans. Having grown used to anti-Soviet graffiti, the

Soviet garrisons in Poland to their surprise were suddenly meeting with unexpected warmth. In formerly German territories their post-war Polish settlers were crossing out such slogans as 'Russians go home.'[11] The irony was that these very same worried Poles were often refugees or children and grandchildren of refugees from former Polish territories in the east annexed by the Soviet Union. Victimized by the Soviet Union, they generally resented and hated the Russians, but the prospect of German reunification made their fear of the Germans more imminent and acute than their wish to get rid of the Russians. They did not want to be displaced once again, this time by returning Germans. 'It is quite a change,' said a Soviet lieutenant, 'before they were quite rude and said nasty things to us, now they smile and act friendly.'[12]

Besides the Poles, the Jews also displayed a heightened degree of sensitivity and discomfort with the approach of the East German vote and the presumed German reunification. They were anxious that a united Germany should continue to remember and educate its people about the Nazi crimes and set up various safeguards against a danger of their repetition sometime in the future. In German eyes such anxiety, just like the Polish anxiety, was sometimes excessive and unjustified.

An exchange of views between Chancellor Kohl and Rabbi Marvin Hier, dean of the Simon Wiesenthal Center for Holocaust Studies in Los Angeles, was especially illuminating of both the German and Jewish views on the matter. Kohl had a history of long-term sensitivity to Jewish concerns, as Rabbi Hier confirmed, and he had spoken frankly of Nazi crimes, yet he also took forthright issue with the often expressed anxieties and doubts about the Germans because of their Nazi past. Critics had frequently pointed out that the East Germans in particular had not faced or learned and become aware of the Nazi past. Kohl claimed that the East Germans, through their experience of Communism, were 'immune to any new totalitarian temptations'. The West Germans in turn were well aware of 'the causes and consequences' of Nazi tyranny, he said, and voiced 'deep disappointment at how little many opponents of German unity take note' of it. He pointed out the West German laws against 'crimes of hatred' which included the 'instigation of racial hatred or defamation of Nationalist Socialist victims, especially by the denial of the Holocaust'. Kohl further stated to Rabbi Hier that 'I understand the anxiety expressed by some victims of the Nationalist Socialist dictatorship in view of the prospect of German unity,' but 'it needs to be asked whether such anxiety is essentially justified, whether its roots lie not only in the past but also in the present. In this respect, our views evidently differ.'

In Kohl's view, Americans needed to become more aware of 'the positive things that have happened in Germany since 1945'. He also referred to the record of the Bundesrepublik in maintaining close ties with Israel.

Rabbi Hier in turn stated, 'Victims of Nazism have earned the right to be concerned about the unification of Germany and the Chancellor is politically naïve if he expects such anxiety to disappear.' Kohl had been accused of many things during his long political career, but to be accused of being politically naïve must have stunned both him and his past and present political rivals. Rabbi Hier further suggested that a united Germany should establish a Holocaust museum and special governmental bodies for the supervision of education and learning about the Holocaust in school curricula and textbooks, as well as a commemoration of the Wannsee conference where the Nazis had plotted the extermination of the European Jews. He also said, 'We need a mechanism to ensure that the democracy of reunified Germany will not be an inch deep.'[13]

Not all Jews saw Germany the same way. The Israeli President Chaim Herzog affirmed in an interview given in connection with an official visit to Finland that he was not afraid of a united Germany since the Bundesrepublik was 'in every way a healthy society'. He was nevertheless concerned with anti-Semitic rumbles in the East.[14]

Parallel to the Jewish reactions, Polish concerns continued to be raised. Pressure was building up on Kohl both abroad and within the Bundesrepublik to meet the Poles on the border issue. The leading Free Democrats Genscher and Otto Lambsdorff, in addition to the Social Democrats, were either openly disagreeing with him or criticizing him directly on the matter. The Social Democrats accused Kohl of endangering German interests by his stand. Kohl himself persisted in seeking to gain some reaffirmation of earlier Polish agreements on renouncing claims of war reparations from Germany and on rights of the German minority in Poland in exchange for a border treaty.

In internal German politics it was tactically astute not to give up these claims for nothing in return. If the precedent was set with the Poles abandoning reparation claims, others would have weaker grounds for demanding them – 'An extremely shrewd move by Herr Kohl,'[15] a German newspaper commented.

What were the attitudes of the Germans closest to the border? Judging from random impressions, the East Germans who lived next to the Poles and the former German territories did not entertain any hope of regaining the lost lands. They appeared ready to accept the losses as permanent, although many had roots east of the present border. Yet they also commonly held Poles generally in low esteem. Many seemed to think that the Poles were lazier, less tidy, and less disciplined and organized than the Germans, and that the shrewder ones among them tried to get by through questionable trading and business transactions rather than by honest hard work.

Some East Germans who had grown up in the territories lost to Poland at the end of the Second World War had been back to see their old homes or what was left of them. They spoke with some anger but more with nostalgia and sadness about their experiences and impressions, about the run-down condition of the homes and surroundings of their childhood and youth. Typically, they thought that the new Polish owners had not taken care of or kept up the properties. Common observations were that paint was peeling, front steps and pathways crumbling, and gardens were a mass of weeds.

Such visits by Germans to see their former homes made their present occupants nervous. Some sensitive Poles who lived in former German houses said that they woke up at night from dreams where the Germans had returned to reclaim their lost properties. Adding to the Poles' nervousness were stirrings and reassertions of their German identity among Polish citizens with a German background.

With the collapse of Communism in the DDR and the promise of German reunification, a renewed ethnic self-confidence awoke among this long-frustrated, thrifty, and hardworking minority which had felt held back by the long decades of Communism in Poland. The reassertion of its ethnic identity by the German minority came as an unpleasant and unwelcome surprise to many Poles. Many had become accustomed to overlooking and ignoring the long-suppressed German heritage and identity among hundreds of thousands of the inhabitants of former German territories.[16]

Yet the clash between the German and Polish past and ways of life had not disappeared, even though the German identity had been forced into a private and inner life. Their different and very opposite roles as participants in tragic recent history alone had created a deep and wide gulf between Germans and Poles which was hard to bridge. Whereas the Germans remembered most of the Second World War period as a time when they led a privileged life compared with the Poles, the latter remembered the deprivation, oppression and violence they had suffered at German hands. Conversely, the Germans had vivid memories of rapes and killings by Soviet soldiers and looting and repression by Poles at the end and in the aftermath of the war.[17]

As the turmoil around the border issue intensified, Bonn eventually came to terms with it on 6 March 1990. Kohl and Genscher were concerned that the agreement with Poland would be at risk if Polish claims for reparations stirred up nationalism among the Germans already apprehensive about the cost of reunification. By dropping demands on a Polish waver of reparations, Bonn resolved that 'the Polish people shall know that its right to live in secure borders will not be put in doubt now or in the future by us Germans through territorial claims', though it still persisted with Kohl's notion that the formal and final word belonged to a united Germany. It further declared that prior Polish agreements on war reparations and the rights of the German minority in Poland made to the Bundesrepublik and the DDR also applied to a united Germany. Conceding that 'mistakes were made on every side, including by me', Kohl expressed full agreement with the resolution – though he was definitely not contrite and commented, 'Foreign countries must grasp where German interests lie. We do not need any tutoring here.'[18] There was no mistake about it. The time was long past when Germany was on its knees; now it was standing tall and confident. The German resolution was passed by the Bundestag on 8 March.[19] It did not fully meet the Poles' demands, but it gave them some reassurance and seemed to satisfy many other concerned parties.

Kohl also moved to quell uneasiness and dissatisfaction among those allies of the Federal Republic which had been unhappy about their exclusion from the two-plus-four negotiating process on German reunification. Addressing them, Kohl sought to reassure while also remaining assertive. 'German interests must be taken into account but so also should those of our partners and allies,' he said. Replying to questions, he commented caustically that NATO had always favoured German unification 'when no one thought it would happen . ... Now it is here and we are all being taken at our word.'[20] Kohl's reactions and words reflected his frustration over the gap between past verbal affirmations of allied support to German unification and their actual recent actions and behaviour with regard to reaching it.

The Poles continued to insist that the Bundesrepublik recognize through a treaty the post-war German–Polish border before German unification, and pressed to participate in the two-plus-four negotiations. They received support from the French. During a visit to Paris on 9 March 1990, the Polish leaders Jaruzelski and Mazowiecki gained the backing of Mitterrand, who thought the West German declaration on the border too vague.[21] Mitterrand pleased his guests with his words and won their gratitude, but he once again displeased his powerful neighbours. It did not help matters that his Foreign Minister Roland Dumas, echoing his master, announced that German unification could be achieved only if it was accepted by all European countries.[22] Kohl was disappointed with Mitterrand. For years they had co-operated closely and had regular friendly meetings, but it seemed to count for little in the end. In contrast, Bush and even Thatcher had accepted the German resolution on the border, and the Soviets also acknowledged it positively.[23]

Calling his long-time friend Jacques Delors, the President of the EC Commission, and complaining about French policy, Kohl said he would accelerate German unification and expected those he had known for a long time to support him. He was depressed, and Mitterrand's call to inform him of his talks with the Poles did not improve his mood. Criticizing the Poles' behaviour, he noted they had made no positive moves, in contrast to Havel.

Not only the Poles' but also German feelings had to be considered. Mitterrand was perhaps taken back by Kohl's forthrightness, but he thanked him for speaking so openly. He was beating a retreat, anxious to restore good personal relations (at least officially). Kohl felt relieved.[24] Yet the Poles' persistence paid off in that they were invited to join the 'two-plus-four' process when it dealt with the German–Polish border. In the long run German displeasure would perhaps be more important to the French than Polish gratitude.

The Germans were not unhappy only with Mitterrand. They were also angry with Mrs Thatcher. In their view 'the iron lady', motivated by narrow British nationalism and rivalry, had continually thrown obstacles into the path of German unification. She had certainly tried to slow down the process, and she had emphasized the concerns of nations other than Germany in the matter. For many Germans who were in a hurry and afraid that the opening of the historic opportunity for unity might not last long, that was enough to stamp her as an opponent of reunification.

Notes

1 Cf. *Die Wirtschaft*, 6, 1990, p. 1, and Otto Singer, 'The Politics and Economics of German Unification: From Currency Union to Economic Dichotomy', *German Politics*, 1, pp. 78–80.
2 Witt, in *Newsweek*, 26 Feb. 1990.
3 Cf. 'The New Germany', *The Economist*, 30 June 1990, pp. 14–15; DIW, *Gesamtwirtschafliche und unternehmerische Anpassungsprozesse in Ostdeutschland, Bericht I*, 1991, p. 31; Uwe Andersen, 'Economic Unification', in Dieter Grossen (ed.), *German Unification: The Unexpected Challenge*, 1992, pp. 119–20.
4 Cf. Grzegorz Ekiert, 'The Return of the German Minority to Poland', *German Politics and Society*, Summer, 1992, p. 93.
5 *Libération*, 19 Feb. 1990.
6 *FAZ*, *IHTr*, *SZ* and *Die Welt*, 3 Feb. 1990; Teltschick, 1991, pp. 150–51; *IHTr*, 23, 24 Feb. 1990.
7 Kohl and Bush, in *IHTr*, 26 Feb. 1990.
8 Simon and Pell, in *NYT*, 28 Feb. 1990.
9 *Rzeczpospolita* according to *NYT*, 28 Feb. 1990.
10 *NYT*, 28 Feb. 1990.
11 *IHTr*, 22 Mar. 1990.
12 Ibid.
13 Hier and Kohl, in *NYT*, 2 March 1990.
14 Herzog in *Suomen Kuvalehti*, 20, 1990.
15 *Stuttgarter Zeitung*, 3 March 1990.
16 Ekiert, 'The Return of the German Minority to Poland', *German Politics and Society*, Summer, 1992, pp. 90–108.
17 Impressions from both sides of the German–Polish border in Feb.–March 1990.
18 See, e.g., *FAZ*, *IHTr*, *SZ* and *Die Welt*, 7, 8, 9 March 1990.

19 *FAZ* 9 March 1990.
20 Kohl, in *IHTr*, 9 March 1990.
21 *Le Monde*, 10 March 1990.
22 Dumas, in *Le Monde*, 13 March 1990.
23 Teltschick, 1991, p. 171.
24 Ibid., pp. 172, 174–5.

10 The March Elections

During the winter of 1990 the East Germans were increasingly in a hurry to make sure that reunification proceeded as smoothly and as quickly as possible. Even Modrow conceded that the DDR tottered on the brink of bankruptcy in his talks with Kohl on 13 February. The question was whether his regime could survive until the elections on 18 March. Kohl faced a dilemma. Something needed to be done quickly to help the East Germans; in less than two weeks in February alone some 100,000 had moved to the west, but he saw little reason to prop up Modrow.[1] Instead, he was becoming personally involved in the election campaign in the DDR.

His first DDR rally drew some 150,000 people in Erfurt, a tradition-laden old stronghold of the German Social Democrats. They received him waving a sea of German flags, and in turn inspired Kohl with enthusiasm. He was especially pleased by a large turnout of workers and youth. The essence of Kohl's message was to build up confidence. He said that difficulties lay ahead, but promised success and security in the end. The successful rally also boosted his confidence in an election victory despite contrary findings in the polls, which favoured the Social Democrats. His final election rally attracted a huge turnout of 320,000 people in Leipzig.[2]

The East Germans were clearly increasingly rallying around Kohl. Indicating mounting support for the Christian Democrats in public opinion polls before the March elections, they were confounding the pundits who had predicted a stronger showing for the Social Democrats. Many commentators, with lingering residual sympathies toward socialism of some kind, had not realized the extent of the East Germans' anger with the very term and all the failures and frustrations that they associated with it.

The East German Social Democrats were originally clearly ahead of the Christian Democrats in the polls. They were untainted by collaboration with the Communists since they had not existed as a party in the DDR after their early absorption by the Communists. In contrast, a co-opted Christian Democratic party had continued to exist but *was* tainted by collaboration. It was slower in getting organized for the election campaign and in receiving help from the West Germans, but the closer the election drew, the more it gained in strength from the large number of previously uncommitted voters. A few days before the elections the Christian Democrat-led Allianz für Deutschland, or Alliance for Germany, was running neck and neck with the Social Democrats.[3]

This success was due in no small measure to the personal campaigning of Kohl. In his repeated campaign forays to East Germany, Kohl was greeted by massive, wildly enthusiastic crowds. They saw in him a symbol and the best guarantee of reunification and prosperity, and frequently spontaneously burst out singing the German national anthem at his rallies.

Furthermore, they were singing the traditional first verse, 'Deutschland, Deutschland über alles, über alles in der Welt,' (Germany, Germany above all, above all in the world) rather than the third verse adopted in the Bundesrepublik after the Second World War. The melody by Joseph Haydn was, of course, the same, but the words mattered in giving expression to deeply felt emotions. The East Germans felt above all German. The misleading talk of an East German nation that was common in the West, in particular in the American media, was lacking a foundation in reality. In the hearts and minds of the East Germans, the people of the DDR were not a nation in the sense of something beyond the artificial state structure that separated them from the rest of the German nation.

They remembered that it was Kohl who had first transformed the dream of unification into an attainable political reality. With his November plan he had put German unity firmly on the international agenda from which it could no longer be removed, despite the unhappiness of many. After Kohl's action, and with continuing massive popular demonstrations and the economic and political crises in East Germany, reunification was now certain, although bickering continued about its timing and form. Yet Kohl's and Genscher's political acumen and skills were a major asset for the overcoming of the lingering resistance and remaining obstacles in both the East and the West.

Kohl's role in the campaign became all the more important after two leading East German figures of the Alliance for Germany were discredited. Wolfgang Schnur, the leader of the Democratic Awakening, was exposed as a Stasi informer and, after admitting it, resigned four days before the elections on 14 March, while it turned out that Pastor Hans-Wilhelm Ebeling from Leipzig had kept his church doors locked during the demonstrations in the autumn of 1989 when other churches served as rallying points for the meetings of the demonstrators.[4]

Although such scandals hampered Kohl's coalition, its Social Democratic rivals suffered from their own problems. So discredited had the very term 'socialism' and its traditional claims for achievement become in East Germany that the Social Democrats played down their association with it. As the campaign went on and the election drew closer, they increasingly echoed the promises of the Christian Democrats. Grasping the tail of a flying kite was a desperate rather than a winning strategy.

Very popular as he was personally, even the Social Democrats' elder statesman Willy Brandt, with all his natural charm and charisma, could not block and turn the tide, although he campaigned with gusto to the very end. Holding rallies up to the eve of the elections in the north in Mecklenburg on the Baltic coast, Brandt was fighting to the end like a lion to win over the undecided voters.[5] He had good reason for his determined, last-minute efforts. Only a couple of days before the election roughly half of the electorate had not yet made up their minds, and the latest forecasts indicated a third each supporting Kohl's coalition and the Social Democrats. The West German political heavyweights dominated the campaign, overshadowing the East German leaders.

Only the Communists, running as the Party of Democratic Socialism, were left to defend the past. Playing upon fears of unemployment and loss of pensions and housing, they appealed especially to those with a heavy stake in the old order. Such fears rested on a widespread perception that East German society was simply falling apart. Soldiers were leaving their units without authorization, and those remaining frequently refused to obey orders or went on strike. Declining to go on manoeuvres, they instead demonstrated for democracy and turned the barracks into discussion and debating forums.[6] Former Stasi members were keeping a low profile, spending much time hiding in their homes. Stressed people suffering from various psychosomatic symptoms were flooding health centres seeking relief from their *angst* about an uncertain future.

The election results were a smashing victory for Kohl's coalition. Voter participation was massive, with 93.2 per cent of the eligible voters entering the polling booths, a new experience for most after the ritualistic sham elections under the Communist system. The elections benefited from mild spring weather, and a clear sense of elation was notable among the East German men and women who were opting by their votes for the speediest possible reunification and a market economy.

The clear victory of the Alliance for Germany took many by surprise. The Christian Democrat-led coalition swamped the Left, in particular in its alleged regional stronghold in the industrial south of East Germany. Altogether the Alliance for Germany attracted 48.1 per cent of the vote (193 of 400 seats), which was over twice the 21.8 per cent (87 seats) cast for its nearest rival the Social Democrats. The former Communists, renamed as the Party of Democratic Socialism, ran third, gaining 16.3 per cent (65 seats) and the Liberal Alliance 5.3 per cent (21 seats).[7] Genscher had campaigned eagerly for the Liberals but, like Brandt, he had been unable to translate his great personal popularity into a more substantial vote.

The levels of support for the principal contenders varied a good deal from region to region. The Alliance for Germany was strongest by far in the south. Ironically, it made its strongest showing in Karl-Marx-Stadt and Erfurt, a cradle of German Social Democracy, with 61 per cent of the vote. The Social Democrats fared best in East Berlin and the surrounding areas and in the north where Brandt had campaigned vigorously to the end. The former Communists also achieved their best results in East Berlin, with its heavy concentration of functionaries and beneficiaries of the old regime. Their local vote of 30 per cent was clearly larger than the Alliance for Germany's 22 per cent, making East Berlin the only district where the Alliance was left in third place.[8]

The election brought forth to the centre stage new East German leaders. The leader of the East German Christian Democrats, Lothar de Maizière, a quiet, small and slightly built, reserved and shyly smiling man, emerged as the leading candidate for the post of East German Prime Minister. Speaking with a soft voice and with a slight lisp, he mumbled rather than shouted and appealed to the intellect rather than to the emotions. A musician turned lawyer, he came from a distinguished family of French Huguenot origin, members of which had served in prominent positions, including an uncle in West Germany. He had become known for defending dissidents and conscientious objectors.[9] The election results dashed the hopes of Ibrahim Böhme, leader of the East German Social Democrats, an articulate jack-of-all-trades who had been repeatedly gaoled by the Stasi for his deviations from the prevailing orthodoxy. In the campaign this orthodoxy had no supporters left, as even the former Communists declared that they would work for a market economy although they continued to emphasize social issues.

The Communists also knew that after over 40 years under their thumb, most East Germans had had enough of the dogmas of both Communism and socialism. For the first time since the early 1930s the East Germans had a free election, and the results stripped away the cloak of pretensions of legitimacy behind which the Communists for decades had hidden their lack of genuine popular support among the population. In this sense the results should also have provided a lesson to many observers and pundits in the West who in the past had frequently written about the way the DDR had succeeded in creating a new socialist East German identity and genuine attachment and loyalty for itself. Such attachment and loyalty, in the end result, touched precious few – mainly only the primary beneficiaries of the DDR, the Communist *apparatchiks*.

The results were a blow to the Communist hold on power everywhere in revealing how narrow its popular base had actually been despite all its assumptions and pretensions. The stark revelation of how small a minority had repressed the will of a vast majority shook the Communists clinging to the remnants of their authority and credibility in Europe. Wherever they faced free elections, the East German precedent sent shivers through them. Next in line was Hungary, where elections were scheduled for 25 March 1990, when a centre-right party, the Hungarian Democratic Forum, imitating the success of the Alliance for Germany, and the other democratic forces buried Communism.[10]

The Communists as the collective emperor had been found naked. In contrast Kohl was successfully being fitted for new clothes. With his moves towards German unification and through active campaigning, Kohl had taken considerable personal risks which were richly rewarded. The bold seemed to inherit the earth in Germany. 'This is a happy moment for Germans,' Kohl declared to his countrymen on television when the election results were clear.[11] So it was for most and certainly for Kohl; the chancellor of West Germany was well on his way to shouldering the mantle of the chancellor of a united Germany. The East German election was also something of a rehearsal for an all-German election in that it dashed the Social Democrats' hopes and promised Kohl a victory in the next test. Lafontaine had hoped to receive a boost for his candidacy from East Germany but instead received a blow which destroyed whatever chance he had of victory. It was of little consolation that he had not been alone in hoping for a boost from the east which never came.

The election results were a personal triumph and vindication for Kohl. He had been the driving force behind the forging of the victorious coalition and, drawing massive crowds, he had made a decisive personal contribution to his coalition's success. East German voters had greeted him with fervour on his campaign appearances. Perhaps the very things for which many Western intellectuals tended to belittle Kohl made him easier to identify with for the ordinary East German. Neither a sophisticate nor a slick, smooth-talking salesman, the homely Kohl was a reassuring and familiar type. He was no perfect performer but he could read and sense his audience, and intuitively he knew their instincts better than more removed poll counters.

German reunification, how quickly it could and should take place and its impact on employment, incomes, prices, pensions, property, rents and social security, these had been the dominant themes of the election campaign. Such internal German issues had overshadowed international concerns like the future place of a united Germany in Europe and its relations with the superpowers and international organizations such as the European Community.

The election victory of the Alliance for Germany had increased the prospects of a speedy reunification, and to this end the Alliance for Germany invited the Social Democrats to participate in a broad coalition government. The Social Democrats, however, declined to join a government which included the conservative German Social Union, the smaller partner of the Christian Democrats in the Alliance for Germany. This complicated a smooth and quick advance towards reunification. Without the Social Democrats an East German government would not have the two-thirds majority in the legislature necessary for constitutional changes, including immediate merger with the Bundesrepublik, though with the Free Democrats, their liberal allies, the Alliance for Germany had an absolute majority and could in any event thus proceed to form a government.[12]

As the leader of the Christian Democrats, by far the largest component of the Alliance for Germany, Lothar de Maizière had risen to prominence as the likely new Prime Minister of the DDR. He was not previously widely known among the public, and in the boisterous election victory celebrations he appeared ill at ease.[13] Anything but an extrovert, he had fallen under the large shadow of Kohl during the election campaign. He had another shadow hanging over him. His uncle, General Ulrich de Maizière, had risen to the very top ranks of the Bundeswehr, the West German army. This had affected Lothar de Maizière's life, making him an object of special interest to the Stasi and the East German regime.

The ghost of the Stasi hovered as a dark cloud over the efforts to construct a government for the DDR. Werner Fischer, a member of an investigating committee set up by the East German government to disband the Stasi, and West German publications reported allegations that Lothar de Maizière, along with a number of emerging East German politicians, had co-operated with the Stasi. According to Fischer, a code name 'Scerny' had been discovered for de Maizière in the Stasi archives, but he also said that accusations against de Maizière could be part of a deliberate campaign to discredit him politically, though he did describe the discoveries as serious. According to him they came from the same source as in the case of Wolfgang Schnur, the former leader of Democratic Awakening, a partner in the Alliance for Germany.[14]

It was not only the Alliance for Germany which was hit by such accusations and revelations. The cloud of suspicion had also fallen on Böhme, the leader of the East German Social Democrats. *Der Spiegel*, the widely read and influential West German weekly, had cited an unnamed Stasi officer who claimed that he had been for ten years the controller of Böhme, who had served as an informer.[15]

Both de Maizière and Böhme vehemently denied these allegations. De Maizière said that in his capacity as a lawyer he inevitably had to have contacts with the Stasi, as did other lawyers, but he angrily denied having worked for the security police. According to him, he had never signed a contract to co-operate with the Stasi or received any money from them. He also announced on 23 March that he was willing to serve as the Prime

Minister of the DDR.[16] Böhme also professed his innocence to the allegations in an open letter to the public: 'I never worked for or co-operated with the Ministry for State Security,' he said, and 'I reject such suspicions as slander,' though he resigned as party leader a mere week later, on 2 April, unable to convincingly document his innocence.[17]

The charges of co-operation with the Stasi were not limited to the new top politicians of the DDR. Similar allegations spread about many lesser lights among the politicians and other East Germans. Charges and rumours circulated about so many of the newly elected legislators that moves were made to subject them all to an investigation of their possible Stasi contacts in order to clear the air. The Social Democrats demanded an investigation but were resisted by Modrow's outgoing government, de Maizière, and Hans-Jürgen Joseph, the chief state prosecutor of the DDR. They claimed that such an investigation would clash with the constitution if it were conducted before the convening of the legislature. There the matter rested. The 'Stasicheck' would have to wait.[18]

The organization which during its existence had destroyed countless lives and careers went on doing the same after its presumed demise. With some 100,000 full-time employees and several hundreds of thousands of collaborators, the Stasi left a trail of over 100 kilometres of documents, among them numerous deliberate plants of misinformation. Its activity lasted until the very end of the SED regime, including the Modrow government.[19] Its massive files contained information on at least five million East Germans out of a total population of some sixteen millions. It had truly been all-pervasive. No wonder some, fearing an endless witch-hunt, thought it best to destroy the files. The long-time head of the Stasi, Erich Mielke, had declared on the collapse of the old Communist order, 'I love you all really,'[20] but his fellow countrymen somehow were not convinced that loving care lay behind all those endless files tucked away in the Stasi labyrinths.[21]

Notes

1 Teltschick, 1991, pp. 144–5.
2 *FAZ* and *Die Welt*, 21 Feb. 1990; Infas, *Report Wahlen DDR 1990. Wahl der Volkskammer der DDR am 18. März 1990*, March 1990; Teltschick, 1991, pp. 153–4; *FAZ* and *Die Welt*, 15 March 1990.
3 See, e.g., M. Jung in *Aus Politik und Zeitgeschichte*, June 1990, pp. 3–15.
4 *FR* and *SZ*, 15 March 1990.
5 See, e.g., Brandt, *Reden zu Deutschland – 'was zusammengehört'*, 1990.
6 See, e.g., *Kölner Stadt-Anzeiger*, 8 March 1990.
7 *FAZ*, 19 March 1990.
8 *FAZ*, *FR* and *Die Welt*, 19 March 1990.
9 *FAZ* and *Die Welt*, 19 March 1990.

10 See, e.g., *The Economist*, 31 March 1990.
11 Kohl, on German television, 18 March 1990.
12 *FAZ* and *SZ*, 20 March 1990.
13 German television, 18 March 1990.
14 See, e.g., *Köln Express*, 24 March 1990.
15 *Der Spiegel*, 26 March 1990.
16 *FAZ*, *FR* and *SZ*, 23, 24 March 1990.
17 ADN, 25 March; *FAZ* and *Die Welt*, 3 April 1990.
18 *FR* and *SZ*, 24 March 1990.
19 Schäuble, *Der Vertrag*, 1991, pp. 272–3.
20 Herles and Rose (eds), *Parliaments-Szenen einer deutschen Revolution*, 1989, p. 193.
21 For more information on the Stasi, see, e.g., Gauck, *Die Stasi-Akten*, 1991; Gill and Schröter, *Das Ministerium für Staatssicherheit*, 1991; von Lang, *Erich Mielke*, 1991; Schell and Kalinka, *Stasi und kein Ende*, 1991; Bürgerkomitee Leipzig (ed.), *Stasi Intern*, 1991.

11 International Reactions

While internal and inter-German matters had largely preoccupied the Germans in connection with the March elections, others were primarily concerned with their international ramifications. Their first reactions to the election results reflected these concerns. Washington welcomed the success of the Christian Democrats as signalling support for German membership of NATO. Moscow declared its acceptance of the results, but urged the new East German leaders to move slowly in the matter of unification and to respect the obligations of the DDR and Soviet interests. Reunification should not lead to NATO membership of a unified Germany as this would shake the balance in Europe. The chairman of the EC Commission, Jacques Delors, said that the Bundesrepublik could not proceed with unification without negotiating with its EC partners. According to Delors, German reunification presupposed consent of the other EC members as in practice it introduced East Germany into the EC. Warsaw in turn immediately announced that it wanted to begin negotiations with both Germanies about a border treaty.[1]

German reunification, which the election results hastened, was the single most important change for Europe since the Second World War. It symbolized and was the focal point of a fundamental transformation of the Cold War alignment. The long-oppressed and repressed East Germans were the catalysts for this change and found themselves unexpectedly in the driver's seat. Through their actions, first through the massive haemorrhage to the West and then through their votes, they were in practice largely setting both the course and speed of German unification. These actions and the East German economic collapse were hastening a quick currency union with economic and political unification close upon its heels. The very momentum and necessity of these developments in turn put narrow limits and constraints on outsiders' influence and reduced their options for creating obstacles and road blocks. Even any efforts along such lines were risky both in terms of their immediate and long-term results. They might create immediate inestimable economic havoc, even chaos, and sow potentially dangerous and long-lasting bitterness in the strongest economic power in Europe.

Washington had come to recognize such dangers. It was quickly passing the word out that it favoured speediest possible German reunification. This was in sharp contrast to its earlier go-slow advice and cautions. It wished to overcome any bad feelings generated among the Germans by such previous approaches. Bush also let Kohl know that they were on the same wavelength on the thorny question of the German Polish border. Prior to meeting the Polish prime minister Mazowiecki in Washington on 21 March 1990, he informed Kohl of his intended message to the Pole on the border issue. To German satisfaction it reflected their line without an 'if and but'.[2] Seeking to placate and to reassure the Germans, Washington was further serving notice that, while it wished Germany to stay in NATO, this was a German decision.[3]

Moscow had rejected a united Germany's NATO membership repeatedly. Although Gorbachev had categorically ruled it out publicly on West German television on 6 March 1990, other Soviet officials were hedging. Thus the Soviet Union was staking out a tough bargaining position in order to win maximum concessions in return for eventual agreement. But there was more to it. German NATO membership was also a difficult matter for the Soviet Union for reasons of its internal politics. This was why Gorbachev's and Shevardnadze's public statements on the matter were tougher than their attitudes in private. They were guarding themselves against internal attacks by hard-liners.[4]

A curious example of this dual approach took place at a meeting of the Warsaw Pact in Prague in March 1990. At the very climax of the East German election campaign the Soviet-led Warsaw Pact members were arguing in Prague over whether a united Germany could be a member of NATO. Czechoslovakia, Hungary and Poland were acting in concert and defying the Soviet Union. They asserted their own independent foreign policy over the German issue. Moscow insisted upon German neutrality, but Budapest, Prague and Warsaw accepted Germany's NATO membership.[5]

Geography, economic needs, history and political fears determined their stand. Inhabiting a geographical region between Germany in the west and the Soviet Union in the east, the Poles, Czechoslovaks and Hungarians had always lived in the shadow of both Germans and Russians. They badly needed massive foreign investment and know-how which they realized they could, to a large extent, only obtain from Germany. Witnessing the internal disintegration and economic collapse of the Soviet Union, they knew they could no longer count on their traditional economic ties with the Soviets. Both as their most important source of raw materials, above all oil, and as the largest market for their industrial exports which were unable to compete in the West, the Soviet Union seemed an undependable partner in the near future. In need of a new, powerful economic partner, they did not want to offend Germany.

Yet it was not only their wish to get along with the Germans that shaped their attitude to German membership of NATO. The Poles and the Czechs also feared the Germans. Sharing common borders with a united Germany and possessing large, formerly German-inhabited territories, they worried about future German ambitions. To them a neutral but unrestrained Germany seemed more dangerous and threatening than Germany bound to and by NATO. This reassurance seemed all the more important to them as they wanted to rid their territory of Soviet troops. Czechoslovakia and Hungary had already signed treaties to that effect, and Poland would have eagerly followed their example if it were not for its lingering border and territorial concerns. The Czechoslovak foreign minister Jiri Dienstbar thought a neutral Germany the 'worst alternative' and his Polish colleague Krzysztof Skubiszevski said it would 'not be good for Europe'.[6]

In the disintegrating Warsaw Pact, the Soviet Union had become isolated in its opposition to German membership of NATO. This put Soviet Foreign Minister Shevardnadze out on a limb. Still insisting that NATO membership for a united Germany was 'impossible', he also sought to shift the focus of attention on future German armaments. Although Shevardnadze had spoken harshly against German NATO membership, in private he afterwards expressed his appreciation that several states had been for it. Their stand could serve as a shield for him and Gorbachev against the hard-liners in the internal Soviet debate on Germany.[7]

The Germans welcomed signs of Soviet flexibility. They encouraged close contacts with the Soviet leadership by being receptive to Soviet desires and requests. Kohl indicated to Gorbachev that Soviet troops could remain for a limited time in East Germany even after unification without the simultaneous presence of German troops. He also promised the fulfilment of the DDR's economic obligations to the Soviet Union within the limits of feasibility.[8]

There was nevertheless a limit to Kohl's accommodation. He repeatedly rejected tentative Soviet proposals to weaken or undo Germany's commitment to NATO. Such Soviet proposals varied from full German neutrality to trying to keep the Germans tied both to NATO and the Warsaw Pact or establishing a demilitarized zone in the heart of Germany. Moscow also dangled before the Germans an arrangement like the French had with NATO, but made it clear that if Bonn persisted with NATO membership the rights of the Warsaw Pact similarly had to be upheld in the DDR.[9] However, the very fact that Moscow was actively proposing different solutions to German membership indicated its willingness to compromise.

Germany's immediate eastern neighbours shared its western neighbours' anxiety to keep a unified Germany in NATO as a form of check or control on it (though controlling a member, Germany, certainly could not be an admitted purpose of NATO's existence or even one of its openly avowed missions). Yet with the receding Soviet threat, NATO clearly needed a new reason for its existence, or at least a redefinition of its mission. The Americans had talked about turning the defence alliance into a broader political organization, but it was the German attitude to membership which was the key to NATO's future. Without the Germans it had none, at least in the sense in which it had existed in the past. Furthermore, how long would the Germans see a need for it when the last Soviet troops left Germany? How long after that would they welcome or even tolerate a foreign military presence on their territory? When would they tell the Americans to take their noisy jets, the object of frequent complaints, elsewhere? These were anxious questions increasingly aired in European capitals and Washington.

Anxiety about Germany could not serve as a reason for NATO's continued existence, and anxiety about the Soviet Union was rapidly becoming passé. What, then, would bind the alliance together? The Americans might leave without being asked to withdraw their forces. They had often talked about reducing their troops in Europe, and many Americans had long resented the costs incurred, though successive Washington administrations had never seriously considered total withdrawal. Bush, however, faced a different situation from any of his post-war predecessors in the White House. Not only was the credibility of the Soviet threat waning rapidly but the EC, spearheaded by Germany, was increasingly emerging as a major economic rival of the United States. How long would American taxpayers put up with contributing to the security of such an increasingly prosperous rival?

Bush and the American foreign policy establishment saw NATO and some continued American military presence in Europe as a lever with which to assert and protect American political and economic interests. The question being increasingly asked was how long they could sell that notion to the American voters. Kohl's success in the East German elections pushed such nagging questions to the background for a while, as it cooled the speculation and debate about German NATO membership, but the issue of NATO's future and Germany was likely to come back to haunt the policy-makers. A united Germany was unlikely to welcome or even tolerate foreign troops on its soil indefinitely.[10]

American, British and others' anxiety over NATO's future was spurred on by Genscher. He talked of an eventual replacing of the existing alliances in Europe with a new, comprehensive, collective security structure. When Genscher spoke along those lines at a meeting of the WEU, the Western European Union, on 23 March 1990, the very forum alarmed the Americans in particular. They saw in the WEU, as a potential European defence organization excluding the United States, a possible rival to NATO. Genscher had also spoken in terms that had been used by the Soviets, which further added to the American and British sense of alarm.[11]

Kohl reacted angrily to Genscher's words, which departed from his repeated affirmation and pledges of German NATO membership. He feared that his Western allies could misunderstand them as signalling German linkage with the Soviet Union, and informed Genscher that he would not allow such statements to become Bonn's policy.[12] Genscher's utterances could have undermined Kohl's credibility and even suggested German duplicity, though they may actually have benefited rather than harmed the German cause. By adding to the Western allies' anxiety, Genscher's comments may have increased their disposition to humour the Germans and were undoubtedly music to Russian ears.

At least for the time being, Kohl and the Germans were eager to reassure everyone who possibly harboured doubts about a new united Germany. Immediately after the East German elections Kohl had praised the Americans and the other Western allies for contributing to German reunification. He had also paid tribute to Gorbachev's policy of *perestroika* for allowing the first free elections in East Germany. Kohl also sought to calm worries about German domination of the EC or, alternatively, fears that the reunification of Germany would slow down and damage the plans for a single market in 1992 and European economic, monetary and political union.[13] These apprehensions derived from alarm over a resurgence of German nationalism resulting from reunification and future German preoccupation with rebuilding the badly damaged economy of eastern Germany.

The East German elections symbolized a giant step towards German unity. They also brought forth a resurgence of strong emotional reactions among those who most feared and opposed it. The strongest reactions, predictably and understandably, could be found among Jews who had suffered most at German hands. The most extreme talk of Germans and Germany ranged from the notion of a specific defective German genetic flaw to evils of the German national character, though more sober minds sought to calm it. 'You can't talk about something genetically wrong with the German people,' said Moshe Zimmerman, professor of German history at Jerusalem's Hebrew University, but it was Václav Havel, the Czechoslovak president, who perhaps most compellingly put such speculation about the national character in a historical perspective. Speaking about the Germans to his countrymen he said, 'to condemn them only because they are Germans, to be afraid of them only because of that, is the same as to be anti-Semitic'.[14]

Among the major powers France stood to be most directly affected by German reunification. President Mitterrand had sought to block or, failing that, to curb its advance. After repeated failure to achieve either he pinned his hopes on a Social Democratic victory in the East German elections, hoping that it might slow down the process of unification.[15] Foreseeing power in Europe slipping more and more to a united Germany in the future, the French sought to tie Germany to the further political and monetary integration of the EC as soon and as thoroughly as possible. To them it was a form of reassurance. Because the French at the same time tried to preserve what they could of their leadership role within the EC, they faced a delicate task. Their situation was unenviable as they walked a tightrope between a fear of Germany cut loose and fear of German domination of the EC.

Kohl attempted to calm such fears. 'No one needs to be worried about German dominance in the European Community,' he vouched. Pledging that a united Germany would be a reliable and solid partner who would adhere to the timetable and the aims of the economic and political integration of the EC, he also said that a unified Germany was only possible with a more united EC. He maintained, furthermore, that German unification would speed European integration.[16] Kohl made his soothing statement in Brussels where Jacques Delors, the French President of the European Commission, had invited him to give reassurances in the EC headquarters.

It was not the first time that he had given such pledges. He had given similar assurances at least twice before, at the EC summit meetings in Paris and Strasbourg the previous autumn, yet as the process of German reunification accelerated it generated new waves of anxieties that had to be taken into account. Not only the very speed and fact but the manner of reunification alarmed European leaders. President Mitterrand was annoyed that he had to read in the papers and hear on television news about reunification of which he expected to have been appraised. His own actions in turn may have accounted for such a lack of communication, as the Germans had become wary of him. They had not taken kindly Mitterrand's trips to confer in Berlin with Modrow, the last Communist Prime Minister of the DDR. Mitterrand's meeting with Gorbachev in Kiev in December had also increased Germany's uneasiness, as did his support of Poland on the border issue.

The prospect of reunification and the East German election results brought worries about Germany to the surface elsewhere. Officials in Britain, Italy and the smaller EC nations in part shared the French concerns. One result was a warming of relations between France and Britain despite their deep disagreements about the future direction and course of the EC. The tentative Franco–British embrace involved military matters[17] and reflected the lasting formative impact of the Second World War on their leaders. More widespread within the EC were concerns about the economic impact of German unification. Uppermost were questions of the integration of East Germany with the EC.

The concern was not so much about the immediate costs of the economic reconstruction of eastern Germany – funds and investment for that were largely expected to flow from West Germany. Rather it had to do with indirect costs, such as its possible impact on interest rates or inflation in

Germany. Because of the economic weight and power of Germany and the Deutschmark, on which other European currencies were heavily dependent, a rise in German interest rates or inflation was expected and feared to drag along the rest of Europe in its wake.

The West Germans would pay the lion's share of the costs of reconstruction in East Germany, though their more prosperous EC partners would have to contribute a smaller share via the regional development and social funds if East Germany was classified as poor. In EC parlance this meant living standards less than 75 per cent of the EC average. However, the reconstruction of East Germany opened up a new, potentially attractive market for other nations as well as the Germans, but this tended to be overlooked by them. Concern and even fear still seemed to dominate over a recognition of the opportunities.

Hovering in the background behind such economic concerns lay concerns of a longer-term nature. When and how would a united Germany assert political power corresponding to its economic power?

The integration of the East German economy into the EC after reunification remained a sore point with those who feared ending up footing part of the bill one way or another. In particular Prime Minister Thatcher was wary and reluctant to include East Germany. Kohl's reassurances did little to console her as, in contrast to Delors and Mitterrand and many other EC leaders, she did not favour further integration of the EC.

Soon after the East German elections, Kohl moved to mend fences with both Mitterrand and Mrs Thatcher. Recognizing Kohl's enhanced stature, the inevitability of German unification, and the further future rise in German power, both Mitterrand and Thatcher were willing to go along with him. In a television interview on 25 March 1990, Mitterrand sought to repair the Franco–German rift.[18] To Mitterrand's relief, Kohl had agreed with him on accelerated EC integration.

With Mitterrand, Kohl had the benefit of close past co-operation and consultation to build on. The two leaders had customarily met twice a month before the rift which accompanied the beginning of the rapid drive towards German unification. In contrast, relations between Kohl and Mrs Thatcher had never been close but rather cool. Although both were conservative, no real personal empathy had evolved between them.

Indeed, mutual snubs had punctuated their relationship. Mrs Thatcher continued that tradition in an interview published on Kohl's home ground in the widely read weekly *Der Spiegel* a few days before a scheduled meeting between her and Kohl on 29 and 30 March 1990. Criticizing Kohl, she took him to task on the German–Polish border issue. This was rubbing salt in an open wound, as Kohl's handling of the matter had already come under heavy attack from many quarters both at home and abroad. She revealed to the great joy of Kohl's enemies: 'and I heard Helmut say, "No, I will not guarantee, I will not recognize future boundaries." I have heard it myself in Strasbourg after dinner.'[19]

It sounded a bit like a strait-laced schoolgirl reporting on a badly behaved classmate. Nevertheless, coming on top of much earlier criticism, it stung. Kohl sought to overcome it by repeatedly expressing his support of the German resolutions to respect the German–Polish border. Mrs Thatcher may also have regretted going too far, and sought to backtrack from her criticism of Kohl when the two met later.

She may not have liked Kohl, as British officials admitted, but she had to recognize the changed realities about both Kohl and Germany. Kohl's success in the East German elections with their implications for German reunification and subsequent German elections, Washington's shift to support his drive to German unity after previously siding with Britain and France, and Kohl's public acceptance of the Polish border counted heavily among them. In short, Mrs Thatcher was grappling with the new realities of power in Europe. As she herself put it: 'We have to get used to having one country in Europe that is far stronger than the rest. ... Everyone has to accept that there is a bigger Germany.'[20]

She also acted accordingly. During Kohl's visit she was clearly making amends and on her best behaviour. She claimed that Britain had done as much for German unity as others, and their meeting certainly improved relations between the two leaders. When Thatcher insisted that a united Germany had to remain in NATO, Kohl said he would not pay the price of neutrality for unification. He complimented her on British television as 'a wonderful lady' and found her to be impressive and stimulating: she knew her facts, was specific and concrete in asking questions, and listened – though he admitted that she could also be difficult to deal with, showing little sensitivity to her partner. Kohl thought the old saying that England had no friends or enemies, only interests, applied to her. He had found her 'a fighter' and 'a magnificent woman'.[21]

Kohl also challenged her by saying, 'Those who want a united Germany to be firmly integrated into European structures must logically support further progress in European unification.' When Mrs Thatcher disagreed, he felt confident enough to smile and complimented her: 'Margaret Thatcher is a great lady – a very strong-minded lady,' he noted, but added that, 'I have my own ideas, too; my opponents have been underestimating me for years.'[22] Kohl's confidence rested by then both on the progress made towards German reunification and on his own contributions to it, as well as on the support he was receiving from Bush. After the East German elections Washington had increasingly supported Kohl's unification drive, and the Soviet Union was also coming around.

Foreign and domestic critics had repeatedly castigated Kohl for unduly rushing reunification but the election outcome in the DDR strengthened his hand in dealing with them. Kohl was clearly the man of the hour. The loud East German endorsement of his leadership to achieve speedy reunification not only made him the likely chancellor of a united Germany in the near future. It also gave him added weight and authority in the coming negotiations with other countries on the future place of Germany in Europe and the emerging new order on the continent.

At decisive times on the difficult path towards German unity Kohl had acted with determination. Either through instinct or shrewd calculation he had made bold choices that had turned out to be the right choices. After recognizing the opportunity to achieve unification as a result of the popular revolution in the DDR, he persisted in moving ahead over all the obstacles put in his way. If Kohl had reason to be satisfied with his record, it inevitably also influenced his fellow players and negotiating partners.

This held true concerning his dealings with both domestic and foreign issues. Kohl's success subdued previous talk of his coalition partners, the Free Democrats, possibly deserting for the opposition Social Democrats. It also persuaded the Social Democrats to be less inclined to diametrically oppose Kohl's plans and timetable for reunification. The East German election results were the writing on the wall, spelling danger to those who were perceived to be dragging their feet on the issue of national unity. It had put fear into many Social Democrats, acutely aware of the national elections in December, with regard to how the voters might punish them for their past policies on unity.

Kohl's stronger position versus the other players encouraged him to move forward with confidence. By the beginning of April 1990 he was talking of a definite date for the withdrawal of Soviet troops from eastern Germany and the stationing of and extending conscription for the Bundeswehr, the federal army, over all of Germany. He advised the Poles of his readiness for the final regulation of the German–Polish border, but also brought up his interest in German minority rights in Poland and its renunciation of German reparations, though he did not specifically tie them to a treaty on the border.[23]

Meanwhile, during his visit to Washington on 6 April, Shevardnadze made it clear that the Soviet Union was dropping its demand of neutrality for a unified Germany, though he persisted in rejecting unified Germany's NATO membership.[24] The continuing collapse of the Warsaw Pact influenced Soviet views on Germany and NATO. Moscow found it difficult to accept the continuation and even potential expansion of the rival alliance when its own alliance system was disintegrating. Yet the serious weakening of its economy, its need of economic and financial help, and the aspirations of its minority nationalities undermined the Soviet ability and will to resist concessions. The Baltic peoples' fervour to reassert their independence and growing nationalist rumblings among Ukrainians, by far the largest Soviet national minority, were unnerving Moscow.

As a compromise, the Soviets had floated the idea that Germany could be simultaneously a member of both NATO and the Warsaw Pact, but no one had picked it up. To others it seemed impractical and unrealistic. They saw it as a sign of Soviet desperation in finding an alternative to unified Germany's NATO membership when faced with solid resistance to German neutrality. Bush and Thatcher increased their pressure on the issue, repeating their earlier demands on German NATO membership, though they also upheld German rights to full control of all its territory and full sovereignty.[25]

Moscow continued, however, serving notice of its reservations on the German question, including the pace at which reunification was proceeding. Besides wanting further real concessions, Gorbachev still needed to engage in shadow boxing for the sake of his domestic critics. Depending on its spokesman, and sometimes even delivered by the same person, Moscow's positions kept changing. Without totally abandoning its opposition to German NATO membership, it was nevertheless signalling its will to continue to negotiate. Shevardnadze had stressed the need for compromise on 10 April.[26] Moscow had clearly travelled some distance from its original rather arrogant stand.

The Soviets were also buttressing their bargaining position by reasserting themselves in the DDR against the de Maizière government. Summoning the prime minister to his presence as an inferior, the Soviet ambassador made it clear who was still the boss and insisted on fulfilment of all DDR contracts and obligations to the Soviet Union and the other Comecon countries.[27]

Such an insistence on economic obligations was also a reflection of the Soviet Union's worsening economic problems. Kohl was apprehensive that these difficulties, together with the acute tension between Lithuania and Moscow, could create obstacles to German unification. He saw the Soviet economic problems as the key to overcoming Moscow's resistance. German economic aid and co-operation would be more important to Moscow than opposing German membership of NATO. On 23 April he proposed negotiations to Gorbachev on an extensive treaty of co-operation, including DDR obligations. Evoking historical co-operation between Germany and Russia, the proposal suggested a fundamental improvement and warming of relations between the two countries, parallel in importance with European integration.[28] It was an important step towards a German–Soviet deal.

Kohl was also keen on reassuring France and its smaller neighbours of Bonn's continuing interest in European integration and that German reunification was no obstacle to it. Acting together, Kohl and Mitterrand proposed an EC meeting about European political union to complement meetings on economic and monetary union. Both leaders wanted to speed up preparations and work for these aims in order to have them ready for ratification by the beginning of 1993. They also envisaged the political union to include European foreign, defence and security policy.[29] This could reduce the future importance of both NATO and the United States for Europe, which had been a long-term French aim, preceding but also continued by Mitterrand.

Like Kohl, Mitterrand also wished to resume Franco–German co-operation particularly for the purpose of further European integration. He wanted it badly enough to initiate a major effort to make amends, as he now had little reason for thinking that anything could stop German unification. The only thing that remained was to make the best of it for France. When the two leaders met in Paris on 25 April, Mitterrand toasted German unification and praised the 'great' German people. He was obviously both eager to please Kohl in private and to display good relations between the two in public, though he also pleaded with Kohl for French troops to stay in Germany until further progress took place on general disarmament and Soviet stability. Kohl was pleased with Mitterrand's overtures, and in turn talked of Franco–German friendship and his wish for European unity.[30]

At the time, however, Kohl's primary interest lay in German reunification, although he also sincerely wanted further European integration. Furthermore, the latter contributed to the former, as it could reassure many of Bonn's partners in the EC who may have been concerned about the Germans. While France believed that German reunification increased the need for European integration as a way of retaining control over German actions, Britain did not share this view. It preferred to achieve the same ends via NATO.

Most EC nations supported the Franco–German initiative for further European integration, although (including France and Germany) they held many and in part different visions about the nature of future political union. Some were willing to transfer more power to the European organs than others. The Germans wanted to strengthen the European Parliament and the role of democratic decision-making within the EC, while the French were bent on strengthening the role of the Council of Ministers.

The Franco–German proposal was aired at an EC summit meeting in Dublin on 28 April which had originally been called to discuss the implications of German reunification for the Community. Kohl told the meeting that German and European unification were two sides of the same coin. He also soothed the assembled EC leaders' possible worries concerning the potential economic costs of German reunification to its EC partners by promising that the Germans would pay for it by themselves. He said that they did not plan to put their hands into the EC wallet. Jacques Delors, the President of the European Commission, had proposed EC aid to the East Germans but was blocked by Margaret Thatcher.

The EC leaders' response greatly pleased Kohl, who was all smiles. They endorsed German unification in positive terms and agreed upon moves for needed modification in the EC. Mitterrand did his share, as well as other European leaders such as the Italian prime premier Giulio Andreotti, who had previously been critical of German reunification but who now became very supportive. The choice was whether to be run over or jump on the train. Kohl was particularly satisfied with Mitterrand's stance.[31]

Not only Germany's EC partners gave new and renewed signals of their agreeability and needs. So did Washington, alarmed over all the recent talk of European political union and a common EC foreign, security and defence policy and its implications for the American presence and role in Europe. Changes were taking place in Europe which pointed towards a reduced American influence there in the future. Not only had the rapidly diminishing threat from the east undermined the importance of NATO, but the grafting of a common security policy onto the EC and talk of an all-European security structure, based on the Conference on Security and Co-operation in Europe, or the CSCE consultations, could also weaken the American impact.

Washington had some reason to worry. Having largely lost their fear of the Russians, many Europeans were less enthusiastic about the continued American presence on their continent than at any other time since the Second World War. Some Europeans were still apprehensive, and even entertained fears of the Germans. They and many others continued to welcome the continued existence of NATO and an American presence as a counterweight to a powerful, unified Germany. Washington used these fears by associating its future contribution to European defence and security with the viability of NATO, but the crucial unanswered question remained how long the Europeans would respond in the same way.

As long as the Soviet situation stayed unsettled and uncertain, all the European NATO members would cling to the organization as a guarantee of safety for lack of a viable alternative. What would happen with the emergence of an alternative solution to their security problems? Would they then still see value in NATO? Having existed for so long, over forty years, NATO was likely to continue its existence in some form even after its original mission and essential functions had disappeared. The force of continuity, old habits and institutional dynamics, sheer lethargy and fear of the unknown could allow it to linger while it slowly withered, but to remain the kind of viable and vital organization on which the United States could base its role in Europe in the future, NATO needed a credible mission and purpose. In the long run, Washington's need of it could not alone either keep it a going concern or keep the Europeans interested in it.

Many Germans and other Europeans had already been and were talking about creating alternatives to NATO as solutions to European problems of security. Among them were influential figures such as Genscher and leading German Social Democrats, and French and East European leaders, including Gorbachev and Shevardnadze. While the possible alternatives remained vague, they alarmed Washington enough for it to move to thwart the threats to the role of NATO. At the same time, Washington continued its search for a new mission, a political role for the organization which would maintain the United States as a player in Europe.[32]

For the preservation of NATO as an organization of key importance in Europe, continued German membership was essential. Thus Washington thought it important to keep the Germans happy by supporting German unification, lest they be tempted by Moscow's talk of alternative security arrangements as a price for unification. At the NATO foreign ministers' meeting in Brussels on 3 May 1990, Baker declared that a stable, united Germany was a loss to no one. The Americans were, of course, not the only ones eager to keep the Germans in NATO, and had ample backing in this aspiration among its other members. The meeting was also generally positive on German unification.[33] Coming so soon after the supportiveness of the EC summit, this was a double boost for the Germans. They were riding high.

From the NATO meeting Baker went to Bonn and emphasized Bush's concerns directly to Kohl. Bush wanted to strengthen NATO's political role and keep the United States 'a major player' in European politics. As if to underline the seriousness of this desire, Baker tied it to significant American military presence in Europe. Desirous of keeping a close rapport with Bush, Kohl in turn reassured Baker and strongly disassociated himself from efforts to bring about an American withdrawal from Europe.[34] The very same day that Baker was passing on Bush's concerns to Kohl, Bush himself also forcefully expressed similar views in a speech in Oklahoma. He said that 'the Unites States should remain a European power in the broadest sense, politically, militarily and economically' and that 'the foundation for American engagement in Europe has been and will continue to be NATO'. Speaking in support of a continued American military presence in Europe, he claimed that it demonstrated better than words an enduring political compact between the United States and Europe.[35]

Washington had many reasons for wishing to remain an active and influential player in Europe. It feared that an American military withdrawal would lead to a loss of political influence which in turn could lead to restrictions on American exports and investment activities in Europe. Washington also thought that continued American military commitment was necessary because of the unsettled situation in the Soviet Union. While Washington was vocal about the Soviet factor, it said little of its wish to guarantee and guard American economic interests as a reason for its continued political and military engagement in Europe. It and other NATO members said even less in public about a remaining factor – Germany. A strongly felt need still existed in Washington, as in other NATO capitals, to keep the Germans in check and contained within the Western alliance. Many felt that a strong American role in Europe was needed even more to balance the increasingly powerful Germans. This was talked about far more in private than in public, and such sensitivity to German feelings already indicated the German's growing power.[36]

Such sensitivities reflected the spreading conviction that German unification was already inevitable. The Germans themselves were moving rapidly forward with economic and monetary union, though serious problems remained unsettled over a unified Germany's place in the security structure of Europe. Concerning these remaining problems, the Soviet Union was out of step with the other involved powers. German NATO membership remained the most serious bone of contention. On the German–Polish boundary there was a meeting of minds in principle, but some irritation lingered over the timing of its final recognition. Kohl wanted to wait until after the German local and national elections, in order to prevent potential extremist electioneering exploitation of that sensitive issue.

On the eve of the first so-called two-plus-four talks about German unification between the foreign ministers in Bonn on 5 May 1990, the participants were manoeuvring for position. Moscow was signalling to Bonn its receptiveness to a deal with the Germans. An article in *Pravda* indicated that unified Germany's NATO membership was likely and not necessarily a disaster.[37] Immediately following Baker, Shevardnadze had gone to see Kohl, bringing Gorbachev's warm greetings and a message of his readiness to meet Kohl in July.

Shevardnadze came basically as a supplicant, although he still held some bargaining leverage. If the Soviet reforms had no success, he predicted that total anarchy or a dictatorship would ensue. As Kohl repeated his earlier proposals for far-reaching co-operation between unified Germany and the Soviet Union, Shevardnadze emphasized his own and Gorbachev's responsiveness to Kohl's proposals. He said that they favoured German unification and, although the Soviet Union could not accept unified Germany's NATO membership, a compromise could be found.

Its nature became evident when, in conclusion, he asked Kohl for Bonn's credit guarantees for the Soviet Union. A fair degree of anxiety accompanied the Soviet request. This became clear when Shevardnadze proceeded to assure Kohl that the Soviet Union was basically a rich country, so the credits would involve no risk. Kohl indicated his wish to help but did not commit himself to a promise.[38] Without explicitly admitting it, the Soviet Union was in fact asking for money as partial payment for its acceptance of a settlement on the German question. No wonder the Germans concluded that Moscow was ready for an understanding. The credit request meant that it was looking for a deal and not for a confrontation. Kohl was quite pleased with his talks with both Shevardnadze and Baker. He wanted to help Gorbachev with credits without delay, thinking that, together with the earlier German food aid, it would help to smooth the way for a political understanding.[39]

In the two-plus-four talks the Soviet Union had a difficult row to hoe. Alone, it faced both the Germans and their Western allies. The one thing it had going for it was the others' wariness of pushing Gorbachev too hard for fear of endangering his leadership of the Soviet Union. He had, after all, been willing to co-operate with them, and any alternative to him would be an unknown quantity. Shevardnadze tried to make the most of this by indicating that Gorbachev had little room for concessions because of internal Soviet pressures. He could not give more without also gaining something.

Shevardnadze came with alternative proposals to German NATO membership. Besides again proposing a new European-wide security system, based on the 35-nation Conference on Security and Co-operation in Europe, the CSE, he also suggested the uncoupling of the external and domestic issues of German unification. This second proposal came as a total surprise and caused quite a stir. It was a clear departure from past Soviet policy. Shevarnadze was signalling to the Germans to proceed with unification before solutions had been found to the disputes concerning its international or external aspects. There was, however, a drawback. Until a solution to them was found, the four wartime allies could retain rights in Germany.[40]

The German reception of Shevarnadze's proposal was divided. Genscher welcomed it, saying that it paved the way for rapid German reunification. Kohl rejected it. He felt it was merely an opening bid in a continuing game. 'Did anyone really believe the Soviet Union would put all its cards on the table?' he wondered.[41] Shevardnadze's proposal implied continued restrictions on German sovereignty, a prospect which held little appeal for a nation riding high on expectations of its unification. The German desire to have full sovereignty restored to them found support with Baker. He warned against any kind of discrimination against the Germans as it could cause resentment, conflict and instability. Even the French Foreign Minister Roland Dumas expressed similar sentiments, saying it was not for the wartime

Allies to decide for a sovereign and unified Germany what alliance it could join.[42]

As if making amends, Shevardnadze adopted a conciliatory tone in the concluding press conference of the two-plus-four meeting. Vouching for constructive Soviet co-operation, he also mentioned its intention to speed up the process of German unification.[43] This was another departure from a long-standing Soviet position. Previously, Moscow had repeatedly complained about the Germans moving too fast. The Soviet Union clearly did not wish to appear as the spoiler to the Germans when Bonn's Western allies gave it vocal support. Something resembling a bidding match was evolving. The Germans had reason to feel satisfied and confident of the eventual outcome.

Encouraged by the two-plus-four meeting and Shevardnadze's comments, Kohl concluded that all-German elections could perhaps be held that same year. He had reason to feel confident. Gorbachev sent him a message a few days later, on 9 May 1990, indicating how pleased he was over Kohl's talk with Shevardnadze and how he wished to quickly solve the remaining problems.[44]

What, then, lay behind the new Soviet emphasis on speeding matters up? While Gorbachev and Shevardnadze had to talk tough in public to appease the Soviet hard-liners, they increasingly needed German economic help and co-operation to shore up their positions. The Soviet economic chaos and, most recently, the May Day demonstrations had served notice to both of their vulnerability. They probably felt that they could not afford to stall much longer on a deal with the Germans.

Notes

1 See, e.g., *The Economist*, 24 March 1990; *Newsweek* and *Time*, 26 March 1990.
2 Teltschick, 1991, p. 179.
3 *IHTr*, 22 March 1990.
4 Teltschick, 1991, p. 180.
5 *FAZ*, *SZ* and *Die Welt*, 19 March 1990.
6 *IHTr*, 19 March 1990.
7 Teltschick, 1991, pp. 184, 201.
8 Ibid., pp. 180, 188.
9 Ibid., pp. 180, 186.
10 Cf. Emil Kirchner and James Sperling, 'The Future of Germany and the Future of NATO', *German Politics*, vol. 1, no. 1, April 1992, pp. 50–77.
11 *FAZ*, *IHTr*, *SZ*, *The Times* and *Die Welt* 24 March 1990; Teltschick, 1991, p. 182.
12 Teltschick, 1991, pp. 182–3.
13 *FAZ* and *Die Welt*, 20 March 1990.
14 Zimmerman and Havel in *Time*, 26 March 1990.

15 *IHTr*, 20, 22 March 1990.
16 Kohl, in *Time*, 26 March 1990, and *IHTr*, 24 March 1990.
17 *The Economist*, 24 March 1990, p. 51.
18 Mitterrand, on French television, 25 March 1990.
19 Thatcher, in *Der Spiegel*, 26 March 1990.
20 Thatcher, in *IHTr* and *The Times*, 31 March 1990.
21 Ibid.; Kohl, on BBC, 30 March 1990; Kohl, in Teltschick, 1991, pp. 189–90.
22 Kohl, BBC, 30 March 1990, and *Time*, 2 April 1990.
23 Teltschick, 1991, pp. 190, 192.
24 *Welt am Sonntag*, 8 March 1990.
25 *IHTr* and *The Times*, 14 April 1990.
26 Shevardnadze, Novosti, 10 April 1990.
27 Teltschick, 1991, p. 198.
28 Ibid., pp. 204–6.
29 *IHTr*, *Le Monde* and *Die Welt*, 21 Feb. 1990.
30 Teltschick, 1991, pp. 207–8; *FAZ*, *Le Figaro*, *Le Monde* and *Die Welt*, 26 April 1990.
31 *Welt am Sonntag*, 29 April 1990; *Der Spiegel*, 30 April 1990; *The Economist*, 5 May 1990; Teltschick, 1991, p. 211.
32 Kirchner and Sperling, 'The future Germany and the future of NATO', *German Politics*, 1, 1992, pp. 50–77.
33 *FAZ*, *IHTr*, *SZ* and *Die Welt*, 4 May 1990.
34 Teltschick, 1991, p. 217.
35 Bush in *IHTr*, 4 May 1990.
36 Views expressed by several Western diplomats in the spring of 1990.
37 *Pravda*, 3 May 1990.
38 Teltschick, 1991, pp. 218–21.
39 Ibid., p. 221.
40 Shevardnadze, Novosti, 5 May 1990.
41 *IHTr* and *Die Welt*, 8 May 1990; *The Economist*, 12 May 1990.
42 *IHTr*, 5 May 1990; *Welt am Sonntag*, 6 May 1990; *Der Spiegel*, 7 May 1990; Szabo, 1992, pp. 82–4.
43 *FAZ* and *SZ*, 7 May 1990.
44 Teltschick, 1991, pp. 224, 228.

12 Monetary and Economic Union

While the politics of German reunification captivated the world, German business had started on the practical aspects of building unity. The booming West German economy had ample funds for investment.[1] Along with the leading politicians, leading German businessmen also recognized the imperative of moving rapidly to meet the East Germans' hopes of a better future. They saw the obstacles posed by the run-down and outmoded East German infrastructure and factories, but they took the long view and foresaw a vast emerging market and a potential for rapid and strong economic growth after the initial hardships of adjustment to a modern market economy. Some also regarded East Germany as a bridge for economic expansion further east. East Germany could serve as a training ground for dealing with people unfamiliar with the ways of a market economy, but with the advantage of at least sharing the same language. Because of its past close economic and trading ties with Eastern Europe and the Soviet Union, it could also provide knowledge of and ease of access to their markets.

Some giants of the West German economy such as Volkswagen, Daimler-Benz, and the Deutsche Bank moved quickly into East Germany,[2] occasionally with additional impetus coming from their executives' East German roots, as was the case among politicians. Prominent among them were Carl Hahn and Edzard Reuter, respectively the heads of Volkswagen and Daimler-Benz, and Foreign Minister Genscher.

The surge of West German business to the East had started well before the March elections in the DDR but the outcome accelerated it. Anticipating that a new East German regime would remove any remaining obstacles to the free operation of market forces and speedy monetary and economic union, hopes rose of a repetition of the *Wirtschaftswunder*, the rapid West German post-war economic recovery in the 1950s.[3] The needs of East Germany were expected to stimulate the West German economy, and such expectation would in turn attract massive foreign investment and result in a surge in the value of the Deutschmark.

Confirmation was quick to follow. Strong demand from the DDR indeed helped to speed up the economy of the Bundesrepublik, and economists revised their growth estimates up to 4 per cent for 1990.[4] New life also stirred in the sickly economy of East Germany. West German investments and a reawakening of local ingenuity helped to spark new initiatives. Moves were made to reclaim and rebuild former family firms and to start new ventures and enterprises. Some massive and poorly managed industrial combines showed signs of breaking up into more manageable components.

A considerable problem facing this new burst of activity was ignorance of the workings of a market economy. Having grown up with a state-controlled system of guaranteed markets and prices, the East German managers' main worry had simply been to meet the quantitative quotas assigned to them; quality mattered less. Now they had to face the new and unfamiliar challenge of trying to sell their products in a new highly competitive market which put a premium on quality.

Changing ingrained attitudes and ways of thinking would be perhaps the biggest obstacle to rebuilding the East German economy. Money was relatively freely available as credits and loans from both public and private sources in the Bundesrepublik, but many state-owned firms were thought to be beyond rescue while others would have to reduce their workforce.[5] New companies were necessary to take up the slack. They would have to offer employment and help to revive the economy. The Communists had so long discouraged private enterprise through their propaganda and tax system that both words and deeds of encouragement were needed to overcome the burden of that past.

The East Germans had lived in an authoritarian command system which had ingrained into them the habit of waiting for orders telling them what to do. Some were used to sliding by with less than a full effort in their daily jobs, and doing their private errands during work hours. West Germans complained about the East Germans' work habits, accusing them of keeping short hours, slowness and absenteeism. They also thought that the East Germans needed improvement in such traditional Germanic virtues as being reliable and punctual in their work.[6] These complaints and accusations did not go down well with many East Germans who had had a reputation in the former Soviet sphere of possessing the very qualities which they now were said to lack.

Whatever shortcomings the East German workforce may have had in West German eyes, it was by most standards well educated and trained. In general, European business leaders saw in reunification a great bonus to the German economy. It would give German companies a larger home market and a stronger base from which to compete with outsiders. In the long run it would greatly compound German economic power and weight when the productivity of the East Germans caught up with the West Germans. Then the leading larger German companies would emerge as even more formidable competitors in European and world markets.

Difficulties of integration and reconstruction were expected to absorb some of the capital, energy and attention which the Germans otherwise might devote to other markets. This would give others a temporary relief from the keenest edge of the German export drive. Some of Germany's neighbours were also enthusiastic about participating in the rebuilding of East Germany. Foreseeing the need of enormous investment in the East German infrastructure, they anticipated opportunities and profits from construction to communications.[7]

Cherishing hopes of decisive economic improvement, the East Germans had voted heavily for the Alliance for Germany, seeing in it the best promise of rapid unification. The election outcome helped to lower their urge to leave home and their exodus westwards dropped sharply. It reflected both a renewal of faith in a better future at home and the cooling of the welcome to newcomers in the west. The passing of the Communist regime in East Germany removed a constant frustration spurring people to seek a better life elsewhere and reduced the generosity of their reception in the west, where the newcomers' strain on the available resources had caused increasing tensions and resentments towards them. Some wives and children still moved west to join their husbands and fathers who had left earlier to find jobs and housing, but otherwise the earlier flood to the west clearly ebbed.[8]

It was replaced by a flow of people and traffic in the opposite direction, from west to east. West German businessmen, investors, speculators and would-be claimers of lost properties were heading east. The early interest in East German real estate had mushroomed even before its acquisition was legal by people other than the East Germans themselves. Looking like a worn old coat full of patches and holes, East German buildings and houses may not have appeared to be worth having but, despite their almost universally sad appearance, the western lust after them was great, in particular in East Berlin and other choice locations. Grabbing at the run-down structures going at ridiculously low prices by West German standards, many expected to make a killing soon after the anticipated reunification.

Former owners and their descendants were paying visits to municipal offices and enquiring about their lost properties and their present residents. They were haunting their or their parents' old neighbourhoods to the dismay and panic of the present occupants who feared either losing their homes or having to pay higher rents. Among them were all kinds of claimants. Most were looking for their former homes, but some were getting ready to lay claim to substantial real estate holdings, apartment and office buildings as well as factories. Not a few former members of the once influential land-owning nobility east of the Elbe were looking over their ancestral estates and Schlosses (castles). A roller-coaster swirl of strong and mixed emotions often accompanied such returns of native sons and daughters.

Emotions were running high everywhere in the DDR. The expected currency union, the next major step towards German reunification, caused much emotional turmoil. Kohl had announced his intention to seek monetary and economic union with the DDR in early February 1990, just before his trip to Moscow. His cabinet unanimously embraced his proposal and Karl Otto Pöhl, the head of the Bundesbank, the West German central bank, went along with it. Kohl's action and its timing reflected and was in part motivated by the impending economic collapse in the DDR, which was at the point of bankruptcy.[9]

A Bundesbank plan for the exchange rate between the West German Deutschmark and the East German Ostmark was announced at the end of March 1990. It allowed the East Germans to exchange up to 2,000 Ostmarks at a one-for-one rate for the far more valuable western currency. For the rest, including wages and pensions, a two-for-one rate would prevail.[10]

Deep disappointment and anger resulted in the DDR. 'It's a swindle,' said one irate East Berliner, speaking for many others. People demonstrated on the streets against the plan, and officials of the DDR protested about and criticized it. Many claimed that Kohl and other Bonn officials and politicians had promised a one-for-one rate to East Germans with small savings during the election campaign in the DDR. Modrow, its lame duck prime minister, went so far as to claim that the election result was the result of these promises, and nothing else. He insisted that the East Germans had assumed that the promises also extended to wages.[11] Even a one-for-one exchange rate would have left the average East German wage about one-third of the average West German wage, and a two-for-one ratio reduced it to a mere sixth. The pensioners' lot would have been even more pitiful, although a promise was made to raise the pensions in order to soften the impact.[12]

The economists of the Bundesbank, the independent central bank, preferred the less generous exchange rate. Fearing for the stability of the Deutschmark and massive unemployment in the east, they thought that their plan would help to control inflation and assist the less efficient and productive East German companies to compete.[13] To expect the East Germans to live with one-sixth of the West German average wage in the same country was hardly realistic, however. At least part of the difference had to be made up in one way or another, and soon. Subsidies and payments of various kinds would have to try to cushion the exchange rate.

So far it was all only a plan devised by the Bundesbank professionals, and this left the Kohl government free not to adopt it should it not wish to do so. The politicians had to consider the human consequences and potential voter reactions, and the politicians, after all, had the last word. The immediate stakes were heightened for them by their acute awareness of the approaching elections. They had to walk a tightrope. Greater generosity towards the East Germans could translate to resentment by the West Germans, since they would have to pay the bill. A niggardly attitude towards the east might satisfy some in the west, but it would also renew the now unwished flood of migration from east to west and cause resentment. It would also further drain the east of human potential and reduce her ability to recover and catch up with the west. Some feared it could contribute to making the east possibly a permanent ward of the west. In the east, the West German politicians faced a united front on this issue as all the East German parties favoured a one-for-one exchange rate. To them it was a matter of political survival.

When the newly elected legislators of the DDR met for their first session on 5 April 1990 they were keenly aware of their fellow citizens' feelings about the proposed exchange rate. The same day that the parliament met, some 10,000 people protested outside the building, and tens of thousands were out on the streets of other cities in the DDR.[14] Not only anger but also a very real fear for their livelihoods and existence was bringing them together.

The demonstrations put pressure on the politicians to quickly come up with a new government for the DDR which could without delay proceed to deal with Bonn over the currency issue. What emerged after intense negotiations was a broadly based coalition government. It included all the major political forces in the DDR except the Party of Democratic Socialism, the heir of the Communists. Headed by Lothar de Maizière, the leader of the Christian Democrats, the new government also incorporated the other partners in the Alliance for Germany, the conservative Democratic Awakening and the more right-wing German Social Union. The other coalition partners were the Social Democrats and the Liberals.[15]

A major aim of this government was to secure the one-for-one exchange rate. That meant a direct clash with the position taken by the Bundesbank, and some kind of compromise would have to be worked out. In introducing his government's programme the new prime minister de Maizière presented and sought to justify the East German position. He demanded that the one-for-one exchange rate should apply to wages, pensions and savings, but he also indicated flexibility concerning the last category. This was not all. He also made detailed demands for guarantees of a network of social security in East Germany, and insisted that the post-war land reform in East Germany, which involved the larger landed estates, was irreversible.[16] The East Germans clearly did not want to reverse some aspects of the social revolution in their past.

The East German demands were bound to cause some headaches and irritation among the politicians in Bonn. They were keenly aware of and anxious about potential resentment arising among their West German voters if the costs of unity hit their pockets too hard. Many feared for the soundness of the West German social security system if it was faced with new and concerted pressures. In addition, former owners of property in the east demanded their return.

As if anticipating resistance in the west, de Maizière sought to justify his demands by appealing to the West German sense of fairness and solidarity. He noted how East Germany had been saddled with heavy reparations and compensation after the war and how it had been left to cope alone with these burdens and reconstruction without the benefit of Marshall Aid, in contrast to the west.[17] Such evocations of post-war memories also served the purpose of giving self-confidence to the East Germans in reminding them of their past achievements in coping with large obstacles and heavy burdens. It gave weight to the basic East German demand for both freedom and equality with the West Germans as the future citizens of a united Germany. They did not want to become second-class Germans.

The East German demands met with some understanding in Bonn which, after some haggling, made further concessions. On 23 April 1990 the Bonn government proposed a one-for-one swap of the two currencies as a way to clear the path to monetary union by 1 July. The reluctant Bundesbank was dragged along with this proposal, but its officials must have swallowed hard. It was a government spokesman who announced that the Bundesbank 'fully accepted' the government's proposal. The proposal offered the one-for-one exchange rate for all wages and pensions and up to 4,000 marks in savings. A two-for-one rate would apply on other transactions and on all debts. A day after Bonn's offer, Kohl and de Maizière agreed on a currency, economic and social union. It hardly amounted to the *diktat* that some described it to be.[18]

Although not exactly meeting the East German demand for an overall one-for-one exchange, the proposal was generous. Exceeding many times the prevailing unofficial black market rates, it largely met East German expectations. Its limits on savings set a very favourable exchange rate for the savings of most East German families and individuals as the limit was personal and allowed families to multiply its effects. Furthermore, the proposal offered to raise East German pensions to western levels to help meet anticipated increases in living costs – East German pensions averaged only 420 Ostmarks as against approximately 1,100 Deutschmarks in West Germany.[19]

In fact, Bonn's offer was so generous that it alarmed investors on the money markets. When the news broke, many an investor's heart started pounding. The Frankfurt market dropped broadly and sharply, as did to a lesser extent the Deutschmark. Behind this drop lay fears of accelerated inflation, a weaker mark, and higher interest rates. Such fears reflected the prior alarm of the Bundesbank which had preferred and fought for a much less generous exchange rate.[20]

In contrast, the ordinary East Germans had reason to smile, for their most immediate fears had been allayed by the offer. However, many economists were concerned with its longer-term impact. They feared that the offered exchange rates would cut the competitive advantage of East German companies and force them into bankruptcies, resulting in massive unemployment.[21]

The politicians who supported the plan were not unaware of such prospects or immune from similar fears, but other matters affected them more. Smooth and uninterrupted progress to national unification was the top priority for many, and there were also important tactical considerations at stake. The politicians were now focusing on the East German local elections on 6 May and were also keen on stemming and reducing the flood of would-be migrants from east to west by increasing their buying power at home.

Ultimately the problem boiled down to low East German productivity, which was only about one-third of the West German level per worker. The average wage was 1,100 Ostmarks as against 3,300 Deutschmarks, but if East German wages were kept on the level of productivity compared with West Germany, a massive emigration westward would be inevitable, in particular by the younger and more ambitious workers. If the wages were set clearly above productivity, inflation and unemployment threatened. The dilemma facing the decision-makers was difficult indeed.

At first glance, East German wages seemed to reflect the lower productivity, but with economic unification this situation could not last. Whatever advantage low East German wages may have had for some investors would soon disappear. With a free national labour market and growing costs of living in the east, East German wages were bound to begin slowly to approach West German levels.

Bonn's offer amounted to a massive transfer of income and wealth from West to East Germany, in the interests of achieving national integration and solidarity. As, at least in the short term, the West Germans had to give and the East Germans gained according to the plan, it naturally found less favour with the former than with the latter. In opinion polls, only 19 per cent of West Germans supported the one-for-one exchange rate[22] and, in view of this scant support, Kohl's government displayed a good deal of political courage in embracing it. Kohl did his best to counter doubts and to build up confidence concerning monetary and economic union. He pointed out that Germany had never before been better prepared for the challenges involved. West Germany had experienced seven years of strong economic growth and the prognosis for continued future growth was favourable. While he granted that the completion of economic and monetary union would initially give rise to a difficult adjustment process, it would also stimulate further economic growth. As the state finances were also in good shape, Kohl did not see any need for tax increases which would undermine the necessary investment for the reconstruction of East Germany.[23] Besides seeking to reassure the West Germans, he also had his eyes on the forthcoming East German local elections in May.

Further negotiations between East and West Germany led to some additional changes and fine-tuning of the plan before the East Germans accepted it on 2 May. These changes increased the amount that East Germans aged sixty or more could change at the one-for-one rate to 6,000 marks, but limited children of fourteen or under to 2,000 marks. This gesture aimed to ease the fears of the elderly who had accumulated savings in anticipation of retirement and its needs. They feared that their life savings would dramatically lose value with an unfavourable exchange rate, at the same time that living costs would sharply increase. Black market exchange rates of ten-for-one and even twenty-for-one greatly increased such fears.[24]

Once the decisions about the West German offer had been made and the East Germans had accepted it, with certain modifications, the Bundesbank also had to make the best of it. Although it had initially resisted the one-for-one rate it professed itself pleased with the agreement and pledged its strong support. Such a public turnaround reflected both the Bank's sense of responsibility for subsequent economic developments and the broad national consensus and cohesion about the historic opportunity for reunification of the country.

Awareness that in just three days the foreign ministers of the two Germanies were scheduled to meet their American, British, French and Soviet colleagues for the 'four-plus-two' talks about future Germany spurred the Germans to an early agreement between themselves. The more united they faced the four wartime allies, the stronger their bargaining position would be in those negotiations. At stake were Germany's future status and security arrangements for Europe, including German involvement in NATO.

Bonn's concessions and generosity to the East Germans were also eased by an economic boom in the Bundesrepublik. Output was rising and unemployment declining, and Bundesbank officials sounded confident. They spoke soothing words of reassurance to other countries worried about the impact of the German currency union on worldwide interest rates and inflation and thus upon their own economies.

The financial agreements between East and West Germany had left some matters unresolved on which Bonn was pushing for a quick solution. The main unsettled issues involved the nuts and bolts of introducing a market economy into the east, East German foreign trade with the former Soviet bloc, the adaption of East German farming to EC regulations, and social welfare regulations.

Despite the generosity of many aspects of the financial agreements, the East Germans were not exactly beside themselves with joy. Day by day they were learning in concrete, everyday terms what the introduction of a market economy meant in their lives. The currency union and free markets involved big changes in their day-to-day existence. The removal of subsidies from food prices and rents implied unknown threats and dangers, especially to the lowest income groups.

Many of them were pensioners. Where the average East German wage was almost 1,000 marks, many pensioners got less than half that. They feared an even further lowering of living standards and ending up in the poverty trap. To the elderly, such a prospect was all the more bitter and disheartening as they had already experienced extreme poverty once in their lives during the immediate post-war years. Then they had at least been young, but now the resiliency and optimism of their youth was replaced by the fears and pessimism of old age.

The working East Germans increasingly worried about how they would fare in the labour market under capitalism. They feared not only for the future of the companies and institutions which employed them but for themselves on a more personal plane. They were mulling over in their minds whether as individuals they would measure up to free market demands of working pace, efficiency and production. What intensified such worries was the great unknown and the ignorance connected with it. Few East Germans had any real knowledge about these matters. Most had some vague and hazy ideas about them which fed and exaggerated rumours when they exchanged notes and 'information'. From such stuff further fears were born.

When West Germans sometimes expressed doubts about the East Germans' ability to cope with the work requirements of a market economy, they touched on a raw nerve. Injured feelings and anger was the result. Even those East Germans who harboured similar doubts about their adequacy found such comments by West Germans arrogant. Those East Germans who were self-confident about their abilities found them intolerable.[25]

Many people were working harder and longer hours. Even their health seemed to have become better, at least judging by the lowered rate of absenteeism and sick leave. Doctors recounted how, in contrast to the past, they had little to do during a normal day. Working patients wanted to have appointments after working hours. Much of it, of course, had to do with anxiety to hold on to one's job in the anticipated grim dog-eat-dog days of capitalism ahead. Many workers were simply eager to impress upon their bosses that they were the ones who should stay on in a job even if others were laid off. Others were simply resigned and depressed and suffered from nightmares. Besides worrying about their jobs, people fretted about the future cost of living increases. The growing anxiety and tensions took their toll in increased marital feuding, divorce and crime rates.

The emergence of a sort of economic interregnum in the DDR intensified the alarm. The centralized planned economy was collapsing but it had not been replaced by a market economy. A period of waiting, amounting to a partial economic and legal vacuum, prevailed. Both individuals and companies were waiting for monetary and economic unification and new economic legislation. Meanwhile, they were to a great extent ignoring the old plans and legislation still technically in force.

Like many of their employees, managers of companies were uncertain or fearful of their future. Former Communist bosses had been dismissed or barely hung on to their jobs. Their former assets, such as old party connections and knowledge of a Marxist planning economy, were useless in the new economic environment. New leaders had replaced some of the old, and others were on the make. Some companies were trying to prepare themselves for a market economy by firing workers or refusing to sell and deliver their products at the old fixed prices. The resulting fear, desperation and shortage of goods in the shops fanned dissatisfaction and unrest.

East German economic anxiety led to demands for further concessions and reassurances from Bonn, and demonstrations and strikes gave them additional thrust. In fact, a growing panic was gripping the DDR. The largest wave of strikes and demonstrations since the opening of the borders was sweeping East Germany. On 15 May 1990 tens of thousands of demonstrators and strikers were demanding guarantees of their economic and social security in the form of additional subsidies and protection from the markets.[26]

Although small in comparison to the massive demonstrations preceding the opening of the wall in the autumn of 1989, this new wave of demonstration alarmed some authorities in the DDR. Interior Minister Peter-Michael Dienstel requested riot control equipment from the Bundesrepublik. It was a curious request – the DDR was hardly lacking in riot control equipment or weaponry – but it did help to alert Bonn to the degree of East German desperation. Dienstel also predicted that the currency union would throw up to four million East Germans out of work. This contrasted sharply with West German talk of one or two million.

The request reflected the East German government's fears and warnings of grave social consequences if monetary, economic and social unification lowered the living standards and security of the East Germans. Reacting to mass protests and restiveness, it tried to win additional concessions from Bonn. Pressed by the trade unions, its Social Democratic ministers in particular argued for a better deal for the East German workers and pensioners. They even threatened to leave de Maizière's government if Bonn did not grant additional subsidies to sections of East German industry and increase the amount of money that the pensioners could exchange at the favourable one-for-one rate to 10,000 Ostmarks.[27]

The Bonn Finance Ministry backed by the Bundesbank, was resisting additional concessions. Finance Minister Theo Waigel quipped rather provocatively that the Bundesrepublik was not a 'self-service store to overcome forty years of mismanagement' in the DDR.[28]

The Kohl government was being squeezed by both the East Germans and the growing resistance and resentment among the West Germans of further concessions and costs. The mushrooming West German resistance became more visible and concrete, in particular in the campaigns and voters' responses in the local state elections of Lower Saxony and North Rhine–Westphalia in May 1990.

The Social Democratic candidate for chancellor and challenger to Kohl, Oskar Lafontaine, campaigned trying to exploit and to capitalize on these sentiments. They echoed and reflected his earlier positions on reunification and gave his candidacy a boost. Sensing his chance to make inroads in the popularity of Kohl and the Christian Democrats at the national level, Lafontaine beavered away with the help of local worthies. He pictured Kohl as a sugar daddy who refused to disclose his bill to the voters. A Social Democratic success in the elections could thus give a new lift to the Lafontaine candidacy.

After thirty hours of bargaining and negotiating between East and West German experts in Bonn, a proposal was finally hammered out for currency, economic and social union acceptable to both by 13 May. The East Germans had pressed for improvements in the conditions of pensioners and students, both threatened by dire poverty and even more heavily dependent on subsidized low prices of necessities than other East Germans. In exchange, the West Germans had demanded extended rights for West Germans to buy land and other property in East Germany without the delays desired by the East Germans. The issue of property ownership had grown in urgency with the approach of economic union and the extension of a market economy to East Germany. It had to be solved in a manner satisfactory to the West Germans before they would commit badly needed investment in the east.[29]

Some disputed matters remained unsolved. They included questions of property rights and the restructuring of industries and agriculture, which were to return to plague the Germans. These open matters would have to be settled before the respective parliaments could ratify the treaty scheduled to go into effect on 1 July 1990. The most awkward remaining issue concerning property rights involved former West German owners' claims on East German property and the disposition of state properties.

Notes

1 Cf. *Die Zeit*, 9 March 1990; Uwe Andersen, 'Economic Unification', in Dieter Grosser (ed.), *German Unification*, 1992, p. 114.
2 *Die Zeit*, 16 March 1990; 'The New Germany', *The Economist*, 30 June 1990, p. 16.
3 See, e.g., Otto Singer, 'The Politics and Economics of German Unification: From Currency Union to Economic Dichotomy', *German Politics*, April 1992, pp. 84, 89; Heinz-Peter Spahn, 'Das erste und das zweite Wirtschafstswunder', *Wirtschaftsdienst*, Feb. 1990, pp. 73–9.
4 *FAZ*, 8 April 1990.
5 *SZ*, 19 March 1990.
6 See, e.g., *Nürnberger Nachrichten*, 3 March 1990.
7 Impressions from conversations with North European businessmen, March 1990.
8 Cf. Thomas Mayer, 'Immigration into West Germany: Historical Perspectives and Policy Implication', in Lipschitz and McDonald (eds), *German Unification: Economic Issues*, 1991.
9 *FAZ* and *Die Welt*, 7 Feb. 1990.
10 *FAZ*, 31 March 1990.
11 Modrow, in *Wall Street Journal*, 2 April 1990.
12 *FR*, 31 March 1990; *The Economist*, 7 April 1990.
13 Deutsche Bundesbank, *Monatsberichte*, July, 1990, pp. 14–29.
14 *FR*, 6 April and *Der Spiegel*, 9 April 1990.
15 *FAZ*, *SZ* and *Die Welt*, 11 April 1990.
16 *FAZ* and *FR*, 20 April 1990.
17 Ibid.
18 *FAZ*, *FR*, *SZ* and *Die Welt*, 24, 25 April 1990.
19 Ibid.
20 *Handelsblatt*, 24, 25 April 1990.
21 *The Economist*, 28 April 1990.
22 German television, 24 April 1990.
23 *FAZ* and *Die Welt*, 3 May 1990.
24 *SZ*, 3 May 1990.
25 Impressions from Germany in May and summer 1990.
26 *FR* and *SZ*, 16 May 1990.
27 *Der Spiegel*, 7, 14 May 1990; *Stuttgarter Nachrichten*, 4 May 1990.
28 Waigel, in the *Wall Street Journal*, 14 May 1990.
29 Wolfgang Stinglwagner, in *Das Parlament*, 11 May 1990; *Rheinischer Merkur/Christ und Welt*, 11 May 1990; *FAZ*, *FR*, *SZ* and *Die Welt*, 14 May 1990.

13 Politics, Property, Currency

The very same date, 13 May 1990, that the results of the joint labours of East and West German experts for a treaty of economic and social unification was announced, the voters of Lower Saxony and North Rhine–Westphalia went to the polls. The results reflected the changing mood among the West Germans about reunification. After initial elation and enthusiasm, they had become increasingly preoccupied and concerned with its economic and financial costs. According to a poll conducted by *Der Spiegel*, 80 per cent of West Germans had come to believe that unification hurt them financially.[1] This growing concern translated into two defeats for Kohl's Christian Democrats.

The vote in Lower Saxony and North Rhine–Westphalia involved some 40 per cent of the West German voters and thus amounted to a major test of Chancellor Kohl's reunification policy, which had become an important issue in the campaign. The Social Democrats succeeded in exploiting voters' fears of the costs of reunification, which were still wrapped in a veil of uncertainty. They claimed that the costs were undermining the Bundesrepublik's social security system and pointed an accusing finger at Kohl.[2]

The results were interpreted as a danger signal for Kohl in the national elections the following December. More immediately, they caused complications for him by costing him his majority in the Bundesrat, the upper house of the parliament. A majority there would enable the Social Democrats to block much legislation and force Kohl to bargain with them and, as German reunification would require new legislation, they would have their say in shaping it.

The loss of Lower Saxony was especially alarming to Kohl and his Christian Democrats, as they had controlled it for 14 years. Kohl called the defeat 'painful'. The outgoing Christian Democratic premier of the state, Ernst Albrecht, whose rule had been plagued by scandals and which may also have been on the voters' minds and influenced the results, put the blame on the Social Democrats' encouragement of voter apprehension concerning the bills for reunification. He called the outcome a 'victory for selfishness'. Rather easier for Kohl to bear was the defeat in North Rhine–Westphalia, where the popular Social Democrat and long-serving Minister-President Johannes Rau had been widely expected to win.[3]

Painful as they may have been to the Christian Democrats and welcome encouragement to the Social Democrats, the election results signalled no major change in voter sentiments if compared with the previous state elections. The Social Democrats picked up and the Christian Democrats lost a couple of percentage points of support in Lower Saxony, with respectively 44.2 (+2.1) and 42.0 (–2.3) per cent, while the Free Democrats remained at 6 and the Greens were down with 5.5 (–1.6) per cent. The Social Democrats actually lost and the Christian Democrats gained votes in North Rhine–Westphalia, receiving respectively 50.0 (–2.1) and 36.7 (+0.2) per cent with the Free Democrats down to 5.8 (–0.2) per cent and the Greens up with 5 (+0.4) per cent.[4]

While the figures as such were no cause of major alarm for Kohl, the resulting Social Democratic majority in the Bundesrat gave him something to think about. It could complicate his life by obstructing the laws necessary for the newly negotiated economic and monetary union. The election results also in general cheered and emboldened Kohl's critics. Objectors to the cost of reunification had new grist for their mill. They were encouraged to press their demands for the total cost of the bill for the economic, monetary and social union, although no one could reliably estimate it. Kohl had claimed that tax increases were not needed to pay for unification, but those promises met with increasing scepticism.

The spreading West German resistance to concessions and the rapidly deteriorating economic situation in the DDR made some East German demands seem unrealistic or unfeasible if true relief lay in rapid economic unification. Anything blocking or slowing down progress towards it became, to many, an obstacle to the ultimate solution.

A specific angel of salvation took the shape of a fund appropriately called 'Deutsche Einheit' or German Unity. Its godparents were Kohl and the heads of the *Länder*, member states of the Bundesrepublik, who after an hour-long meeting gave their blessing to the newborn child on 16 May. This DM115 billion fund would in the first place help with the DDR's massive budget deficit, which was estimated at DM30 billion in 1990 and DM50 billion in 1991. These enormous sums were to help to meet the rising cost of unemployment and social welfare resulting from the difficulties of economic adjustment to a market economy. Thê fund was scheduled to pump DM22 billion into the DDR in 1990, DM35 billion in 1991, DM28 billion in 1992, DM20 billion in 1993, and DM10 billion in 1994. After five years, or by 1995, the territories of the former DDR were supposed to stand on their own feet.[5]

In addition to the Unity Fund, the Bonn government allocated additional billions and expert advice to modernize East German industries and as contributions to social welfare.[6] Large as these contributions were, no one could exactly estimate to what extent they would cover East German needs, and how large the costs would ultimately become, before the benefits of unification would become apparent.

The announcement of the massive aid package to the East Germans came on the eve of the scheduled signing of the state treaty between the Bundesrepublik and the DDR concerning economic union on 18 May 1990. The signing ceremony took place in the Gobelin Hall in the Schaumburg palace at Bonn. The very place evoked memories of an earlier agreement between the Bundesrepublik and the DDR. In 1973 they had signed a treaty of co-operation there sponsored by Chancellor Willy Brandt. It was the culmination of his Ostpolitik, for which he came under heavy criticism for supposedly confirming by the treaty the division of Germany for all time. Seventeen years later, that division was coming to an end.

Beaming with joy and raising their sparkling wine glasses for a toast, Kohl and de Maizière with their respective Finance Ministers Theo Waigel and Walter Romberg celebrated the decisive step to German reunification. Delighted, Kohl spoke of a dream that was on its way to becoming reality, a dream of a united Germany but also of a united Europe. 'This is the moment of birth of a free, united Germany. Forty-five years after the painful division we are taking the first important step towards reunification,' he said. De Maizière called German reunification irreversible and said that it agreed with the East German people's longing for freedom and well-being.[7]

Kohl's and de Maizière's assessments were correct. Economic unification could hardly be separated from political unification. The treaty of economic union was also a decisive political treaty. It transferred control and responsibility over key economic, monetary and social matters in East Germany to Bonn. Inherent in this arrangement was the need for East Germans to also gain a voice in the decisions of the body which would decide their future, and such a voice they could only acquire as voters in a united Germany. Conversely, only German unification could persuade West Germans to make the needed investments and bear the sacrifices necessary for the reconstruction and regeneration of the east.[8]

It was a decisive step. The Germans were facing a historical opportunity, and they grasped it. Yet while many were grappling with it with confidence and trust in their ability to overcome the remaining hurdles on the way to national unity, many others were worrying and deploring the resulting problems.

The high tide of national enhancement had clearly receded since the high of the previous autumn. Both West and East Germans had increasingly focused on the economic and financial costs and results of the unification and how these affected them personally. Such concerns lay behind frequent calls for slowing the pace towards unification which were raised in Germany. Its delay, however, was also risky. Not only could unforeseen international obstacles emerge over time but a fundamental reform of the East German economy could hardly wait without further complications resulting.

No sooner had the treaty of monetary, economic and social union between the two Germanies been signed than it ran into criticism from both east and west. In the DDR the intellectuals of New Forum claimed that it was socially and democratically unbalanced. The heirs of the East German Communists, with the acid tongue of their leader Gregor Gysi, called it subjugation.[9] These voices, however, represented a small minority. More serious in their potential repercussions were the fears of the mass of ordinary East Germans who worried about their jobs and security. The East German Labour Minister Regine Hildebrandt further fuelled such sentiments by voicing her own gloom. She feared the worst as she thought the economic change was too abrupt and without an adequate transition phase.[10]

In the Bundesrepublik the chairman of the Social Democrats, Jochen Vogel, thought the treaty gave too little protection to East Germany against West German competition in business and industry. The Social Democrats voiced threats to block the acceptance of the treaty by the West German parliament unless East Germany received more consideration – though they also complained somewhat contradictorily about the costs of the treaty to the taxpayers.[11]

Drawing a realistic conclusion from the Social Democrats' gains, Kohl appealed for their support for the treaty of German economic, monetary and social union. His majority in the Bundestag, the lower house of the parliament, guaranteed the passage of the treaty there but with their newly won majority control of the Bundesrat the Social Democrats could postpone its ratification. Theo Waigel, Kohl's finance minister, took up the cudgels against the Social Democrats. He reminded them that the East German negotiators had also included Social Democrats and warned of the consequences of reopening arguments about the treaty. He said it would endanger the East German economy and create an explosive social situation. Opposing the treaty threatened reunification in the near future, he claimed.

While not threatening to postpone the ratification of the treaty, Vogel nevertheless demanded changes and additions to it. The candidate for chancellor, Lafontaine, went further. Criticizing Kohl for an excessive rush towards reunification, he called the monetary union 'a first-class mistake' and claimed that research results showed that both East and West Germans thought Kohl had advanced too fast.[12]

In fact, a rift was developing among the Social Democrats concerning the handling of the treaty. The more moderate majority, led by Vogel, was ready to accept the treaty with certain additions. In a sharp departure from this line, Lafontaine demanded that the party should vote against the treaty in the Bundestag but accept it in the Bundesrat. The Bundestag vote would be a demonstration against Kohl's unification policies but would not affect the treaty since it would still have majority support in the lower house.[13]

The fancy political footwork of Lafontaine's plan left most of his colleagues cold. It made some sense from the point of view of Lafontaine's personal candidacy, as his chances of success could depend on how clearly he profiled himself as offering another policy towards unification than Kohl.

Aware of the opposition to his plan, Lafontaine underlined the seriousness of his demands by threatening to resign as the party's candidate for chancellor unless it backed him up. This angered many leading Social Democrats, some of whom wanted to take Lafontaine at his word and pick a new candidate. Vogel also threatened to resign. He was supported by the East German Social Democrats, who criticized Lafontaine's electioneering tactics and appealed to the West German party to support ratification of the treaty.[14] Beneath the heat and acrimony lay an inherent conflict. Lafontaine did not share the national enthusiasm for the prospect of unification which also elated many Social Democrats.

Seeing his opportunity to gain Social Democratic support for the treaty, Kohl signalled his receptiveness to new ideas and additions to it. These were hammered out between Kohl, Vogel, and the liberal leader Count Otto Lambsdorff on 29 May 1990. The Social Democrats' demands were well thought out and appealed to a broad spectrum. Besides additional support for East German enterprises and companies to prevent bankruptcies and to protect employment, the demands included measures for cleaning up the environment, and confiscation of the property of the East German Communist Party and its successor as well as the property of other former East German parties and the Stasi. In addition, the Social Democrats wanted a broad consensus about further measures and policies toward reunification.[15]

The parliament of the DDR promptly put these West German agreements into practice. It passed legislation on 31 May which transferred the property of political organizations to governmental control. The main target was the former Communists who had amassed by far the largest fortune during the decades in which they had exercised a stranglehold on power. Predictably their leader, Gregor Gysi, raised the most anguished and vehement protest, wailing in the televised parliamentary session that the government wished to eliminate the opposition.[16] The measure was hugely popular: a prominent revolutionary demand in the autumn of 1989 had been to deprive the Communist operatives of their remaining power base and comfortable existence. 'The parasites have got their due' was a widely repeated comment.

Such sentiments were all the more powerful and prevalent as many prominent former Communists seemed to be doing quite well, to the frustration of ordinary East Germans. Many still held their old choice jobs, while others succeeded in landing lucrative positions as representatives of West German companies, benefiting from their contacts in and knowledge of the workings of the East German bureaucracy. They knew how to get things through it and this made them valuable to their new employers. The sight of such individuals in expensive fashionable clothes and in new, expensive, Western cars, exasperated and infuriated other East Germans struggling to get by and concerned about their and their families' future.[17]

Worries abounded not only in Germany but also elsewhere. Germany's long record of holding inflation at bay was expected to translate into substantially higher interest rates, as Germany would pay for the costs of reunification with an expansionary fiscal policy combined with a tight monetary policy. Because of their dependency on or links to the powerful German economy and currency, this would force others to make an uncomfortable choice. They would have to choose between raising their own interest rates or devaluing their currencies against the Deutschmark. Higher interest rates could curtail growth and devaluation would invite inflation. Germany's problems were becoming everybody's problems.

With the treaty on monetary, economic and social union, Helmut Kohl had lived up to the promises he had made during the March election campaign in the DDR, and he had done so at some risk to his own future political fortunes. He had used his political weight to prod the Bundesbank and its President Karl Otto Pöhl to give up their earlier positions.

The difference between Kohl's one-for-one and the Bundesbank's two-for-one conversion rate was not as sharp as it appeared at first sight. If the total of East German personal savings were counted in, the exchange rate would average at about one-and-half-for-one. Furthermore, the overall exchange of the Ostmarks to Deutschmarks added about 14 per cent to the West German monetary stock. This addition roughly equalled the ratio between the two gross domestic products, as far as that could be at all reliably estimated for the DDR at the time.[18] This alone hardly justified the frequently expressed fears about the fundamental stability of the Deutschmark. Its value would obviously fluctuate but not necessarily significantly beyond its recent limits.

Then there were the intangible and unquantifiable yet nevertheless important matters that affect economies in a powerful manner, such as that the Germans were savers rather than spenders. Unlike consumers in many other modern advanced free market societies, they were not perennially up to their ears in debt to credit card companies, as credit cards had found only cautious and guarded acceptance among the Germans. They simply earned and saved more than they spent. The result was both high personal saving and a West German national surplus.

One of the most vexing matters in the negotiations for the monetary, economic and social union between the two Germanies had been the question of property. Time after time a solution to it had to be postponed. Even after the agreement on the basic treaty, the issue remained to be settled after further consultation in an appendix to the treaty.

After a long struggle, de Maizière's government had accepted Bonn's demand that West Germans and foreigners could buy land and other real estate for commercial and industrial use in the DDR. Fearing wholesale dispossession at bargain basement prices, the East Germans had resisted this stubbornly, but Bonn had argued that it was necessary to secure the badly needed investment required for economic reconstruction. The ninth appendix to the treaty which purported to settle the matter was nevertheless so vague in its wording that it left matters essentially unsettled. While it stipulated that East German industrial and commercial property was available for purchase, it also left the eventual price open-ended, to be decided later when the value of East German property had become clarified. De Maizière said, 'There would be no give-aways'.[19]

The lack of a final and conclusive settlement concerning property ownership left many living in a limbo. Successive waves of property confiscations in East Germany had left a rapidly rising avalanche of claims. Claims by West Germans alone were said to threaten the homes of potentially some five million East Germans.[20] On top of this figure came the impact of internal East German claims of restoration of old property rights. Many property claims conflicted with one another; being based on chronologically successive waves of expropriation and redistribution of property, they had left many groups of victims and beneficiaries.

The first massive post-war expropriations in East Germany were carried out at the direct order of the Soviet authorities immediately at the end of the war, from 1945 to 1946. It involved the take-over of all landed estates larger than 100 hectares. These were first divided among small farmers. Subsequently, beginning in 1952 and at accelerated pace after 1958, they were forced into collectives and eventually into very large state farms.

The process had left owners of the original larger estates, the *Junkers* or the landed gentry, as well as other prosperous landowning families as claimants to their ancestral homes. It also established another much larger group, which had at first benefited from the distribution of the estates, with claims on the very same lands. What further complicated matters was that many people in this second group had lost their own farms in the eastern territories that were ceded to Poland at the end of the Second World War. This gave them a moral right to claim some compensation.

Successive waves of expropriation also hit properties other than landed estates. At first they concentrated on the property of people accused of being war criminals. After the birth of the DDR, the state took over the largest enterprises. From the mid-1960s onwards state control was extended to an ever wider scope of economic activity until by 1972 all medium-sized and even smaller businesses of any significance were taken over. The state similarly took control of private residences which belonged to the multitudes of people who fled to the west.

Settling all the claims on expropriated and lost property would take a vast amount of time. Conflicting claims and repayment of compensation received by claimants would cause drawn-out negotiations and litigation. Meanwhile, potential investors in East German property would clamour for security of title, as would their lenders.[21] It could all evolve into a horrendous mess which would hold back reconstruction and recovery in the east for years.

The East Germans told and repeated horror stories about West German former owners emerging in person or through letters to claim back their old properties and sometimes demanding compensation, with interest, for damage and wear and tear.[22] Seeking to protect themselves the East Germans were resisting at least the return of the large properties redistributed at the very end of the Second World War before the establishment of the DDR. In general they were also much less receptive to claims for West Germans than to restoring properties to their former East German owners. Formerly family-owned firms were generally willingly returned at easy terms.

The artificially controlled very low rents and uncertainty over the status of much of the East German real estate hampered any attempts at improving the general appearance of the East German cities, towns, and villages. Their grey, drab, unpainted, and run-down look would not change until rents were raised at least to the level of paying for the upkeep of the properties and until people felt secure enough in ownership to invest in it.[23]

For this, the East and West Germans would have to come to an agreement about the property rights. West German concepts of the sanctity of property rights locked horns here with East German long-time occupancy and the resulting sense of squatters' rights. Difficult as it was, the issue would have to be settled one way or another before the flow of investment from the west and the reconstruction of East Germany could go ahead at full speed. Investment would not flow freely until investors felt that the title to their new properties was secure against unknown future claims against them. The unknown could be a powerful obstacle.

So could a growing awareness of the environmental mess in East Germany. Acid rain, corrosive soot and chemical toxins had been fouling its air, soil and waters relentlessly. They had poisoned people, dirtied and corroded buildings, and killed forests. Pollution had given East German towns and villages an overall grey-brownish, grubby and gloomy look. It did not amount to a visually attractive place in which to invest or move with one's family from the west.[24]

The brown coal that provided the bulk of East Germany's energy needs was largely responsible. Locally abundant and cheaply available, it powered factories and heated homes, offices, schools and hospitals. Although it contaminated the environment and caused various illnesses, little or next to nothing had been done to control or reverse these sad results. The Communists had shown little concern with the damage and, because of years of neglect, it now amounted to a ticking time bomb. East Germany, along with neighbouring Poland and Czechoslovakia and various parts of the Soviet Union, was the worst-polluted place in Europe. The clean-up would cost a very great deal of money. The prospect of the need for such heavy investment also held back investors.

Aside from brown coal, its chemical industry was the leading poisoner of the environment and people in the DDR. A centre of the East German chemical industry, Bitterfeld, was about as bitter a place to grow up and live in as its name suggested. The grimy town offended the eyes and noses of both visitors and natives, and most trees around it had died. Childhood diseases and abnormally short life spans characterized the pasty-faced residents. While Bitterfeld was perhaps the worst case of pollution in the DDR, other horror stories abounded. Estimations of the investment and time needed for a clean-up to bring East Germany in line with the standards of the Bundesrepublik varied, but the sums quoted were enormous. They amounted to hundreds of billions of Deutschmarks and ten to twenty years of effort.[25]

These were daunting estimates but something could and would have to be done, and done quickly. East German pollution was not just an East German problem but travelled freely in the air and in rivers to West Germany and elsewhere. Some important sources of pollution could soon be replaced, however, including East German Trabant cars. Each one of them was said to pollute the air as much as a hundred cars with catalytic converters. For other reasons as well, having to do with status, power and style, their owners were itching to replace them as soon as they could with Western vehicles.

In addition to the unsettled property issues and environmental pollution, the sorry state of the East German communications infrastructure discouraged and hampered new West German investment. The antiquated and outmoded telephone network was the most serious single impediment in this respect. Telecommunications with West Germany were deplorable or non-existent, and only 7 per cent of East German households had telephones in contrast to virtually each one in the west. In addition, enormous investment was needed for roads, railways, bridges, airports, canals and harbours. They had to be built, rebuilt, or at least repaired to bring the transportation network to the West German level. Cost estimations of all this reconstruction varied widely but there was no mistaking the German determination to meet the challenge.[26]

As the day of German monetary, economic and social union came in sight, anticipation, anxieties, reassurances and admonitions intensified and multiplied. It was the unknown which lay ahead that perhaps more than anything else accounted for the highly charged emotions. Never before had a state with a socialist planning economy been changed overnight into a capitalist market economy. The sensation many experienced was like expecting to be thrown into cold water without knowing whether they could swim or even float. A general expectation was emerging that some third of the East German companies would go under and another third might sink in a market economy. Accordingly, estimations varied widely concerning the resulting unemployment. The higher estimates amounted to 25 per cent unemployed.

National leaders appreciated and empathized with the mixed public sentiments but sought to guide them into constructive channels. Seeking to reassure the nervous East Germans, they criticized negative predictions of massive unemployment for millions in East Germany.

According to West German Finance Minister Theo Waigel, any prognosis about production and employment was 'pure speculation' in view of the unprecedented change in the economic system of East Germany, and he therefore considered that no one should go about the country with gloomy prognoses about a wave of bankruptcies throwing onto the labour market millions of workers. Waigel's comments were aimed in particular at leftist predictors of doom and gloom who had sought to make use of the widespread public uncertainties and fears, in particular the discredited Communists and their heirs, who had found in it a way to try to build visibility and some credibility for themselves. Waigel's words were also backed up by a leading Social Democrat, the Mayor of West Berlin, Walter Momper, who said even more emphatically about the impending change: 'Anyone who says he knows what will happen is lying.'[27]

Waigel also sought to give courage to and reassure the East Germans. Emphasizing the traditions of industrial experience, education and training in the DDR, he said the East Germans shared the same basic preconditions for success with the West Germans. His fundamental message was one of optimism, proclaiming that those who had faith in themselves, and invested capital, or in their own education and training need not worry about the future.[28] Nobody knew with any certainty how East Germany would fare in the next few months, although the longer-term prognosis was optimistic.

Neither could anyone tell with certainty how much the reconstruction of East Germany would cost, but there was widespread faith that eventually East Germany would get on its feet through very rapid economic growth and reach the living standards of West Germany.

It was belived that, initially, East German needs and demands would spur on the already formidable rate of West German economic growth. East German growth was later expected to even bypass that growth and contribute mightily to the general German economy. Optimistic talk about a new German Wirtschaftswunder was thick in the air. A highly respected German economic institute, IW, predicted an annual economic growth rate of up to 7.5 per cent for East Germany, assuming the transition to a market economy succeeded, and that accordingly the East Germans would reach West German living standards by year 2000.[29] Some estimates talked about even more rapid economic growth in East Germany. The West German Economics Minister, Helmut Hausmann, predicted on 29 May 1990 that it would reach between 7 and 10 per cent annually in the ensuing years. He certainly expected a new Wirtschaftswunder.[30] Such comments raised the hopes of the East Germans, though they did not like Hausmann's admonitions of their need to accept lower wages and longer working days than the West Germans.

Such optimism was fanned by a deliberate campaign. The Information Agency of the Bundesrepublik placed full-page advertisements in the newspapers a few days before the consummation of the economic union in late June in which Kohl, Waigel, and de Maizière assured the readers of a bright future 'in freedom and unity'. They claimed that continuing economic growth provided the needed foundation for German unification and that the unique opportunity would benefit everybody.

Nevertheless, money spoke louder than words and the East Germans would receive an immediate, tangible and concrete benefit from economic and monetary union when it took place. They would receive 'real money', as some put it. With their new Deutschmarks they could buy many things not available for their Ostmarks. There was a party mood to it all. On the eve of the economic union and at the beginning of the massive money swap accompanying it, there was something abroad akin to the feeling children have about Christmas: excitement mixed with anticipation. Beer and sekt, or sparkling wine, was flowing and fireworks dazzled. People were getting ready to exchange their allotted amount and planned what to do with it. In preparation they had first cleaned out the shelves of East German shops in a last-minute rush to buy cheap items, such as basic foods, with their soon superfluous Ostmarks. The shops in turn had been getting ready for the new era by stocking massive amounts of West German goods, anticipating high demand for them.

Many economic soothsayers had predicted a wild spending spree by the East Germans once they laid their hands on their Deutschmarks, and such predictions had fanned fears in political circles of its possible inflationary impact. In the last days of June preceding the economic and monetary union, both East and West German political leaders were admonishing the East German consumers to refrain from excessive spending of their new monies.

They need not have bothered. The East Germans behaved by and large as one might expect of orderly, prudent and sober Germans. Except for partying and a mêlée at the Alexanderplatz in the heart of East Berlin, where a Deutsche Bank office opened exceptionally early for the exchange that took place on Saturday night, it proceeded smoothly. At the Alexanderplatz masses of people were jostling each other and shouting and whistling, to the delight of the news media, but elsewhere they were dutifully lining up on the Sunday morning to patiently wait their turn with the cashier. Although everyone knew that the people moving on the streets carried unusually large amounts of cash on them, no rise in the number of muggings was reported.

In many places long lines stretched outside banks with people waiting in rainy weather to get in, but they did not seem to mind. They were used to queuing patiently. Their comments revealed much of their mood and expectations. 'Now there is finally something worth waiting in a queue for,' a woman commented. A man added that he had come 'to witness history and to take part in it'. Others spoke of the specifics they intended to do with their money. Most of it would just go for ordinary living costs, but some planned to fulfil a long-cherished dream to travel in the west. Beside native prudence, uncertainty as to future employment, prices and rents kept people cautious. Many East Germans had also already satisfied their first great urge for Western delicacies and goods by shopping in West Germany after the opening of the borders. Only a few felt that they could afford to spend on luxury goods, although many wished they could buy a Western car.[31]

Many older people had arrived early on Sunday morning before the banks opened, to reserve places in the queues. They did not expect to do any immediate shopping with their new money but were driven by memories of disappointments. They thought it best and surest to get their Deutschmarks while they could, before any possible sudden new restrictions or changes.[32] As veterans of the scarcities and arbitrariness of life under Communism, they did not like to take chances.

One elderly, well-known East German couple with substantial savings also made known their wish to change their funds to Deutschmarks. These were the former first couple of the DDR, Erich Honecker and his wife Margot. Their lawyer announced that their cash hoard of some 290,000 Ostmarks had accumulated by savings from their salaries. The Honeckers had to share the same uncertainty as many others. Their funds had been confiscated pending the outcome of corruption and other charges against them.[33]

Uncertainties about the future also preoccupied business leaders and politicians. Both were relieved by the prudence ordinary East Germans showed about handling their new Deutschmarks; to them they were not only symbols of their new freedom but the best guarantee for their future security and well-being. Although the East Germans' behaviour was reassuring, however, businessmen continued to be cautious about releasing money for major production investments, with a few notable exceptions such as Volkswagen, Siemens, or Daimler-Benz. Many announcements of new plans to invest in East Germany were made, but much of it had to do with sales and services rather than new production capacity. Furthermore, new production plants would take time to materialize, far more time than setting up sales and service offices and networks. Thus, while many new, large, colourful signs were put up and products displayed, few new production lines were started.

Kohl had repeatedly urged West German business and industrial leaders to invest in East Germany. He had appealed to their sense of national solidarity to create new working and training opportunities there. He had tried time after time to hammer home to West Germans the need to make sacrifices for the sake of the unity and equality of all Germans.[34]

Politicians were now growing impatient with businessmen, urging them to move faster, while some businessmen blamed their hesitations on the politicians. They said the politicians had not solved the issues which were holding back investments, such as settling the matter of property rights. Money was not the problem, as the booming Federal Republic possessed ample capital supplies for financing the required investments.

In addition to the problem of property rights and disputes, other bureaucratic matters slowed down new investment and the birth of new businesses in East Germany. The stiff and rigid *verboten* mentality and endless bureaucratic pettiness had a tight grip on others as well as Communists. Both officials and ordinary East Germans had for long lived under this system and knew no other, and they therefore put up with and accepted long delays caused by complex and often senseless rules and regulations. The filling in and handling of innumerable forms and endless correspondence, however, were discouraging and intolerable for many West German entrepreneurs who had alternative uses for their investment funds than East Germany.[35]

Yet for all its complications and risks, the economic, monetary and social union already amounted in most eyes to the *de facto* reunification of Germany. So confident and secure did the German leadership and establishment feel about it that some gave in to the luxury of venting their frustrations about their neighbours' attitudes towards reunification. A multi-page special advertising section on Germany in the *Wall Street Journal* took Britain and France to task. It pointed out,

> For decades, British and French leaders had assailed the Berlin Wall. ... Yet some of them, to judge by their reactions, seemed to miss it as soon as it was gone.
>
> Germany's closest neighbors, West and East, have reacted to the rapid pace of the unification process with a barely disguised mixture of jealousy and anxiety. The sudden fall of the hated Wall triggered few celebrations in the West. But it did set off a remarkable round of shuttle diplomacy between West Germany's erstwhile NATO allies and their pro forma Warsaw Pact adversaries in Poland and Czechoslovakia.
>
> The surprising retreat of Soviet and American power brought the unspoken truth about Europe closer to the surface than at any time since the outbreak of World War II.
>
> Some West Germans felt betrayed by their friends. German leaders notched up the decibels of soothing verbal reassurances they have been issuing for foreign consumption throughout the post-war period.[36]

While releasing pent-up German emotions and frustrations and clearing the air, such advertisements also added to the discomfort felt by her neighbours. The process of German reunification brought in its wake much emotional baggage which would have to be sorted out in the future.

Notes

1 *Der Spiegel*, 28 May 1990.
2 *FR* and *SZ*, 14 May 1990.
3 Kohl, on German television, 13 May 1990; *FAZ, SZ* and *Die Welt*, 14 May 1990.
4 Ibid.
5 *FAZ*, 17 May 1990; Uwe Andersen, 'Economic Unification', in Dieter Grosser (ed.), *German Unification*, 1992, p. 131.
6 *FAZ*, 17 May 1990.
7 German television, 18 May 1990; *FAZ, SZ* and *Die Welt*, 19 May 1990; the treaty is published in *Die Verträge zur Einheit Deutschlands*, 1990, pp. 1–23.
8 Robert Leicht, in *Die Zeit*, 18 May 1990.
9 *Neues Deutschland*, 19 May 1990.
10 *FR, Neues Deutschland* and *SZ*, 19 May 1990.
11 Ibid.
12 For this debate, see, e.g., *FAZ, FR, SZ* and *Die Welt*, 21, 22, 23 and 27 May 1990.
13 *Welt am Sonntag*, 27 May 1990; *Der Spiegel*, 28 May 1990.
14 *FR, SZ* and *Die Welt*, 28, 29 May 1990; *Der Spiegel*, 28 May 1990.
15 *FAZ, FR* and *SZ*, 30 May 1990.
16 German television, 31 May 1990; *FAZ* and *SZ*, 1 June 1990.

17 Impressions from East Germany, May and summer 1990.
18 'Survey: The New Germany', *The Economist*, 30 June 1990, p. 10.
19 Ibid., pp. 14–15.
20 *The Economist*, 9 June 1990, p. 27.
21 Cf. Uwe Andersen, 'Economic Unification', in Dieter Grosser (ed.), *German Unification*, 1992, pp. 119–20, 126.
22 Information based on talks with Germans, summer 1990.
23 Impressions from Germany, 1989–90.
24 Cf. Petschow, Meyerhoff, Thomasberger (eds), *Umweltreport DDR*, 1990.
25 Cf. Lipschitz and McDonald (eds), *German Unification: Economic Issues*, 1990, p. XV; Uwe Andersen, 'Economic Unification', in Dieter Grosser (ed.), *German Unification*, 1992, pp. 127–8.
26 Cf. *FAZ* and *Die Welt*, 27 June 1990.
27 Momper, in the *Wall Street Journal (Europe)*, 29 June 1990.
28 *FAZ*, *SZ* and *Die Welt*, 27 June 1990.
29 *FAZ* and *Die Welt*, 30 May 1990.
30 *FAZ*, 30 May 1990.
31 Impressions from Germany, summer 1990.
32 Ibid.
33 *Die Bild Zeitung*, 29 June 1990.
34 *FAZ* and *Die Welt*, 22, 29 June, 2 July 1990; Kohl, on German television, 1 July 1990.
35 Information based on talks with Germans, summer 1990.
36 'The German Monetary Marriage', *Wall Street Journal (Europe)*, 2 July 1990.

14 The End Game

The Germans felt confident, yet before Gorbachev's and Kohl's meeting in July 1990 cleared the last remaining major hurdle from the path of German reunification, some surprises still lay in store and many problems still had to be solved.

Both German politicians' and business leaders' confidence owed much to a Moscow visit by leading West German bankers at Kohl's instigation in mid-May 1990. Hilmar Kopper and Wolfgang Röller, respectively the heads of the Deutsche Bank and the Dresdener Bank, together with Kohl's foreign policy adviser Horst Teltschick, had confidential meetings with Soviet leaders in the Kremlin on 14 May. Soviet requests for credit guarantees from Kohl had brought the German bankers to Moscow to assess Soviet creditworthiness from an economic point of view.

The Soviet leaders put their best face on things as loan applicants. Soviet Premier Nikolai Ryzhkov, Shevardnadze, and in the end Gorbachev himself gave their sales talk. Thanking the Germans for their quick and confidential reaction and for the possibility of talking over their problems and for possible help, the Soviet leaders spoke positively of the developing German–Soviet political and economic ties. They needed economic help to keep Soviet living standards from falling to the point of endangering the reform policy and the future of the world, they said. They also argued that the Soviet Union was a rich country with a great potential when it came out of its transition. The Germans felt the Soviets presented their economic situation candidly, to the point of producing a list of their major creditors in descending order. West Germany headed it, followed by Japan, Italy, France, Austria, and Britain. It was an interesting list – notable was the absence of the United States.[1]

The Soviet leaders' response to the German delegation confirmed that Kohl was on a right track. Upon its return he decided to help Gorbachev with some DM5 billion worth of credit guarantees. In addition, he sought to enlist Bush for further aid during a visit to Washington on 17 May. Outlining to Bush the deteriorating economic situation and rapidly rising unemployment in East Germany and anticipating further problems with monetary union, Kohl wanted to bring forward the anticipated all-German elections to early December, but for that he needed Gorbachev's co-operation. Bush hesitated because of the Lithuanian–Soviet conflict, but agreed with Kohl that the Lithuanian issue should not determine the West's policy when Kohl pointed out that a successor to Gorbachev would probably be no improvement.[2]

Kohl spoke candidly of his concerns, but so did Bush. As before, he said that the Soviet troop withdrawal should not be tied up with American withdrawal. Furthermore, he would not wish to leave American troops where they were not wanted. It was not that the Americans had to feel loved in order to stay, but Bush was concerned about the future development of American and German opinions as he was fighting growing isolationism. Kohl did his best to reassure Bush and compared his own situation to that of a farmer who wished to bring in the hay before a possible thunderstorm. The two men had developed considerable trust in each other and afterwards publicly confirmed their agreement about achieving German reunification. Bush came out for unrestricted German sovereignty over all its territory and an end to all Allied post-war rights. 'We both want a united Germany', he said, 'which enjoys full sovereignty, a united Germany which is a full member of the Western community and of NATO.' Kohl in turn thanked Bush for his support of German unification.[3]

Just before seeing Bush, Kohl had received a jolt from the local elections in North Rhine–Westphalia and Lower Saxony on 13 May. On past experience he had reason to believe that he would fare better in all-German than mere West German elections. This gave him an additional reason to push for early unification, and his coalition partners favoured these aims for the same reasons. This upset the Social Democrats, who expected in contrast to succeed better in the West German elections. Polls showed them gaining ground and on 21 May a poll indicated that Lafontaine could beat Kohl. They also thought that the prolonged economic problems and dislocation associated with unification could benefit them in the long run and therefore wanted to delay the eventual all-German elections.[4]

Another potential concern was the attitudes of Germany's neighbours, among whom public support for German unification was declining. According to EC polls, support for it since the fall of the wall had waned in France from 80 to 66, in Britain from 71 to 64, in the Netherlands from 76 to 59, and in Belgium from 71 to 61 per cent. In West Germany the percentage of people supporting unification had remained stable, going from 78 to 77 per cent.[5] It was ironic. While public support for German unification was declining among her neighbours, the originally reluctant British and French leaders had come around to backing it because of its seemingly unstoppable dynamics.

Kohl thus had ample reason to strongly pursue his aim of rapid unification. He made it known to Gorbachev that he regarded the credits as part of a package for progress in the two-plus-four talks, and held out the promise of help with further Western credits and wide-ranging German–Soviet economic co-operation. In return he expected Moscow to contribute to a constructive solution of the German issue before the end of the year.[6]

The Soviet leaders had been demanding treaty-bound limits on German armed forces and continued to resist German membership of NATO. Moscow further talked of the need of a peace treaty with Germany, originally gaining some support from Paris for this notion. Bonn opposed it determinedly, believing that it could lead to all kinds of complications and delays and put the Germans in an inferior position as the defeated power. The Germans instead wanted talks between equals.

Kohl's message to Gorbachev was followed up by Genscher meeting Shevardnadze. Genscher brought with him a bag of presents and concessions in exchange for Soviet recognition of German unification and NATO membership. They included massive credits and promises of more, specific East German deliveries to the Soviet Union including uranium, and funds for the upkeep and pay of Soviet troops in East Germany.[7]

The Soviet leaders did not buy the offer at once. During a Moscow visit by Mitterrand on 25 May, Gorbachev indicated increased Soviet intrasigence in disarmament negotiations if a united Germany became part of NATO. As a compromise he proposed a similar arrangement for Germany as France had with NATO. He was also suggesting to the West the uncomfortable notion that the West's insistence on German NATO membership signalized its distrust of the Germans.[8] In view of Mitterrand's past activities, Gorbachev may have hoped to gain his support, but times and the situation had changed.

Gorbachev was looking for a way in which he could deliver enough to secure the aid he needed and wanted, without risking a serious internal political backlash. In a *Time* interview preceding his trip to Washington in May, he predicted a narrowing of differences between himself and Bush on the German question.[9] He also attempted to drive a wedge between the Germans and their Western allies, saying that some in the West pretended to be more enthusiastic about German unity than they really were, hoping that the Soviet Union would put the brakes on and get the blame.[10]

Shevardnadze was also making soothing overtures to the Germans. He talked about the need to search for solutions to the German issue that were acceptable to all, while also indicating Soviet agreeability to the accelerated German timetable. Furthermore, he underlined the importance of future good Soviet–German relations, including those with a united Germany.[11] It was all connected with money. The German offer of DM5 billion in credits was something concrete of which the Soviet leaders were eager to take advantage. Genscher reported to Kohl that Shevardnadze had reacted 'euphorically' to it and had signalled his readiness to settle the remaining issues.[12] Shevardnadze also proceeded to prepare the ground in the Soviet Union for its eventual acceptance of German membership of NATO.[13] Stopping off in Ottawa on his way to Washington, Gorbachev pursued the same line, expressing optimism over an eventual agreement on the matter.[14] Meanwhile, Kohl and Bush kept in close touch with one another, co-ordinating strategies. Kohl wanted to make sure that Gorbachev gained an impression of American–German unity on the issues involved. Having discerned the possibility of a deal with Gorbachev, he was keen on propping him up sufficiently for him to stay in power. Kohl therefore wanted Gorbachev to emerge well from the Washington summit so that his position *vis-à-vis* his internal foes would strengthen. He repeatedly stressed the importance of this to Bush, who basically agreed with his approach.[15]

The summit, however, brought no breakthrough on the German question. Gorbachev criticized Washington both for trying to dictate its views and for the lack of any new ideas, but both leaders also expressed optimism. Apparently keen on not jeopardizing his relations with Bonn, Gorbachev said that the Soviet Union did not wish to obstruct German unification. Bush informed Kohl of the progress and outcome of the summit. Reporting that Gorbachev had asked for massive economic help with American participation, he indicated agreement on condition that progress was made on the German question among other issues.[16]

Bush and Kohl were in fact consulting so closely with one another over the German question that they seemed to work in tandem. The American establishment clearly wanted good relations with a future united Germany, as did the Soviet leadership. Early in June Kohl was again back in the United States receiving a Harvard honorary doctorate and a standing ovation both before and after his speech thanking the American people for what they had done on behalf of the Germans.[17] He also met Bush. Upon his return to Bonn, Kohl told the assembled Christian Democratic politicians that Bush had represented German interests as no other American president had done before, and commented on a friendly attitude in Congress and in the country in general towards Germany.[18]

That was quite a change from the previous autumn, when Washington seemed to have been out of touch with the mood and events in Germany. Bush had early recognized the Bundesrepublik as the most important American ally in Europe, but had hesitated and floundered for a certain period when facing the novel situation arising out of the events in East Germany in the autumn of 1989. The fall of the Berlin Wall and the sudden prospect of German reunification took him by surprise, as they did so many others. However, he recognized the new European and German realities faster than some other international leaders, and his policy rapidly became one of resuming and continuing close co-operation with Kohl.

What the Germans wanted from the United States and the West in general was further economic help for the Soviet Union, and progress in the disarmament negotiations in order to facilitate Soviet agreement on the German issue. Almost simultaneous meetings of the Warsaw Pact and NATO in early June opened up new possibilities for a removal of the remaining obstacles. The meeting of the Warsaw Pact in Moscow on 7 June signalled its continuing dissolution. Moscow could clearly no longer dictate its will to its other members as in the past. Neither Gorbachev's proposals to revitalize the Pact nor his renewed suggestion that a united Germany should be tied to both NATO and the Warsaw Pact found much appeal with its other members.[19] Gorbachev's bargaining power was rapidly running out, being essentially reduced to the leverage he could squeeze from his very weakness, the perceived vulnerability and tenuousness of his hold on power in the Soviet Union.

The simultaneous NATO meeting at Turnberry on 8 June declared all its members' support for the unrestricted sovereignty of a united Germany, including its right to NATO membership.[20] Pressure was clearly increasing on the Soviet Union and Gorbachev to stop delaying on the German issue. Talk could be heard in political and diplomatic circles that continued Soviet resistance on the German and NATO issue put at risk Moscow's chances of gaining German and Western aid and credits. The possibility of German interference with energy and water supplies to the Soviet garrisons in East Germany was also mentioned. The potential long-term negative impact on future relations between a united Germany and the Soviet Union which could arise from continued procrastination loomed as an additional cloud on the horizon in the minds of some Soviet officials.[21]

Whatever the reasons, the Soviet leaders started to display increasing flexibility. Gorbachev got in touch with Kohl by letter on 11 June. Thanking him for his aid in overcoming Soviet economic problems, he pleaded for Kohl's help in securing additional large long-term credits from other countries as well. He reaffirmed their mutual agreements of 10 February and assured him of his confidence in rapidly finding solutions to the international ramifications of the German issue, and proposed direct contacts.[22]

It was an encouraging communication for the Germans. So was a meeting between Genscher and Shevardnadze in Brest on the same day that Kohl received Gorbachev's letter. It was a symbolic reconciliation of a sort between Germany and the Soviet Union from the tragedies of the Second World War. The two foreign ministers together visited the grave of Schevardnadze's brother who had fallen on the first day of the war. Seeking a solution to Germany's membership of NATO in a transformation of NATO and the Warsaw Pact from military to political organizations associated with each other, they ran into problems over specific details.

Shevardnadze insisted on the preservation of the wartime Allies' rights in Germany until the completion of the Soviet military withdrawal and reciprocity in thc withdrawal of Soviet and Western troops. Genscher rejected both conditions.[23]

The Soviet leaders' bargaining position was not enviable. Internationally they were isolated, as their former allies or subject states had slipped out of their hands and abandoned them. Domestically their room for manoeuvre was shrinking, for their popularity at home was sinking as the Soviet economy deteriorated. They still held out against accepting united Germany's membership of NATO, but few thought that Gorbachev even now was aiming at German withdrawal from NATO; rather, he was simply trying to arrange the best possible deal he could get. The Germans believed that money would make all the difference, although they officially denied it to spare Soviet sensitivities, and that Gorbachev could not afford to wait much longer. They also wanted to strike a deal while Gorbachev still could deliver it. The Soviet Union, however, was no longer in a position to block German unification. Even its possible insistence on keeping troops in East Germany could no longer guarantee its ability to dictate to the Germans. Isolated and demoralized, these troops were rapidly losing their value as a bargaining asset but instead increasingly turned into a liability for Moscow.

No wonder the German leaders felt ever more confident of settling matters soon. Internally they were preparing to move as quickly as possible to unification. The re-emergence of the *Länder* in East Germany corresponding to the West German *Länder* assisted rapid unification. This could occur under Article 23 of the constitution of the Bundesrepublik without any time-consuming and complex legal and constitutional disputes.[24]

On the international aspects of unification the road might be more awkward. While the Bundesrepublik appeared to be willing to pay what it could, other nations were clearly less forthcoming with the credits and aid that Gorbachev seemed to be holding out for. They were no more eager to help when they witnessed how the Russians were falling behind on the payments on credits they had already received. Loans were no longer as easily accessible to the Soviets as they had been. The Russians were met with scepticism when they claimed that their problems were of a passing nature. While they managed to roll over short-term credits, they had little success in raising large new loans. Soviet officials had to get used to the humiliation of knocking in vain on bankers' doors in European financial centres. Warily received, they often had to leave with empty pockets or to agree to much higher interest rates and more guarantees if they did manage to get any results. In desperation the Soviets were offering gold deposits as security.[25]

Clearly the value of money was increasing as a bargaining lever with Moscow.

Gorbachev announced new proposals in a speech to the Supreme Soviet on 12 June. He could accept Germany's NATO membership with limitations, he said, if it also remained a Warsaw Pact associate and changes took place in both organizations which resulted in *rapprochement* between them towards an all-European security structure. Broadcast directly on TV, Gorbachev's speech was intended to prepare Soviet opinion for greater flexibility and signal to the West and the Germans his own willingness to find solutions. Both Kohl and Bush rejected Gorbachev's new proposals.[26]

Gorbachev's internal position was at the same time rapidly becoming increasingly precarious. Under pressure from the hard-liners, he was also confronted by a growing challenge from Boris Yeltsin. Yeltsin's power increased greatly at one blow, as the elected President of the Russian Federation when it declared its 'sovereignty', on the same day that Gorbachev was making his proposals.[27]

While Gorbachev's position was weakening, Kohl was moving determinedly ahead to speed up German unification. He was acting on several fronts simultaneously in order to advance his basic aim. The day after Gorbachev's speech he dispatched letters to his EC and Group of Seven partners, the participants in the world economic summits. He was preparing the ground, asking them to help in dealing with the Soviet economic problems. Kohl thus sought to set an agenda for the forthcoming EC and Group of Seven summits in Dublin and Houston which could be helpful to German unification.[28] He was trying to meet Gorbachev's request for additional massive Western credits.

Internally, he was building consensus for the final and conclusive acceptance of the Polish–German boundary on the Oder–Neisse line as a necessary condition for unification. Those who would not abandon territorial claims were putting unification at risk, he said, and announced publicly that the border would be guaranteed.[29] Poland's acceptance of Soviet troops within its territory until it had received satisfactory German border guarantees may have been on his mind.

The following day Kohl was sitting on the balcony of the East German parliament when the proposal came up to immediately join the Bundesrepublik. It passed easily with an overwhelming majority of 267 to 92. Although it was later set aside for additional study and preparation, the clear majority for the motion added to the pressure for speedy unification.[30] It was a prod to the wartime Allies and it bolstered Kohl's wish for fast action; his guiding hand was seen behind the vote.

Kohl wasted no time in taking advantage of the East German measure and predicted that an all-German government would emerge before the end of the year.[31] He was speeding along towards national German unity, driven both by a genuine general desire for it and by tactical considerations. The tactical considerations had both internal German and international dimensions. The internal aspects involved election calculations based on the economic prospects in East Germany. Kohl was thought to stand a better chance the earlier the all–German elections took place, such thoughts being based on gloomy expectations of economic dislocation in East Germany in the wake of monetary union.

The international considerations concerned mainly German fears that Gorbachev would not or could not deliver owing to his increasingly shaky position in the Soviet Union. Furthermore, some of the pronouncements of Bonn's Western allies were not altogether reassuring to the Germans. French Foreign Minister Roland Dumas, for example, was clearly making amends for past French behaviour in an interview in *Der Spiegel* in mid-June, but still felt free to say that the Germans were in too much of a hurry. This was not altogether reassuring to the Germans in view of Dumas's past pronouncements. The Germans also remembered that the Nazis had executed Dumas's father during their occupation of France, and Dumas was very close to Mitterrand.[32] At about the same time British Prime Minister Margaret Thatcher reiterated in public her concerns about German unification. She expressed her worries over German economic and political domination of the European Community, evoking the memory of the two world wars.[33]

German apprehensions of Gorbachev's position became aggravated by the Communist hard-liners' heavy attacks on the Soviet leader. His main enemy, Yegor Ligachev, criticized him for his handling of the German question. Hard-pressed, Gorbachev was forced to seek an alliance with another old foe, the Russian President Boris Yeltsin.[34] This indicated the seriousness of Gorbachev's troubles as the two were divided not only by old feuds but also by bad personal chemistry.

Gorbachev's problems manifested themselves in additional hurdles on the path to German unification. Shevardnadze tied the Soviet troop withdrawals from the DDR to the reduction of other foreign forces in Germany, and proposed an upper limit of 200,000 to 250,000 to the German armed forces. Furthermore, he wanted to maintain the wartime Allies' rights and troops in Germany and the DDR's treaty obligations to the Warsaw Pact for at least five years after unification, but this made little sense in practice and was immediately rejected by the Western allies and Bonn. They saw Shevardnadze's proposals as a sop to the Soviet hard-liners.[35] Shevardnadze himself indirectly encouraged the dismissal of his proposals by repeatedly indicating his willingness to compromise.[36]

The Germans and the Western allies knew that Moscow's ability to press its demands was rapidly weakening. Popular protests against the increasingly demoralized Soviet troops were emerging in East Germany and Gorbachev's need for economic help was growing ever more urgent. After German economic union in July, Bonn was to pick up the DDR's obligations for the support and upkeep of the Soviet troops and their dependants in East Germany. This meant that what had been considered an élite part of the Soviet army would depend on Bonn for its daily existence. The Soviet military also became dependent on Bonn in another way, as a partner, when Bonn became responsible for the DDR's obligations, including providing the Soviets with elements of high technology.[37]

Meanwhile, Kohl continued systematically to work for an eventual deal with Gorbachev. He secured the simultaneous acceptance by both German legislatures of German economic union and a recognition of the German–Polish border. The latter he justified as necessary to achieve German unity, but once again demanded rights for the German minority in Poland.[38] A formal recognition of the border was hard on many Germans. They held cherished and intimate memories of the lost lands connected with their youth and childhood, memories of childhood friends, parents and grandparents, and lost homes. Many felt these losses to be unjust.

To German annoyance, the French had supported the Poles on the border issue, and settling it also thus removed an irritant from Franco–German cooperation. By June, Mitterrand was increasingly eager to get along with Kohl, making amends for his past attitudes and confirming the Franco–German alliance and friendship. While, for example, Bush was holding back on American economic help to Gorbachev despite Kohl's earnest pleas for it, Mitterrand became receptive and helpful. He publicly advocated an agreement on an aid package at the forthcoming EC and world economic summits respectively in Dublin and Houston.[39] In Dublin, Mitterrand backed Kohl's efforts to gain international financial aid for Gorbachev but Mrs Thatcher forthrightly refused. This was despite the rapport that allegedly existed between her and the needy Russian, but she could be frugal and had never been enthusiastic about German unity, to put it mildly.

The British saw no reason to rush with aid to the Soviet Union. After all, the Russians were not starving, they said, only standing in queues.[40] Instead of immediate aid, the EC summit merely agreed to provide it in principle, subject to further study.[41] This was something, but not the quick shot in the arm that Gorbachev had been looking for, in the form of rapidly available credits in their billions. He badly needed to have something substantial to show in the way of achievement before the fast-approaching Congress of the Soviet Communist Party, where he was expected to come under heavy attack, but at least Kohl had measured up to his word to try to enlist international help to Gorbachev beyond the promised billions of German credits. He would also soon have another chance at another forum at the forthcoming Houston economic summit in early July.

Kohl gained more immediate results from the NATO summit in London. Immediately preceded by but largely simultaneous with the Congress of the Soviet Communist Party, it made the kind of reassuring noises and gestures towards the Soviet Union which Kohl and the Germans were after. The idea was to reassure Gorbachev and bolster him against the Soviet hard-liners, in order to advance Moscow's acceptance of united Germany's NATO membership. Just before and during their own meeting, the NATO summit participants were exposed to reports of the hard-liners' show of strength and blistering attacks against Gorbachev. Shevardnadze, speaking early in the Soviet meeting, was on the defensive and appeared nervous. Where he talked in favour of co-operation with a unified Germany, whose division he called artificial and unnatural, the leader of the hard-liners, Ligachev, advocated the use of strong armed forces, to the sound of loud applause.[42]

The question of united Germany and NATO was the central issue confronting the London summit, and was in turn closely connected with the role of the United States in NATO and Europe and the possible future evolution of the organization. Its preservation was a top priority to the Americans, as it provided their main foothold and bridgehead in Europe. Without Germany the organization could no longer fulfil such a role.

Gorbachev tried to influence the summit. Sending a message to Mrs Thatcher as its hostess, he said that its results would influence Soviet attitudes on German unification, and once again tried to obtain Western economic aid. It did nothing to harm his cause,[43] and the East Germans did their share to impress upon the summit the urgency of dismantling the military confrontation in Central Europe. East German Defence Minister Rainer Eppelmann demanded the withdrawal of Soviet troops from the DDR. He said that their continued presence caused rising tension between them and the local people which had resulted in open confrontations and some violence.[44]

The NATO summit basically delivered what the Germans wanted. It sent conciliatory and friendly signals to Gorbachev to help him in overcoming hard-line resistance to acceptance of German unity and NATO membership. All the summit participants spoke of the importance of united Germany's NATO membership, but also agreed on a series of reassuring overtures to Moscow, which included several steps designed to emphasize the defensive and peaceful character of NATO. Among them were proposals for new disarmament measures, changes in strategic doctrine, and buttressing the role of the Conference on Security and Co-operation in Europe as a means of including the Soviet Union more closely in a new security structure for the continent. The Germans, supported by the French, had championed the last point. They also signalled their acceptance of new upper limits on their armed forces as a further reassuring gesture.

The Americans went far to meet German desires at the summit, connecting it with their own future in Europe. Bush re-emphasized the wish of the United States to remain a European power in politics, militarily, and in economics, and noted that the United States, more than any others, had welcomed German unification. Stressing his wish to continue the American presence in Germany, he at the same time soothed the Germans by saying that the future size of the German armed forces was up to them. Kohl in return pledged future German loyalty to NATO.[45] The Germans had reason to be pleased with the results of the summit. It had gone along with their wish to help Moscow.

The EC and NATO summits in Dublin and London had already displayed the Germans' enhanced status and role, and in the Houston economic summit of the Group of Seven this became even more visible. Helmut Kohl arrived after the other participants, together with the Italian Prime Minister Giulio Andreotti directly from the World Cup final in Rome, where this former centre forward of his high school's soccer team had seen his compatriots win the world soccer championship. It caused a new emotional high among the Germans, accompanied by fervent flagwaving and celebrations. Kohl shared the triumphant emotions, as the tears in his eyes and his happy face clearly revealed on television to the hundreds of millions of people around the world watching the final. It also revealed that only with the German team did all its members consistently sing the words to their national anthem when it was played. With other teams only some, typically a minority, participated this way.[46]

It could be taken as one indication of patriotism or nationalism and as such flew in the face of the polls which suggested that patriotism and nationalism had a weaker grip on young Germans than on their counterparts in many other countries around them.

Germany was clearly being empowered in politics and sports as well as in the economic matters on the agenda in Houston. In May the Bundesrepublik, together with Japan, had been granted the second most voting power in the International Monetary Fund after the United States. This was a formal recognition of its increased economic influence, putting it ahead of its third-ranked European rivals Britain and France – or, as Bonn's Finance Minister Theo Waigel put it, the Germans and Japanese had won silver while Britain and France got bronze. The Deutschmark had also become, after the US dollar, the second most important reserve currency in the world, reflecting the Bundesrepublik's leading status as an exporter. Under the circumstances, it was no wonder the Germans were expected to flex their muscles.[47]

As the leader of the strongest and wealthiest European country, Kohl acted accordingly. On issues displaying the world's factual division into three leading economic areas, the other Europeans tended to support the Germans, the British being the frequent exception. All the summit participants vouched support for German reunification and pledged co-operation with Soviet efforts to move to a free market economy. Yet key economic powers such as the United States and Japan stopped short of promising the kind of quick financial aid to Moscow that Kohl, closely supported by Mitterrand, was advocating. This rift was disguised in a unanimous agreement to study the matter further, in an echo of the Dublin EC summit.[48]

The Soviet Communist Party Congress had continued its bickering parallel with the Houston summit. After its rocky start Gorbachev had succeeded in reasserting his leadership.[49] With the immediate danger to Gorbachev's position removed, Bush had less reason to agree to contribute credits or funds, while the Japanese first wanted their two disputed islands in the Kurils from the Soviets before they would join in.

Time after time the British had been most reluctant to rally to the Germans. Nevertheless, an interview by Nicholas Ridley, the Trade and Industry Secretary in Mrs Thatcher's cabinet, when he candidly gave his views on Germany and the Germans, caused something of an uproar. Exposing the secret (and not so secret) British views of their neighbours in colourful and blunt language in public, it startled, pleased, embarrassed and angered people, depending upon their point of view. Speaking of the EC, Ridley divulged: 'This is all a German racket designed to take over the whole of Europe. It has to be thwarted. This rushed take-over by the Germans on the worst possible basis, with the French behaving like poodles to the Germans, is absolutely intolerable.' Referring to Kohl he said: 'He'll soon be coming over here and trying to say that this is what we should do on the banking front and this is what our taxes should be. I mean, he'll soon be trying to take over everything.'[50]

Ridley looked back over a long past when Britain had succeeded in keeping a balance of power in Europe which 'never had been more necessary than now, with Germany so uppity. … It's the German people. They're already running most of the Community. I mean they pay half of the countries. … But being bossed by a German – it would cause absolute mayhem in this country, and rightly, I think.'[51]

What gave extra force to Rodley's pugnacious words was the nature of his relationship with Mrs Thatcher. They were very close. Ridley was Thatcher's closest ally in the cabinet, and his outspokenness was thought to reveal Mrs Thatcher's real views, since she had earlier opposed German unification.[52] As *The Economist* put it, 'the shock among his colleagues will be less at his sentiments, more that he has been found out'.[53]

Ridley was not just whistling in the wind. His words mirrored many of his compatriots' gut feelings. Many Conservative MPs rallied to defend him against calls for his resignation, arguing that his views represented 'a significant segment of public opinion in both the House of Commons and the country'.[54] Were they right? In April a poll in Britain had found that 50 per cent of the people were concerned about a united Germany emerging as the dominant power in Europe, and of them 53 per cent feared the re-emergence of Nazism or Fascism.[55] Polls taken immediately after Ridley's comments tended to confirm these findings, although in some polls a clear majority of the respondents distanced themselves from his language. According to a *Sunday Times* poll, 55 per cent would worry if a united Germany 'became the dominant power in Europe', but only 37 would not.[56] In another poll, 33 per cent agreed and 60 disagreed that 'the French were behaving like poodles to the Germans', while only 28 per cent agreed and 66 did not that Kohl 'will soon be trying to take over everything'.[57] In contrast leading tabloids, including the *Sun*, the daily with the largest circulation in the country, reported overwhelming support among their readers for Ridley's anti-German opinions.[58] Despite such sentiments, other polls published almost simultaneously indicated that 64 per cent approved of German unification and trusted the Germans.[59]

Mrs Thatcher at first stood by her friend, resisting demands for his resignation but putting it on record that Ridley's views did not represent her own or the government's views.[60] Ridley himself said he would not resign if Mrs Thatcher did not wish it. Under growing pressure, however, he had to go; as well as the Labour Party, most conservative MPs also demanded it. Mrs Thatcher's position weakened when the Ridley interview was followed by eye-catching new revelations of official British attitudes towards the Germans and reunification. A leaked confidential report about a brainstorming session on Germany, held by Mrs Thatcher, her foreign policy adviser David Powell, Foreign Secretary Douglas Hurd and six experts at her country retreat, Chequers, on 24 March hit the press on 15 July. Written by Powell, it exposed what many had suspected.

Attempting to assess what a united Germany would be like, the report enumerated certain alleged German characteristics and traits. Having appeared in the past these traits, such as insensitivity, self-obsession and self-pity, might reappear in the future. Among other traits, '*angst*, aggressiveness, bullying, egotism, inferiority complex' were mentioned as an 'abiding part of the German character'. Further worries emerged concerning a German tendency to overestimate their capabilities and power. The meeting had recognized reassuring changes in Germany but feared a possible repeat of past patterns. Thus, while Germany was no longer bent on world conquest, 'the way in which Germans currently used their elbows and threw their weight about in the European Community suggested that a lot had still not changed'. Yet the participants saw consolation in that 'the more assertive Germany became, the easier it ought to become to construct alliances against Germany on specific issues in the Community'.[61]

The session had also expressed admiration and envy of German achievements as well as concerns about German reactions during a serious economic crisis. While not seriously wary of the current German leadership, the participants speculated on the re-emergence of negative characteristics within the next 10 to 15 years. Even the more optimistic ones expressed fear concerning the impact of unification on German attitudes. Germany was expected to change as a result of it and to focus more on Eastern Europe and to dominate it economically. The meeting also thought that West and East Europeans shared certain identical interests in security matters in preventing a re-emergence of German militarism. It wanted continued American military presence in Europe as a counterweight to German military power as well as restrictions on that power. The participants also anticipated that in the long term the reformed Soviet Union was the only power in Europe that could balance Germany. They also further speculated on whether the German commitment to European political unity was tactical or genuine.

As a balance there were also reminders of the harm caused to Europe in the past by British–German disputes. The report concluded on a more hopeful note that the Germans had changed in important ways, they were no longer bent on territorial conquest, and that Britain should be 'nice' to them.[62]

With the publication of this report suspicions increased that Mrs Thatcher not only shared Ridley's views but might actually have originally encouraged him to give his interview. Foreign Secretary Hurd sought to deny this and tried to minimize the damage done. Concerning the leaked report he said, on the one hand, that its comments should not be taken seriously, and on the other hand he emphasized the positive conclusion about the reassuring changes that had taken place in Germany.[63] He had an unenviable and painful task. Mrs Thatcher's memoirs show that she actually shared many of the views leaked from the Chequers seminar.[64]

Outwardly, the Germans took the whole episode quite calmly but it left fences difficult to mend and wounds hard to heal, at least as long as Mrs Thatcher remained in office. To overcome these would take more than words. Bonn's spokesmen tried to underplay the incident, though there were also some cutting comments. An official from the Chancellor's Office claimed: 'What Ridley said was so stupid that we refused to believe that his comments reflected the view of the British establishment.'[65] More important and substantial matters concerning Germany soon overshadowed the Ridley episode and the Chequers report in connection with Helmut Kohl's visit to Gorbachev.

Notes

1 Teltschick, 1991, pp. 230–35.
2 Ibid., pp. 236–7.
3 Ibid., pp. 238–9; *FAZ* and *IHTr*, 18 May 1990.
4 *FAZ, FR, SZ* and *Die Welt*, 16, 22 May 1990.
5 Karlheinz Reif, Director of Surveys, Research, and Analysis for the EC Commission, Milan, Reuters, 17 May 1990.
6 Teltschick, 1991, pp. 243–4.
7 *FAZ, IHTr, SZ* and *Die Welt*, 22, 23, 24 May 1990.
8 *Le Monde, FAZ, IHTr* and *Pravda*, 26 May 1990.
9 Gorbachev, in *Time*, 26 May 1990.
10 Ibid.
11 Shevardnadze, in *Welt am Sonntag*, 27 May 1990.
12 Teltschick, in *Welt am Sonntag*, 27 May 1990.
13 Shevardnadze, in *Izvestia*, 29 May 1990.
14 Gorbachev, in *Toronto Star*, 30 May 1990.
15 Teltschick, 1991, pp. 237–9, 253.
16 *FAZ, IHTr, SZ* and *Die Welt*, 1, 2, 4 June 1990; *Welt am Sonntag*, 3 June 1990; Teltschick, 1991, pp. 255–8.
17 *Boston Globe* and *Die Welt*, 8 June 1990; Kohl, in *Bulletin*, 74, 13, June 1990, p. 642.
18 Teltschick, 1991, pp. 262, 264.
19 *FAZ, IHTr, SZ* and *Die Welt*, 8 June 1990; *Der Spiegel*, 11 June 1990.
20 *Der Spiegel*, 11 June 1990.
21 Soviet officials in Stockholm, June 1990.
22 Teltschick, 1991, p. 264.
23 Ibid., pp. 268, 273–4.
24 For a debate on these matters, see, e.g., Glaessner, *The Unification Process in Germany*, 1992, pp. 16–17 and the cited sources.
25 *The Economist*, 16 June and the *Wall Street Journal (Europe)*, 15–16 June 1990.
26 *FAZ, IHTr, SZ* and *Die Welt*, 13 June 1990.
27 Ibid.
28 Teltschick, 1991, pp. 274–5.
29 *Welt am Sonntag*, 17 June 1990.
30 *FAZ, SZ* and *Die Welt*, 18 June 1990.
31 Ibid.
32 Dumas, in *Der Spiegel*, 4 June 1990.
33 Thatcher, on the BBC, 18 June 1990; *the Times*, 19 June 1990.
34 *FAZ, IHTr, SZ* and *Die Welt*, 21 June 1990.
35 *FAZ, IHTr, SZ* and *Die Welt*, 23 June 1990; Teltschick, 1991, p. 285.
36 E.g. Shevardnadze in *Neues Deutschland*, 27 June 1990.
37 Article 13, section 2 of the treaty of German monetary, economic and social union pledged to honour the DDR's foreign trade contracts, *Bulletin, Presse - und Informationsamt der Bundesregierung*, 133/1900.
38 *FAZ* and *Die Welt*, 22 June 1990.
39 Mitterrand, in *Le Monde*, 20 June 1990.
40 Reuters, 25 June 1990.
41 *IHTr* and *The Times*, 27 June 1990.
42 Reuters, 3 July 1990.
43 *IHTr* 6 July 1990.

44 AFP, 5 July 1990.
45 For the NATO summit, see, e.g., Teltschick, 1991, pp. 298–304; *FAZ, IHTr, The Times, SZ* and *Die Welt*, 6, 7 June 1990; Szabo, 1992, pp. 88–92.
46 Based on television coverage in June and July 1990 of the tournament in Italy.
47 *Wall Street Journal (Europe)*, 9 July 1990.
48 *FAZ, Financial Times, Handelsblatt* and *Wall Street Journal (Europe)*, 9–13 July 1990; *The Economist*, 14 July 1990.
49 *FAZ, IHTR, SZ* and *Die Welt*, 10–14 July 1990.
50 Ridley, in the *Spectator*, 14 July 1990.
51 Ibid.
52 *Spectator*, 14 July 1990; Thatcher, 1993, p. 722.
53 *The Economist*, 14 July 1990, p. 33.
54 As Quoted in the *Wall Street Journal (Europe)*, 13–14 July 1990.
55 Ibid.
56 *Sunday Times*, 15 July 1990.
57 *Sunday Telegraph*, 15 July 1990.
58 *Sun, Daily Express* and *Daily Star*, 13 July 1990.
59 *The Independent*, 13 July 1990.
60 Thatcher, in *The Times*, 13 July, and Ridley, on the BBC, 14 July 1990.
61 *Independent on Sunday*, 15 July 1990.
62 Ibid.
63 Hurd, on the BBC, 15 July 190.
64 See, e.g., Thatcher, 1993, pp. 769, 791, 798, 813–15.
65 Quoted in the *Financial Times*, 16 July 1990.

15 The Solution

Kohl flew to Moscow at the head of a large delegation on 14 July 1990. Having prepared the ground during the previous weeks' summits for his much anticipated trip, he had good reason for optimism about its results. Although he had not succeeded in immediately raising the billions that Gorbachev hoped for and felt he needed, Kohl had made a visible effort to deliver. Added to the *de facto* unification of Germany which had just taken place with its economic, monetary and social union, this might be just enough to convince Gorbachev that the deal he could make with his guest would get no better by waiting. Gorbachev could also anticipate that Kohl would not be arriving empty-handed; it had actually been spelled out by a Bonn spokesman.[1] Such outspokenness could have embarrassed the Russian leader. By contrast, a more sensitive Genscher tried his best to soothe Soviet sensitivity and pride by stating that Bonn 'has never believed that German unity could be bought'.[2] It was a sore point with the Russians.

Knowing that he had not only been invited to Moscow but to Gorbachev's home ground north of the Caucasus, Kohl had reason to expect success. He also knew that Gorbachev was back in the saddle for the time being, having overcome his hard-line foes in the party congress. How firmly and for how long remained an open question, but at least for a time he had gained a longer leash and more room to manoeuvre and to make deals.

Kohl was also aware of Gorbachev's continuing financial needs as the Soviets were making full use of the five billions of Deutschmarks in credits that they had previously received.[3] Together with the delays and hesitations that the EC and Group of Seven summits had revealed in the granting of further assistance to the Soviet Union, this was a reliable indication of the financial and economic pressures on Gorbachev. It was significant that Kohl's party included Finance Minister Theo Waigel as well as Foreign Minister Genscher. Clearly, economic and financial matters stood high on its agenda.

The German Chancellor was in high spirits when flying eastwards over the same Russian plains through which German soldiers had slogged during the war, but his occasionally too loud joking revealed his inner tension.[4]

This was perhaps inevitable, as he realized that he was probably on the most important foreign mission in his life. The Germans had to overcome two major obstacles to German unification and the restoration of full sovereignty: the securing of Soviet agreement to its NATO membership, and renunciation of the wartime Allies' rights in Germany. The two were connected. Winning Soviet agreement to them would clear the way for treaties with Bonn's Western allies as well.

When Kohl's party landed in Moscow, Foreign Minister Shevardnadze was at the airport to greet them. Horst Teltschick, Kohl's foreign policy adviser, felt his welcome to be extraordinarily warm. The welcome made Kohl confident that the visit would go well.[5] Meeting Gorbachev the following day in a turn-of-the-century neo-Gothic mansion belonging to a wealthy pre-revolutionary businessman, they found the Soviet leader friendly and earnest.[6] As an opening Kohl referred to a saying by Bismarck that one must seize the mantle of history, thus emphasizing the historic opportunity the two leaders faced. Seeking an emotional common bond, he then reminded Gorbachev that they both belonged to the generation which had been affected by the Second World War, yet were too young to feel guilt. With their common experiences, they should make the most of their chance.

Agreeing with Kohl's words, Gorbachev picked up and developed the same theme. Emphasizing the importance of rebuilding closer German–Russian relations, he equated their importance with the relations between the Soviet Union and the United States. In return, Kohl promised to conclude an extensive agreement of co-operation with the Soviet Union, subject to solution of the existing problems. He also reminded him that all the efforts towards financial and economic co-operation, referring to the EC, NATO and Group of Seven summits, were part of a general package or solution to the German question. To buttress his case, he also described the rapidly deteriorating economic situation in the DDR. Gorbachev could empathize with this and quipped that Kohl was living through his own *perestroika*, adding that therefore there should be mutual help.

Keeping his eyes on the essentials, Kohl then proceeded to outline what still needed to be accomplished to keep on track and to the planned timetable. He listed the settlement on Soviet troop withdrawals from the DDR, united Germany's NATO membership, and future limitations on its armed forces. The end result had to be a fully sovereign Germany.[7] How the one-sided troop limitations accorded with full German sovereignty remained unexplored.

Gorbachev then complimented Kohl for influencing Bush to pursue better relations with the Soviet Union. Kohl in turn emphasized the importance of no suspicions emerging in Washington concerning the German–Soviet relationship. It had to be made clear that good German–Soviet relations were also in the American interest.[8] This was the other side of the coin to the earlier, often-repeated Western assurances to Gorbachev that a united Germany's membership of NATO was also to the advantage of the Soviet Union. Gorbachev also expressed his appreciation of the direction NATO was moving, referring to the reassuring and soothing sounds emitted at the NATO London summit about co-operation with the Soviet Union and no longer regarding it as an adversary.[9]

Then he followed up with the decisive concessions. After expressing his assumption that the reunited Germany would be confined within the existing West and East German borders and of Germany's renunciation of nuclear, biological and chemical weapons, he reached the heart of the matter. NATO's military structure was not to be extended to DDR territory, a transition period of three to four years was needed for Soviet troop withdrawal and, to Kohl's direct question, he expressed agreement with united Germany's full sovereignty. He accepted its NATO membership with the restriction on East Germany, and the end of the wartime Allies' rights and responsibilities in Germany without a transition period after the conclusion of the two-plus-four talks. For the withdrawal of Soviet troops, he wanted a separate treaty.

Kohl repeated Gorbachev's comments to make sure that there had been no misunderstanding.[10] It was a historic breakthrough. Gorbachev had provided the solution to the remaining obstacles to final German reunification.

Gorbachev afterwards expressed his appreciation for the five billion credit guarantees from Bonn. 'This master stroke had come at the right moment. He valued this step ... therefore very highly.'[11] It was a telling comment. Hearing it, Kohl must have felt pleased that he had followed his instincts by responding immediately and positively to Gorbachev's requests some two months earlier. It had paid off handsomely.

Economic and financial matters in fact occupied a crucial role in the talks and the emerging settlement between Bonn and Moscow. Bonn's Finance Minister Waigel had a large role in the Moscow talks, and Gorbachev also emphasized the importance of economic co-operation and trade to Soviet–German relations at the press conference following the first stage of his talks with Kohl. He underlined his expectations of their future importance by stressing that the Bundesrepublik had been the largest Western and the DDR the largest Eastern trading partner of the Soviet Union.[12] Waigel's talks with his Soviet counterparts dealt with potential extensive aid programmes both directly by Bonn or via the International Monetary Fund where Bonn carried increased weight. They also involved guarantees for long-term German–Russian trade contracts as well as the costs associated with the withdrawal of Soviet troops from the DDR and their relocation in the Soviet Union. These would come on top of the costs to which Bonn had already earlier agreed covering the upkeep of these troops after monetary union, including providing Deutschmarks for their wages.

After their first day of talks in Moscow, Gorbachev and Kohl headed southwards to Stavropol and the Caucasus. They had both exuded *bonhomie* at the press conference and, while assuring everyone that their talks were going well, they did not fully reveal how well. Many details, of course, still remained to be settled or, as Gorbachev put it in concrete terms, 'We have got a few small nuts to crack, but we have got very good teeth. We will crack them.'[13] It was a fitting comment from the man who had been said to have iron teeth.

Much of what remained to be settled would be tackled in a serene environment in the high mountains of the Caucasus. After landing at Stavropol, Gorbachev's home town during his many years as the first secretary of the Communist Party in the region, where they had a friendly encounter with Soviet war veterans, they continued their journey to a mountain resort. They arrived at sunset in the midst of a beautiful flowery meadow surrounded by snowcapped mountains. Wading into the meadow, Raisa Gorbachev picked a few of the flowers and smilingly handed them to Kohl.[14] It was a charming gesture which said a great deal.

Kohl's and Gorbachev's talks continued in an informal atmosphere and setting. Interspersed with walks and strolls, their talks progressed well and in a good mood. Reiterating their aims and conditions, and the agreements from Moscow, they plunged into greater detail, engaging in some bargaining and explaining more their reasoning and thinking. While agreeing that a fully sovereign Germany could choose her own alliances, including NATO, Gorbachev did not want NATO mentioned specifically in a treaty. This, together with the exclusion of NATO troops from eastern Germany as long as Soviet troops remained there, would help to gain acceptance among his compatriots for united Germany's NATO membership. Shevardnadze also specified that, after the Soviet troop withdrawal, NATO structure and in particular nuclear weapons should not be placed in former DDR territory against Soviet wishes.[15]

There seemed to be some discrepancy in the views or lack of co-ordination between the two Soviet leaders, as in some of their past pronouncements on the German question, with Gorbachev being more agreeable to the Germans than Shevardnadze. This was evident when Gorbachev reiterated that both its NATO membership and the extension of the NATO area into eastern Germany after the Soviet troop departure was the business of Germany alone. Yet he did not want it on paper. The Soviet Union assumed, however, that nuclear weapons were not to be introduced there and that its security was not reduced. The troops of a unified Germany could, however, be stationed in eastern Germany.

There was further agreement on the stationing of allied troops in Berlin until the Soviet departure. Gorbachev also agreed to Genscher's comment about the extension of NATO security guarantees to cover eastern Germany after unification. German troops could be stationed there before the departure of the Soviet troops although they should not be integrated with NATO forces. After the Soviet withdrawal they could be put under its command.

Some bargaining followed concerning the duration and costs of Soviet troop withdrawal and the limitations on future German armed forces. Gorbachev now wanted a five- to seven-year timetable for the withdrawal, while Kohl thought that three to four years would be sufficient. Kohl prevailed, promising support, retraining and housing for the troops. Gorbachev justified the support for the Soviet troops as preventing restlessness among the soldiers which could spread to the whole army.[16] He may have been worried over its impact on his own future position, but raising the issue also served the purpose of obtaining more money from the Germans.

While the withdrawal of Soviet troops and the restoration of a fully sovereign Germany was of the utmost importance to the Germans, the economic and financial returns for their agreement loomed as obviously high on the Soviet leaders' list. Going beyond the German assumption of the DDR's economic and financial obligations to the Soviet Union (and they had been many), Gorbachev, as ever a skilful salesman, held out the promise of glowing economic opportunities for the Germans in the Soviet Union. Kohl sought to reassure him with promises of new levels of co-operation and pointed out his record of efforts to gain wider international support for Gorbachev's reform policies than the Germans alone could provide. Becoming more specific, Gorbachev also brought up the matter of Soviet real estate in the DDR, for which he wanted compensation.

On the question of German troop limitation, Shevardnadze mentioned the figure of 350,000. The Germans were prepared to come down to 370,000 men within four years. Genscher connected the reduction with general progress on the disarmament talks taking place in Vienna, trying to avoid the singling out of Germany, and Kohl tied it to the withdrawal of Soviet troops from eastern Germany. Gorbachev had previously asked Kohl during their flight south how far Kohl would go and received the figure of 370,000 as an answer. Saying he had expected more, he nevertheless accepted Kohl's figure.[17] It was far above the original 200,000 to 250,000 men the Soviets had mentioned earlier, yet it still represented a substantial reduction from previous levels of combined German armed strength as well as from the then existing West German forces of 480,000. Finally, Gorbachev also agreed to Kohl's request to see to the situation of the Soviet Germans.[18]

At the ensuing press conference, confronting curious and anxious journalists who had been waiting impatiently for a historic news story, Kohl and

Gorbachev gave the principal results of their talks. Visibly pleased and all smiles, Kohl stressed their historic significance not only for Germany and the Soviet Union but for Europe as a whole. Gorbachev sounded somewhat defensive. Stressing the preceding summit meetings' and notably the NATO summit's significance to the outcome, he also said: 'Whether we like it or not the time will come when a united Germany will be in NATO if that is its choice.' He also added that the Soviet Union could not deny the Germans what others were conceding to it.[19]

The tenuousness of Gorbachev's hold on the Soviet Union was graphically displayed the very same day with the Ukraine's simultaneous formal declaration of its sovereignty.[20] It served as a reminder of the many pressures under which Gorbachev was operating. As indicated by his and Kohl's demeanour on television at their first encounter in Moscow and by his exceptional hospitality, he rather than Kohl appeared to be seeking favour. Whereas Kohl had appeared confident, the normally self-confident Gorbachev had seemed uncertain. Both their postures and facial expressions had signalled their mood when facing the bargaining that lay ahead.[21] Kohl probably felt that German unification was by then unstoppable and only the bill for it had to be settled. Gorbachev was under pressure to extract as much as he could from Kohl not only because of immediate economic and financial needs but because he was being accused of giving up the fruits of the Soviet victory in the Second World War. He was fighting not just to save face against accusations of selling out but for his job and, indeed, his political future.

Yet when he relinquished East Germany, Gorbachev was not really giving up anything concrete that was not already lost or of little remaining value to the Soviet Union. After its loss of control over Poland and Czechoslovakia, its troops in East Germany had in fact become a potentially vulnerable hostage to the West and, as such, a liability. The practical reality was not the only thing that mattered, however. In history and politics symbolism also has its role and, as a primary trophy and symbol of Soviet power resulting from the victory in the Second World War, East Germany had great value and its loss hurt Soviet pride. Appearances also mattered.

In agreeing to extensive economic co-operation and a build-up of trade with the Soviet Union, the Germans were making no sacrifices in the long run. Rather, besides securing German unification, it was an investment in a potentially massive future market for their products.[22] It was a means of ensuring that Germany's already clear lead in the vast Russian markets would not only continue but grow in the future.

The Germans felt euphoric after the breakthrough in the Caucasus. Kohl received congratulations from world leaders and lesser notables, from the Nazi-hunter Simon Wiesenthal to Prince Louis Ferdinand of Prussia. Bush was impressed and complimented him for outstanding leadership and excellent results.[23] The German press greeted him as a conquering hero.[24]

Not everyone shared that enthusiasm. Although both Kohl and Gorbachev had given assurances that German–Soviet co-operation was not aimed against any other country, guarded nervousness initially coloured many reactions. There were hurried and often vague recollections of earlier occasions when the Germans and the Russians had drawn together, such as the Rapallo treaty of 1922 and even the Nazi–Soviet pact of August 1939 which triggered first the German and then the Soviet invasion of Poland and the Second World War.

Such recollections were enough to make some suspect the worst, yet the precedents hardly warranted or justified the fears. At Rapallo two alienated and ostracized outsiders in the then international community had allied themselves for mutual self-help. The image did not apply to or fit Germany and the Soviet Union in 1990, and neither did the Nazi–Soviet pact; Kohl was no Hitler and Gorbachev no Stalin.

Fears are nevertheless often beyond the realm of reason. Outwardly, official reactions in other countries were polite and sometimes even sounded enthusiastic, but this often hid a deep uneasiness. To some a new power axis seemed to be emerging connecting Germany and Russia, and this would require adjustment from others. Apprehension about this was wide spread.

What mattered most, however, were the reactions of the United States, France and Britain because of their greater weight and power. Washington, London and Paris felt left out of the limelight. The Kohl–Gorbachev deal had reduced the remaining two-plus-four negotiations and meetings to a sideshow; Western leaders first learned about the historic breakthrough from the media, which certainly did not please them. Clearly a new era was beginning with German unification and the Soviet retreat from Central Europe. This alone caused uneasiness and even foreboding, but for those who were accustomed to be the prime players and to perform the main roles, to be left out of the spotlight at such a time intensified their unease. It was hard to be denied real participation at such a turning-point in post-war history.

When the two-plus-four talks convened in Paris on the heels of the Caucasus meeting, the participants were largely reduced to simply registering things that had already been agreed. The remaining issue was the German–Polish border. The Germans felt some bitterness about the final renunciation of territories which amounted to roughly a quarter of pre-war Germany but accepted it as the inevitable price of their unity.[25]

Prepared to pay that price, they were incensed at the Polish demand that the wartime Allies retain their rights in Germany until a unified Germany recognized the existing German–Polish boundary. By insisting on it, the

Poles expressed their suspicions regarding the dependability of the resolutions and pledges of the parliaments and governments of both German states to accept the permanency of the border. The Germans thought that it amounted to undermining the foundations of future co-operation between the neighbours.[26] In the end an agreement was reached that the German government would sign a border treaty with Poland immediately after unification. The Germans also promised economic help to the Poles.[27]

The bills were mounting for the Germans over their unification. Anxiety was growing in the DDR as its economy continued to decline and dissolve at a dramatic rate. Some 224,000 lost their jobs during the first two weeks following monetary and economic union, and 30,000 to 40,000 shared their fate each week. In addition, some half a million had only part-time work by the second half of July. This forced Bonn to quickly pump additional money into East Germany.[28]

The growing East German anxiety emerged in increasing demonstrations and short strikes. The strikers knew that they received half or a third of the corresponding West German wages and at the same time were confronting rapidly increasing living costs. Unemployment hit women especially hard, and among some a feeling of having been deceived and treated unfairly was spreading. Women in particular were also upset over the closing of some social services, such as kindergartens, which added to their burdens.[29]

In part the East Germans were themselves directly responsible for their plight as they preferred to buy West German products to their own goods, including basic foods. This accelerated the drying up of even the local markets, further lowered production, and threw increasing numbers of people out of work. Yet people wanted Western cars and gadgets as well as Western clothes and equipment. Western chains and wholesalers also at times insisted on exclusively providing their own products to their East German outlets, thus shutting out the local products. When East German products could compete neither at home nor abroad, for often they could not immediately meet Western specifications, the East German economy inevitably disintegrated rapidly.

The disintegration was taking place faster and going much further than earlier calculations had predicted. By the end of August the unemployed had passed the 400,000 level and the figure continued to rise at the rate of some 25,000 per week. Another million or so had only part-time or no work although still classified as employed.[30] Since unemployment was a new experience to most East Germans, they were ill prepared to cope with their new situation.

In the midst of this economic malaise, Reiner Gohlke, the man in charge of the economic reforms in the DDR, resigned for lack of adequate Western investment and because of former Communist officials' resistance to reforms.[31] This contributed to growing scepticism about the DDR government's ability to carry out the necessary economic reforms.

Adding to the heightening sense of a deep crisis in the DDR was the break-up of its ruling coalition. Together with the increasing and intensifying economic chaos, it led to moves to further speed up reunification. The Volkskammer, the DDR parliament, voted by an overwhelming majority of 294 to 62 on 23 August for German reunification to take place on 3 October 1990. The vote reflected growing public pressure (recent polls showed an even clearly higher share, nine out of ten) for speedy reunification. Responding warmly to the vote, Kohl spoke of a day of joy for all Germans. He stressed how unification had occurred 'without war, without blood, in full unanimity' with Germany's partners in East and West, calling it unique in contemporary history.[32]

The vote brought a sigh of relief from the Germans. Many thought it would encourage investment and eventually relieve unemployment in East Germany. Quick unification was believed to be the best guarantee of narrowing and then closing the gap between the West and East Germans' standard of living.[33]

One sizable group of East Germans, however, did not, and did not have reason to, look to their personal future with such optimism. These were the many officials of the DDR, some 1.6 million strong, Stasi collaborators and informers, administrators for the old Communist rulers. Many of them would be deprived of their jobs and they could start to empty their desk drawers. Even those kept on would only be on probation. This meant that they faced an uncertain future. To join the ever growing ranks of the unemployed would be a new experience for them.

Others who looked forward to a future full of uncertainty were Soviet soldiers and their dependants stationed in the DDR. Pressures were building up among the East Germans to get rid of these unwanted guests sooner rather than later. Graffiti demanding 'Russen raus', Russians out, were appearing and the Russians were meeting with increasingly chilly treatment by local people. The East Germans were venting long-pent-up emotions of resentment for the past high-handedness of the Soviets.[34]

The Soviet troops were rapidly becoming demoralized. Not only were they facing local hostility but they were becoming increasingly conscious of the ideological and economic defeat that their homeland had suffered in the long rivalry and struggle with the West. All around them people were rejecting Communism and its symbols with gusto and the shops were newly flooded with goods of variety and quality not available in the Soviet Union. Facing departure from this 'chocolate-land', as they revealingly called it, they could not even be sure of a roof over their heads upon their eventual return to the motherland, because of housing shortage and competition from other returning troops and their dependants.

The Soviet troops' unhappiness was a growing concern to Gorbachev. Passing the word to Bonn that their withdrawal would take at least five to seven years, Shevardnadze reminded the German government that the withdrawals were tied to German help and complained that it was inadequate. Threatening to slow down the withdrawals, he made other demands concerning security and economic, scientific and technical co-operation between Germany and the Soviet Union.

To spur on the Germans, the Kremlin also conveyed a message that the situation in the Soviet Union was acute and the leadership at a critical juncture. Support for the Soviet troops was essential as otherwise a military revolt could not be excluded in the absence of means for new housing, transport costs and subsistence in the DDR. Kohl decided to be forthcoming as regards Soviet requests for housing but tough on support for the troops. This could both provide a carrot for the troops to leave and a stick to discourage them from lingering in Germany. He also prepared to provide food from the DDR for the Soviet needs worth some one billion Deutschmarks.

These measures did not settle the matter, however, and some tough bargaining over money lay ahead. The Soviets presented a bill in some detail for the Deutschmarks they hoped to collect. They wanted 3.5 billion for troop support over four years, 3 billion for transport, 11.5 billion for new housing, kindergartens, shops and new infrastructure, 500 million for retraining, and 17 to 17.5 billion for the Soviet real estate in the DDR. It was quite a bill and came on top of a telephone request by Bush to Kohl for German financial help to cover the costs of the Kuwait crisis.

Kohl personally called Gorbachev and offered him a total package of 8 billion for the troop withdrawal. The Soviet leader reacted toughly, rejecting the offer as not nearly enough, but showed some flexibility. He wanted 11 billion alone for housing and infrastructure. When the troops' transport and support costs were added, the sum would be substantially higher. Without a financial solution the two-plus-four treaty was endangered, he said. Facing the unmistakable underlying threat, Kohl sought to lighten the tone by saying that, with good will on both sides, a solution could be found, while Gorbachev called the situation alarming. Kohl then suggested that they should both think it over during the weekend.

The game was now approaching its end, as the two-plus-four representatives were supposed to meet in Moscow on 12 September to sign the treaty of German reunification. Two days before that, Kohl again called Gorbachev. Now he offered a total of 11–12 billion. Saying that he did not want to haggle, Gorbachev asked for 15–16 billion. Neither did he, said Kohl, and referred to the other good things to come through joint Western efforts. Gorbachev then described the internal pressures he was under and stuck to the 15 billion figure, saying that since it could not be met almost everything had to be thought over. At that time Kohl threw in another 3 billion in interest-free credits.[35]

It did the trick. The bargaining over the money had been tougher than had the amiable meeting in the Caucasus, perhaps because of additional as well as renewed domestic pressures on Gorbachev. Both leaders declared their unwillingness to haggle but haggle they did and rightly so, as it was their duty as national leaders to look after the interests of their people and the stakes were high.

The settling of the issue between Kohl and Gorbachev cleared the way for the signing of the Treaty on Final Arrangements in Relation to Germany. Although not in name, it was in practice a peace treaty. It re-established full German sovereignty with the end of the wartime Allies' rights, deriving from their defeat and occupation of Germany almost half a century earlier. It had been a long wait for the Germans. They were, however, to be rattled by a last-minute hitch. This time the British held back. They baulked at signing the treaty, insisting upon rights of manoeuvre on East German territory which the treaty denied. Informed about the British demand, Shevardnadze passed the word that 'there would be no treaty' if they persisted, and the angry Germans were reminded of the Ridley affair. Eventually the British backed down, clearing the way.[36]

The final signing of the treaty on 12 September 1990 called for some speech-making. Perhaps the most apt comment was made by Shevardnadze, who said: 'We cannot continue to live in the past. We have to think about the future.'[37] Indeed, the new treaty clearly marked the closing of one era and the beginning of another in the long history of Europe.[38] In a sense it marked the end of the tragedy-filled twentieth century and the dawn of the twenty-first century.

It was accompanied the next day by the initialling of a German–Soviet treaty of broad co-operation. Including pledges of non-aggression against each other and annual summits, expanded trade and investment, and scientific and technical co-operation, it helped Gorbachev and Shevardnadze to sell the settlement with Germany for ratification to the partly reluctant and hostile Supreme Soviet.[39]

After the final clearance of the remaining obstacles on the path of German reunification and the restoration of its full sovereignty, a scramble to adjust to the new reality ensued. Bonn increasingly became a point of attraction to foreign delegations and visitors seeking contact with this rising centre of influence and power. For the future of Europe and in particular the EC, relations between Bonn and Paris remained the most critical. While asking Kohl permission for French troops to remain in Germany, and eager for continuing Franco–German co-operation towards an economic, monetary and political union of Europe, Mitterrand tried to make amends for the past year. In accordance with his European policy, Kohl wisely reassured him on his concerns.[40]

Behind these concerns lay an apprehension that German reunification would result in profound changes in the general mood and perceptions in Europe. The waning Soviet threat and the withdrawal of Soviet troops (and in time probably the Americans as well) from Germany could weaken the ties of cohesion in Western Europe which had originally been a response to the challenge from Moscow.

With the common enemy and shared fears gone, alliances often fall apart. Would this happen again? Would it lead in turn to an increasing emphasis on national interests at the expense of the common good and, especially in Germany, to a preoccupation with the challenging task of internal reconstruction and healing of wounds? Such questions hung in the air and were anxiously aired and discussed in many places in the face of German reunification.

After the initial clear majority of popular support in France for German reunification immediately after the fall of the Berlin Wall, second thoughts had at times come to the fore. Whereas in January 61 per cent of the French had supported and 15 per cent opposed German unity, a poll published just before reunification indicated that 37 per cent welcomed it while 27 per cent felt uneasy about it. Yet another poll taken a little after reunification found 58 per cent were for and only 9 per cent were against it, while 28 per cent were indifferent.[41] The polls could vary considerably, depending upon their timing and the exact wording of the questions, among other things. An endless debate had been carried out on the issue for months in the media, bombarding the public with worried messages. Typical was the question posed by *Le Figaro*, a conservative paper, just before reunification. It read: 'Should we be afraid of Germany?'[42] No matter how such questions were treated and answered they obviously contributed to public uneasiness.

Yet the French public still remained clearly less alarmed and more positive about a unified Germany than many members of their élite which was more preoccupied with national status and power. Trained to stress the rational, they could not get away from the evidence of the statistics which gave united Germany an overwhelming lead over France in those matters which could be so measured. The one increasingly questionable exception in terms of its actual value was the French nuclear arsenal.

In Britain a somewhat similar gap persisted between the broader public and segments of the élite, although there also mass readers of the tabloid newspapers endorsed the gut feelings of the élite doubters. Historical memories, traditional prejudices and new fears united them. Feelings of being overrun and ignored in the German unification process angered some leaders. Even the German emphasis on the connection between their national and European unification annoyed rather than reassured those who opposed further European integration. Yet much of the leading British media stressed repeatedly how different contemporary democratic Germany was from the enemy of the past, and a clear majority of the British accepted German unity.[43]

The Americans had offered the most consistent and strongest support to the Germans' pursuit of unity and had least trepidation about it. Yet preoccupation with the Kuwait crisis was leading to resentment in Washington concerning the level of German support for the American efforts there against Iraq, although there was some recognition of the heavy German obligations to the Soviet Union and internal reconstruction. The broader American public continued to favour German reunification. Just before it was formalized, an ABC News telephone poll indicated that 80 per cent of Americans supported it and 79 per cent saw in Germany no threat. Even among the over 65 age group of the Second World War generation, eight out of ten approved. Many German Americans were very pleased, while many Jews were apprehensive.

Although, of the major powers, the Soviet Union had most vocally opposed German reunification, it looked forward to future co-operation. Seeing in Germany its main Western trading partner and source of help and investment, its leaders and spokesmen referred to this former deadly enemy as a partner and even ally.[44] Polls taken in Moscow indicated that the Muscovites favoured by a 50 to 30 majority the unification process.[45] In fact, the Russian overtures were causing some nervousness in Bonn concerning its ability to fulfil all the expectations.

Sharing borders with both Germany and the Soviet Union, the Poles felt uncomfortably caught in between the German–Russian bear hug. Of all Europeans they were least well disposed to or comfortable with German reunification, the reasons involving both historical and current anxieties. The Poles were understandably keenly anxious over the Kohl–Gorbachev deal, as historically they had many a time ended up paying the bill for a German–Russian understanding.

For the future relations between the Germans and their allies and neighbours, not only were the allies' and neighbours' attitudes towards German reunification important, but the Germans' perceptions of them were as well. Polls conducted among Germans around the time of reunification give some interesting clues.

The West and East Germans were asked separately about their allies' and neighbours' stand on unification. For the most part their perceptions were similar but differed clearly on the English and the Poles. Both agreed that the Americans were by far most in favour and least opposed to German reunification while at the opposite end were the Poles, and to lesser degree the English.

While agreeing that a clear majority of the Americans, the French and the Soviets were for reunification, the West Germans thought that almost as many of the English were against as for it, but the East Germans clearly thought that more were for than against. The West Germans believed that a higher proportion of Poles than the English were for reunification, but the East Germans thought that only among the Poles was a clear majority opposed to it. The extremities of the estimates varied from the West German perception of 74 per cent of Americans favouring and the East German perception of 60 per cent of the Poles being against reunification.[46]

The Germans were quite naturally mainly concerned with their internal unification, and all the more so when the outside obstacles fell by the wayside. Yet their mood was not the same as when the wall came down. The party could not last for ever and the initial great wave of joy had become mixed increasingly with anxiety about costs and jobs. Monday morning had followed the weekend partying and celebrations. The very physical contrast between East and West Germany remained stark. The drab gloom of East Germany struck one continually as another world from the well-kept and tidy West.

It was not just the physical contrast between the two which was striking; the difference was in mentality as well. The distance between the more open and enterprising West Germans and the grimness of many in the East, the lingering 'Verboten' mentality with all its authoritarianism and submissiveness, caused tension. It could not be easily or quickly resolved as it involved two long, separate journeys through time. The different experiences of two generations during close to a half a century, and the marks they had left, could not be wiped out or be overcome easily. The pressures to adjust fell lopsidedly on the East Germans, putting them at a distinct disadvantage and under much greater strain, and as a result the tension and its symptoms were far greater among them.

The West Germans often treated their poorer eastern cousins as somewhat embarrassing, unsophisticated poor relatives. They bemoaned the inefficiencies and technical backwardness of the eastern firms and institutions. They complained about the rundown, dilapidated, and unkept buildings and the lack of modern communications. Some behaved like colonial masters among the natives they had come to tutor and train, and a few concluded that the East Germans were somehow inherently less capable and unable to manage and work effectively.

The East Germans resented being made to feel second class. Very few among them missed the DDR but uncertainty and tension clouded their joy over reunification. They were happy to be free, free to travel and to speak their mind, but their uncertainty over their economic future prevented them from taking full advantage of the new freedom. They were hurt by westerners looking down on them and telling them how to run their affairs. Many saw the westerners who descended upon them as sharpers and sharks who were out to exploit and trick them because of their inexperience with the workings of the market.

Many westerners went to the east motivated by a genuine desire to help. They brought much-needed skills and knowledge, helping to educate and train the easterners in the new ways and techniques of doing things. Often they had eastern roots which could add to their understanding and intensify their empathy with the people and problems of the east. The easterners sometimes found it easier to accept and welcome them and they became important bridge-builders across the gap that separated the two parts of Germany.[47]

Although they recognized the inferiority of their living standards and environmental and health conditions, as well as their levels of science and technology, education and vocational training, the majority of the easterners felt they had also been better off in some ways. A clear majority believed that they had had greater equality between men and women as well as more protection against crime and more social security,[48] but in the new conditions they faced this offered scant comfort.

They were somewhat in the position of children or immigrants in a new land or strangers in their own land in the sense that they had many new things to learn to be able to fully function in their new society. The challenges they faced were not easy to overcome. While many would eventually find and gain what they had been hoping and looking for in unification, others were destined to be gravely disappointed.

Like immigrants they discovered that their customary ways of doing things were no longer adequate or even acceptable. Much of what they had learned in their past lives had little relevance or use in the present and the future. They had to meet problems they had never faced before and which often bewildered them. They came across and had to cope with new customs and behaviour, a new value system and institutions, laws and regulations and commercial practices, which often differed dramatically from what they were used to and knew. The very novelty and strangeness of the new options available made every act or choice seem critically important, which added to the tension and strain. In short, many easterners were experiencing a culture shock. No wonder their self-esteem was severely tested and that they felt less self-confident and more easily discouraged, more helpless and anxious than the westerners in the new conditions of a united Germany.[49]

They also, of course, had very real material reasons to feel the way they did. Sharp contrasts existed between the easterners and the westerners concerning both the levels of unemployment and perceptions of their job security. Unlike the western stereotypes of them, however, the easterners displayed a greater willingness than the westerners to regard their lives as challenges into which they were prepared to put a great deal of effort. In contrast, twice as many westerners as easterners were willing to settle back and enjoy their lives, troubling themselves no more than was necessary.[50]

The easterners wanted to be neither drones nor drudges. By far the most important matters in their lives were love and family happiness, followed by speaking their minds openly and honestly.[51] The strength of the urge to speak freely was a telling testimony to the inner forces and drive which had led them to successfully challenge the repression they had lived under, and it put to shame those who had mocked their thirst for freedom as a hunger after bananas and Deutschmarks.

Despite the many differences between them and the resulting tensions, most Germans welcomed reunification. Older people generally greeted it as a natural coming together of the two parts of the nation, the division of which had always been utterly artificial to them. Polls conducted among the Germans shortly before reunification on 3 October indicated greater joy over it among the easterners. Only 12 per cent of them were negative about it, in comparison to 25 per cent among the westerners. In line with this, a higher proportion of the easterners were also more optimistic about their prospects of catching up with the westerners.[52]

Whatever their worries and expectations most Germans joined wholeheartedly in the celebrations of national unification starting on 3 October and continuing for many through the night and the next day. On the eve of the celebrations, Helmut Kohl addressed his compatriots on television. He spoke of a dream which had become reality and how the moment was one of the happiest of his life. Thanking the people of the DDR who had made reunification possible, he also expressed his appreciation of the United States and above all President Bush, as well as friends in France and Britain and reformers in Hungary, Poland and Czechoslovakia, and President Gorbachev, without whom unification would not have been possible on that date. He also appealed for solidarity among the Germans to overcome the difficulties which he warned lay ahead.[53]

Unlike the creation of the German empire 120 years earlier, German reunification was not celebrated with displays of military power. Instead, it was accompanied by music, singing, dancing, fireworks, and with the ringing of church bells and solemn services. These were ceremonies which should have been reassuring to watchful neighbours, nervous over signs of aggressive German nationalism. The festivities centred on the floodlit

Reichstag building in the heart of Berlin, around which enormous, happy crowds milled in high spirits. They were entertained by folk and classical music from the great German musical tradition, including pieces by Bach, Beethoven, Brahms and Mendelssohn, conducted appropriately by Kurt Masur, representing the people of Leipzig.

The crowd greeted the arrival of Kohl as the first chancellor of reunited Germany with waves and cheers and calls of 'Helmut' and a sea of black, red and gold German flags. At midnight, when reunification was officially proclaimed, Kohl, the German President Richard von Weizsäcker, and former Chancellor Willy Brandt among other leaders joined the crowd in the singing of the national anthem while a huge floodlit German flag rose towards the sky. It was during this moment that people seemed most overcome with emotion. Most Germans, from their leaders to the ordinary people, were moved by experiencing the realization of what had long been a mere dream to many.

In contrast, a few thousand leftists staged counter-demonstrations against reunification, engaging in rock throwing, window smashing and the tearing down of German flags. Whatever little impact they might have had was nullified by a series of earlier revelations of co-operation between leftist West German terrorists responsible for notorious assassinations and the universally despised Stasi. The not uncommon view was that the leftist demonstrators resorting to violence and the terrorists were kindred souls mainly motivated by resentment and hatred. Their actions were counter-productive in that they merely offended, but gained no sympathy from, most of those few who took any notice of them at all in the midst of their own celebrations of German unity.

Notes

1 Dieter Vogel, Reuters, 29 June 1990.
2 Genscher, in *Die Welt*, 29 June 1990.
3 Teltschick, 1991, p. 316.
4 Ibid.
5 Ibid., pp. 318–19.
6 Klein, *Es begann im Kaukasus*, 1991, provides detailed accounts and apt observations of the physical settings and atmosphere of the German–Soviet talks.
7 Teltschick, 1991, pp. 319–20. Teltschick's diary offers the only available detailed account of these historic talks.
8 Ibid., p. 322.
9 Ibid.
10 Ibid., pp. 323–4.
11 Ibid., p. 325
12 *FAZ*, *SZ* and *Die Welt*, 16 July 1990.

13 Gorbachev, in *IHTr*, 16 July 1990.
14 Teltschick, 1991, pp. 329–30.
15 Ibid., pp. 333–5.
16 Ibid., pp. 335–6.
17 Ibid., pp. 336–8.
18 Klein, *Es begann im Kaukasus*, 1991, pp. 259–60.
19 A full description and the text of the press conference appears in Klein, 1991, pp. 269–86, 303–23; Gorbachev, in the *Financial Times* and the *Wall Street Journal (Europe)*, 17 July 1990.
20 *IHTr*, 18 July 1990.
21 German television, 15 July 1990.
22 Robert Gerald Livingston, in *IHTr*, 16 July 1990.
23 Teltschick, 1991, p. 343.
24 See, e.g., *Bild Zeitung*, *FAZ* and *Die Welt*, 17 June 1990.
25 See, e.g., *Der Tagesspiegel*, 18 July 1990.
26 See, e.g., Bernt Conrad, in *Die Welt*, 19 July 1990.
27 *FAZ* and *SZ*, 18 July 1990.
28 ADN, 19 July 1990.
29 Gertrude Schaffner Goldberg, 'Women on the verge: winners and losers in German unification', *Social Policy*, Fall, 1991, pp. 34–44.
30 Ibid., 1 Sept. 1990.
31 *Bild Zeitung*, 20 Aug. 1990.
32 *FAZ, IHTr, SZ* and *Die Welt*, 24 Aug. 1990.
33 Ibid.
34 Impressions from East Germany, summer 1990.
35 For this bargaining process, see Teltschick, 1991, pp. 352–5, 358, 360–62.
36 Shevardnadze, *The Future belongs to Freedom*, 1991, pp. 146–7; *Der Spiegel*, 17 Sept. 1990, pp. 19–20.
37 Shevardnadze, in *NYT*, 13 Sept. 1990.
38 Treaty of the Final Settlement with Respect to Germany, 12 September 1990, *Documents of German Unity*, 1990.
39 317–1 'Treaty on good neighbourliness, partnership and co-operation between the Federal Republic of Germany and the Union of Soviet Socialist Republics', 13 Sept. 1990, *Bulletin, Presse- und Informationsamt der Bundesregierung*. 133/1900.
40 Teltschick, 1991, pp. 367–9; *SZ* and *Le Monde*, 19 Sept. 1990.
41 *The Economist*, 27 Jan. 1991; *Le Figaro*, 1 Oct. 1990; *Spiegel Spezial*, I, 1991, p. 27.
42 *Le Figaro*, 1 Oct. 1990.
43 Cf. *The Economist*, *Financial Times* and *The Independent*.
44 Shevardnadze, in *Newsweek*, 8 Oct. 1990.
45 *Spiegel Spezial*, I, 1991, p. 24.
46 Ibid., p. 25.
47 Impressions from East Germany in 1990 and 1991.
48 See, e.g., the statistics in *Spiegel Spezial*, I, 1991, p. 46.
49 Ibid., pp. 66, 68, 70–71.
50 Ibid., pp. 58–9, 69.
51 Ibid., p. 67. These were 'very important' to respectively 85 and 70 per cent of the East Germans, while having a job where one could earn much money was 'very important' to only 29 per cent.
52 *Spiegel Spezial*, I, 1991, pp. 21, 23, 80.
53 Kohl, on German television, 2 Oct. 1990.

16 Epilogue

Growing ties between the two Germanies and a certain revival of a sense and reassertion of German national identity had preceded reunification during the 1980s. These were due to no small extent to a German determination not to become the main victims in a possible conflict between the United States and the Soviet Union. Such fears, connected with the missile crises, led to efforts in both Germanies to loosen their dependencies upon the two superpowers.

This in turn became possible with their relative weakening. Far more pronounced in the case of the Soviet Union, it brought internal Soviet reforms under Gorbachev. It also resulted in the Soviet withdrawal from the war in Afghanistan after a decade-long but futile effort to dominate that country, the last four years of it under Gorbachev's aegis. This concrete double example of the Soviet loss of both ability and will to maintain the old order internally and imperialist domination abroad did not escape notice. The people who lived against their will under Soviet domination in Europe, including the East Germans, drew their conclusions from both. The result was a wave of liberalization among some, followed next by liberation everywhere from the old Communist order and Soviet power.

These large international transformations and dramatic changes were also a necessary precondition and accompaniment for East German liberation and German reunification. Adding specifically to the tensions in the DDR was Honecker's unwillingness to emulate Gorbachev's reforms, to the extent of banning reformist Soviet publications from his domains. This left little hope of a compromise between the regime and the desires for a liberalizing change.

At the same time, conditions ripened inside the DDR for a fundamental internal challenge to the leadership and a subsequent transformation. There, as elsewhere in the Communist world, a basic conflict existed between the ruling ideology and reality: the preaching of utter equality and the factually prevailing strict hierarchy in the distribution of power and privilege. A self-perpetuating élite had become increasingly out of touch with the desires and mood of the masses, despite massive Stasi surveillance which seemed to drown in the very volume of the material that it gathered.

Democracy and unification promised greater political equality and equity, although they would also bring more differentiation in wealth and incomes. The sometimes bemoaned loss of equality among the East Germans as a result of the demise of the DDR overlooked fundamentals: its gross inequalities in political rights and power inherent in the utter lack of freedom and democracy. With this, basic preconditions for any true and meaningful equality or equity were missing.

Contributing to the chasm between the rulers and the ruled in the DDR was another gap. It separated illusions and false perceptions, based on lying media and statistics, from the East Germans' real mood and the reality of their standards of production and material conditions. Vastly increased East German visits to the West, typically with families left behind as hostages, added dramatically to the dissatisfaction and frustration. It reflected another gap. This was the vast difference between East and West German standards of living.

As a result of improved East and West German relations and a *rapprochement* between Kohl and Honecker, obstacles to inter-German visits were reduced in the mid-1980s. This led to a dramatic increase in East German visits to the West. The number of East German visitors leaped by roughly two million annually, until about every third East German had travelled in the West by 1988. This relatively sudden and enormous increase in first-hand exposure of the East Germans to the West hardly made them more satisfied with the conditions in the DDR. Instead, it added to their existing dissatisfaction. It immediately preceded the open eruption of demands for change in the DDR in 1989, and the connection in timing was not coincidental. Instead of reconciling the East Germans to their lot and their regime, the lowering of travel restrictions increased their appetite for more freedom and better material standards. This contributed to the events of 1989, validating some of the premises of the Ostpolitik and helping along eventual German reunification.

Yet the step from dissatisfaction and frustration to action was a long one. To defy the repressive regime with all its means of suppression and coercion took great courage; and especially so before it became clear that challenges would not be met with bullets. To some, challenging the regime meant overcoming not only physical fears but also the lingering grip of the ruling ideology on their minds. The comment of a couple from East Berlin on this was both telling and tragicomic. They said: 'Within our limits we are as angry as we can afford to be and still remain socialists.'[1]

The East Germans who braved the streets with their demands for freedom were also the main catalysts for German reunification. Eminent among them were the people of Leipzig, who set the example for others by being the first, the most consistent, and the greatest number to take the risk of defying the Communist regime. A measure of the courage demanded from the earlier demonstrations is that they were carried out with the Chinese massacre on the Square of Heavenly Peace still fresh in the memory. Ordered by the Chinese authorities against demonstrators, this terrible action received the plaudits of the DDR leaders. The early East German demonstrators had no way of knowing that their approbation would not translate into similar bloody repression in the face of a challenge. Their actions demanded bravery and solidarity.

The collective popular forces, the people on the move, their desires and determination drove the major players. The people shaped and often decided their own options and timetables. The East German popular action on a massive scale was a necessary precondition for Chancellor Kohl's and Foreign Minster Genscher's well-timed and decisive actions in the international arena. Important to their success in the international game were Bush's wish for the United States to remain a major player in Europe and Gorbachev's need of financial and economic help. Both Bush and Gorbachev saw in Germany an important partner to secure these aims and needs, and Bush's and eventually Gorbachev's willingness in turn to meet the German desire for reunification doomed any potential opposition to it to failure.

There lay an irony of history here. German reunification would be accompanied by the Soviet exit not only from eastern Germany but from the lands located between the Germans and the Russians as well. Historically long contested between the two, they were moving away from the Russian and towards the German sphere. Gorbachev had talked a great deal about the construction of a common European house, but he dealt the Soviet Union and the Russians out of many rooms of their former apartment in it without gaining access to the rest of the house as an accepted member of the club. In short, the Soviet exit from Germany may also have meant Russian withdrawal from Europe itself.

German reunification would also be accompanied by an anticipated gradual American retreat from Germany and Europe. Declining German and European needs of American military protection and diverging economic and trade interests could undermine and weaken old commitments and loyalties. Thus, Bush's actions on German unification could in the long term have results for America which were the opposite of his aim to retain a major American presence and role in Europe. Yet neither Bush nor Gorbachev may have had any realistic and viable alternative than to go along with the Germans. There was no mistaking it. Reunification did mean a major redivision of power in Europe. This was a fact. It meant the end of both American and Soviet domination of the continent. It also meant a redistribution of power among the leading nations of the European Community. United Germany gained and France and Britain lost in relative power, and this foreseeable result inevitably caused tension, anxieties, and efforts to struggle against it.

While the British and French efforts to hold back the Germans had little success, they were understandable actions of perceived national interest. In essence the British and the French leaders, Thatcher and Mitterrand, saw themselves defending their nations' and their own position and status. In their own eyes they were undoubtedly only doing their duty as the leaders of their nations. Rather than giving up without a fight, they chose to struggle. Another matter is whether they made a wise choice.

Events moved so fast that the pace alone at times made it difficult for opposition to reunification to coalesce and become organized. The quickness and ease of the collapse of the DDR caused widespread surprise, which can be explained in part by a human tendency to accept matters that have lasted a long time as more or less natural and viable, rather than hold them to be artificial and therefore fragile and vulnerable.

The DDR had existed for two generations, long enough to establish it in many minds (especially outside Germany) as a more or less regular and solid European state. This left many blind to the thinness of the ropes which held it together and how stretched and strained they had become. The Berlin Wall might have looked formidable but both the building and the opening of it were measures of desperation by a regime with no legitimacy in the eyes of the people who lived behind it and were hemmed in by it.

In the end only a small minority wanted the DDR to continue to exist, just as only a small minority felt that it had more to lose than gain from its demise and from German reunification. They made more noise and they received more attention than their small numbers warranted, because they included a disproportionate number of the articulate and the assertive. Some were mainly motivated by dreams of a third way between capitalism and communism. They wanted a society not only of equality and freedom, but also free from the excesses of the market-place. Others simply feared the loss of their privileges based on the old order and sought their perpetuation. Both were in a position to air their feelings in public forums.

What helped them to gain attention had much to do with the earlier actions of some among them and with the receptiveness of the Western media. Some had early called for reforms though without supporting the destruction of the DDR and reunification. They appealed to like-minded Western leftists who in turn secured them attention in the media. The result was an optical illusion. Some confused the frequency of views expressed in public with views actually held by the vast majority of the East German people on reunification.

What emerged was an informal alliance of views between some original East German intellectual opponents of the old order, outright Communist backers of that order, and West German leftist intellectuals who disliked the Bundesrepublik and feared that reunification would lead to the reassertion of extreme German nationalism.

The same fear, of course, had haunted many among the allies and neighbours of Germany and influenced their reactions to the reunification process. More real among them were fears of German economic and eventually political predominance. Polls conducted among the Germans gave scant basis for fears of expansive and assertive German nationalism which would seek to dominate others. In a *Der Spiegel* poll, only 23 per cent of the West Germans and 22 per cent of the East Germans favoured future German hegemony in Europe. In contrast, 43 and 60 per cent were against while 33 and 12 per cent were indifferent.[2]

Such polls provided much evidence neither of assertive German nationalism in general nor of exceptionally strong feelings of nationalism among the East Germans. Yet the latter was becoming a widely held belief.

Another poll, which asked which country the Germans admired most and wanted their own country to be like, also showed a clear aversion to becoming a dominant great power. Most Germans answered Switzerland or Sweden.[3] That they picked the prime examples and symbols of peacefulness, prosperity and egalitarianism in Europe, or the whole world for that matter, was revealing of most Germans' values and aspirations. Like the Swiss and the Swedes, they wanted to cultivate their well-ordered and tidy gardens, not conquer and dominate others. In time, of course, matters could change. In life and history conditions and views evolve and change; there were no guarantees that today's wishes would be tomorrow's desires.

With the dissolution of the Soviet bloc and German reunification, the German strategic position and security improved dramatically. Two opposing front-line states of two antagonistic alliances had fused into one state far more powerful than any of its immediate neighbours. East of them the Germans found themselves facing a power vacuum consisting of would-be allies and clients, instead of enemies belonging to a hostile power bloc. They therefore no longer depended for their own security upon the ultimate protection of the United States.

The new opportunities which opened up with such a fundamental transformation would naturally in time affect the German outlook and views of their proper role in the world. Temporarily, the needs of reconstruction in the eastern section of their country would absorb most German attention and energy; eventually they could gradually spare both more attention and investment for their needy eastern neighbours. Clearly, they had already invested in the region more than anyone else, and complained that others made splendid speeches about providing aid and investment to the east but did little. France and Britain did not like to be left behind German penetration and growing influence in the region but were hard put to follow its example. Both Mitterrand and Thatcher wanted to take up the German challenge in the region.[4] Shortage of cash and expertise in the area as well as geography were against them. The Germans seemed predestined to gain and keep the upper hand there, and this signalled fears of German domination in many minds.

Clear variations existed in the relations between the Germans and their immediate eastern neighbours. They were best with the Hungarians, for both longer-term historic and recent reasons. The Germans and the Hungarians had fought on the same side in both world wars and the Germans appreciated the Magyar role as catalysts in the collapse of the DDR. German–Czech relations were more uneasy. They suffered from greater historical burdens, including occupation during and expulsion of the local Germans after the Second World War. The Czech President Václav Havel's timely and generous pronouncement in favour of German reunification was important for German–Czech reconciliation, and similarities in culture and work habits eased economic co-operation in particular. The German–Polish relationship was the most difficult and problematic of the three. The burdens inherited from both the distant and the recent past were heavier than with the others, for repeated German participation in the historic divisions of Poland and the horrors of the Second World War coloured everything. Sharp differences in culture and temperament caused additional difficulties.

Yet all four of these nations realized their need to work with one another closely as neighbours. In practice, this meant above all an extension of German influence upon the others. As a result, the traditional geographical concept of Central Europe was reborn and revived, after a moribund existence through its years of division during the Cold War.[5]

Russia had been the power which historically had challenged German influence in the region lying between them. As long as the Soviet Union lasted, it tried to maintain a lingering grip on it, even after its troops were in full retreat. For example, it tried to block its former satellites' efforts to join any alliance that it construed was aimed against itself, though, with the collapse and disintegration of the Soviet Union, such efforts were doomed. All three of the Germans' immediate eastern neighbours were anxious to join the European Community and even NATO. They saw in Germany a potential sponsor of these ambitions which further strengthened German influence upon them.

The more rational and real fears of German domination had to do rather with economics than with politics or military matters. The basic strength of Germany rested on its productive capacity rather than in its political or military power. In an era when economic power rather than military might increasingly determined the pecking order between nations and their influence upon one another, Germany's economic strength both frightened and attracted other nations. It was both a formidable source of export competition and provider of credits, investment and markets.

In addition to the East German people, West German economic strength and financial reserves had been the major weapons in Chancellor Kohl's arsenal in bringing about reunification. They had enabled him first to provide incentives to and later to meet Gorbachev's pleas for credits and economic and financial aid. At the time of the final deal, they had enabled Bonn to offer a package to Moscow which it neither wanted to nor could turn down. Finally, they made it possible for the Bundesrepublik to hold out the promise of massive help and economic improvement in the future for the East Germans after reunification. It was evident, despite the subsequent agony, that if any country could afford the costs of unification, integration and reconstruction of eastern Germany, then the Bundesrepublik could and would meet the bill.

Kohl had promised that German reunification would not result in new economic burdens upon its EC partners because of the inclusion of East Germany in the Community. Germany would itself pay for it.[6] This would indeed formally be the case, but indirectly the reconstruction of East Germany affected not just the other EC countries but much of the rest of Europe as well. This it did through the *de facto* German impact on the European economies through the EMS, the European Monetary System, which was dominated by the Deutschmark.

Bonn had such economic and financial power that by keeping its interest rates high it could indirectly not only influence other economies but attract them to make a contribution to reconstruction in eastern Germany. Together, high German interest rates and the reputation of the Deutschmark for strength, soundness and stability, attracted foreign investments. It worked like honey on bees.

Nevertheless, German reunification was not just a matter of economics. It had more to do with longings for freedom and dignity, freedom from fear, freedom to speak one's mind, and freedom to pursue one's dreams and a better life. It was the result of human actions based on such longings and fired by courage. This courage was inspired by the courage of neighbouring peoples and Gorbachev's unwillingness, indeed refusal, to use raw force to suppress the emerging challenges to Soviet domination west of its borders.

It was important for Germany and especially important for the future soundness of democracy in the east that reunification was the result of popular wishes and desires. Unlike several previous occasions in German history, this time popular participation, democracy and freedom accompanied a remarkable German success and empowerment. Democracy had earlier often been associated with German failure, defeat and national humiliation. Now the victory and extension of democracy among the Germans was intimately intertwined with the victory of national aspirations and an accompanying sense of joy, pride, achievement and power.

This change in the emotional associations between democracy and the fate of Germany, at a watershed in German history which deeply affected people and their attitudes and emotions, had far-ranging significance. Reunification was an emotionally intense and defining national collective experience. People would remember its essence and pass it on in their own attitudes to their children and grandchildren.

Although popular collective desires, determination and actions brought about unification to a great extent, individuals occupying key positions and playing major roles in the unfolding drama also mattered a great deal. They put an imprint upon and shaped their nations' official actions and reactions. Thus the roles of Kohl, Gorbachev and Bush or Mitterrand and Thatcher became inseparable from the roles of the Bundesrepublik, the Soviet Union and the United States or from France and Britain. Their mutual relations also influenced and reflected their nations' relations and attitudes to one another.

The more effective among these key players in achieving their aims were not only those who represented the strongest countries but those who most clearly acted according to the wishes of a clear majority of their compatriots. This was the case above all with Kohl, but also with Bush and Gorbachev, although to a lesser extent. Mitterrand and Thatcher at times acted against the apparent wishes of most of their compatriots or, depending on the representativeness of polls, represented highly divided, and sometimes rather evenly divided, constituencies on the German question.

Some leaders and main players who were averse to German reunification deprecated ordinary people's support of it. Not only were they averse to the aim, they seemed to disapprove of ordinary people making important historic decisions. Gorbachev and Andreotti said that decisions about Germany should not be made on the streets. Mitterrand doubted, or claimed that he doubted, whether the East Germans even wanted unification, even when they had already made their wish for it quite clear. At various times these leaders and Thatcher, and even Bush early in the game, said the decision concerning reunification was not just a German matter but needed to be subjected to the approval of other powers. In short, they were questioning the East Germans' right to freely decide their fate.

This implied that they were also questioning and throwing doubt on the very principles of freedom, democracy, popular sovereignty and national self-determination. This was a tall order. It could not and would not work. It was an unsellable notion in particular in the Western societies in whose very cores and ethos these principles lay and who had elevated them to the level of articles of faith, to close counterparts of a modern religion.

This was the fundamental cause of the rift between the attitudes of the ordinary people and some of their leaders and élites towards German reunification. The views of the ordinary people reflected more faithfully the core values of their societies than did the leaders' perceptions of national interest. They therefore baulked at endorsing efforts to block the popular East German and German wish for freedom, the right of self-determination, and unity. Their stand effectively circumscribed their leaders' options on the issue, and thus the influence of public opinion abroad helped the East German people to gain the right to decide about their future and the cause of German reunification.

It also helped Helmut Kohl's and Hans-Dietrich Genscher's efforts to make reunification a reality, but although they could point at and had the benefit of popular support for their cause in their dealings with other leaders, they still had many obstacles to overcome. At least Kohl repeatedly used the evidence of popular pressure for reunification in his dealings with the other major players. Pointing it out and emphasizing its strength and irresistibility, he undermined and weakened the potential resistance to reunification by other players.

No Western leader faced greater challenges than Kohl in the course of 1989 and 1990, and none met them with greater skill and determination. His two great challenges were German reunification and staying in power after the elections scheduled for December 1990. In tackling these aims, Kohl displayed striking accomplishments as a power broker in both domestic and international politics. He had already had a well-established and solid reputation as a formidable master of domestic politics. He had less of a reputation as a player of international politics before his role in the achievement of German unity. As late as the spring of 1989, Anglo–American critics had accused him of being panic-prone and jelly-like in facing both the Soviets and domestic critics over arms reduction negotiations, ignoring the fact that Kohl had different priorities.

Kohl's great accomplishment was his contribution to convincing both the Western allies and the Soviet Union that German reunification was inevitable and reassuring them through promises and payments. In politics few things are inevitable but nobody wants to fail, and to oppose something that is inevitable amounts to failure. Kohl reassured his uneasy Western allies, never enthusiastic about German reunification, by promising and insisting that a unified Germany would remain faithful to NATO and the EC and would not court neutrality as the price of reunification. The Soviet Union he bought off by making use of its economic misery. The deal became easier because of Gorbachev's perception that, by letting go of East Germany, he was selling something that was in any event slipping from Soviet control.

After his success in orchestrating German reunification, Kohl eventually received lavish praise from past major actors on the international political stage. They had watched his performance with fascination and with eyes sharpened by their own experiences. Henry Kissinger, the former American secretary of state, rightly complimented Kohl's 'great sense of timing', and said 'he was correct in pushing for fast unification'. Expressing his admiration of and confidence in Kohl, he predicted that Kohl would 'go down in history as a great man'.[7] Kissinger's colleague as a practitioner of international relations at a high level, former French Foreign Minister Jean François Poncet, was equally generous in heaping praise on Kohl's performance. According to Poncet, Kohl was 'one of the great European leaders of the post-war period', and he added, 'he hasn't made a single significant mistake'.[8]

Kohl played with skill a historic political game in order to secure German reunification. His role in that process invited comparison with the accomplishments of two nineteenth-century European masters of domestic and international politics, Otto von Bismarck and Camillo di Cavour. As chancellor of Prussia, Bismarck engineered German unification under Prussian leadership. As the prime minister of the small north Italian state of Piedmont, Cavour brought about Italian unification.

Kohl was naturally often more easily compared with Bismarck, the first chancellor of a unified Germany. Like Kohl, Bismarck was a physically imposing figure, a big, powerfully built man who towered over his surroundings. Both men were quick to see and to make use of political opportunities, often way ahead of their rivals and opponents, but in some ways there are clearer parallels in Kohl's and Cavour's roles and contributions in helping along their respective nations' unification.

Kohl, unlike Bismarck, could not rely on superior military virtuosity and power, as the ultimate enforcer and guarantor of his political and diplomatic designs. He had no Helmuth von Moltke, the military genius of his age, or a Prussian army to lean on for support. Instead, he had to rely on his political instincts and skills, the will, boldness and enthusiasm of the German people, and the prosperity and wealth of the Bundesrepublik. His assets resembled those of Cavour whose primary assets, besides his own political acumen, were popular Italian enthusiasm for unification and the reputation of Piedmont as a model to the rest of Italy.

Like Bismarck and Cavour, Kohl made skilful use of international constellations to advance his cause of unification. He wanted to make use of the window of opportunity while it lasted, though he was sometimes criticized for having pressed matters too quickly. Yet at the very time of the Moscow benediction of the reunification in September 1990, widespread rumours circulated of unexplained troop movements around Moscow as preparation for a hard-line military coup. Crack paratroop units were suddenly flown in by a wave of transport planes, wearing full battle gear with helmets, arms, live ammunition and flak jackets. Somehow Defence Minister Dmitri Yazov's official explanation that they came to pick potatoes did not seem convincing.[9]

The coup did not take place then, but if it had it would certainly have justified Kohl's speed. Instead it came the following August, involving the same Yazov, and failed – but it did result in the departure of Gorbachev from power, and it was in Gorbachev that both Kohl and Genscher had heavily invested their hopes and efforts to achieve German reunification.

United Germany had to immediately face conflicting expectations and demands from abroad. Their nature was sometimes ironic in view of the often expressed fears of a re-emergence of German nationalism and domination during the drive towards reunification. In essence they amounted to both an expectation of and demand for a greater German assertiveness and role in international affairs. The Germans would not be allowed to turn into Swiss or Swedes.

Furthermore, the allies and neighbours of Germany were not merely demanding mere words and cash but German military action abroad, which had been unacceptable in the past as a matter most easily and readily associated with reviving and inflaming nationalist passions and the ghosts of history. When during the Gulf crisis and war the Germans provided cash though not arms and fighting men, they became the object of a fair amount of abuse for evading their international duty in the crusade against Saddam Hussein of Iraq. Emotions ran high, especially in the US Congress, to the effect that the Germans were ingrates who did not reciprocate American support for their reunification. Overlooked, however, were the enormous obligations the Germans were already shouldering with their commitments to the Soviet Union and the reconstruction of the eastern part of their country.

In contrast, when soon afterwards the Germans became more assertive on behalf of the Slovenes and Croats in the break-up of Yugoslavia, the French and the British suspected and accused them of new hegemonical aspirations in Eastern Europe. The Germans could have wondered, and many did, that no matter how they behaved, they would be an object of suspicion and a butt of criticism. At the same time, of course, they were trying to look after their interests.

That they did it more assertively than before in the post-war period was alone bound to grate on some who were accustomed to different German behaviour. When the Germans not only got away with it but also exerted their will on others, levels of unease and suspicion were heightened, in particular among those used to leading in the past. This was the case when the Germans persuaded the EC to recognize the independence of Croatia and Slovenia; the British and the French did not approve of this, as they had originally seemed to favour the Serbs, perhaps partly for reasons of history going back to the two world wars.

With the Soviet withdrawal, Germany was clearly becoming the dominant power in the lands located between the two powers and there was not much anybody could or would do about it. The cards seem stacked in the Germans' favour in the region. It was not so much a matter of the Germans moving in aggressively but of being insistently invited by the locals, in desperate need of help, investment, know-how and trade. The Germans were closest and seemed most able and willing to provide for these and for Russian needs as well, even when pressed by the costs and tasks of reconstruction at home. With the most urgent demands of that job over, they were expected to provide more for their eastern neighbours.

When faced with what they perceived to be German challenges closer at home, the British and the French grew more concerned. Kohl had by and large persuaded the French that he was a good European genuinely in favour of further European integration, but when he suggested that the German language be given corresponding status with French and English in the EC, signs of irritation were clear among the British and the French. The Germans felt that they were at a disadvantage in EC dealings because of problems connected with language, and pointed out that they were, after all, clearly the largest language group within the Community. They had a case which was difficult to deny on grounds of fairness, but to the British and the French it was nevertheless upsetting. They took it as an effort to diminish their relative status and to enhance the Germans'.

Related issues of social psychology, status and power were at stake with the possibility of Germany, together with Japan, gaining a permanent seat on the Security Council of the United Nations. The British and French did not like it and Mrs Thatcher rejected it outright. It remained to be seen how long the permanent membership of the Security Council could continue to be restricted to the principal victors of the Second World War when it no longer corresponded to the actual distribution of power in the world among the major nations. The example of the old League of Nations as originally an organization of the victors in the First World War did not provide a reassuring antecedent in this respect.

At least for the time being, however, the Germans were more preoccupied with their internal unification than they were with their status in the world. Its economic, financial and psychological costs climbed higher than most had foreseen. This resulted in greater hardship for the East Germans and heavier obligations for the West Germans than many had expected. The West Germans had to dig deeper in their pockets than they had thought and the east did not bloom as soon as the East Germans had hoped. The West Germans were not happy at having to subsidize the East Germans' employment, their unemployment, health and other social benefits, and their retirement benefits and pensions. The unsurprising consequence was frustration and dissatisfaction among both, and it was these that lay behind much of the tension and acrimony between them.

With attention focusing on the economic dislocation and havoc in East Germany resulting from reunification, one basic fact was often overlooked. The fundamental cause of the East Germans' economic miseries was not reunification but rather the previous decades of mismanagement and neglect of the economy in the DDR. The failures of the past were only now fully revealed. The rigid, centrally controlled planning economy of the DDR had not adjusted and adapted to changing demand and the requirements of time. As a result it had become increasingly obsolete and uncompetitive compared with its more flexible and responsive rivals in the international markets of which East Germany became a part with reunification. With the walls of protection and artificial subsidies gone, behind which the true extent of its incompetence and decay had long remained hidden, the tottering state of the East German economy had simply become exposed to the light of day.

In addition to this sad inheritance, parallels with the reunification caused additional woes. The old protected markets for East German goods vanished with the disassembling of the former Soviet bloc. With it went Comecon, its trading umbrella. It had helped to oversee and maintain trade at often artificial prices in return for guaranteed markets for goods and products often unable to compete on free world markets. In addition, rising wage pressures among the East Germans still employed further aggravated the situation faced by many East German firms.

Meanwhile, large numbers of unsolved property claims continued to hamper and slow down new investment. It was becoming clear that it would take longer than originally expected for the living standards in the east to catch up with the west. The east faced a major problem in the scarcity of qualified professionals in many fields, and relatively few westerners were willing to relocate there, often for sheer lack of amenities. The run-down housing and shortage of attractive restaurants and other such mundane matters were uninviting to them.

Despite its difficulties, united Germany proved an irresistible magnet to would-be refugees and immigrants. Its liberal and generous policies of admission based on its constitution, together with its prosperity, high material standards of living, and its relatively advanced and generous social policies attracted large numbers of people from far and wide. Germany received and admitted far larger numbers of newcomers than any other country in Europe, which in itself often led to resentment and at times to violent backlash.

The extremely high levels of unemployment among East Germans and the havoc and dislocation accompanying unification gave rise to a volatile situation. A vast and rapidly growing influx of newcomers from abroad with no end in sight, competing for and sharing already stretched and strained resources, was bound to result in turmoil in these highly charged conditions.

Neo-Nazi skinhead attacks against foreigners received wide attention as being connected to the German Nazi past. Massive protests were staged against the skinhead violence, however, and these attracted many times the numbers involved in anti-foreign protest actions. Repeatedly urging other countries to partake more in the intake of the rapidly growing refugee flow, the Germans felt that they were doing more than their share. With the exception of their immediate smaller neighbours, a positive response was rather lacking, although criticism of the German violence and its handling had been considerable.

The very same things that attracted masses of refugees to Germany also ensured that the unemployed East German multitudes did not live in dire destitution, as might have been inferred from some foreign reporting on Germany. Germany was, after all, an advanced welfare state, and decades earlier the old German Empire had had social legislation which had served as a model for many other parts of Europe, including the Nordic countries, the subsequent pathbreakers and pioneers in the field.

Germany may have lost its position in the vanguard of advanced social legislation. Its social policies may not have been as progressive in equalizing and levelling the human material condition, its safety net not as far flung or its floor of security not as high as those in the Nordic countries. It was nevertheless clearly ahead of the United States, as well as the United Kingdom, in most matters of this kind. The East Germans who became citizens of the Bundesrepublik certainly did not end up in a *laissez-faire* capitalist jungle, dog-eat-dog type of society, as was sometimes portrayed.

By most standards German social benefits were generous, the working hours short, and vacations long. While these benefits and conditions were not that different from other prosperous European societies, the average vacations were, for example, two and a half times as long as in the United States. Thus the equalizing and redistributive features of the German welfare society were helping to ease the East Germans' hardships. They provided for and guaranteed the basics – food, shelter, medical care, plus a few extras – and they also narrowed in practice the distinctions between the Germans' standards of living and quality of life.

With the passage of time the differences between east and west would diminish. They could become less significant than the older and historically more important divisions between north and south Germany or Protestants and Catholics. Even after the flow of special funds earmarked for the reconstruction in the east slowed down, the German federal system of revenue sharing could help to bridge the remaining inequities between east and west. It had marked built-in features of solidarity affecting both individuals and the different *Länder*, the member states. The German system redistributed and readjusted incomes and services available to them through progressive taxation and social policies as well as revenue sharing.

Preoccupied with the immediate difficulties associated with reunification, both the Germans themselves and many foreign observers often took a gloomy view of the situation in Germany, though the long-term prospects were not that grim. Certainly the process of economic, social and psychological unification would continue for many years, but gradually old wounds would heal and many scars fade. People belonging to different age groups did not experience the changes brought by reunification in the same way. For some in the east, the changes came too late in their lives for a happy adjustment. They constitute a lost generation. To the ever growing numbers of younger people reaching adulthood, however, united Germany is not only a promise but a reality of something much better than the fading memory of the DDR.

Notes

1 Comment from August 1990.
2 *Spiegel Spezial*, I, 1991, p. 48.
3 *SZ*, 4 Jan. 1991, or Childs, *Germany in the Twentieth Century*, 1991, p. 269.
4 Thatcher, 1993, p. 798.
5 Cf. István Deák, 'German Unification: Perceptions and Politics in East Central Europe', *German Politics and Society*, summer, 1990, pp. 22–30.
6 See, e.g., *Financial Times*, 31 July 1990.
7 Kissinger, in *Vanity Fair*, Dec., 1990, p. 240.
8 Poncet, in the *Wall Street Journal*, 30 Nov. 1990.
9 *Komsomolskaya Pravda* and Reuters, 4 Oct. 1990.

Bibliography

Journals, Magazines, Newpapers, Periodicals

(Articles are cited only in the notes)

Aus Politik und Zeitgeschichte
Aussenpolitik
Aussenpolitik und Zeitgeschichte
Berliner Tagesblatt
Berliner Zeitung
Bild Zeitung
Boston Globe
Bulletin, Presse- und Informationsamt der Bundesregierung
Bulletin of the European Community
Business Week
Current Policy
Daily Express
Daily Star
Daily Telegraph
Deutsche Bundesbank – Monatsberichte
Deutschland Archiv
The Economist
Europa-Archiv
L'Express
Le Figaro
The Financial Times
Foreign Affairs
Frankfurter Allgemeine Zeitung
Frankfurter Rundschau
General-Anzeiger
German Comments
German Historical Institute's Bulletin
German History

German Politics
German Politics and Society
German Studies Review
The Guardian
Handelsblatt
The Independent
International Herald Tribune
International Affairs
International Security
Izvestija
Junge Welt
Kieler Nachrichten
Komsomolskaya Pravda
Köln Express
Kölner Stadt-Anzeiger
Libération
Le Monde
Neue Gesellschaft / Frankfurter Hefte
Neuen Berliner Illustrierten
Neues Deutschland
New York Review of Books
New York Times
Newsweek
Nürnberger Nachrichten
Nürnberger Zeitung
Osteuropa Wirschaft
Das Parlament
Le Point
Politics and Society in Germany, Austria and Switzerland
Pravda
Rheinischer Merkur/Christ und Welt
Rheinische Post
Social Policy
Sovetskaya Rossiya
Spectator
Der Spiegel
Stern
Stuttgarter Zeitung
Sunday Express
Suomen Kuvalehti
Survival
Süddeutsche Zeitung

Der Tagesspiegel
Die Tageszeitung
Time
The Times
Toronto Star
Vierteljährshäfte für Zeitgeschichte
Wall Street Journal (Europe)
Washington Quarterly
Westdeutsche Allgemeine
Die Welt
Die Wirtschaft
World Politics
Die Zeit

Books

The following list includes publications which appeared too late to benefit this book but which could be useful for readers interested in further information.
(Articles are cited only in the notes)

Abel, E., *The Shattered Block: Behind the Upheaval in Eastern Europe*, Boston, 1990.

Abelshauser, W., *Wirtschaft in Westdeutschland, 1945–1948*, Stuttgart, 1975.

Adam, J., *Economic Reforms in the Soviet Union and Eastern Europe Since the 1960s*, New York, 1989.

Adenauer, K., *Erinnerungen*, Stuttgart, 1967.

Adenauer, K., *Memoirs*, London, 1966–68.

Albers, D., Deppe, F., Stamm, M., *Fernaufklärung: Glastnost und die bundesdeutsche Linke*, Cologne, 1989.

Albrecht, W. (ed.), *Kurt Schumacher. Reden-Schriften-Korrespondenzen, 1945–1952*, Berlin and Bonn, 1985.

Allen, B., *Germany East: Dissent and Opposition*, Montreal, 1989.

Andert, R. and Herzberg, W., *Der Sturz: Erich Honecker im Kreuzverhör*, Berlin and Weimar, 1990.

Appel, R. (ed.), *Helmut Kohl – wer sonst? Über die Alternativen deutscher Politik*, Munich, 1990.

Arato, A., *Crisis and Reform in Eastern Europe*, New Brunswick, NJ, 1991.

Ardagh, J., *Germany and the Germans*, New York, 1988.

Arnold, K-H., *Die ersten hundert Tage des Hans Modrow*, Berlin, 1990.

Aron, R. and Lerner, D., *France Defeats the EDC*, New York, 1957.

Artner, S.J., *A Change of Course: The West German Social Democrats and NATO, 1957–1961*, Westport, Conn., 1985.
Ash, T.G., *'Und du willst nicht mein Bruder sein': Die DDR heute*, Reinbek, 1981.
Ash, T.G., *The Magic Lantern: The Revolution of '89*, New York, 1990.
Ash, T.G., *The Uses of Adversity: Essays on the Fate of Central Europe*, New York, 1990.
Ash, T.G., *In Europe's Name: Germany and the Divided Continent*, New York, 1993.
Asmus, R., *German Perception of the United States on the Eve of Unification*, Santa Monica, Calif., 1991.
Augstein, R., and Grass, G., *Deutschland, einig Vaterland?* Göttingen, 1990.
Backer J.H., *The Decision to Divide Germany: American Foreign Policy in Transition*, Durham, NC, 1978.
Bahr, E., *Zum europäischen Frieden*, Berlin, 1988.
Bahr, E., *Sicherheit für und vor Deutschland*, Munich, 1991.
Bahrmann, H. and Links C., *Wir sind das Volk: Die DDR zwischen Okt. und 17. Dec. 1989. Eine Chronik*, Weimar and Wuppertal, 1990.
Bahro, R., *Die Alternative. Zur Kritik des real existierenden Sozialismus*, Cologne and Frankfurt am Main, 1977.
Baier, L. *Volk ohne Zeit*, Berlin, 1990.
Baker, K., Dalton, R.J. and Hildebrandt, K., *Germany Transformed*, Cambridge, 1981.
Balabkins, N., *Germany Under Direct Control*, New Brunswick, NJ, 1964.
Balfour, M., *Four Power Control in Germany and Austria, 1945–1946*, London, 1956.
Balfour, M., *West Germany: A Contemporary History*, London, 1982.
Bandulet, B., *Adenauer zwischen Ost und West*, Munich, 1970.
Baring, A., *Aussenpolitik in Adenauers Kanzlerdemokratie*, Munich, 1969.
Baring, A., *Uprising in East Germany, June 17, 1953*, Ithaca, NY, 1972.
Baring, A., *Machtwechsel: Die Ära Brandt–Scheel*, Stuttgart, 1982.
Baring, A., *Im Anfang war Adenauer*, Munich, 1988.
Baring, A., *Unser neuer Grössenwahn: Deutschland zwischen Ost und West*, Berlin, 1988.
Baring, A., *Deutschland was nun?,* Berlin, 1991.
Bark, D.L. and Gress, D.R., *A History of West Germany*, 2 vols, 2nd edn, Oxford, 1993.
Barzel, R., *'Zur Deutschlandpolitik der neuen Bundesregierung', Texte zur Deutschlandpolitik*, Bonn, 1985.
Baumann, E. et al., *Der Fischer Weltalmanach, Sonderband DDR*, Frankfurt am Main, 1990.

Beck, T., *Liebe zum Sozialismus – Hass auf den Klassenfeind: Wehrmotiv und Wehrerziehung in der DDR*, Lüneburg, 1983.
Beck, U., *Jenseits von Rechts und Links*, Frankfurt am Main, 1992.
Becker, J.M., *Ein Land geht in den Western: Die Abwicklung der DDR*, Munich, 1990.
Becker, J. von, and Hillgruber A. (eds), *Die deutsche Frage im 19. und 20. Jahrhundert*, Munich, 1983.
Becker, U., Becker, H. and Ruhland, W., *Zwischen Angst und Aufbruch: Das Lebensgefühl der Deutschen in Ost und West nach der Wiedervereinigung*, Düsseldorf, 1992.
Belwe, K., *Psychosoziale Befindlicheit der Menschen in den neuen Bundesländern nach der Wende im Herbst 1989*, Bonn, 1991.
Bender, P., *Neue Ostpolitik. Von Mauerbau bis zum Moskauer Vertrag*, Munich, 1986.
Bender, P., *Deutsche Parallelen*, Berlin, 1989.
Bender, P., *Unsere Erbschaft: Was war die DDR – was bleibt von ihr?*, Hamburg, 1992.
Benz, W., ed., *Die Vertreibung der Deutschen aus dem Osten. Ursachen, Ereignisse, Folgen*, Frankfurt am Main, 1985.
Berghahn, V., *The Americanization of West German Industry, 1945–73*, Leamington Spa, 1986.
Berghahn, V. and Karsten, D., *Industrial Relations in West Germany*, Oxford, 1987.
Berghahn, V.R., *Modern Germany: Society, Economy and Politics in the Twentieth Century*, Cambridge, 1990.
Bergmann-Pohl, S., *Abschied ohne Tränen: Rückblick auf das Jahr der Einheit*, Berlin and Frankfurt am Main, 1991.
Beschloss, M., *The Crisis Years: Kennedy and Khrushchev, 1960–1963*. New York, 1991.
Beschloss, M.R. and Talbott, S., *At the Highest Levels: The Inside Story of the End of the Cold War*, Boston, 1993.
Besier, G. and Wolf, S. (eds), *'Pfarrer, Christen und Katoliken.' Das Ministerium für Staatsicherheit und die Kirchen*, Neukirchen, 1992.
Besson, W., *Die Außenpolitik der Bundesrepublik*, Munich, 1970.
Der Besuch von Generalsekretär Honecker in der Bundesrepublik Deutschland. Dokumentation zum Arbeitsbesuch des Generalsekretärs der SED und Staatsratsvorsitzenden der DDR, Erich Honecker, in der Bundesrepublik Deutschland im September 1987, Bonn, 1988.
Beyme, K. von, *The Political System of the Federal Republic of Germany*, Aldershot, 1984.
Beyme, K. von, and Zimmermann, H., *Policymaking in the German Democratic Republic*, New York, 1984.

Beziehungen der Deutschen Demokratischen Republik zur Bundesrepublik Deutschland. Dokumente 1971–1988, Berlin, 1990.
Biermann, W., *Demokratisierung in der DDR?,* Hattingen, 1982.
Binder, D., *The Other German: Willy Brandt's Life and Times*, New York, 1975.
Birke, A., *Britain and Germany*, London, 1987.
Birke, A., *Nation ohne Haus*, Berlin, 1989.
Birnbaum, K.E., *East and West Germany: A Modus Vivendi*, Westmead, 1973.
Blackburn, R. (ed.), *After the Fall: The Failure of Communism and the Future of Socialism*, London / New York, 1991.
Blaessner, G-J., *Die andere deutsche Republik*, Opladen, 1989.
Blanke, T. and Erd, R., *DDR – Ein Staat Vergeht*, Frankfurt am Main, 1990.
Blankenhorn, H., *Verständnis und Verständigung*, Frankfurt am Main, 1980.
Blechman, B.M. and Fisher, C. (eds), *The Silent Partner: West Germany and Arms Control*, Cambridge, Mass., 1988.
Bohley, B. et al., *40 Jahre DDR...und die Bürger melden sich zu Wort*, Frankfurt am Main, 1989.
Bolling, K., *Republic In Suspense*, London, 1964.
Bölling, K., *Die fernen Nachbarn*, Hamburg, 1985.
Borneman, J., *After the Wall*, New York, 1991.
Borneman, J., *Belonging to the Two Berlins: Kin, State, Nation*, New York. 1992.
Bower, T., *Blind Eye to Murder*, London, 1983.
Bracher, K.D., *Deutscher Sonderweg – Mythos Oder Realität?*, Munich, 1982.
Bracher, K.D. et al. (eds), *Geschichte der Bundesrepublic Deutschland*, 7 vols, Stuttgart and Mannheim, 1981–7.
Brandt, H., *The Search for a Third Way*, Garden City, NY, 1970.
Brandt, W., *Aussenpolitik, Deutschlandpolitik, Europapolitik*, Berlin, 1968.
Brandt, W., *Begegnungen und Einsichten: Die Jahre 1960–1975*, Hamburg, 1976.
Brandt, W., *People and Politics*, London, 1978.
Brandt, W., *Reden über das eigene Land: Deutschland*, vol. 2, Munich, 1984.
Brandt, W., *Reden zu Deutschland – '...was zusammengehört'*, Bonn, 1990.
Brandt, W., *My Life in Politics*, New York, 1992.
Braunthal, G., *The West German Social Democrats, 1969–1982*, Boulder, Col., 1983.
Bredow, W. von, and Brocke, R., *Das deutschlandpolitische Konzept der SPD*, Erlangen, 1987.
Breuilly, J. (ed.), *The State of Germany: The national idea in the making, unmaking and remaking of a modern nation-state*, London, 1992.

Brigoulleix, B. and Rovan, J. (eds), *Que devient l'Allemagne?*, Paris, 1986.
Brown, J.F., *Eastern Europe and Communist Rule*, Durham, NC, 1988.
Brown, J.F., *Surge to Freedom: The End of Communist Rule in Eastern Europe*, Durham, NC, 1991.
Bruns, W., *Deutsch-deutsche Beziehungen: Prämissen, Probleme, Perspektiven*, Opladen, 1984.
Bruns, W., *Von der Deutschland-Politik zur DDR-Politik? Prämissen, Probleme, Perspektiven*, Opladen, 1989.
Brus, W., *From Marx to Market: Socialism in Search of an Economic System*, New York, 1989.
Bryson, P. and Melzer, M., *The End of the East German Economy*, Basingstoke and London, 1991.
Buchheim H., *Deutschlandpolitik, 1949–1972: Der politisch-diplomatische Prozess*, Stuttgart, 1984.
Buchstab, G. (ed.), *Adenauer: Es musste alles neu gemacht werden*, Stuttgart, 1986.
Bugajski, J. and Pollack, M., *East European Fault Lines: Dissent, Opposition, and Social Activism*, Boulder, Col., 1989.
Bulmer, S. and Paterson, W., *The Federal Republic of Germany and the European Community*, London, 1987.
Burdick, C. et al. (eds), *Contemporary Germany: Politics and Culture*, Boulder, Col., 1984.
Burens, P.C., *Die DDR und der Prager Frühling*, Berlin, 1981.
Bürger Ulrich, *Das sagen wir natürlich so nicht!*, Berlin, 1990.
Bürgerkomitee Leipzig (ed.), *Stasi intern. Macht und Banalität*, Leipzig, 1991.
Buschmann, A. (ed.), *Kaiser und Reich: Klassische Texte und Dokumente zur Verfassungsgeschichte der Heiligen Römischen Reiches Deutscher Nation vom Beginn des 12. Jahrhunderts bis zum Jahre 1806*, Munich, 1984.
Buttlar, W. von, *Ziele und Zielkonflikte der sowjetischen Deutschlandpolitik, 1945–1947*, Stuttgart, 1980.
Calleo, D., *The German Problem Reconsidered. Germany and the World Order, 1870 to the Present*, Cambridge, 1980.
Calleo, D.P., *Beyond American Hegemony: The Future of the Western Alliance*, New York, 1987.
Calleo, D.P. et al., *Geteiltes land – Halbes Land?*, Frankfurt am Main, 1986.
Campbell, E.S., *Germany's Past and Europe's Future*, Washington, 1989.
Carr, J., *Helmut Schmidt: Helmsman of Germany*, London, 1985.
Cate, C., *The Ideas of August: The Berlin Wall Crisis 1961*, New York, 1978.
Catudal, H.M., Jr, *A Balance Sheet of the Quadripartite Agreement on Berlin*, Berlin, 1978.

Catudal, H.M., *Kennedy and the Berlin Wall Crisis*, Berlin, 1980.
Childs, D., *From Schumacher to Brandt: The Story of German Socialism, 1945–1965*, Oxford, 1966.
Childs, D., *East Germany*, London, 1969.
Childs, D. (ed.), *Honecker's Germany*, London, 1985.
Childs, D., *East Germany to the 1990s: Can it Resist Glasnost?,* London, 1987.
Childs, D., *The GDR: Moscow's German Ally*, 2nd edn, London, 1988.
Childs, D., *Germany on the Road to Unity*, London, 1990.
Childs, D., *Germany in the Twentieth Century*, New York, 1991.
Childs, D. and Johnson, J., *West Germany: Politics and Society*, London, 1981.
Childs, D., Baylis, T.A. and Rueschemeyer, M. (eds), *East Germany in Comparative Perspective*, London/New York, 1989.
Christ, P. and Neubauer, R., *Kolonie im Eigenen Land: Die Treuhand, Bonn und die Wirtschaftskatastrophe der fünf neuen Länder*, Berlin, 1991.
Clay, L.D., *Decision in Germany*, Garden City, NY, 1950.
Clemens, C., *Reluctant Realists: the CDU/CSU and West German Ostpolitik*, Durham, NC, 1989.
Conradt, D., *The German Polity*, 4th edn, New York, 1989.
Cooney, J.A., Craig, G., Schwarz, H-P. and Stern, F. (eds), *The Federal Republic and the United States: Changing Political, Social, and Economic Relations*, Boulder, Col., 1984.
Cooney, J., Friedrich, W-U. and Kleinfeld, G., *Deutsch-Amerikanische Beziehungen*, Jahrbuch 1, Frankfurt am Main, 1989.
Craig, G., *From Bismarck to Adenauer*, New York, 1989.
Craig, G.A., *The Germans*, New York, 1991.
Dahl, R., *After the Revolution?,* New Haven, Conn., 1990.
Dahrendorf, R., *Society and Democracy in Germany*, London, 1968.
Dahrendorf, R., *Reflections on the Revolution in Europe*, New York, 1990.
Dalton, R., *Politics in West Germany*, Boston, 1989.
Darnton, R., *Berlin Journal, 1989–1990*, New York, 1991.
Davison, W.P., *The Berlin Blockade*, Princeton, NJ, 1958.
De Zayas, A., *Nemesis at Potsdam: The Expulsion of the Germans from the East*, 3rd edn, Lincoln, Nebr., and London, 1989.
Dean, R.W., *West German Trade with the East: The Political Dimension*, New York, 1974.
Dehio, L., *Germany and World Politics in the Twentieth Century*, New York, 1967.
Demandt, A. (ed.), *Deutschlands Grenzen in der Geschichte*, Munich, 1990.
Dennis, M. (ed.), *The GDR Approaches the 1990s: The View from Britain*, Bakersfield, Calif., 1988.

Dennis, M., *German Democratic Republic: Politics, Economics, and Society*, London, 1988.
DePorte, A.W., *Europe between the Superpowers: The Enduring Balance*, New Haven, Conn., 1979.
Deppe, R., Dubiel, H. and Rödel, U. (eds), *Demokratischer Umbruch in Osteuropa*, Fankfurt am Main, 1991.
Deuerlein, E., *DDR 1945–1970: Geschichte und Bestandsaufnahme*, Munich, 1972.
Deuerlein, E., *Deutschland 1963–1970*, Hanover, 1972.
Deutsch, K.W. and Edinger, L.J., *Germany Rejoins the Powers*, Stanford, Calif., 1959.
Diedrich, T., *Der 17 Juni 1953 in der DDR: Bewaffnete Gewalt gegen das Volk*, Berlin, 1991.
Ditfurth, C. von, *Blockflöten: Wie die CDU ihre realsozialistische Vergangenheit verdrängt*, Cologne, 1991.
Dittman, K., *Adenauer und die Widervereinigung Deutschlands. Die politische Diskussion des Jahres 1952*, Düsseldorf, 1981.
Diwald, H., *Deutschland einig Vaterland. Geschichte unserer Gegenwart*, Frankfurt am Main, 1990.
Diwald, H., *Gesamtwirtschaftliche und unternehmerische Anpassungsprozesse in Ostdeutschland. Bericht 1*, Kiel, 1991.
Dockdrill, S., *Britain's Policy for West German Rearmament, 1950–1955*, Cambridge, 1991.
Doder, D. and Branson, L., *Gorbachev: Heretic in the Kremlin*, New York, 1991.
Doering-Manteuffel, A., *Die Bundesrepublik in der Ära Adenauer*, Darmstadt, 1983.
Dohnanyi, K. von, *Das deutsche Wagnis: Über die wirtschaftliche und sozialen Folgen der Einheit*, Munich, 1991.
Dornberg, J., *The Other Germany*, New York, 1968.
Dorpalen, A., *German History in Marxist Perspective: The East German Approach*, London, 1986.
Drummond, G.D., *The German Social Democrats in Opposition, 1949–1960*, Norman, Okla., 1982.
Dubiel, H., Frankenberg G. and Rödel, U., *Die Demokratische Frage*, Frankfurt am Main, 1989.
Duhnke, H., *Stalinismus in Deutschland: Die Geschichte der sowjetischen Besatzungszone*, Cologne, 1955.
Dönhoff, M., *Foe into Friend: The Makers of the New Germany from Konrad Adenauer to Helmut Schmidt*, London, 1982.
Döring, H. and Smith, G. (eds), *Party Government and Political Culture in Western Germany*, New York, 1982.

Eckert, R., Kuttler, W. and Seeber, G. (eds), *Krise – Umbruch – Neubeginn: Eine kritische und selbstkritische Dokumentation der DDR: Geschichtswissenschaft 1989/90*, Stuttgart, 1992.
Economic Assistance in the New German Länder, Bonn, 1991.
Edinger, L.J., *Kurt Schumacher*, Stanford, Calif., 1965.
Edinger, L.J., *Politics in Germany*, Boston, 1977.
Edinger, L.J., *West German Politics*, New York, 1986.
Edwards, G.E., *GDR Society and Social Institutions: Facts and Figures*, London / New York, 1985.
Efforts of the German Government and its Allies in the Cause of German Unity, 1955–1966, Bonn, 1966.
Ehring, K. and Dallwitz, M., *Schwerter zu Pflugscharen: Friedensbewegung in der DDR*, Reinbek, 1982.
Elm, L., *Nach Hitler, nach Honecker: Zum streit der Deutschen um die eigene Vergangenheit*, Berlin, 1991.
Engelberg, E., *Bismarck. Urpreusse und Reichsgründer*, Berlin, 1985.
Eppelmann, R., *Wendewege: Briefe an meine Familie*, Bonn, 1992.
Erdmenger, K., *Das folgenschwere Missverständnis. Bonn und die sowietische Deutschlandpolitik 1949–1955*, Freiburg im Breisgau, 1967.
Erhard, L., *Prosperity through Competition*, London, 1958.
Erler, F., *Democracy in Germany*, Cambridge, Mass., 1965.
Falcke, H., *Die unvollendete Befreiung: Die Kirchen, die Umwälzung in der DDR und die Vereinigung Deutschlands*, Munich, 1991.
Feis, H., *Churchill, Roosevelt, Stalin*, Princeton, NJ, 1957.
Feld, W., *Reunification and West German–Soviet Relations*, The Hague, 1963.
Felf, W.J., *West Germany and the European Community: Changing Interests and Policy Objectives*, New York, 1981.
Filmer, W. and Schwan H., *Helmut Kohl*, Düsseldorf, 1985.
Fischer, A., *Die Deutsche Demokratische Republik*, Freiburg, 1988.
Fischer, J., *Die Linke nach dem Sozialismus*, Hamburg, 1992.
Förster, P. and Roski, G., *DDR zwischen Wende und Wahl: Meinungsforscher analysieren den Umbruch*, Berlin, 1990.
Foschepoth, J. (ed.), *Kalter Krieg und Deutsche Frage. Deutschland im Widerstreit der Mächte, 1945–1952*, Göttingen, 1985.
Frauen in den neuen Bundesländern im Prozess der deutschen Einigung, Bad Godesberg, 1991.
Freund, M., *From Cold War to Ostpolitik*, London, 1972.
Frey, E.G., *Division and Détente: The Germanies and Their Alliances*, New York, 1987.
Fricke, K.W., *Politik und Justiz in der DDR: Zur Geschichte der politischen Verfolgung 1945–1968*, Bericht und Dokumentation, Cologne, 1979.

Fricke, K.W., *Opposition und Widerstand in der DDR: Ein Politischer Report*, Cologne, 1984.
Fricke, K.W., *Die DDR-Staatssicherheit: Entwicklung, Strukturen, Aktionsfelder*, 3rd edn, Cologne, 1989.
Fricke, K.W., *MfS intern. Macht, Strukturen Auflösung der DDR-Staatssicherheit*, Cologne, 1991.
Friedmann, W., *The Allied Military Goverment of Germany*, London, 1956.
Friedrich, W-U. (ed.), *Die USA und die deutsche Frage 1945–1990*, Berlin, 1991.
Friend, J.W., *The Linchpin: French–German Relations, 1950–1990*, New York, 1991.
Fritsch-Bournazel, R., *Die Sowietunion und die deutsche Teilung: Die sowjetische Deutschlandspolitik, 1945–1979*, Opladen, 1979.
Fritsch-Bournazel, R., *Das Land in der Mitte: Die Deutschen im europäischen Kräftefeld*, Munich, 1986.
Fritsch-Bournazel, R., *Confronting the German Question*, Oxford, 1988.
Fritsch-Bournazel, R., *Europe and German Unification*, New York, 1992.
Fulbrook, M., *The Divided Nation: A History of Germany, 1945–90*, New York, 1991.
Fulbrook, M., *The Divided Nation: A History of Germany, 1918–1990*, New York, 1992.
Fulbrook, M., *The Two Germanies, 1945–1990: Problems of Interpretation*, Basingstoke and London, 1992.
Furniss, E.S., *France: Troubled Ally*, New York, 1960.
Fursdon, E., *The European Defence Community: A History*, London, 1980.
Gaddis, J.L., *The United States and the Origins of the Cold War, 1941–1947*, New York, 1972.
Gaddis, J.L., *Strategies of Containment: A Critical Appraisal of Postwar National Security Policy*, New York, 1982.
Gaddis J.L., *The Long Peace: Inquiries into the History of the Cold War*, New York, 1987.
Gallis, P.E., *The Unification of Germany: Background and Analysis of the Two-Plus-Four Talks*, Washington, DC, 1990.
Gasteyger, C., *Die beiden deutschen Staaten in der Weltpolitik*, Munich, 1976.
Gatzke, H.W., *Germany and the United States: A Special Relationship?*, Cambridge, Mass., 1980.
Gauck, J., *Die Stasi-Akten. Das unheimliche Erbe der DDR*, Reinbek, 1991.
Gauss, G., *Texte zur deutschen Frage: Mit den wichtigsten Dokumenten zum Verhältnis der beiden deutschen Staaten*, Darmstadt-Neuwied, 1981.
Gauss, G., *Wo Deutschland liegt. Eine Ortsbestimmung*, Munich, 1986.
Gedmin, J., *The Hidden Hand: Gorbachev and the Collapse of East Germany*, Washington, DC, 1992.

Geipel, G. (ed.), *The Future of Germany*, Indianapolis, 1990.
Geissler, H., *Zugluft-Politik in stürmischer Zeit*, Munich, 1990.
Gelb, N., *The Berlin Wall: Kennedy, Khrushchev, and a Showdown in the Heart of Europe*, New York, 1968.
Gelb, N., *The Berlin Wall*, London, 1986.
Genscher, H-D., *Unterwegs zur Einheit. Reden und Dokumente aus bewegter Zeit*, Berlin, 1991.
Gerlach, M., *Mitverantwortlich: Als Liberaler im SED-Staat*, Berlin, 1991.
Gerster, F. and Stobbe, D., *Die linke Mitte heute*, Bonn, 1990.
Geschichte der Deutschen 1949–1990. Eine Chronik zu Politik, Wirtschaft und Kultur, Frankfurt am Main, 1990.
Giersch, H., Paque, K-H. and Schmieding, H., *The Fading Miracle: Four Decades of Market Economy in Germany*, New York, 1992.
Giesen, B. and Leggewie, C. (eds), *Experiment Vereinigung: Ein sozialer Grossversuch*, Berlin, 1991.
Gill, D. and Schröter, U., *Das Ministerium für Staatssicherheit: Anatomie des Mielke-Imperiums*, Berlin, 1991.
Gillingham, J., *Coal, Steel, and the Rebirth of Europe 1945–1955. The Germans and French from Ruhr Conflict to Economic Community*, Cambridge, 1991.
Gimbel, J., *The American Occupation of Germany: Politics and the Military, 1945–1949*, Stanford, Calif., 1968.
Glaessner, G-J., *Herrschaft durch Kader. Leitung der Gesellschaft und Kaderpolitik in der DDR am Beispiel des Staatsapparates*, Opladen, 1977.
Glaessner, G-J. (ed.), *Die DDR in der Ära Honecker. Politik – Kultur – Gesellschaft*, Opladen, 1988.
Glaessner, G-J., *Die andere deutsche Republik*, Opladen, 1989.
Glaessner, G-J., *Der schwierig Weg zur Demokratie*, Wiesbaden, 1991.
Glaessner, G-J. (ed.), *Eine deutsche Revolution. Der Umbruch in der DDR, seine Ursachen und Folgen*, Frankfurt am Main, 1991.
Glaessner, G-J., *The Unification Process in Germany: From Dictatorship to Democracy*, New York, 1992.
Glaessner, G-J. and Scherer, K-J., *Auszug aus der Gesellschaft. Gemeinschaften zwischen Utopie, Reform und Reaktion*, Berlin, 1986.
Glaessner G-J. and Reissig, R. (eds), *Das Ende eines Experiments: Umbruch in der DDR und Deutsche Einheit*, Berlin, 1991.
Glaessner, G-J. and Wallace, I. (eds), *The German Revolution of 1989: Causes and Consequences*, Oxford, 1992.
Glenny, M., *The Rebirth of History: Eastern Europe in the Age of Democracy*, London / New York, 1990.
Gleye, P., *Behind the Wall: An American in East Germany, 1988–89*, Carbondale, Ill., 1991.

Glotz, P., *Der Irrweg des Nationalstaates*, Stuttgart, 1990.
Goeckel, R.F., *The Lutheran Church and the East German State: Political Conflict and Change Under Ulbricht and Honecker*, Ithaca, NY, 1990.
Golay, J.F., *The Founding of the Federal Republic of Germany*, Chicago, 1958.
Goldman, G., *The German Political System*, New York, 1974.
Goldmann, K., *Détente: Domestic Politics as Stabilizer of Foreign Policy*, Princeton, NJ, 1984.
Gorholt, M. and Kunz, N.W. (eds), *Deutsche Einheit, deutsche Linke: Reflexionen der politischen und gesellschaftlichen Entwicklung*, Cologne, 1990.
Götz, H.H., *Honecker – und was dann*, Herford, 1989.
Grabner, W-J., Heinze, C. et al. (eds), *Leipzig im Oktober: Kirchen und alternative Gruppen im Umbruch der DDR*, Berlin, 1990.
Grafe, P., *Tradition und Confusion*, Frankfurt, 1991.
Graml, H., *Die Allierten und die Teilung Deutschlands: Konflikte und Scheidungen, 1941–1948*, Frankfurt am Main, 1985.
Gransow, V. and Jarausch, K. (eds), *Die deutsche Vereinigung: Dokumente zu Bürgerbewegung, Annäherung und Beitritt*, Cologne, 1991.
Grass, G., *Deutscher Lastenausgleich. Wider das dumpfe Einheitsgebot: Reden und Gespräche*, Frankfurt am Main, 1990.
Grass, G., *Two States – One Nation?*, San Diego, 1990.
Grewe W.G., *Rückblenden, 1976–1951*, Frankfurt am Main, 1979.
Grewe, W.G., *Die deutsche Frage in der Ost-West Spannung: Zeitgeschichtliche Kontroversen der achtziger Jahre*, Herford, 1987.
Griffith W.E., *The Ostpolitik of the Federal Republic of Germany*, Cambridge, Mass., 1978.
Griffith, W.E. (ed.), *Central and Eastern Europe: The Opening Curtain?*, Boulder, Col., 1989.
Grosser, A., *West Germany from Defeat to Re-armament*, London, 1956.
Grosser A., *Germany in Our Time*, London, 1971.
Grosser, A., *Geschichte Deutschlands seit 1945*, Munich, 1974.
Grosser A., *Das Deutschland im Western. Eine Bilanz nach 40 Jahren*, Munich, 1988.
Grosser, A., *Frankreich und seine Aussenpolitik, 1944 bis heute*, Munich, 1989.
Grosser, D. (ed.), *Der Staat in der Wirtschaft der Bundesrepublik*, Opladen, 1985.
Grosser, D. (ed.), *German Unification: The Unexpected Challenge*, Oxford, 1992.
Gruner, W.D., *Deutschland mitten in Europa*, Hamburg, 1991.
Gruner, W.D., *Die deutsche Frage – Ein Problem der europäischen Geschichte seit 1800*, Munich, 1992.

Grünwald, L. (ed.), *Sudetendeutsche – Opfer und Täter*, Vienna, 1983.
Gwertzmann, B. and Kaufman, M.T., *The Collapse of Communism*, New York, 1990.
Gysi, G. and Falkner, T., *Sturm auf das grosse Haus. Der Untergang der SED*, Berlin, 1990.
Habermas, J., *Die nachholende Revolution. Kleine politische Schriften VII*, Frankfurt am Main, 1990.
Hacke, C., *Weltmacht wider Willen: Die Aussenpolitik der Bundesrepublik Deutschland*, Stuttgart, 1988.
Hacker, J., *Deutsche unter sich*, Stuttgart-Degerloch, 1977.
Hacker, J., *Deutsche Irrtümer: Schönfärberei und Helfershelfer der SED-Diktatur im Westen*, Berlin, 1992.
Haftendorn, H., *Sicherheit und Entspannung*, Baden-Baden, 1983.
Haftendorn, H., *Security and Détente: Conflicting Priorities in German Foreign Policy*, New York, 1985.
Haglund, D.G., *Alliance within the Alliance: Franco–German Military Co-operation and the European Pillar of Defense*, Boulder, Col., 1991.
Hahn, A. et al. (eds), *Protestdemonstration Berlin DDR – 4/11/89*, Berlin, 1990.
Hahn, R., *Ausgedienst: Ein Stasi-Major erzählt*, Halle, 1990.
Hallet, G., *The Social Economy of West Germany*, London, 1973.
Hamerow, T.S., *The Social Foundations of German Unification, 1858–1871*, 2 vols, Princeton, NJ, 1969, 1972.
Hamilton, D., *After the Revolution: The New Political Landscape in East Germany*, German Issues, 7, Washington, DC, 1990.
Hancock, M.D., *West Germany: The Politics of Democratic Corporatism*, London, 1989.
Hancock, M.D. and Welsh, H.A. (eds), *German Unification: Process and Outcome*, Boulder, Col., 1993.
Hangen, W., *The Muted Revolution*, London, 1968.
Hanhardt, A.M., *The German Democratic Republic*, Baltimore, 1968.
Hanrieder, W.F., *West German Foreign Policy, 1949–1963: International Pressure and Domestic Response*, Stanford, Calif., 1963.
Hanrieder, W.F., *West German Foreign Policy: 1949–1979*, Boulder, Col., 1980.
Hanrieder, W.F. (ed.), *Helmut Schmidt: Perspectives on Politics*, Boulder, Col., 1982.
Hanrieder, W.F, *Germany, America, Europe: Forty Years of German Foreign Policy*, New Haven, Conn., 1989.
Hanrieder, W.F., *Deutschland, Europa, Amerika. Die Aussenpolitik der Bundesrepublik Deutschland 1949–1989*, Paderborn, 1991.

Hardach, K., *The Political Economy of Germany in the Twentieth Century*, Berkeley, 1980.
Harris, J.F. (ed.), *German–American Interrelations. Heritage and Challenge*, Tübingen, 1985.
Hartley, A., *Germany East/West*, London, 1968.
Hartrich, E., *The Fourth and the Richest Reich*, New York, 1980.
Hartung, K., *Neunzehnhundertneunundachtzig*, Frankfurt am Main, 1990.
Havel, V. et al., *The Power of the Powerless*, Armonk, NY, 1990.
Heep, B., *Helmut Schmidt und Amerika*, Bonn, 1990.
Heidenheimer, A., *Adenauer and the CDU*, The Hague, 1960.
Heidenheimer, A., *The Governments of Germany*, 4th edn, New York, 1977.
Heine, M. et al. (eds), *Die Zukunft der DDR-Wirtschaft*, Reinbek bei Hamburg, 1990.
Heisenberg, W., *German Unification in European Perspective*, London, 1991.
Heitzer, H., *GDR: An Historical Outline*, Dresden, 1981.
Helwig, G., *Die letzten Jahre der DDR: Texte zum Alltagsleben*, Cologne, 1990.
Henrich, R., *Der vormundschaftliche Staat: Vom Versagen des real existierenden Sozialismus*, Reinbek bei Hamburg, 1989.
Hentilä, S., *DDR, valtio ilman kansaa*, Helsinki, 1992.
Herf, J., *War by Other Means: Soviet Power, West German Resistance and the Battle of the Euromissiles*, New York, 1991.
Herles, H. and Rose E. (eds), *Parlaments-Szenen einer deutschen Revolution. Bundestag und Volkskammer im November 1989*, Bonn, 1989.
Herles, H. and Rose E. (eds), *Vom Runden Tisch zum Parlament*, Bonn, 1990.
Hersh, S.M., *The Price of Power: Kissinger in the White House*, New York, 1983.
Hettlage, R. (ed.), *Die Bundesrepublik. Eine historische Bilanz*, Munich, 1990.
Hildebrand, K., *Geschichte der Bundesrepublik Deutschland: Von Erhard zur Grossen Koalition, 1963–1969*, Stuttgart, 1984.
Hildebrand, K. and Pommerin, R. (eds), *Deutsche Frage in europäisches Gleichgewicht. Festschrift für Andreas Hillgruber zum 60 Geburtstag*, Cologne, 1984.
Hillgruber, A., *Deutsche Geschichte, 1945–1982. Die 'deutsche Frage' in der Weltpolitik*, Stuttgart, 1983.
Hillgruber, A., *Die Last der Nation*, Düsseldorff, 1984.
Hillgruber, A. and Hildebrand, K., *Kalkül zwischen Macht und Ideologie*, Zürich, 1980.
Holm, H.A., *The Other Germans: Report from an East German Town*, London, 1971.

Honecker, E., *Aus meinem Leben*, Berlin, 1982.
Honecker, E., *Zu den dramatischen Ereignissen*, Hamburg, 1992.
Horn, G., *Freiheit die ich meine: Erinnerungen des ungarischen Aussenministers, der den Eisernen Vorhang öffnete*, Hamburg, 1991.
Horn, H. and Mampel, S. (eds), *Die deutsche Frage aus der heutigen Sicht des Auslandes*, Berlin, 1987.
Hornsby, L., *Profile of East Germany*, London, 1966.
Huelshoff, M.G., Markovits, A.S. and Reich, S. (eds), *From Bundesrepublik to Deutschland*, Ann Arbor, 1993.
Humann, K. (ed), *Wir sind das Geld,* Reinbek bei Hamburg, 1990.
Iggers, G.G., *The German Conception of History: The National Tradition of Historical Thought from Herder to the Present*, rev. edn, Middletown, Conn., 1983.
Implications of the Treaty of Final German Settlement for NATO Strategy and US Military Presence in Europe, Hearing, Committee on Armed Services, Senate, October 4, 1990, Washington DC, 1991.
Infas-Report Wahlen DDR 1990. Wahl der Volkskammer der DDR am 18 März 1990. Analysen und dokumente, Bonn-Bad Godesberg, 1990.
Jacobson, J., *Locarno Diplomacy: Germany and the West, 1925–1929*, Princeton, 1972.
Jäger, W. and Link, W., *Geschichte der Bundesrepublik Deutschland: Republik im Wandel*, Stuttgart, 1987.
Jahn, H.E., *Die deutsche Frage von 1975 bis heute. Der Weg der Parteien und Regierungen*, Mainz, 1985.
James, H. and Stone, M., (eds), *When the Wall Came Down: Reactions to German Unification*, New York, 1992.
James, H.A, *A German Identity, 1770–1990*, New York, 1990.
Janka, W., *Schwierigkeiten mit der Wahrheit*, Reinbek, 1990.
Janson, C-H., *Totengräber der DDR: Wie Günter Mittag den SED-Staat ruinierte*, Düsseldorf, 1991.
Jaspers, K., *The Future of Germany*, Chicago, 1967.
Jeffries, I. and Melzer, M. (eds), *The East German Economy*, London, 1987.
Jesse, E. and Mitter, Armin (eds), *Die Gestaltung der Deutschen Einheit: Geschichte, Politik, Gesellschaft*, Bonn, 1992.
Joesten, J., *Germany: What Now?,* Chicago, 1948.
Jonas, M., *The United States and Germany: A Diplomatic History*, Ithaca, NY, 1984.
Just, G., *Zeuge in eigener Sache. Die fünfziger Jahre*, Berlin, 1990.
Kaiser, K., *German Foreign Policy in Transition: Bonn between East and West*, London, 1968.
Kaiser, K., *Deutschlands Vereinigung: Die internationalen Aspekte*, Bergische Gladbach, 1992.

Kaiser, K. and Lelleouche, P. (eds), *Deutsch-Französische Sicherheitspolitik*, Bonn, 1986.
Kaiser, K. and Morgan, R. (eds), *Britain and West Germany: Changing Societies and the Future of Foreign Policy*, London, 1971.
Kaiser, K. and Roper, J. (eds), *British–German Defence co-operation*, London, 1988.
Katzenstein, P. (ed.), *Industry and Politics in West Germany*, Ithaca, NY, 1989.
Katzenstein, P., *Policy and Politics in West Germany: Toward the Third Republic*, Ithaca, NY, 1989.
Katzenstein, P.J., *Policy and Politics in West Germany: The Growth of a Semi-sovereign State*, Philadelphia, 1987.
Keithly, D.M., *Breakthrough in the Ostpolitik*, Boulder, Col., 1986.
Kelleher, C.M., *Germany and the Politics of Nuclear Weapons*, New York, 1975.
Kennedy, P., *The Rise of Anglo–German Antagonism, 1860–1914*, London, 1980.
Kennedy, P., *The Rise and Fall of the Great Powers*, New York, 1989.
Kiesinger, K., *Stationen 1949–69*, Tübingen, 1969.
Kiesling G., *Neutralität ist kein Verrat*, Erlangen, 1989.
Kimball, W.F., *Swords or Ploughshares? The Morgenthau Plan for Defeated Nazi Germany, 1943–1946*, Philadelphia, 1976.
Kirchner, E.J. and Sperling, J. (eds), *The Federal Republic of Germany and NATO: 40 Years After*, London, 1992.
Kirschey, P., *Wandlitz Waldsiedlung – die Geschlossene Gesellschaft*, Berlin, 1990.
Kissinger, H., *The White House Years*, Boston, 1979.
Kissinger, H., *The Years of Upheaval*, Boston, 1982.
Klein, H., *Es begann im Kaukasus: Der entscheidende Schritt in die Einheit Deutschlands*, Berlin, 1991.
Klemperer, K. von, *Germany's New Conservatism*, Princeton, NJ, 1957.
Klessmann, C., *Die doppelte Staatsgründung: Deutsche Geschichte 1945–1955*, Bonn, 1982.
Klessmann, C., *Zwei Staaten, eine Nation: Deutsche Geschichte 1955–1970*, Göttingen, 1988.
Klier, F., *Abreisskalender: Ein deutsch-deutsches Tagebuch*, Munich, 1989.
Klier, F., *Lüz-Vaterland: Erziehung in der DDR*, Munich, 1990.
Kloss, G., *West Germany: An Introduction*, Basingstoke and London, 1990.
Knabe, H. (ed.), *Aufbruch in eine andere DDR: Reformer und Oppositionelle zur Zukunft ihres Landes*, Reinbek bei Hamburg, 1989.
Koch, H.W., *A Constitutional History of Germany in the Nineteeth and Twentieth Centuries*, New York, 1984.

Koch, P., *Konrad Adenauer: Eine politische Biographie*, Reinbek, 1985.
Kock, K. (ed.), *West Germany Today*, London, 1989.
Kohl, H. (ed.), *Konrad Adenauer 1876–1976*, Stuttgart, 1976.
Kohl, H., *Reden und Erklärungen zur Deutschland Politik*, Bonn, 1990.
Kohler-Koch, B. (ed.), *Die Osterweitung der EG: Die Einbeziehung der ehemaligen DDR in die Gemeinschaft*, Baden Baden, 1991.
Kohn, H., *The Mind of the Germans: The Education of a Nation*, New York, 1960.
Kolinsky, E. (ed.), *The Federal Republic of Germany: The End of an Era*, Oxford, 1991.
Koop, V. and Schössler, D., *Erbe NVA – Eindrücke aus ihrer Geschichte und der Tagen der Wende*, Waldbröl, 1992.
Krejci, J., *Social Structure in Divided Germany*, London, 1976.
Krenz, E., *Wenn Mauern fallen: die Friedliche Revolution: Vorgeschichte – Ablauf – Auswirkungen*, Vienna, 1990.
Krieger, L., *The German Idea of Freedom: History of a Political Tradition*, Boston, 1957.
Krisch, H., *German Politics under Soviet Occupation*, New York, 1984.
Krisch, H., *The German Democratic Republic: The Search for Identity*, Boulder, Col., 1985.
Krisch, H., *Politics and Culture in the German Democratic Republic*, Ann Arbor, 1988.
Krockow, C.G. von, *Nationalismus als deutsches Problem*, Munich, 1976.
Kroh, F. (ed.), *'Freiheit ist immer Freiheit...': Die Andersdenkenden in der DDR*, Frankfurt am Main / Berlin, 1988.
Kuby, E., *Der Preis der Einheit: Ein deutsches Europa formt sein Gesicht*, Hamburg, 1990.
Kuczynski, J., *Schwierige Jahre – mit einem besseren Ende?,* Berlin, 1990.
Kuhn, E. *Der Tag der Entscheidung: Leipzig, 9 Oktober 1989*, Berlin, 1992.
Kuklick, B., *American Policy and the Division of Germany: The Clash with Russia over Reparations*, Ithaca, NY, 1972.
Ködderitzsch, P. and Müller, L., *Rechtsradikalismus in der DDR*, Göttingen, 1990.
Köhler, H. (ed.), *Deutschland und der Western: Vorträge und Diskussionsbeiträge des Symposions zu Ehren von Gordon A, Craig*, Berlin, 1984.
Königsdorf, H. (ed.), *Adieu DDR – Protokolle eines Abschieds*, Reinbek bei Hamburg, 1990.
Kurz, R., *Honeckers Rache: Zur politischen Ökonomie des wiedervereinigten Deutschlands*, Berlin, 1991.
Laird, R.F. (ed.), *Strangers and Friends: The Franco–German Security Relationship*, London, 1989.
Laird, R.F., *The Soviets, Germany, and the New Europe*, Boulder, Col., 1991.

Laitenberger, V., *Ludwig Erhard: Der Nationalökonom als Politiker*, Göttingen, 1986.
Lang, J. von, *Erich Mielke: Eine deutsche Karriere*, Berlin, 1991.
Lang, R. (ed.), *Das Umbaupapier (DDR): Argumente gegen die Wiedervereinigung*, Berlin, 1990.
Lange, K. (ed.), *Aspekte der Deutschen Frage*, Herford, 1986.
Langguth, G. (ed.), *Berlin von Brennpunkt der Teilung zur Brücke der Einheit*, Berlin, 1990.
Lapp, P., *Die 'befreundeten Parteien' der SED: DDR-Blockparteien heute*, Cologne, 1988.
Laqueur, W., *Germany Today: A Contemporary History*, New York, 1982.
Laqueur, W., *Germany Today: A Personal Report*, London, 1985.
Larrabee, F.S. (ed.), *The Two German States and European Security*, New York, 1989.
Lau, K., *Deutschland auf dem Weg zur Einheit: Dokumente einer Revolution*, Brunswick, 1990.
Leaman, J., *The Political Economy of West Germany, 1945–85*, London, 1988.
Le Gloannec, A-M., *Die deutsche-deutsche Nation: Anmerkungen zu einer revolutionären Entwicklung*, Munich, 1991.
Lemke, C., *The Quality of Life in the GDR*, Armonk, NY, 1989.
Lemke, C., *Die Ursachen des Umbruchs 1989: Politische Sozialisation in der ehemaligen DDR*, Opladen, 1991.
Lemke, C. and Marks, G. (eds), *The Crisis of Socialism in Europe*, Durham, NC, 1992.
Lentz, M., *Die Wirtschaftsbeziehungen DDR–Sowietunion*, Opladen, 1979.
Leonhard, W., *Child of the Revolution*, Chicago, 1967.
Leptin, G., *Die deutsche Wirtschaft nach 1945: Ein Ost-West Vergleich*, Opladen, 1970.
Leptin, G. and Melzer, M., *Economic Reform in East German Industry*, London, 1978.
Liebert, U. and Merkel, W. (eds), *Die Politik zur Deutschen Einheit: Probleme, Strategien, Kontroversen, Leverkusen*, Opladen, 1991.
Links, C. and Bahrmann, H., *Wir sind das Volk: Die DDR im Aufbruch*, Berlin / Wuppertal, 1990.
Lippman, H., *Honecker and the New Politics of Europe*, New York, 1972.
Lipschitz, L. and McDonald, D. (eds), *German Unification: Economic Issues*, Washington, DC, 1990.
Livingston, R.G. (ed.), *The Federal Republic of Germany in the 1980s*, New York, 1983.
Lochner, A. (ed.), *Linke Politik in Deutschland*, Hamburg, 1990.

Loest, E., *Die Stasi war mein Eckermann oder mein Leben mit der Wanze*, Göttingen, 1991.

Loth, W., *Die Teilung der Welt. Geschichte des Kalten Krieges 1941–1955*, Munich, 1978.

Loth, W., *Ost-West-Konflikt und deutsche Frage. Historische Ortbestimmungen*, Munich 1989.

Loth, W., *Der Weg nach Europa*, 2nd edn, Göttingen, 1991.

Löw, K. (ed.), *Ursachen und Verlauf der deutschen Revolution 1989*, Berlin, 1991.

Ludwig, M., *Polen und die deutsche Frage*, Bonn, 1990.

Ludz, P.C., *The German Democratic Republic from the Sixties to the Seventies*, Cambridge, Mass., 1970.

Ludz, P.C., *The Changing Party Elite in East Germany*, Cambridge, Mass., 1972.

Ludz, P.C., *Die DDR zwischen Ost und West*, Munich, 1977.

Mahnke, H.H. (ed.), *Dokumente zur Berlin-Frage, 1967–1986*, Munich, 1987.

Maier, C.S. (ed.), *The Origins of the Cold War and Contemporary Europe*, New York, 1978.

Maier, C.S., *The Unmasterable Past: History, Holocaust, and German National Identity*, Cambridge, Mass., 1988.

Maier, C.S. and Bischof, G. (eds), *The Marshall Plan and Germany*, New York, 1991.

Mann, A., *Comeback: Germany 1945–1952*, London, 1980.

Marcuse, P., *Missing Marx: A Personal and Political Journal of a Year in East Germany, 1989–1990*, New York, 1991.

Markovits, A.S. (ed.), *The Political Economy of West Germany*, New York, 1982.

Markovits, A.S. (ed.), *The Politics of West German Trade Unions: Strategies of Class and Interest Representation in Growth and Crisis*, Cambridge, 1986.

Maron, J. and Schedlinski, R., *Innenansichten DDR. Letzte Bilder*, Reinbek bei Hamburg, 1990.

Marsh, D., *The Germans: Rich, Bothered and Divided*, London, 1989.

Marsh, D., *The New Germany*, London, 1990.

Marsh, D., *Bundesbank: The Bank that Rules Europe*, London, 1992.

Marshall, B., *The Origins of Post-war German Politics*, London, 1988.

Martin, E., *Zwischenbilanz: Deutschlandpolitik der 80er Jahren*, Stuttgart, 1986.

Maser, W., *Helmut Kohl: Der Deutsche Kanzler*, Berlin, 1990.

Mattox, G.A. and Shingleton, A.B. (eds), *Germany at the Crossroads: Foreign and Domestic Policy Issues*, Boulder, Col., 1992.

Mattox, G.A. and Vaughan, J.H., Jr, *Germany Through American Eyes*, Boulder, Col., 1989.

May, B., *Kosten und Nutzen der deutschen EG-Mitgliedschaft*, Bonn, 1982.

McAdams, A.J., *East Germany and the Détente: Building Authority after the Wall*, Cambridge, 1985.

McAdams, A.J., *Germany Divided: From the Wall to Reunification*, Princeton, 1993.

McCauley, M., *Marxism–Leninism in the German Democratic Republic: The Socialist Unity Party (SED)*, New York, 1979.

McCauley, M., *East Germany: The Dilemmas of Division*, London, 1980.

McCauley, M., *East–West German Relations: A Turning Point?,* London, 1983.

McCauley, M., *The German Democratic Republic since 1945*, New York, 1983.

McElvoy, A., *The Saddled Cow: East German Life and Legacy*, London, 1992.

McGhee, J.J., *At the Creation of a New Germany*, New Haven, Conn., 1989.

Meier, C., *Deutsche Einheit als Herausforderung: Welche Fundamenta für welche Republik*, Munich, 1990.

Meier, C., *Die Nation die keine sein will*, Munich, 1991.

Meinel, R. and Wernicke, T., *Mit tschekistischem Gruss. Berichte der Bezieksverwaltung für Staatssicherheit Potsdam 1989*, Potsdam, 1990.

Meissner, B. (ed.), *Die deutsche Ostpolitik: 1961–1970*, Cologne, 1970.

Mellor, R., *The Two Germanies: A Modern Geography*, London, 1978.

Menge, M., *"Ohne uns geht nichts mehr": Die Revolution in der DDR*, Stuttgart, 1990.

Menges, C.C., *The Future of Germany and the Atlantic Alliance*, Washington, DC, 1991,

Merkel, W. and Wahl, S., *Das geplünderte Deutschland: Die wirtschaftliche Entwicklung im östlichen Teil Deutschlands von 1949 bis 1989*, Bonn, 1991.

Merkl, P.H., *The Origin of the West German Republic*, New York, 1963.

Merkl, P.H., *Germany: Yesterday and Tomorrow*, New York, 1965.

Merkl, P.H., *German Foreign Policies: East and West*, Santa Barbara, 1974.

Merkl, P.H. (ed.), *The Federal Republic of Germany at Forty*, New York, 1989.

Merkl, P.H. and Glaessner, G.J., *German Unification in the European Context*, University Park, Penn., 1993.

Merritt, R.L., *Politics, Economics and Society in the Two Germanies, 1945–1975*, Urbana, Ill., 1978.

Meuschel, S., *Legitimation und Parteiherrschaft. Zum Paradox von Stabilität und Revolution in der DDR 1945–1989*, Frankfurt am Main, 1992.

Meyer, G., *Die DDR-Machtelite in der Ära Honecker*, Tübingen, 1991.
Middleton, D., *The Struggle for Germany*, New York, 1950.
Mittag, G., *Um Jeden Preis: Im Spannungsfeld zweier Systeme*, Berlin and Weimar, 1991.
Mittenzwei, I., *Friedrich der II und Preussen*, Berlin, 1979.
Mitter, A. and Wolle S. (eds), *'Ich liebe euch doch alle!' Befehle und Lageberichte des MfS Januar–November 1989*, Berlin, 1990.
Modrow, H., *Aufbruch und Ende*, Hamburg, 1991.
Moersch, K., *Kurs-Revision: Deutsche Politik nach Adenauer*, Hof, 1978.
Mommsen, W.J., *Two Centuries of Anglo–German Relations: A Reappraisal*, London, 1984.
Momper, W., *Grenzfall: Berlin im Brennpunkt deutscher Geschichte*, Munich, 1991.
Moreton, N.E., *East Germany and the Warsaw Alliance: The Politics of Détente*, Boulder, Col., 1978.
Moreton, N.E. (ed.), *Germany between East and West*, Cambridge, 1987.
Morgan, R., *The United States and West Germany 1945–1973*, London, 1973.
Morgenthau, H., *Germany is Our Problem*, New York, 1945.
Morris, E., *Blockade: Berlin and the Cold War*, London, 1973.
Morrison, J., *Boris Yeltsin: From Bolshevik to Democrat*, New York, 1991.
Muller, S. and Schweigler, G.L. (eds), *From Occupation to Cooperation: The United States and United Germany in a Changing World Order*, New York, 1992.
Müller, M. and Kanonenberg, A., *Die RAF-Stasi Konnexion*, Berlin, 1992.
Müller-Enbergs, H., Schulz, M. and Wielgohs, J. (eds), *Von der Illegalität ins Parlament: Werdegang und Konzept der neuen Bürgerbewegungen*, Berlin, 1991.
Naumann, G. and Trumpler, E., *Von Ulbricht zu Honecker*, Berlin, 1990.
Naumann, G. and Trumpler, E., *Der Flop mit der DDR-Nation*, Berlin, 1991.
Nawrocki, J., *Relations between the Two States in Germany*, Bonn, 1985.
Nelson, B., Roberts, D. and Veit, W. (eds), *The European Community in the 1990s. Economics, Politics, Defence*, Oxford, 1992.
Nesselrode, F. von, *Germany's Other Half*, London, 1963.
Nettl, J.P., *The Eastern Zone and the Soviet Policy in Germany, 1945–1950*, London, 1951.
Neubert, E., *Eine protestantische Revolution*, Osnabrück, 1990.
Neues Forum Leipzig, *Jetzt oder Nie – Demokratie! Leipziger Herbst, 1989*, Leipzig, 1989.
Neumann, T., *Die Massnahme: Eine Herrschaftsgeschichte der SED*, Reinbek bei Hamburg, 1991.

New German Critique. Special Issue on German Unification, no. 52, Winter 1990.

Niethammer, L., von Plato, A. and Wierling, D., *Die Volkseigene Erfahrung: Eine Archäologie des Lebens in der Industrieprovinz der DDR*, Berlin, 1991.

Ninkovitch, F.A., *Germany and the United States: The Transformation of the German Question Since 1945*, Boston, 1988.

Noack, P., *'Deutschland, deine Intellektuellen': Die Kunst, sich in Abseits zu stellen*, Stuttgart, 1991.

Nolte, E., *Deutschland und der Kalte Krieg*, 2nd edn, Stuttgart, 1985.

Oberdorfer, D., *The Turn: From the Cold War to a New Era – The United States and the Soviet Union, 1983–1990*, New York, 1991.

Obst, W., *Reiz der Idee – Pleite der Praxis: Ein deutsch-deutscher Wirtschaftsvergleich*, Osnabrück, 1983.

Oktober 1989 – Wider den Schlaf der Vernunft, Berlin, 1989.

Orlow, D., *A History of Modern Germany*, Englewood Cliffs, NJ, 1987.

Osmond, J., *German Reunification: A Reference Guide and Commentary*, Harlow, 1992.

Osten, W., *Die Aussenpolitik der DDR*, Opladen, 1969.

Padgett, S. (ed.), *Party Politics in the New Germany*, Aldershot, 1992.

Padgett, S. and Burkett, T., *Political Parties and Elections in West Germany*, London, 1986.

Parkers, K.S., *Writers and Politics in West Germany*, London, 1986.

Paterson, W. and Smith, G. (eds), *The West German Model: Perspectives on a Stable State*, London, 1981.

Paterson, W. and Soutern, D., *Governing Germany*, Oxford, 1991.

Peterson, E., *The American Occupation of Germany*, Detroit, 1978.

Petschow, U., Meyerhoff, J. and Thomasberger, C. (eds), *Umweltreport DDR: Bilanz der Zerstörung – Kosten der Sanierung – Strategien für den ökologischen Umbau*, Frankfurt am Main, 1990.

Pfeiler, W., *Deutschlandpolitische Optionen der Sowjetunion*, Melle, 1987.

Pfetsch, F.R., *West Germany: Internal Structure and External Relations*, New York, 1988.

Philipsen, D., *We Were the People: Voices from East Germany's Revolutionary Autumn of 1989*, Durham, 1993.

Phillips, A.L., *Soviet Policy toward East Germany Reconsidered: The Postwar Decade*, New York and Westport, Conn., 1986.

Picht, R. (ed.), *Das Bündniss im Bündniss. Deutsch-französische Beziehungen im internationalen Spannungsfeld*, Berlin, 1983.

Pierre, A.J. (ed.), *Domestic Change and Foreign Policy: A Widening Atlantic?,* New York, 1986.

Planck, C.R., *The Changing Status of German Reunification in Western Diplomacy*, Baltimore, 1967.
Plock, E.D., *The Basic Treaty and the Evolution of East–West German Relations*, Boulder, Col., 1986.
Plock, E.D., *East German–West German Relations and the Fall of the GDR*, Boulder, Col., 1993.
Poidevin, R. and Bariéty J., *Deutschland und Frankreich: Die Geschichte ihrer Beziehungen, 1815–1975*, Munich, 1977.
Pollack, D. (ed.), *Die Legitimität der Freiheit. Politisch alternative Gruppen in der DDR unter dem Dach der Kirche*, Frankfurt am Main, 1990.
Pond, E., *After the Wall*, New York, 1990.
Pond, E., *Beyond the Wall: Germany's Road to Unification*, Washington, DC, 1993.
Post, G., Jr. (ed.), *German Unification: Problems and Prospects*, Claremont, Calif., 1992.
Press and Information Office of the Federal Government, *The Unification of Germany in 1990. A Documentation*, Bonn, 1991.
Preuss, U.K., *Revolution, Fortschritt und Verfassung. Zu einem neuen Verfassungsverständnis*, Berlin, 1990.
Pridham, G., *Christian Democracy in West Germany*, London, 1977.
Priewe, J. and Heickel, R., *Der Preis der Einheit: Bilanz und Perspektiven der deutschen Vereinigung*, Frankfurt am Main, 1991.
Prittie, T., *Divided Germany*, London, 1961.
Prittie, T., *Konrad Adenauer*, London, 1972.
Prittie, T., *Willy Brandt: Portrait of a Statesman*, London, 1974.
Prittie, T., *The Velvet Chancellors*, London, 1979.
Prolingheuer, H., *'Kirchenwende oder Wendekirche?' Die EKD nach dem 9 November 1989 und ihre Vergangenheit*, Bonn, 1991.
Pronay, N. and Wilson, K. (eds), *The Political Re-education of Germany and her Allies after World War II*, London, 1985.
Przybylski, P. (ed.), *Tatort Politbüro: Die Akte Honecker*, Berlin, 1991.
Raff, D., *A History of Germany*, New York, 1988.
Rehlinger, L.A., *Freikauf. Die Geschäfte der DDR mit politisch Verfolgten*, Frankfurt am Main and Berlin, 1991.
Reich, J., *Rückkehr nach Europa: Zur Lage der deutschen Nation*, Munich, 1991.
Reich, J., *Abschied von den Lebenslugen: Die Intelligenz und die Macht*, Berlin, 1992.
Rein, G. (ed.), *Die Opposition in der DDR – Entwürfe für einen anderen Sozialismus*, Berlin, 1989.
Rein, G., *Die protestantische Revolution, 1987–90: Ein deutsches Lesebuch*, Berlin, 1990.

Richardson, J., *Germany and the Atlantic Alliance*, London, 1966.
Richert, E., *Die Sowjetzone in der Phase der Koexistenz*, Hanover, 1961.
Riste, O. (ed.), *Western Security, the Formative Years. European and Atlantic Defence 1947–1953*, New York, 1985.
Roberts, G.K., *West German Politics*, London, 1972.
Roehricht, K.H., *Lebensverläufe: Innenansichten aus der DDR*, Berlin, 1991.
Rostow, W.W., *The Division of Europe after World War II: 1946*, Austin, Tex., 1981.
Rotfeld, A.D. and Stützle, W. (eds), *Germany and Europe in Transition*, Stockholm, 1991.
Roth, R., *Aussenpolitische Innovation und politische Herrschaftssicherung*, Meisenheim am Glan, 1976.
Rovan J. and Weidenfeld, W. (eds), *Europäische Zeitzeichen. Elemente eines deutsch-französischen Dialogs*, Bonn, 1982.
Rueschemeyer, M. and Lemke, C. (eds), *The Quality of Life in the German Democratic Republic*, New York, 1989.
Rusi, A.M., *After the Cold War: Europe's New Political Architecture*, New York, 1991.
Sanford, G.W., *From Hitler to Ulbricht: The Communist Reconstruction of East Germany, 1945–46*, Princeton, NJ, 1983.
Sanford, J., *The Mass Media of the German-Speaking Countries*, London, 1976.
Sanford, J., *The Sword and the Ploughshare: Autonomous Peace Initiatives in East Germany*, London, 1983.
Saña, H., *Das Vierte Reich. Deutschlands später Sieg*, Hamburg, 1990.
Sauer, H., and Plumeyer, H-O., *Der Salzgitter Report: Die zentrale Erfassungstelle bericht über Verbrechen in SED-Staat*, Esslingen-Munich, 1991.
Schabowski, G., *Das Politbüro: Ende eines Mythos*, Berlin, 1990.
Schabowski, G., *Der Absturz*, Berlin, 1990.
Schädlich, H.J. (ed.), *Aktenkundig*, Berlin, 1992.
Schaffer, G., *Russian Zone*, London, 1947.
Scharf, C. and Schröder, H-J. (eds), *Die Deutschlandpolitik Grossbritanniens und die Britische Zone, 1945–1949*, Wiesbaden, 1979.
Scharf, C.B., *Politics and Change in East Germany: An Evaluation of Socialist Democracy*, Boulder, Col., 1984.
Schäuble, W., *Der Vertrag: Wie ich über die deutsche Einheit verhandelte*, Stuttgart, 1991.
Schell, M. and Kalinka, W., *Stasi und kein Ende: Die Personen und Fakten*, Frankfurt am Main and Berlin, 1991.
Scheuch, E.K., *Wie deutsch sind die Deutschen? Eine Nation wandelt ihr Gesicht*, Bergisch Gladbach, 1991.

Schick, J.M., *The Berlin Crisis, 1958–1962*, Philadelphia, 1971.

Schmid, G., *Entscheidung in Bonn: Die Entstehung der Ost- und Deutschlandpolitik, 1969–1970*, Cologne, 1979.

Schmidt, H., *Menschen und Mächte*, Berlin, 1987.

Schmidt, H., *Die Deutschen und ihre Nachbarn: Menschen und Mächte II*, Berlin, 1990.

Schmieding, H., *German Unification: the Economics of Transition*, working paper 468, Kiel, 1991.

Schneider, E., *The GDR: The History, Politics, Economy, and Society of East Germany*, New York, 1978.

Schneider, E., *Der Nationsbegriff der DDR und seine deutschlandpolitische Bedeutung*, Cologne, 1981.

Schneider, G., *Wirtschaftwunder DDR – Anspruch und Realität*, Cologne, 1990.

Schneider, M., *Die abgetriebene Revolution: Von der Staatsfirma in die DM-Kolonie*, Berlin, 1990.

Schneider, P., *Extreme Mittelage: Eine Reise durch das deutsche Nationalgefühl*, Reinbeck, 1990.

Schneider, P., *The German Comedy*, New York, 1991.

Schneider, R., *Frühling im Herbst: Notizen vom Umbruch der DDR*, Göttingen, 1991.

Schneider, W., *Leipziger Demontagebuch*, Leipzig and Weimar, 1990.

Schnitzer, M., *East and West Germany: A Comparative Economic Analysis*, New York, 1972.

Schönbohm, J., *Zwei Armeen und ein Vaterland: Das Ende der nationalen Volksarmee*, Berlin, 1992.

Schüddekopf, C. (ed.), *'Wir sind das Volk!' Flugschriften, Aufrufe, Texte einer deutschen Revolution*, Reinbek bei Hamburg, 1990.

Schulz, E., *Die deutsche Nation in Europa: Internationale und historische Dimensionen,* Bonn, 1982.

Schulz, E. *Die deutsche Frage und die Nachbarn am Osten*, Munich, 1989.

Schulz, E. and Danylow, P. (eds), *Bewegung in der deutschen Frage? Die ausländischen Besorgnisse über die Entwicklung in den beiden deutschen Staaten*, 2nd edn, Bonn, 1985.

Schulze, H.R. and Kessler R. (eds), *Hans-Dietrich Genscher: Ein deutscher Aussenminister*, Munich, 1990.

Schwartz, T.A., *America's Germany: John McCloy and the Federal Republic of Germany*, Cambridge, Mass., 1991.

Schwarz, H-P. (ed.), *Die Legende von der verpassten Gelegenheit: Die Stalin Note vom 10. März 1952*, Düsseldorf, 1952.

Schwarz, H-P. (ed.), *Konrad Adenauer, Reden: 1917–1967*, Stuttgart, 1975.

Schwarz, H-P. (ed.), *Entspannung und Wiedervereinigung. Deutschlands-politische Verstellungen Konrad Adenauers 1955–1958*, Stuttgart, 1979.
Schwarz, H-P., *Geschichte der Bundesrepublik Deutschland: Die Ära Adenauer, 1949–1957*, Stuttgart, 1981.
Schwarz, H-P. (ed.), *Adenauer und Frankreich: die deutsch-franzsösischen Beziehungen 1958 bis 1969*, Bonn, 1985.
Schwarz, H-P., *Berlinkrise und Mauerbau*, Bonn, 1985.
Schwarz, H-P., *Adenauer: Der Staatsmann, 1952–1967*, Stuttgart, 1991.
Schweigler, G., *National Consciousness in Divided Germany*, London, 1975.
Schweitzer, C.C. et al., *Politics and Government in the Federal Republic of Germany, Basic Documents*, Leamington Spa, 1984.
Seebacher-Brandt, B., *Die Linke und die Einheit*, Berlin, 1991.
Seewald, H. (ed.), *Helmut Kohl: Deutschlands Zukunft in Europa. Reden und Beiträge des Bundeskanzlers*, Herford, 1990.
Seiffert W., *Das ganze Deutschland*, Munich, 1986.
Seiffert W., *Die Deutschen und Gorbatschow*, Erlangen, 1989.
Seiffert W. and Treutwein, N., *Die Schalck Papiere: DDR-Mafia zwischen Ost und West. Die Beweise*, Vienna, 1991.
Sharp, T., *The Wartime Alliance and the Zonal Division of Germany*, Oxford, 1975.
Shears, D., *The Ugly Frontier*, London, 1970.
Sheehan, G., *The Man Who changed the World: The Lives of Mikhail S. Gorbachev*, New York, 1990.
Sheehan, J.J. (ed.), *Imperial Germany*, New York, 1976.
Sheehan, J.J., *German Liberalism in the Nineteenth Century*, Chicago, 1978.
Shevardnadze, E., *The Future belongs to Freedom*, New York, 1991.
Shlaes, A., *Germany: The Empire Within*, New York, 1991.
Siebert, H. and Schmieding, H., *Restructuring Industry in the GDR*, working paper 431, Kiel, 1990.
Sievers, H-J., *Stundenbuch einer deutschen Revolution: Die Leiziger Kirchen im Oktober 1989*, Göttingen, 1990.
Simmons, M., *The Unloved Country: A Portrait of East Germany Today*, London, 1989.
Simonian, H., *The Privileged Partnership: Franco–German Relations in the European Community, 1969–84*, Oxford, 1985.
Slusser, R., *The Berlin Crisis of 1961*, Baltimore, 1963.
Smith, E.O., *The West German Economy*, Beckenham, 1983.
Smith, G., *Democracy in West Germany*, London, 1979.
Smith, G., Paterson, W. and Merkl, P. (eds), *Developments in West German Politics*, London, 1989.
Smith, G., Paterson, W.E., Merkl, P.H. and Padgett, S. (eds), *Developments in German Politics*, Durham, 1992.

Smith, J.E., *The Defense of Berlin*, Baltimore, 1963.
Smith, J.E., *Germany Beyond the Wall*, Boston, 1968.
Smyser, W.R., *Restive Partners: Washington and Bonn Diverge*, Boulder, Col., 1990.
Snell, J.L., *Wartime Origins of the East–West Dilemma over Germany*, New Orleans, 1959.
Sodaro, M.J., *Moscow, Germany, and the West: From Khrushchev to Gorbachev*, Ithaca, NY, 1991.
Solberg, R., *God and Caesar in East Germany*, New York, 1961.
Sontheimer, K., *The Government and Politics of West Germany*, London, 1972.
Sontheimer, K. and Bleek, W., *The Government and Politics of East Germany*, London, 1975.
Sontheimer, K. and Bleek, W., *Die DDR: Politik, Gesellschaft, Wirtschaft*, Hamburg, 1979.
Souchon, L., *Neue deutscher Sicherheitspolitik*, Herford, 1991.
Sowden, J.K., *The German Question 1945–1973*, London, 1975.
Speier, H., *West German Leadership and Foreign Policy*, Evanston, Ill., 1957.
Spence, D., *Enlargement Without Accession: The EC's Response to German Unification*, London, 1991.
Spiro, H.J., *The Politics of German Codetermination*, Cambridge, Mass., 1958.
Spittmann, I., *Die DDR unter Honecker*, Cologne, 1990.
Spittmann, I. and Fricke, K.W. (eds), *17 Juni 1953: Arbeiteraufstand in der DDR*, Cologne, 1962.
Spittmann, I. and Helwig, G. (eds), *Chronik der Ereignisse in der DDR*, 4th edn, Cologne, 1990.
Stahl, W., *The Politics of Post-war Germany*, New York, 1963.
Stares, P. (ed.), *The New Germany and the New Europe*, Washington, DC, 1992.
Staritz, D., *Die Gründung der DDR*, Munich, 1984.
Staritz, D., *Geschichte der DDR 1949–1985*, Frankfurt am Main, 1985.
Starrels, J.M. and Malinckrodt, A.M., *Politics in the German Democratic Republic*, New York, 1975.
Statistisches Jahrbuch der Deutschen Demokratischen Republik 1990, Berlin, 1990.
Steele, J., *Socialism with a German Face: The State that Came in from the Cold*, New York, 1977.
Steininger, R. (ed.), *Chance zur Wiedervereinigung? Die Stalin Note vom 10. März 1952. Darstellung und dokumentation auf der Grundlage unveröffentlicher britischer und amerikanischer Akten*, Bonn, 1985.

Steininger, R., *Eine vertane Chance: Die Stalin-Note vom 10 März 1952 und die Wiederverenigung*, Berlin and Bonn, 1985.
Steininger, R. (ed.), *Deutsche Geschichte: 1945–1961*, 2 vols, Frankfurt, 1987.
Stent, A., *From Embargo to Ostpolitik*, Cambridge, 1981.
Stent, A.E., *Economic Relations with the Soviet Union: American and West German Perspectives*, Boulder, Col., 1985.
Stern, C., *Ulbricht: A Political Biography*, London, 1965.
Stern, F., *The Failure of Illiberalism: Essays on the Political Culture of Modern Germany*, New York, 1972.
Stern, F., *Dreams and Delusions: The Drama of German History*, New York, 1987.
Sternburg, W. von (ed.), *Die deutsche Kanzler von Bismarck bis Schmidt*, 2nd edn. Königstein, 1985.
Stolpe, M., *Schwieriger Aufbruch*, Berlin, 1992.
Stolper, W.F., *Germany between East and West*, Washington DC, 1960.
Stolper, W.F., *The Structure of the East German Economy*, Cambridge, 1960.
Stolz, R., *Der deutsche Komplex: Alternativen zur Selbstverleugnung*, Bonn, 1990.
Strauss, F.J., *The Grand Design*, London, 1965.
Strauss, F.J., *Die Erinnerungen*, Berlin, 1989.
Stulz-Herrnstadt, N., *Das Herrnstadt Dokument*, Reinbek bei Hamburg, 1990.
Stürmer, M., *Dissonanzen des Fortschritts: Essays über Geschichte und Politik in Deutschland*, Munich, 1986.
Stürmer, M., *Die Grenzen der Macht: Begegnung der Deutschen mit der Geschichte*, Berlin, 1992.
Stützle, W., *Kennedy und Adenauer in der Berlin Krise, 1961–1962*, Bonn-Bad Godesberg, 1973.
Suhr, H., *Der Treuhand Skandal: Wie Ostdeutschland geschlachtet wurde*, Frankfurt am Main, 1991.
Süsskind, P., *Angst vor Deutschland*, Hamburg, 1990.
Süssmuth, H. (ed.), *Wie geht es weiter mit Deutschland?*, Baden-Baden, 1990.
Swoboda, J. (ed.), *Die Revolution der Kerzen. Christen in der Umwälzung der DDR*, Wuppertal and Kassel, 1990.
Szabo, F. (ed.), *The Bundeswehr and Western Security*, London, 1990.
Szabo, S.F., *The Changing Politics of German Security*, London, 1990.
Szabo, S.F., *The Diplomacy of German Unification*, New York, 1992.
Teltschik, H., *329 Tage: Innenansichten der Einigung*, Berlin, 1991.
Texte zur Deutschlandpolitik, 3rd Series, Bonn, 1966–89.

Thalheim, K.C., *Die wirtschaftliche Entwicklung der beiden Staaten in Deutschland*, Opladen, 1978.
Thatcher, M., *The Downing Street Years*, London and New York, 1993.
Thaysen, U., *Der Runde Tisch. Oder: Wo bleibt das Volk? Der Weg der DDR in die Demokratie*, Wiesbaden, 1990.
Thierse, W., *Mit eigene Stimme sprechen*, Munich, 1990.
Thies, J. and Wagner, W. (eds), *Das Ende der Teilung: Der Wandel in Deutschland und Osteuropa*, Bonn, 1990.
Thomaneck, J.K.A. and Mellis, J. (eds), *Politics, Government and Society in the German Democratic Republic: Basic Documents*, Oxford, 1989.
Thomas, H., *Armed Truce. The Beginning of the Cold War 1945–46*, London, 1986.
Thränhardt, D., *Geschichte der Bundesrepublik Deutschland, 1949–1984*, Frankfurt am Main, 1986.
Tilford, R., *The Ostpolitik and Political Change In Germany*, Farnborough, 1975.
Tilford, R. and Preece, R.J.C., *Federal Germany: The Political and Social Order*, London, 1969.
Trautmann, G. (ed.), *Die hässlichen Deutschen?,* Darmstadt, 1991.
Treue, W., *Die Demontagepolitik der Westmächte nach dem Zweiten Weltkrieg*, Hanover, 1967.
Treverton, G.F., *America, Germany, and the Future of Europe*, Princeton, NJ, 1992.
Trommler, F., and McVeigh, J. (eds), *America and the Germans: An Assessment of a Three-Hundred-Year History*, Philadelphia, 1985.
Turner, H.A., Jr., *Stresemann and the Politics of the Weimar Republic*, Princeton, NJ, 1963.
Turner, H.A., Jr., *The Two Germanies since 1945*, New Haven, Conn., 1987.
Turner, H.A., Jr., *Germany from Partition to Reunification* (rev. edn of *The Two Germanies since 1945*), New Haven, Conn., 1992.
Turner, I.D. (ed.), *Reconstruction in Post-War Germany: British Occupation Policy and the Western Zones, 1945–1955*, Oxford, 1989.
Tusa, A. and Tusa, J., *The Berlin Blockade*, London, 1988.
Ullmann, W., *Demokratie – Jetzt oder nie! Perspektiven der Gerechtigkeit*, Munich, 1991.
Urwin, D.W., *The Community of Europe. A History of European Integration since 1945*, London and New York, 1991.
Uschner, M., *Die Ostpolitik der SPD*, Berlin, 1991.
Valance, G., *France – Allemagne. Le Retour de Bismarck*, Paris, 1990.
Vali, F.A., *The Quest for a United Germany*, Oxford, 1968.
Venohr, W. (ed.), *Die deutsche Einheit kommt bestimmt*, Bergisch Gladbach, 1982.

Venohr, W., *Die rote Preussen: Vom wundersamen Aufstieg der DDR*, Erlangen, 1989.
Venohr, W. (ed.), *Ein Deutschland wirds es sein*, Erlangen, 1990.
Verheyes, D. and Soe, C. (eds), *The Germans and their Neighbors*, Boulder, Col., 1993.
Vincentz, V., *Privatization in Eastern Germany: Principles and Practice*, Munich, 1991.
Visuri, P. and Forsberg, T., *Saksa ja Suomi. Pohjoismainen näkökulma Saksan kysymykseen*, Porvoo, 1992.
Volkmann, H-E. and Schwengler, W., *Die Europäische Verteidigungs Gemeinschaft. Stand und Probleme der Forschung*, vol. 7., Militärgeschichte seit 1945, Boppard, 1985.
Wallace, I. (ed.), *The GDR Under Honecker, 1971–1981*, GDR Monitor Special Series, no. 1, Dundee, 1981.
Wallace, I. (ed.), *East Germany: The German Democratic Republic*, Oxford / Santa Barbara, Calif., 1987.
Wallach, H.G.P. and Francisco, R.A., *United Germany: The Past, Politics, Prospects*, Westport, Conn., 1992.
Wallich, H.C., *The Mainsprings of the German Economic Revival*, New Haven, Conn., 1955.
Watson, A., *The Germans: Who Are They Now?*, London, 1992.
Wawzrzyn, L., *Der Blaue: Das Spitzelsystem der DDR*, Berlin, 1990.
Weber, G. (ed.), *Die europapolitische rolle der Bundesrepublik Deutschland aus der Sicht ihrer EG-Partner*, Bonn, 1984.
Weber, H. (ed.), *DDR: Dokumente zur Geschichte*, Munich, 1986.
Weber, H., *Geschichte der DDR*, Munich, 1986.
Weber, H., *Die DDR, 1945–1986*, Munich, 1988.
Weber, H., *Aufbau und Fall einer Diktatur: Kritische Beiträge zur Geschichte der DDR*, Munich, 1991.
Weber, H., *DDR: Grundriss der Geschichte 1945–1990*, Hanover, 1991.
Weidenfeld, W. (ed.), *Die Identität der Deutschen*, Munich, 1983.
Weidenfeld, W. (ed.), *Geschichtsbewusstsein der Deutschen: Materialen zur Spurensuche einer Nation*, Cologne, 1987.
Weidenfeld, W. (ed.), *Politische Kultur und deutsche Frage*, Cologne, 1989.
Weidenfeld, W. (ed.), *Die Deutschen und die Architektur des Europäischen Hauses. Materialen zu den Perspektiven Deutschlands*, Cologne, 1991.
Weidenfeld, W., *Deutschland: Eine Nation – doppelte Geschichte: Materialen zum deutschen Selbstverständnis*, Cologne, 1992.
Weidenfeld, W. and Korte, K-R, (eds), *Handwörtebuch zur deutschen Einheit*, Frankfurt, 1992.
Weidenfeld, W. and Zimmermann, H. (eds), *Deutschland Handbuch: Eine doppelte Bilanz 1949–1989*, Munich, 1989.

Weisenfeld, E., *Welches Deutschland soll es sein? Frankreich und die deutsche Erinheit seit 1945*, Munich, 1986.
Weiss, R. (ed.), *Chronik eines Zusammenbruchs: der 'heisse' Herbst 1989 und seine Folgen in der Länder des Warschauer Paktes*, Berlin, 1990.
Weiss-Hartmann, A., *Geschichte der deutschen Spaltung, 1945–1955*, Cologne, 1975.
Weizsäcker, R. von, *Richard von Weizsäcker: Im Gespräch mit Gunter Hoffmann und Werner A. Perger*, Frankfurt, 1992.
Wessell, N.H. (ed.), *The New Europe: Revolution in East–West Relations*, New York, 1991.
Wessels, W. and Regelsberger, E., *The Federal Republic and the European Community: The Presidency and Beyond*, Bonn, 1988.
Wettig, G., *Entmilitarisierung und Wiederbewaffnung in Deutschland 1943–1955*, Munich, 1967.
Wettig, G., *Community and Conflict in the Socialist Camp: The Soviet Union, East Germany, and the German Problem, 1965–1972*, New York, 1975.
Wettig, G., *Die Sowictunion, die DDR und die Deutschland-Frage, 1965–1976*, Stuttgart, 1976.
Wettig, G., *Changes in Soviet Policy Towards the West*, London, 1991.
Weymar, P., *Konrad Adenauer*, London, 1957.
Whetten, L.L., *Germany's Ostpolitik: Relations between the Federal Republic and the Warsaw Pact Countries*, London, 1971.
Whetten, L.L., *Germany East and West: Conflicts, Collaboration, and Confrontation*, New York, 1980.
Whetten, L.L., *Interaction of Political and Economic Reforms within the Eastern Block*, New York, 1989.
Wickert, U., *Angst vor Deutschland*, Hamburg, 1990.
Wiedemann, E., *Die deutschen Ängste: Ein Volk in Moll*, Frankfurt, 1990.
Wild, T. and Jones, P. (eds), *De-Industrialisation and New Industrialisation in Britain and Germany*, London, 1991.
Wildenmann, R., *Volksparteien. Ratlose Riesen?*, Baden-Baden, 1989.
Wildenmann, R. (ed.), *Nation und Demokratie*, Baden-Baden, 1991.
Wilharm, I. (ed.), *Deutsche Geschichte 1962–1983*, 2 vols, Frankfurt, 1985.
Wilke, M. and Hertle, H-H., *Das Genossenkartell: Die SED und die IG-Druck und Papier/IG Medien*, Berlin, 1992.
Wilkening, C., *Staat im Staate: Auskünfte ehemaliger Stasi-Mitarbeiter*, Berlin, 1990.
Willett, R., *Americanisation of Germany, 1945–1949*, London, 1989.
Willis, F.R., *The French in Germany, 1945–1949*, Stanford, Calif., 1962.
Willis, F.R., *France, Germany and the New Europe, 1945–1967*, New York, 1968.

Wilson, M., *Germany at the Crossroads: The Costs of Reunification*, London, 1991.
Windsor, P., *German Reunification*, London, 1969.
Windsor, P., *Germany and the Management of Détente*, London, 1971.
Winkler, G. (ed.), *Frauenreport '90*, Berlin, 1990.
Wirtschaftsreport: Daten un Fakten zur wirtschaftlichen Lage Ostdeutschlands, Berlin, 1990.
Wiskemann, E., *Germany's Eastern Neighbours*, London, 1956.
Wolf, C., *Was Bleibt*, Frankfurt, 1990.
Wolf, M., *Die Troika*, Berlin, 1989.
Wolf, M., *In eigenem Auftrag: Bekenntnisse und Einsichten*, Munich, 1991.
Wolffsohn, M., *West Germany's Foreign Policy in the Era of Brandt and Schmidt. An Introduction*, Frankfurt am Main, 1986.
Wolffsohn, M., *Keine Angst vor Deutschland*, Bonn, 1990.
Wolters, U. (ed.), *Rudolf Bahro: Critical Responses*, New York, 1980.
Woods, R., *Opposition in the GDR Under Honecker, 1971–85*, Basingstoke, 1986.
Wuttke, C. and Musiolek, B. (eds), *Parteien und Politische Bewegungen im letzten Jahr der DDR*, Berlin, 1991.
Zeman, Z.A.B., *Pursued by a Bear: The Making of Eastern Europe*, London, 1989.
Zentrum für Theaterdokumentation und -information, *Wir treten aus unseren Rollen heraus. Dokumente des Aufbruchs Herbst '89*, Berlin, 1990.
Zieger, G., *Die Haltung von SED und DDR zur Einheit Deutschlands, 1949–1987*, Cologne, 1988.
Zimmermann, H. (ed.), *DDR Handbuch*, Cologne, 1985.
Zink, H., *The United States in Germany*, Princeton, NJ, 1957.

Index